Beyond the Code

Beyond the Code

Protection of Non-Textual Features of Software

Noam Shemtov

Senior Lecturer in Intellectual Property
and Technology Law,
Queen Mary, University of London

OXFORD
UNIVERSITY PRESS

Great Clarendon Street, Oxford, OX2 6DP,
United Kingdom

Oxford University Press is a department of the University of Oxford.
It furthers the University's objective of excellence in research, scholarship,
and education by publishing worldwide. Oxford is a registered trade mark of
Oxford University Press in the UK and in certain other countries

© Noam Shemtov 2017

The moral rights of the author have been asserted

First Edition published in 2017

Impression: 1

All rights reserved. No part of this publication may be reproduced, stored in
a retrieval system, or transmitted, in any form or by any means, without the
prior permission in writing of Oxford University Press, or as expressly permitted
by law, by licence or under terms agreed with the appropriate reprographics
rights organization. Enquiries concerning reproduction outside the scope of the
above should be sent to the Rights Department, Oxford University Press, at the
address above

You must not circulate this work in any other form
and you must impose this same condition on any acquirer

Crown copyright material is reproduced under Class Licence
Number C01P0000148 with the permission of OPSI
and the Queen's Printer for Scotland

Published in the United States of America by Oxford University Press
198 Madison Avenue, New York, NY 10016, United States of America

British Library Cataloguing in Publication Data

Data available

Library of Congress Control Number: 2017947641

ISBN 978-0-19-871679-2

Printed and bound by
CPI Group (UK) Ltd, Croydon, CR0 4YY

Links to third party websites are provided by Oxford in good faith and
for information only. Oxford disclaims any responsibility for the materials
contained in any third party website referenced in this work.

For Ino and Daphne

Table of Contents

FOREWORD	xiii
PREFACE	xv
TABLE OF CASES	xvii
TABLE OF LEGISLATION	xxiii
TABLE OF TREATIES, ETC	xxvii
LIST OF ABBREVIATIONS	xxix

1. LICENCE-CREATED MONOPOLIES: CONTROLLING USE THROUGH RESTRICTIVE LICENSING TERMS — 1

1.1 Setting the Scene	2
1.2 Restricting Licensees Through the Use of Technology-Based Solutions	4
1.2.1 The position in the European Union	5
1.2.2 The US position	5
1.2.2.1 *Judicial perspectives*	6
1.3 Reverse Engineering, Reproducing Functional Elements, and Contractual Provisions	10
1.3.1 Contractual prohibitions on reverse engineering and reproduction	11
1.3.2 Licence types	13
1.3.3 Summation	14
1.4 The Case for Freedom of Contract	14
1.5 Contracts of Adhesion	17
1.6 Regulating 'Freedom of Contracts'	19
1.6.1 Limitations based on public policy	19
1.6.2 Regulating the enforceability of contracts of adhesion	21
1.6.3 Misusing a legal right	22
1.7 The Combined Effect of Contracts of Adhesion and Technological Protection Measures	23
1.8 The Special Case of Software	26
1.8.1 The collapse of the copyright–patent dichotomy	26
1.8.2 Software's expressive core	27

1.8.3 Software as a vault		28
1.8.4 Barriers to entry		29
1.8.5 Summation		31

2. LEGAL MECHANISMS FOR MITIGATING THE EFFECT OF RESTRICTIVE LICENSING PROVISIONS — 32

2.1 Introduction	32
2.2 Contract Law–Based Mechanisms	34
2.2.1 Licence or sale?	34
2.2.1.1 *United States*	35
2.2.1.2 *European Union*	38
2.2.2 Contract formation and content	38
2.2.2.1 *Contract formation*	39
2.2.3 Contract content	46
2.2.3.1 *UCITA*	47
2.2.3.2 *Directive on unfair terms in consumer contracts*	47
2.2.3.3 *Directive for the protection of computer programs*	47
2.3 Pre-Emption–Based Mechanisms	51
2.3.1 Statutory pre-emption	51
2.3.2 Constitution pre-emption	54
2.4 Competition Law–Based Mechanisms	56
2.4.1 EU competition law and prohibitions on reproduction of functional software features	57
2.4.1.1 *Article 101*	57
2.4.1.2 *Article 102*	59
2.4.2 US antitrust law	65
2.4.2.1 *Section 1 of the Sherman Act—anticompetitive agreements*	65
2.4.2.2 *Section 2 of the Sherman Act: abuse of dominant position*	66

3. ON REVERSE ENGINEERING AND DECOMPILATION — 70

3.1 Reverse Engineering and Decompilation of Software: A Practical Overview	71
3.1.1 On reverse engineering	71
3.1.2 On software and black box reverse engineering	71
3.1.3 On software, reverse engineering, and decompilation	72

Table of Contents

3.1.4 The various stages of reverse engineering	73
3.1.5 Motivation and methods for reverse engineering	75
3.1.6 Reasons for and benefits of decompilation	78
3.1.7 Interoperability	79
3.1.7.1 *Free and Open Source Software (FOSS)*	80
3.2 Decompilation and Copyright Law	83
3.2.1 Idea-expression dichotomy and decompilation	84
3.2.2 The decompilation exception under the EU computer programs copyright regime	85
3.2.3 Decompilation under the US copyright regime	85
3.2.3.1 *Atari Games Corp. v. Nintendo of America, Inc.*	86
3.2.3.2 *Sega Enterprises v. Accolade*	87
3.2.3.3 *Sony Computer Entertainment v. Connectix*	90
3.3 An Entitlement to Exclude Access to Ideas	93
3.4 Entitlements in the Case of Decompilation of Computer Programs	94
3.4.1 An anomaly?	95
3.5 A Critical Overview of Article 6 as a Means to Enable Decompilation to Achieve Interoperability	96
3.6 A Note on Reverse Engineering in a Cloud Environment	101
4. THE IDEA-EXPRESSION DICHOTOMY AND ITS ROLE IN SOFTWARE-RELATED DISPUTES	**102**
4.1 Introduction	102
4.2 The Idea-Expression Dichotomy: Critique and Justifications	104
4.2.1 A brief note regarding critiques of the idea-expression dichotomy principle	104
4.2.2 Economic and efficiency-based justifications of the idea-expression dichotomy	105
4.2.3 The idea-expression dichotomy and natural laws systems	106
4.3 Idea-Expression Dichotomy: Emergence and Development	108
4.3.1 The emergence of the idea-expression dichotomy on both sides of the Atlantic	109
4.3.2 The development of the idea-expression dichotomy in the United Kingdom	112
4.3.3 The application of the idea-expression dichotomy in recent UK software-related disputes	120
4.3.4 The application of the idea-expression dichotomy in EU software-related disputes	121

	4.3.5 The development of the idea–expression dichotomy in the United States	124
	4.3.6 The application of the idea–expression dichotomy in US software-related disputes	127
5.	THE COMBINED EFFECT OF COPYRIGHT AND RESTRICTIVE LICENSING PROVISIONS	136
	5.1 Exercising A Right in a Manner That Runs Contrary to its Objectives and Social Function	138
	5.2 The US Copyright-Misuse Doctrine	140
	5.3 The 'Function' of Intellectual Property Rights as a Means to Regulate the Manner of their Exercise	149
	5.3.1 The essential function of a patent	150
	5.3.2 The essential function of a copyright	151
	5.3.3 The functions of a trade-mark as a curb on the manner of its exercise: the CJEU setting internal limitation on the circumstances in which a trade mark could be enforced	152
	5.3.4 Applying the 'protectable functions' rationale to software-related scenarios	156
	5.4 A Brief Note on the Prohibition of Abuse of Law in the European Union	158
6.	PATENTING SOFTWARE	160
	6.1 Computer-Implemented Inventions in the United States	161
	6.1.1 Background	161
	6.1.2 Policy trends and judicial interpretation	162
	6.1.2.1 *Policy trends*	162
	6.1.2.2 *The development of case-law*	163
	6.2 Computer-Implemented Inventions at the European Patent Office	178
	6.2.1 Background	178
	6.2.2 Trends and case-law development	179
	6.2.2.1 *The contribution approach*	179
	6.2.2.2 *The 'any-hardware' approach*	180
	6.3 Convergence of the Present Approaches in the United States and European Patent Office	184
7.	PROTECTING USER INTERFACES	188
	7.1 Copyright Protection Over 'Look-and-Feel' Elements	190
	7.1.1 GUI protection under US copyright law	190
	7.1.2 Look-and-feel protection under EU law	193

7.2 Trade-Mark, Trade-Dress, and Unfair-Competition
     Protection for GUIs ... 195
    7.2.1 United States: trade-mark and trade-dress protection to GUIs ... 196
        7.2.1.1 *Rules on eligibility and scope of protection* ... 196
        7.2.1.2 *Applying the rules* ... 202
    7.2.2 European Union: trade-mark protection for GUIs ... 203
        7.2.2.1 *Distinctiveness* ... 203
        7.2.2.2 *Functionality* ... 204
        7.2.2.3 *Infringement* ... 206
    7.2.3 A brief note on unfair-competition laws in
          the European Union ... 206
7.3 Design Patents and Registered Designs ... 207
    7.3.1 Design patents in the United States ... 208
        7.3.1.1 *Eligibility* ... 208
        7.3.1.2 *Infringement* ... 210
    7.3.2 Registered designs in the European Union ... 211
        7.3.2.1 *Eligibility* ... 211
        7.3.2.2 *Infringement* ... 213
7.4 A Brief Note on Patent Protection for GUIs ... 214
    7.4.1 Utility-patent protection in the United States for GUIs ... 214
    7.4.2 Protecting GUIs at the EPO ... 216

8. TRADE SECRETS AND THE SOFTWARE INDUSTRY ... 219

8.1 Introduction ... 219
8.2 Trade Secrets: The Legal Basis of the Right ... 221
8.3 Trade Secrets Protection in the European Union ... 224
    8.3.1 Protection in Member States prior to the
          Trade Secrets Directive ... 224
    8.3.2 The Trade Secrets Directive ... 225
        8.3.2.1 *Background* ... 225
        8.3.2.2 *The Trade Secrets Directive's framework* ... 226
8.4 Trade Secrets Protection in the United States ... 233
    8.4.1 Background ... 233
    8.4.2 Legislative framework ... 234
        8.4.2.1 *The Uniform Trade Secrets Act* ... 235
        8.4.2.2 *A brief note on the Defend the Trade Secrets Act 2016* ... 243

INDEX ... 245

Foreword

Software plays a crucial role in our economy and society. It is the backbone of how we communicate, create, travel, entertain, conduct business, and provide services and, increasingly in an era of 'big data', predicts and shapes our future behaviour. The pervasiveness of software makes it easy to forget that its transformational impact has occurred in just over half a century. The history of intellectual property protection of software is also relatively short, with copyright protection being widely recognized by the early to mid 1980s and patent protection for software related inventions from the 1970s. Like the technology itself, intellectual property issues relating to software have become more complex over time. Yet core areas of contention remain, relating to the scope of copyright protection, the use of contractual and technological mechanisms to protect against copyright infringement, the permissibility of reverse engineering, and the patentability of software. Much ink has been spilled, particularly in United States law journals, about these issues. But it is rare to see a systematic, thoughtful and current account of all of them in one place. This is where Dr Noam Shemtov's book, 'Beyond Code', steps in.

'Beyond Code' is concerned with the protection of non-literal features of software, not simply the code itself, because this is where the more interesting questions arise. The analysis delves into the domains of copyright, patents, trade secrets, trade marks, designs, and contract law, according to both United States and European (Union) law. These jurisdictions are wisely chosen, not least because the United States and Europe are powerhouses of software creation.

A central analytical thread running throughout the book is how to avoid over-protection of software, to ensure vibrant, competitive software industries. As such, the book offers valuable reform proposals, including; improvements to decompilation and reverse engineering exceptions in copyright law, the judicial utilization of a 'misuse' or 'abuse of right' doctrine, and interpretations of contractual enforceability, especially when licence terms conflict with substantive norms of copyright law. Dr Shemtov is to be commended for writing a sophisticated and highly accessible exegesis on intellectual property protection of software. It is an extremely valuable addition to the literature and will make highly beneficial reading for academics, practitioners, and students alike.

Professor Tanya Aplin
July 2017

Preface

My first expression of authorial interest in the legal protectability of software took place during the years of writing my PhD thesis. Ever since, I was fascinated by software's amorphous nature as a legally protectable subject matter. Software plays a crucial role in most parts of today's society. It is now an indispensable feature of the world of business, finance, industry and manufacture, education and research, medicine, government, entertainment, law and daily life in general. Furthermore, software stands at the heart of all disruptive technologies, as predicted at present. Hence, artificial intelligence, automation and robotics, Internet of things, biometric and digital identification and virtual reality, have software at their core.

As a legally protectable subject matter, software always proved to be challenging. None of our intellectual property regimes provide a good fit, and Mr. Bumble's memorable line from Oliver Twist on the law being an 'ass' does sometimes spring to mind when we witness jurists' continuous attempts to fit software within our existing intellectual property landscape in a manner that takes account of right owners' proprietary interest, while bearing in mind broader public welfare considerations.

In light of software's prominence in all walks of life in the 21st century and its unique characteristics as a legally protectable subject matter, it is somewhat surprising that it has not been subject to more analysis as a legally protectable asset, in particular in relation to the law in the European Union, where such works are relatively few and far between.

This book attempts to address this state of affairs by analyzing software's various facets as legally protectable subject matters, with particular emphasis on non-literal software aspects. It examines the protectability of the different aspects of software products or services under various intellectual property, quasi - intellectual property and contract laws, focusing in particular on the laws of the United States and European Union. This focus is due to the fact that, to date, both jurisdictions are not only extremely significant markets for software -based products and services, but also have the most mature software-related legal ecosystems.

My intention in writing this book was to make it of interest to both legal scholars and practitioners. Therefore, it does not only survey the current legal state of affairs in relation to the different areas of coverage, it also attempts to predict how the law is likely to develop in this context. In addition, on occasions I chose to provide a critical viewpoint regarding the legal position at issue while suggesting potential fixes to address such shortcomings, irrespective of whether or not I believe that the said position is likely to change any time soon. To name just two examples in this context, in relation to the combined effect of copyright, restrictive contractual provisions and TPMs, as well as in relation to the implications of the trade secrets regime under the newly enacted directive on software available under beta – test agreements, I provide an analysis of the present legal position and critique as to its inadequacy, but I also point out towards possible workarounds, should the courts be prepared to adopt an activist approach in this regard.

In terms of scoping, the book is intellectual property focused. However, I am of the view that no meaningful discussion could take place, especially with regard to the scope of protection of software under copyright law, without considering the implications of licensing provisions that seek to broaden the protection granted under the former. It is for this reason that the discussion in this book commences with an examination of such restrictive licensing provisions prevalent in the software industry, their origin, purpose and impact, as well as the juridical tools that are currently at the courts' disposal for mitigating the effect of such provisions. From this point onwards the discussion focuses purely on intellectual property law. Copyright law still being the main vehicle for protecting software's 'non-literal' elements is discussed in greater detail, with reference to exceptions and limitation applicable to such scenarios. The discussion then moves to protection available under patent law, trade marks and trade dress law, registered designs and design patents and, finally, trade secrets law.

I decided to include a separate chapter dealing with graphical user interfaces (GUIs). This feature of a software product or service's get-up is decisive to its success, while its legal protectability might be determined with reference to a wide tapestry of intellectual property rights. Questions of GUIs protectability are becoming even more important nowadays, where many software offerings are available as a service over the internet, without any possibility to access its code or architecture. While it is true that some may argue that a GUI includes 'literal' elements and thus, as a whole, might not be considered as non-literal stricto sensu, it is nevertheless discussed here in detail since its protectability is non-code related.

Finally, one could not conclude a personal note written at the first part of 2017 without referring to the looming departure of the United Kingdom from the European Union. By the time that the British public voted to leave the European Union, the vast majority of this book was already written. But even if it were not the case and I would have written the whole book at this very moment, there is little more that I would have done differently as the terms of such departure are far from clear. Hence, subject to a few explanatory comments, rather than enter the realm of political speculation, I opted to address the relevant issues on the basis of the political and legal state of affairs at the time of writing: The United Kingdom being a member state of the European Union.

Noam Shemtov

Table of Cases

United Kingdom

Aerotel Ltd v. Telco Holdings Ltd & Ors Rev 1 [2006] EWCA Civ. 1371, 28 .... 183, 217
Beta Computers (Europe) Ltd. v. Adobe Systems (Europe) Ltd (1996) FSR 367 42
Burnett v. Chetwood 2 Mer. 441, 35 Eng. Rep. 1008 (Ch. 1720) 108
Designers Guild Ltd v. Russell Williams (Textiles) Ltd [2001] 1 WLR 2416; [2001]
  FSR 11; [2001] ECDR 10 (HL) 115–17, 134
Donaldson v. Beckett 1 Eng. Rep. 837 (H.L. 1774) 109
Europemballage Corp, Continental Can Co Inc. v. Commission [1973] CMLR 199 61
Exxon Corp. v. Exxon Insurance Consultants International Ltd [1981] 3 All E.R. 241 120–1
Harman v. Osborne [1967] 2 All ER 324, [1967] 1 WLR 723, at 728 .... 112, 118
Hollinrake v. Truswell [1894] 3 Ch. D 420 .... 109–10, 112–13, 118, 160
Ibcos Computers v. Barclays Mercantile Highland Finance [1994] FSR 275 .... 114–15, 119–20
Kenrick v. Lawrence (1890) 25 QBD 99 112
LB (Plastics) Limited v. Swish Products Limited [1979] RPC 551 .... 112, 114, 118
L'Estrange v. F Groucob Ltd [1934] 2 K.B. 394 45
Ladbroke (Football) Ltd v. William Hill (Football) Ltd [1964] 1 WLR 273 117
McCrum v. Eisner [1917] 87 LJ Ch. 99, 102 112
Millar v. Taylor 98 Eng. Rep. 201 (KB 1769) 109
Navitaire Inc. v. Easyjet Airline Company and Bulletproof Technologies Inc.
  [2004] EWHC 1725 (Ch) 120–1, 128–9
Nova Productions Limited v. Mazooma Games Limited & Others [2007]
  EWCA Civ. 219 .... 103, 121
Poznanski v. London Film Production, Ltd. (1937), MacG. Cop. Cas. (1936–45) 107 112
Reckitt & Colman Products Ltd v. Borden, Inc. and Others [1990] 1 All ER 873 206
Rees v. Melville, (1914) MacG. Cop. Cas. (1911–16) 168 112
Samsung Electronics (UK) Ltd v. Apple, Inc. [2012] EWCA Civ. 1339 214
SAS Institute, Inc. v. World Programming Ltd [2010] EWHC 1829 (Ch) 48, 115, 122, 137, 230
Symbian Ltd v. Comptroller General of Patents [2008] EWCA Civ. 1066 183
Temple Island Collections Ltd v. New English Teas [2012] EWPCC 1 118
Thompson v. LM & S Ry [1930] 1 KB 4.1 43
Thornton v. Shoe Lane Parking [1971] 2 WLR 585 42
University of London Press v. University Tutorial Press [1916] 2 Ch. 601, 610 117

European Union

European Commission

Microsoft (Case COMP/ C- 3/ 37.792) Commission Decision C(2004) 900 97

General Court

Bang & Olufsen A/S v. OHIM Case T-508/08 205

Court of Justice

Adam Opel AG v. Autec AG [2007] ECR I-1017 Case C-48/05................................154
Arsenal Football Club v. Reed [2002] ECR I-10273 Case C-206/01....................... 153, 155
Bezpečnostní softwarová asociace – Svaz softwarové ochrany v. Ministry of Culture
 of the Czech Republic, Case C-393/09........................ 5, 10, 49, 121, 137, 156, 189, 193
Centrafarm v. Sterling Drug [1974] ECR 1147, Case C-15/74 150
Coditel v. Cine Vog Films [1980] E.C.R 881, Case C-62/79 151
Consten and Grundig v. Commission [1966] ECR 299, Cases C-56 and 58/64..................60
Deutsche Grammophon Gesellschaft mbH v. Metro-SB-Grossmärkte GmbH &
 Co. KG [1971] ECR, Case C-78/70...151
Football Dataco Ltd and others v. Yahoo! UK Limited, Case C-604/10 113
Google France SARL and Google Inc. v. Louis Vuitton Malletier SA, Google France and
 Google Inc. v. Viaticum SA and another, and Google France and Google Inc. v.
 CNRRH and others, Joined Cases C-236/08, C-237/08, and C-238/08......................156
Hoffmann-La Roche & Co AG and Hoffmann-la Roche AG v. Centrafarm
 VertriebsgesellschaftPharmazeutischer Erzeugnisse mbH 1978 ECR 1139, 3 CMLR
 217 [1978] Case C-2/77..153
Hofner and Elser v. Macrotron GmbH [1991] ECR I-1979......................................58
IMS Health GmbH & Co. OHG v. NDC Health GmbH & Co. KG. (C-418/01) [2004]
 ECR I-503...62, 64
Infopaq International A/S v. Danske Dagblades Forening [2009] ECR I-6569; [2009]
 ECDR 16 Case C-508.. 113, 115, 156
Kefalas and Others v. Greek State and OAE [1998] ECR 1-2843, Case C-367-96 158
Koninklijke Philips Electronics NV v. Remington Consumer Products Ltd [2002]
 ECR I-5475, Case C-299/99..212
L'Oréal SA v. Bellure NV [2009] ECR I-5185 Case C-487/07 155
La Roche & Co AG and Hoffmann-la Roche AG v. Centrafarm Vertriebsgesellschaft
 Pharmazeutischer Erzeugnisse mbH (Case 102/77) 274..64
Lego Juris A/S v. OHIM, Mega Brands Inc., Case 48/09 204
Microsoft v. Commission (T-201/04) [2007] ECR II-1491................................62, 152
Oscar Bronner GmbH & Co. KG v. Mediaprint Zeitungs - und Zeitschriftenverlag GmbH
 & Co. KG, Mediaprint Zeitungsvertriebsgesellschaft mbH & Co. KG and Mediaprint
 Anzeigengesellschaft mbH & Co. KG. [1998], Case C-7/97 62
Painer Case C-145/10 113
Philips v. Remington Case 299/99 204
RTE v. Commission 1991 ECR II-485 [1991] Case T-69/89 151
RTE and ITP v. Commission (Magill) [1995] ECR I-743, Joined Cases C-24 and
 C-242/91.. 61-2, 64, 151
Storck v. OHIM [2006], Case C-24/05 P 204
The Gillette Company and Gillette Group Finland Oy v. LA- Laboratories Ltd Oy,
 Case C-228/03..232
UsedSoft GmbH v. Oracle International Corp., Case C-128/11 ....24, 38

Volvo v. Eric Veng [1988] ECR 6211, Case C-238/87 .... 61-2, 149
European Patent Office Auction Method/HITACHI (T 258/03) [2004] OJ 2004 181-2
BM/Data Processor Network (1988) T 6/83 180
Circuit Simulation/Infeneon Technologies T 1227/05 [2007] OJ EPO 574 183
Classification Method/COMPTEL (T 1784/ 06) [2012] 182
COMVIK/Two Identities (T 641/00) [2004] EPOR 10 182
DUNS LICENSING ASSOCIATES/ESTIMATING SALES ACTIVITY (T 154/04) [2007]
    EPOR 38 183
IBM/Text Processing (1988) T 115/85 180
Koch and Sterzel/X-Ray Method for Optimum Exposure (1987) T 26/86 180
MICROSOFT/Data Transfer (T 424/03) [2006] 40 EPOR 533 181-2
Vicom/Computer – Related Inventions [1987] OJ EPO 14; (1986) T 208/84, [1987] 2 EPOR 74 ... 179
Pension Benefit Systems (T931/95) OJ EPO 441 180-2

OHIM Invalidity Division
ICD 8225 ASSTECH Assembly Technology GmbH Co KG v. Thomas Nagel (ID 07.09.2011) 214
ICD 8242 Nokia Corporation v. Kalwat Iwona Trak Electronics (ID 28.10.2011) 214

Australia
MacRobertson Miller Airline Services v. Commissioner of State Taxation (WA) (1975)
    8 ALR 131 (High Court of Australia) 42

Netherlands
Coss Holland BV v. TM Data Nederland BV Computerrecht 1997/2, 63-65 44

United States
Abele 684, F.2d 902, 214 USPQ (BNA) 682 (CCPA 1982) 165-6
Acuson Corp. v. Aloka Co. 209 Cal. App. 3d 425, 257 Cal. Rptr. 368 (6th Dist.1989) 239
Al-Site Corp. v. VSI Intern., Inc. 174 F.3d 1308 (1999) 196
Alappat 33 F.3d 1526 (Fed. Cir. 1994) 165-8, 215
Alcatel USA, Inc. v. DGI Technologies Inc.116 F.3d 772 (5th Cir. 1999) 144
Aldrich v. Remington Rand, Inc. 52 F.Supp.732 (N.D. Tex. 1942) 126
Alice Corp. Pty. V CLS Bank Int'l 134 S. Ct. 2347 (2014) 168, 170-5, 177, 185, 215-16, 233
Amdoc (Israel) Ltd v. Openet Telecom, Inc. No. 15-1180 (Fed. Cir. 1 November 2016) 177
Apple, Inc. v. Samsung Electronics Co., Ltd Case: 14-1355
    (Fed. Cir. 18/05/2015) 198-199, 209-10
Apple Computer, Inc. v. Microsoft Corp. 35 F.3d 1435, 1445 (9th Cir. 1994) 193
Aqua Connect, Inc. v. Code Rebel, LLC et al. Case No. CV 11-5764-RSWL
    (CD Cal., 13 Feb. 2012) 240-1
Aspen Skiing Corp v. Aspen Highland Skiing Corp. (1985) 472 U.S. 585 67-8
Assessment Technologies of Wi, Inc. v. WIREdata, Inc. 350 F.3d 640 (7th Cir. 2003) 145
AT&T Corp v. Excel Communication Inc., 172 F.3d 1352 (Fed. Cir. 1999) 166-8, 215
Atari Games Corp. v. Nintendo of America, Inc. 975 F.2d 832 (Fed. Cir. 1992) 53

Table of Cases

Baker v. Selden, 101 US 99 (1879) 109-11, 113, 124-9, 131, 160
BASCOM Global Internet Services, Inc. v. AT&T Mobility LLC, No. 2015-1763, 2016
　WL 3514158 (Fed. Cir. June 27, 2016) 173-4, 177
Bateman v. Mnemonic, Inc. 79 F.3d 1532 (11th Cir. 1996) 146
Bernhart, 417 F.2d 1395, 163 USPQ (BNA) 611 (CCPA 1969) 163
BellSouth Advertising v. Donnelley Information 719 F.Supp.1551 (S.D. Fla. 1988) 67
Bilski 545 F.3d 943 (Fed. Cir. 2008) 168
Bilski v Kappos 561 US 593 (2010) 162, 168-71, 215
Boggild v. Kenner Prods. 776 F.2d 1315 (6th Cir. 1985) 21
Bond v. Blum 317 F.3d 385 (7th Cir. 2003) 146
Bonito Boats, Inc. v. Thunder Craft Boats, Inc. (1989) 141 US 489 .... 70, 237
Bose Corp. 772 F.2d 866, 227 USPQ 1 (Fed. Circ. 1985) 200
Bowers v. Baystate Techs, Inc. 320 F.3d 1317 (Fed. Cir. 2003) 53, 55
buySAFE, Inc. v. Google, Inc. 2014 U.S. App. LEXIS 16987 (Fed. Cir. 3 Sept. 2014) 215
Calif. Fed. Sav. & Loan Ass'n v. Guerra 479 U.S. 272, 278 (1987) 54
Campbell v. Acuff-Rose Music, Inc. 510 U.S. 569 (1994) 91
Chamberlain Group, Inc. v. Skyline Techs., Inc. 381 F.3d1178 (Fed. Cir. 2004) 7
CLS Bank Int'l v. Alice Corp. Pty. Ltd 717 F.3d 1269 (Fed. Cir. 2013) 172
Computer Associates International, Inc. v. Altai, Inc. (1992) 982 F.2d 693, 704
　(2nd Circ.) 128, 131, 190-1
Data general Corp. v. Grumman System Support Corp. (1994) 36 F.3d 1147 (1st Cir.) 67, 241
Davidson & Associates DBA Blizzard Entertainment, Inc.; Vivendi Universal, Inc. v.
　Jung et al., (2005) 422 F.3d 630, 638 (8th Cir.) 8, 51, 55
Davidson & Assocs. v. Internet Gateway 334 F.Supp.2d 1164 (E.D. Mo. 2004) 147
DDR Holdings, LLC v. Hotels.com, LP 773 F.3d 1245 (Fed. Cir. 2014) 173, 215
Diamond v. Chakrabarty, 447 US 303, 309, 206 USPQ 193, 197 (1980) 162
Diamond v. Diehr 450 US 175, 209 USPQ 1 (1981) 164-5, 168-69, 171, 185, 215
DVD Copy Control Ass'n., Inc. v. Bunner 31 Cal. 4th 864, 901 (2003)
　(Moreno J, concurring) 241, 244
Edelman v. N2H2 263 F.Supp.2d 137 (D. Mass. 2003) 8
Enfish, LLC v. Microsoft Corp, No. 2015-1244, 2016 WL 2756255 (Fed. Cir.
　12 May 2016) 173-4, 177, 215-16
Eon Corp. IP Holdings LLC V. AT&T Mobility LLC No. 14-1392 (Fed. Cir. 6 May 2015) 186, 215
Feist Publications, Inc. v. Rural Telephone Services Co. 499 US 340 (1991) 40, 52
Firoozye v. Earthlink Network 153 F.Supp.2d 1115, 1130 (N.D. Cal. 2001) 242
Foster 438 F.2d 1011, 169 USPQ (BNA) 99 (CCPA 1971) 163
Freeman 573, D.2d 1237, 197 USPQ (BNA) 464 (CCPA 1978) 165-6
Gates Rubber Co. v. Bando Chemical Indus., Ltd. 9 F.3d 823, 844-45 (10th Cir. 1993) 128, 236
Gorham Co. v. White, 81 US 511, 528 (1872) 210
Gottschalk v. Benson 409 US 63, 175 USPQ (BNA) 673 (1972) 162-5, 169, 215
Grams 888 F.2d 835 (Fed. Cir. 1989) 165
Harper & Row, Publishers, Inc. v. Nation Enterprises 471 U.S. 539 (1985) 87
High Point Design, LLC v. Buyers Direct, Inc. 730 F.3d 1301, 1319 (Fed. Cir. 2013) 209
Hill v. Gateway 2000. Inc. (1997) 105 F.3d 1147 (7th Cir.) 41
Hutchins v. Zoll Medical Corp. 492 F.3d 1377 (Fed. Cir. 2007) 128
I/P Engine, Inc. v. AOL, Inc. 576 Fed.Appx. 982 (Fed. Cir. 2014) 185
Ingrid & Isabel, LLC v. Baby Be Mine, LLC F.Supp.3d, 2014 WL 4954656 (N.D. Cal. 2014) 198

Table of Cases

Intellectual Ventures I LLC v. Symantec Corp. and Trend Micro Incorporated et al.,
  No. 2015-1769 (Fed. Cir. 30 September 2016)..174–7
Inwood Laboratories, Inc. v. Ives Laboratories 436 US 844 (1982)...........................200
Iwahashi 888 F.2d 1370 (Fed. Cir. 1989) 165
Jobscience v. CV Partners (2014) WL 852477 (ND Cal. 2014)..................................242
Kabahie v. Zoland 102 Cal. App. 4th 513 (2002)..242
Katz Dochtermann & Epstein, Inc. v. Home Box Office (1999) 50 USPQ2d 1957, 1959.......52, 241
Kewanee Oil Co. v. Bicron Corp. 416 US 470 (1974) 237
Lasercomb Am., Inc. v. Reynolds 911 F.2d 970 (4th Cir. 1990) 140–5
Lear v. Adkins 395 US 653 (1969)..20
Lexmark Int'l, Inc. v. Static Control Components, Inc. 387 F.3d 522 (6th Cir. 2004) 7
Lotus Development Corporation v. Borland 49 F.3d 807 (1st Circ. 1995) 819...........30, 84, 128,
                                                                         130–3, 191–2, 194–5
Mahony, 421 F.2d 742, 164 USPQ (BNA) 572 (CCPA 1970) 163
Mayo Collaborative Services v. Prometheus Laboratories, Inc. 132 S. Ct. 1289 (2012) 168–71
Mazer v. Stein, 347 US 201 (1954)..129
MDY Industries v. Blizzard Entertainment 629 F.3d 928 (9th Cir. 2010)
  (14 December 2010) 2013..7
Meehan v. PGP Indus. 802 F.2d 881 (7th Cir. 1986) 21
Microsoft v. Electro-wide (1997) F.S.R. 580 43
Microsoft Corp. v. Harmony Computers & Electronics, Inc. 846 F.Supp.208
  (E.D.N.Y 1994)...35–7
Microsoft Corp. Antitrust Litigation 274 F.Supp.2d 743 (D. Md. 2003).........................68
Mitel, Inc. v. Iqtel, Inc. (1997) 124 F.3d 1366, 1372 (10th Cir.) 132, 191–2
Monge v. Maya Magazines, Inc. (2012) 688 F.3d 1164, 1170 (9th Cir.)..........................134
Morison v. Moat (1851) 9 Hare 241 223
Morton-Norwich Products, Inc. 671 F.2d 1332, 1340–41 (CCPA 1982).........................200
Morton Salt Co. v. GS Suppiger Co. 314 US 488 (1942)................................140–2, 146
Musgrave 431 F.2d 882, 167 USPQ (BNA) 280 (CCPA 1970) 163
Nautilus, Inc. v. Biosig Instruments, Inc. 134 S.Ct. 2120 (2014) 186
Newton v. Rumery 480 US 386, 392 (1987) 19
Nichols v. Universal Pictures Corp. 45 F.2d 119 (2nd Cir. 1930)...........................124–5
Nintendo v. Atari 975 F.2d 832 (Fed Cir. 1992)......................72, 82, 85–7, 133, 140, 238
Oracle Am., Inc. v. Google, Inc. 750 F.3d 1339, 1364 (Fed. Cir. 2014)).......126, 128, 131–5, 191–2
Parker v. Flook 437 U.S 584, 198 USPQ (BNA) 193 (1978) 164–5, 169
Partet, 415 F.2d 1393, 162 USPQ (BNA) 541 (CCPA 1969).......................................163
Peter Pan Fabrics, Inc. v. Martin Weiner Corp, 274 F.2d (2nd Cir. 1960) 125
Polaroid Corp. v. Polarad Elect. Corp. 287 F.2d 492 (2nd Cir. 1961) 198
Practice Management Information Corporation v. The American Medical Association
  121 F.3d 516, 520 (9th Cir. 1997)..144–5
PRC Realty Sys., Inc. v. Nat'l. Ass'n. of Realtors, Nos 91-1125, 91-1143, 1992 U.S. App.
  LEXIS 18017, at 38 (4thbCir. 4 Aug. 1992)..147
ProCD, Inc. v. Zeidenberg 86 F.3d 1447 (7th Cir. 1996)..........................40, 52–3, 241
Qualitex Co. v. Jacobson Prods. Co. 514 U.S. 159 (1995) 199
Richardson v. Stanley Works, Inc. 597 F.3d 1288 (Fed. Cir. 2010) 209
Rosetta Stone Ltd v. Google, Inc. No. 10-2007 (4th Cir. 9 April 2012) 202
Ruckelshaus v. Monsanto Co. (1984) 467 U.S. 986 223

Table of Cases

Saturday Evening Post Co. v. Rumbleseat Press, Inc. 816 F.2d 1191, 1200 (7th Cir. 1987)....... 145
Secure Services Technology v. Time and Space Processing 722 F.Supp.1354 (ED Va. 1989)....238
Sega Enterprises v. Accolade 977 F.2d 1510 (9th Cir. 1992) 28, 72, 82, 85, 87–91, 133, 238
Servo Corporation of America v. General Electric Company 393 F.2d 551 (4th Cir.1968) 236
Softman Products Company v. Adobe Systems Inc. 171 F.Supp.2d 1075 (CD Cal. 2001).......36–7
Sony Computer Entertainment, Inc. v. Connectix Corp. 203 F.3d 596
   (9th Cir. 2000).. 9, 72, 85, 90–2, 133, 238
Spear Marketing Inc., v. BancorpSouth Bank et al. __ F.3d __, 2015 WL 3972246
   (5th Cir. 30 June 2015) 242
Specht v. Netscape Communications Corp. (2002) 306 F.3d 17 (2nd Cir.)....................44–6
State Street Bank & Trust Co v. Signature Financial Group Inc., 149 F.3d 1368
   (Fed. Cir. 1998).. 166–8, 215
Step-Saver Data Systems v. Wyse Technology 939 F.2d 91 (3rd Cir. 1991).....................39
Storage Tech. Corp. v. Custom Hardware, Eng'g & Consulting Inc. 421 F.3d 1307
   (Fed. Cir. 2005)...7
Stowe v. Thomas 23 Fed. Cas. 201 (CCED Pa. 1853) 109
Taylor Instrument Companies v. Fawley-Brost Co., 139 F.2d 98 (7th Cir. 1943) 129
Telerate Systems Inc. v. Caro 689 F.Supp.221 (S.D.N.Y. 1988)..............................239
Tetris Holding, LLC v. Xio Interactive, Inc. 863 F.Supp.2d 394 (D.N.J. 2012) 197–8
Thabet Mfg. Co. v. Kool Vent Metal Awning Corp. 226 F.2d 207, 212 (6th Cir. 1955)............209
Thomas & Betts Corp. v. Panduit Corp., 138 F.3d 277, 285 (7th Cir. 1998) 201
TLI Communications, LLC v. AV Automotive, LLC No. 15-1372 (Fed. Cir. 17 May 2016) 215
TrafFix Devices, Inc. v. Marketing Displays, Inc. 532 US 23 (2001).........................200–1
Two Pesos, Inc. v. Taco Cabana, Inc. 505 US 763 (1992) 196
United Drug Co. v. Theodore Rectanus Co., 248 U.S. 90, 97 (1918)...........................195
United States v. Microsoft Corp. 87 F.Supp.2d 30 (D.D.C 2000) 51 ....29, 80
United States v. Terminal Railroad Ass'n. (1912) 224 U.S. 383 67
United States Gypsum Co. v. National Gypsum Co. 352 US 465; Zenith Radio Corp v.
   Hazeltine Research, Inc. 395 U.S. 100 (1969)..141
United States of America, Appellee v. Microsoft Corporation 253 F.3d 34 (D.C. Cir. 2001) 66
Universal City Studios v. Reminders 111 F.Supp.2d 294 (S.D.N.Y. 2000) 6
Universal City Studios, Inc. v. Corley 273 F.3d 429 (2nd Cir. 2001) 6
Vault Corp. v. Quaid Software Ltd., 847 F.2d 255 (5th Cir. 1988) 54–5
Verizon Communications Inc., Petitioner Vv. Law Offices of Curtis V. Trinko, LLP
   (2004) 540 U.S. 398, 411 68–9
Vernor v. Autodesk, Inc. 621 F.3d 1102 (9th Cir. 2010), 1111................................37–8
Video Pipeline, Inc. v. Buena Vista Home Entm't, Inc. 342 F.3d 191 (3d. Cir. 2003) 146
Videotronics v. Bend Electronics 564 F.Supp.1471 (D. Nev. 1983).............................242
Vornado Air Circulation Systems, Inc. v. Duracraft Corp., 58 F.3d 1498, 1500
   (10th Cir. 1995)..201
Wal-Mart Stores, Inc. v. Samara Brothers, Inc. 529 U.S. 205 (2000).......................196–7
Walter 618, F.2d 758, 205 USPQ (BNA) 397 (CCPA 1980)..................................165–6
Whelan Associates, Inc. v. Jaslow Dental Laboratory, Inc. 797 F.2d 1222, 1248
   (3rd Cir. 1986) 84, 128, 190

Table of Legislation

Australia
Australian Copyright Act 1968
   s. 47D(1)(d) 98–9

European Union (EU)
Directives
Council Directive 93/13/EEC [1993]
   OJ L95/29 ....
   21–2, 46–7
   Art. 2(b) 47
Council Directive 2001/29/EC of the European Parliament and of the Council of 22 May 2001 on the harmonization of certain aspects of copyright and related rights in the information society (Information Society Directive)..............................
   5, 10, 49–50, 119, 123, 137, 149, 156–7, 194–5
   Art. 1(2)(a) 5
   Rec. 2................................. 157
Council Directive 2009/24/EC of the European Parliament and of the Council of 23 April 2009 on the legal protection of computer programs [2009] OJ L111/16 (Software Directive)......................
   5, 46–9, 98–100, 106, 115, 119, 123, 137, 149, 156, 193, 229, 238
   Art. 1(2).................... 48, 85, 103, 119
   Art. 4(2)............................... 38
   Art. 5 .... 5, 11
   Art. 5(2)............................... 10
   Art. 5(3)................ 10, 72, 137, 229–31
   Art. 6 .... 5, 10, 11, 80, 85, 96–100, 137, 195, 227, 229–31
   Art. 6(2)(b).........................99, 227
   Art. 7(1)(c) 5
   Art. 8 .... 10–11, 47–9, 72, 229–32

Rec. 10................................. 79
Rec. 11..........................48, 85, 119
Council Directive 2015/2436 of the European Parliament and of the Council of 16 December 2015 to approximate the laws of the Member States relating to trade marks (Trade Marks Directive)
   Art. 10(2)(a) 153, 206
   Art. 10(2)(b)........................... 206
   Art. 10(2)(c) 206
   Art. 4(1)(e)(ii)......................... 204
   Art. 4(1)(e)(iii)........................ 205
Council Directive 2016/943 of the European Parliament and of the Council of 8 June 2016 on the protection of undisclosed know-how and business information (trade secrets) against their unlawful acquisition, use and disclosure (Trade Secrets Directive)........................
   219, 224–7, 236, 238, 244
   Art. 1(1).............................. 226
   Art. 2 ....226, 235
   Art. 2(1)(a) 228
   Art. 2(1)(c) 230
   Art. 3 .... 226–8, 232
   Art. 3(1)(b) 227–30
   Art. 4 ....226, 232
   Art. 4(2)...........................228–30
   Art. 4(3)(b) 228–30
   Art. 4(4)..........................227–8, 232
   Art. 6 233
   Art. 7 233
   Art. 8 ....233, 238
   Art. 9 ....226, 233
   Art. 10 233
   Art. 12 233
   Art. 13 233

Art. 14 233
Art. 15 233
Art. 16 233
Rec. 14 . . . . 227, 232
Rec. 16 . . . . 226, 228, 230
Rec. 23 226
Rec. 24 226
Rec. 32 226
Dir. 3 225
Dir. 8 225

Regulations

Council Regulation (EC) No. 40/94
   Art. 16(1) 21
Council Regulation (EC) No. 6/2002 . . . .
211
   Art. 3(a) 211
   Art. 3(b) 211
   Art. 4(a) 211
   Art. 5 212
   Art. 6 212
   Art. 8(l) 212
   Art. 10 213
Commission Regulation (EU) No. 316/2014 . . . .
59
Technology Transfer Block Exemption
   Regulation . . . .
59
   Art. 4(1)(d) 59
Technology Transfer Guidelines . . . .
59

France

French Civil Code
   Art. 1101 14
   Art. 1165 16
   Art. 1382 207

Germany

Act on the Protection of Trade Secrets . . . .
224
German Civil Code
   Art. 145 16
Gesetz gegen den unlauteren Wettbewerb
   § 4(3)(b) 207

Palandt (2000) . . . .
   s 145, at 140 14

United Kingdom

Contracts (Rights of Third Parties) Act 1999
   s. 1 43
Statute of Anne . . . .
108

United States

35 USC . . . .
. . . 161
§ 101 214
§171(a) 208
§171(b) 208
§ 112(b) 186
California Civil Code
   ss. 3426–3426.11 240
Californian Trade Secrets Act . . . .
240
Copyright Act 1976 . . . .
. . . 127
Art. 2 . . . . 103, 105, 110–11
s. 102 . . . . 10, 52–3
s. 102(a)(1) 53
s. 102(b) 51, 55, 103, 105, 110–11,
127, 190, 193
s. 103 52–3
s. 106 . . . . 10, 52
s. 107 72
s. 109 2
s. 301 . . . . 51–4, 234, 241–2
s. 301(a) 52
Defend Trade Secrets Act . . . .
219, 234, 243–4
s. 2(b) 243
s. 2(b)(2) 243
s. 2(b)(3) 243
s. 2(f) 243
s. 7 243
Digital Millennium Copyright
   Act 1998 . . . .
55, 84
ss 102(b) 6–7, 86, 93, 128, 130–3
ss 107 . . . . 86–7, 91–2
ss 1201(a) 7, 9

ss 1201(a)(1) 9
ss 1201(c)(1) 6, 8–9
ss 1201(f) 6, 8–9
Economic Espionage Act 1996 . . . .
  234
Lanham Act . . . .
  195, 197, 202, 243
  s. 2 195
  s 32 195
  s. 43(a) 195, 197
  s. 43(a)(1)(A) 198
  s. 43(a)(3) 199
  s. 43(c) 198
Louisiana Software Licensing
  Enforcement Act . . . .
  54–5
Manual of Patent Examining Procedure
  § 1504.01(a)(I)(B) 208
Patent Act 1952 . . . .
  161, 164
  s. 101 . . . . 161, 163, 169, 171,
  174–8, 185
  s. 102 214
  s. 103 214
  s. 171(a) 208
Patent Misuse Reform Act 1988 . . . .
  141
Reinstatement (Seconds) of Contracts
  Art. 178(2) 20
  Art. 178(3) 20
Restatement (Third) of Unfair
  Competition 1995 . . . .
  199
  s. 17(c) 200
Restatement of Torts . . . .
  234–5
  s. 757(b) 235
Sherman Act 1890 . . . .
  s. 1 20

s. 2 20
s. 1 65
s. 2 66–7
Texas Theft Liability Act. . . . .
  242
UCC
  s. 1-201(11) 14
UCD
  s. 109(a) 36
Uniform Commercial Code
  ss. 2–302 22
Uniform Computer Information
  Transactions Act . . . .
  46–7
Uniform Trade Secrets Act . . . .
  233–5, 240, 243
  s. 1 240
  s. 1(1) 237
  s. 1(2) 237
  s. 1(2)(b) 236
  s. 1(4) 235–6
  s. 1(4)(a) 236
US Constitution . . . .
  Art. 1, s. 8 161
  Art. 1, s. 8, cl. 8 86
  Art. VI 234
  Art. VI, cl. 2 . . . . 51, 54
  First Amendment 176
  Fifth Amendment 223

World Trade Organization

TRIPS . . . .
  Art. 8(2) 60
  Art. 9(2) 103, 105
  Art. 39 222

Table of Treaties, etc

Department of Justice and Federal Trade Commission Antitrust Guidelines for the Licensing of Intellectual Property 65
European Commission (EC) Treaty
    Art. 30 151
    Art. 34 .... 60, 150-1
    Art. 36 153
    Art. 82 152
    Art. 101 21
European Patent Convention 178-79
    Art. 52 .... 178-86, 216
    Art. 52(1) 179-1
    Art. 52(2) 180-2
    Art. 52(2)(a) 179
    Art. 52(2)(c) 179
    Art. 52(2)(d) 179
    Art. 52(3) 179
    Art. 56 .... 181-4, 216-17
    Art. 63 178
    Art. 83 186-7
    Art. 84 186-7
Treaty on the Functioning of the European Union (TFEU)
    Art. 36 150
    Art. 101 57-60
    Art. 101(1) 58-9
    Art. 101(1)(b) 59
    Art. 101(1)(e) 59
    Art. 101(3) 59
    Art. 102 .... 59-61, 64, 66

List of Abbreviations

ABC	Hypothetical developer
AFC	Abstraction-filtration-comparison
AG	Attorney General
API	Application programming interfaces
BASCOM	*BASCOM Global Internet Services, Inc. v. AT&T Mobility LLC*, No. 2015-1763, 2016 WL 3514158 (Fed. Cir. June 27, 2016)
BnetD	*Davidson & Associates DBA Blizzard Entertainment, Inc.; Vivendi Universal Inc. v. Jung et al.* 422 F.3d 630 (8th Cir. 2005)
BSA	*Bezpečnostní softwarová asociace – Svaz softwarové ochrany v. Ministerstvo kultury*, C-393/09
CAFC	Court of Appeal for the Federal Court
CCPA	Court of Custom and Patent Appeal
CDR	Council Regulation (EC) No.6/2002 of 21 December 2001, on Community design (consolidated version)
CFI	Court of first instance
CLS	*Alice Corp. Pty. V CLS Bank Int'l* 134 S. Ct. 2347 (2014)
CUTSA	California Uniform Trade Secrets Act
DDR	*DDR Holdings, LLC v. Hotels.com, L.P.* 773 F.3d 1245 (Fed. Cir. 2014)
DMCA	Digital Millennium Copyright Act
DTSA	Defend Trade Secrets Act
ECJ	European Court of Justice
EPC	European Patent Convention
EPO	European Patent Office
EULA	End user license agreement
FOSS	Free and open source software
FSF	Free Software Foundation
GUI	Graphic user interface
HULU	Premium online streaming service
IEEE	Institute of Electrical and Electronics Engineers
IMS	*IMS Health GmbH & Co. OHG v. NDC Health GmbH & Co. KG.*, (C-418/01) [2004] E.C.R. I-503.
IPR	Intellectual property right

ISP	Internet service provider
IT	Information technology
LJ	Lord Justice
MDY	*MDY Industries v. Blizzard Entertainment* 629 F.3d 928 (9th Cir. 2010) (14 December 2010) 2013
MPEP	The Manual of Patent Examining Procedure
OHIM	The Office of Harmonization in the Internal Market
OPEL	Case C-48/05 *Adam Opel AG v. Autec AG* [2007] E.C.R. I-1017
OSI	Open Source Initiative
PRC	*PRC Realty Sys., Inc. v. Nat'l. Ass'n. of Realtors,* Nos 91-1125, 91-1143, 1992 U.S. App. LEXIS 18017, at 38 (4th Cir. 4 Aug. 1992)
ProCD	*ProCD, Inc. v. Zeidenberg* 86 F.3d 1447 (7th Cir. 1996)
PTAB	Patent Trial and Appeal Board
PTO	Patent and Trademark Office
QC	Queen's Counsel
SAAS	Software-as-a-service
SSO	Structure, sequence and organization
SST	*Secure Services Technology v. Time and Space Processing* 722 F.Supp.1354 (E.D. Va. 1989)
TDS	Trade Secrets Directive
TFEU	Treaty on the Functioning of the European Union
TM	Trademark
TPM	Technological protection measures
TRIPS	The Agreement on Trade Related Aspects of Intellectual Property Rights
TSD	Trade Secrets Directive
UCITA	Uniform Computer Information Transactions Act
USPTO	United States Patent and Trademark Office
UTSA	Uniform Trade Secrets Act
VGS	Virtual game solution
VOIP	Voice over Internet Protocol
WPL	*SAS Institute, Inc. v. World Programming Ltd* [2010] EWHC 1829 (Ch)

1

LICENCE-CREATED MONOPOLIES

Controlling Use Through Restrictive Licensing Terms

1.1 Setting the Scene	2
1.2 Restricting Licensees through the Use of Technology-Based Solutions	4
1.2.1 The position in the European Union	5
1.2.2 The US position	5
1.2.2.1 *Judicial perspectives*	6
1.3 Reverse Engineering, Reproducing Functional Elements, and Contractual Provisions	10
1.3.1 Contractual prohibitions on reverse engineering and reproduction	11
1.3.2 Licence types	13
1.3.3 Summation	14
1.4 The Case for Freedom of Contract	14
1.5 Contracts of Adhesion	17
1.6 Regulating 'Freedom of Contracts'	19
1.6.1 Limitations based on public policy	19
1.6.2 Regulating the enforceability of contracts of adhesion	21
1.6.3 Misusing a legal right	22
1.7 The Combined Effect of Contracts of Adhesion and Technological Protection Measures	23
1.8 The Special Case of Software	26
1.8.1 The collapse of the copyright–patent dichotomy	26
1.8.2 Software's expressive core	27
1.8.3 Software as a vault	28
1.8.4 Barriers to entry	29
1.8.5 Summation	31

Beyond the Code: Protection of Non-Textual Features of Software. First Edition. Noam Shemtov.
© Noam Shemtov 2017. Published 2017 by Oxford University Press.

1.1 SETTING THE SCENE

Unlike a book, a musical CD, or most other copyright protected works, software products are rarely being sold to the public.[1] This has a considerable effect on the restrictions that may be put on the end user. In this context, in the case of a sale, the purchaser may be entitled to do with the purchased article as he sees fit, as long as it does not involve copyright infringement.[2] Thus, in the case of a sale, where a buyer's actions do not amount to copyright infringement, a copyright holder does not usually seek to restrict those actions via a contract.[3] Let us take an example of a hard copy of a book being sold under a contract whereby the purchaser takes it upon himself not to lend or resell the book to a third party without the authorization of the seller. First, from a practical perspective, entering into a contract each time a physical book is sold may result in transaction costs that could have rendered the transaction less attractive to both parties. Second, violating the above conditions would not have resulted in copyright infringement. Thus, the copyright holder would not have been able to argue successfully that violation of the above conditions terminated his authorization for using the book, and any subsequent use of the book should therefore result in copyright infringement. Finally, the enforceability of such conditions is questionable in the light of the US First Sale doctrine[4] and the European Union's exhaustion of rights principle. Thus, once the transaction is categorized as a sale, it is usually implicit that the seller is giving up the power to control actions that do not constitute copyright infringement in relation to the sold article; this is even more so in the case of further downstream sales, where the original seller has no contractual relationship with downstream purchasers.

However, should the said transaction be classified as licence rather than sale, the seller might be able to retain his ability to control the type of use being made in respect of the licensed article through various contractual provisions. It follows that many copyright owners have a clear incentive to categorize such transactions as a licence rather than a sale, should the legal option for doing so be available. As we shall see, in the case of software products, the said option represents the norm rather than the exception. Software licences can be of various types, ranging from complex negotiated bespoke agreements concerning

---

[1] This comparison does not refer to software as a service, where users are able to access software applications over the web or the cloud, but rather to software that is downloadable or available on physical media.
[2] Of course, where relevant, it should also not involve the infringement of other intellectual property rights.
[3] On the ever-growing tendency of software proprietors to license rather than sell copies of their products, see M A Lemley et al., *Software and Internet Law* (3rd edn., Santa Monica, CA, Aspen 2009).
[4] The First Sale doctrine, as codified under Section 109 of US Copyright Act.

1.1 Setting the Scene

use and service obligations, to standard form contracts governing the distribution of 'off-the-shelf' mass-market software products.[5] Software licensing has been the preferred model of software distribution since the early days of the software industry. Historically, most of these licences were leases of computer hardware coupled with 'real' licences of intellectual property rights. With time, the software industry has developed and has become more sophisticated, and with it, the licensing business models used therein. For example, there are site licences, network licences, per-seat licences, so-many-users-at-a-time licences, software-as-a-service (SAAS) agreements, etc. These types of software licences often result from the specific nature of software products or as a response to customer demands and quite often a combination of both. However, as a mass market for software products emerged, one might have expected outright sales to be the dominant model of software distribution, as is the case with copies of other types of copyrighted works. This, however, was not the case. For a variety of reasons, licensing became the dominant model for distribution of mass-market software products rather than sale. Admittedly, similar licences are becoming the norm in the distribution of certain digital information goods and therefore are not limited to software products. However, as this chapter illustrates, software products pose a particular challenge owing to the nature of software as a copyrightable subject matter. Using licences in place of sales might enable more flexible distribution models, as well as genuine price discrimination, but it may also clash with public policy considerations underlying our intellectual property regime.

It is noteworthy that another alternative model for making software available to the public has emerged more recently—SAAS. However, this chapter is not concerned with the SAAS model, as it does not involve licensing per se. With SAAS, consumers are able to access software applications over the Internet. Those applications are not downloaded onto the consumer's device but rather are hosted elsewhere by the SAAS provider. Google, Flicker, Twitter, and Facebook are just a few examples of providers using the SAAS model. The contractual arrangement in this case does not involve a licence agreement in the traditional sense but is a per se service contract. Such a contract may give rise to important questions from contractual, regulatory, or consumer protection perspectives, to name but a few, but it has little to do with the main friction points that surround software-licensing agreements.

---

[5] Whether these are in 'shrinkwrap', 'click-wrap', or 'broweswrap' form, they are distinguishable from software as-a-service agreements, which are service contracts rather than licensing agreements.

One of the main questions that this chapter addresses is whether and to what extent contract law may be used in order to override or redefine the exceptions and limitations in our copyright laws.

Except for prohibiting reproduction of any part of the program, whether of functional elements or reproduction designed to enable reverse engineering, by using contractual provisions, a right holder may seek to rely on the application of technological-protection measures (TPMs) and a variety of anti-circumvention provisions in order to achieve a similar goal. Often the application of access control and copy control mechanisms enables the right holders to subject any transaction concerning the licensed software to contractual use restrictions. Thus, TPMs are used in combination with prohibitive contractual provisions and the two are interconnected in their application and effect. The electronic fence erected by right holders may direct non-infringing users to an electronic gateway; there, electronic-standard form contracts, such as click-wrap licences, subject a user to entry/access conditions according to which the user would refrain from certain activities. This is so irrespective of whether or not such activities violate copyright law.

It should be noted that this work is mainly concerned with protectability of non-literal elements of software. Those are usually of interest to commercial enterprises rather than private users, and, therefore, the analysis below will not turn to consumer protection laws.

1.2 RESTRICTING LICENSEES THROUGH THE USE OF TECHNOLOGY-BASED SOLUTIONS

Anti-circumvention laws prohibit hacking of technological measures that are applied to digital works such as access control or copy control mechanisms. Such laws are not limited to a prohibition on hacking of digital right management systems.[6] Thus, both in the United States and the European Union, the language of such anti-circumvention provisions is broad enough so as to potentially encompass techniques such as authentication handshakes, code signing, code obfuscation, and protocol encryption, which may all qualify as TPMs covered by the anti-circumvention provisions. As this work concerns non-literal copying in software products, the focal point of the discussion below is the application of TPMs in order to regulate reproductions of functional features, as well as reproductions done in the context of reverse engineering and decompilation.

---

[6] For example, such as copy protection mechanisms as applied to DVDs.

1.2.1 The position in the European Union

In the European Union, the Information Society Directive[7] provides that it shall have no effect on the protection of computer programs.[8] However, as we will later see, in *BSA*,[9] the CJEU concluded that certain aspects of software products, such as graphical user interfaces (GUIs), are not considered an expression of computer programs and, as a result, are governed under the Information Society Directive rather than the Software Directive. Nevertheless, the ability to access and reproduce GUIs is not likely to be restricted effectively by TPMs, as GUIs are readily available for inspection by lawful users of the software, and could therefore be reproduced by competing developers. Thus, the elaborate anti-circumvention regime that was set under the Information Society Directive is not likely to effectively prevent the reproduction of various elements of GUIs.[10] As regards protection against copying of features of software architecture, it is mainly the Software Directive that regulates the European anti-circumvention regime. Unlike the Information Society Directive, the act of circumvention itself is not restricted under the Software Directive, and it is only the act of trafficking in circumvention tools that is prohibited.[11] Thus, where a right holder applies TPMs to a computer program, circumvention of such measures is not restricted under the Software Directive. As regards to trafficking of circumvention tools, Article 7(1)(c) of the Software Directive, which concerns the trafficking in tools that are designed to facilitate the circumvention or removal of any technical device protecting a computer program, is explicitly stated to be without prejudice to Articles 5 and 6, which deal with reverse engineering and decompilation respectively. Hence, the EU exceptions of reverse engineering and decompilation for achieving interoperability could not be overridden by the application of TPMs.

1.2.2 The US position

In the United States, the position is somewhat different. As discussed below, reverse engineering and decompilation in order to gain access to unprotectable elements

---

[7] Council Directive 2001/29/EC of 22 May 2001 on the harmonization of certain aspects of copyright and related rights in the information society [2001] OJ L167/10 (hereinafter 'Information Society Directive').
[8] Information Society Directive, Art. 1(2)(a).
[9] *Bezpečnostní softwarová asociace - Svaz softwarové ochrany v Ministerstvo kultury*, C-393/09.
[10] Such TMPs may assist in preventing reproduction of visual elements of a GUI in the form of copy and paste, but cannot stop a developer from reproducing such elements while writing his own code.
[11] It is submitted that a party who is sufficiently skilled to reverse engineer a computer program will not usually find circumvention of technological protection measures to be beyond its technical capabilities. Thus, such a party may be able to circumvent technical means without a need to rely on circumvention tools designed by others. Under these circumstances, the anti-circumvention provisions of the Software Directive do not apply.

of a computer program may be permitted under the broad exception of 'fair use', while the reproduction of certain functional elements of software products may be legitimate under the Section 102(b) distinction between protectable expression and non-protectable ideas.

In the context of decompilation, two exceptions to the anti-circumvention regime of the DMCA[12] appear to be particularly relevant. Section 1201(f) allows circumvention and the development of means for such circumvention for identifying program elements necessary for achieving interoperability.[13] What about decompilation for other fair-use purposes? Although before the DMCA, decompilation may have been tolerated under copyright law for purposes other than achieving interoperability, as long as it was done in order to gain access to un-protectable program elements, applying TPMs may now have the effect of limiting the ability of a competitor to decompile a computer program to scenarios involving interoperability.

The legal position on TPMs that may restrict reverse engineering and decompilation done for fair-use purposes other than achieving interoperability, or restricting reproduction of functional elements that may be permissible under Section 102(b), is far from certain. Section 1201(c)(1) states that nothing in Section 1201 affects rights, remedies, limitations, or defences to copyright infringement, including fair use. Hence, it may be argued, since prior to the introduction of the DMCA, reverse engineering and decompilation was permissible under the 'fair-use' defence for a wider range of purposes than merely for achieving interoperability, it may be permissible to circumvent TPMs in order to continue to do so. Similarly, it may be reasoned that since reproduction of certain functional elements is permissible under the copyright limitation of Section 102(b), Section 1201(c)(1) guarantees that, where necessary, TPMs could be circumvented in order to enable such reproduction. However, there is no judicial consensus in relation to the question of whether or not circumvention of TPMs in order to engage in uses that do not amount to copyright infringement is excused under Section 1201(c)(1).

1.2.2.1 *Judicial perspectives*

In *Universal Studios v. Reminder* it was decided that the DMCA does not condone circumvention of TPMs in order to engage in fair use.[14] Subsequently, the Second Circuit followed suit holding that Section 1201(c)(1) is not a 'fair-use' saving provision;[15] thus, the court concluded that circumventing a

---

[12] Digital Millennium Copyright Act 1998, amending 17 U.S.C.
[13] Thus, circumventing technical measures in order to decompile a program with a view to achieve interoperability will be excused under this provision.
[14] *Universal City Studios v. Reminders* 111 F.Supp.2d 294 (S.D.N.Y. 2000).
[15] See *Universal City Studios, Inc. v. Corley* 273 F.3d 429 (2nd Cir. 2001).

technological-protection measure in order to engage in fair-use amounts to a violation of the anti-circumvention provisions, irrespective of whether or not it is followed by copyright infringement.

The above conclusion was not endorsed by all circuit courts. First, in *Lexmark* the Sixth Circuit found in favour of the defendant mainly owing to the program to which the TPM at issue was applied, being functional and therefore not eligible to copyright protection under Section 102(b).[16] The court's reasoning in reaching this conclusion was not particularly coherent but Judge Merritt's concurring opinion on the DMCA applicability in these types of instances should be noted; he stated that unless a plaintiff can show that a defendant 'circumvented protective measures "for the purpose" of pirating works protected by the copyright statute', its infringement claim should fail.[17]

However, it was the Federal Circuit in a case decided two months earlier that explicitly departed from the aforementioned *Reminder* and *Corley* decisions. Thus, in *Chamberlain*, the court found that there must be a nexus between the contested circumvention and copyright infringement.[18] According to the Federal Circuit, where subsequent to circumvention the defendant engages in fair use, and is therefore not liable for copyright infringement, liability under Section 1201 should not to be imposed. As the court put it, interpreting Section 1201(a) as though it concerns only access control regardless of the rights protected under copyright law would be 'both absurd and disastrous'.[19] In a subsequent decision, the Federal Circuit continued to maintain that circumventing TPMs without engaging in copyright infringement should not attract liability under the DMCA.[20]

Thereafter, the pendulum swung back again towards *Reminder* and *Corley*. Explicitly departing from the aforementioned Federal Circuit reasoning, in *MDY v. Blizzard*, the Ninth Circuit stated: 'While we appreciate the policy considerations expressed by the Federal Circuit in *Chamberlain*, we are unable to follow its approach because it is contrary to the plain language of the statute.'[21] Thus, according to the Ninth Circuit Section 1201(a) creates a new anti-circumvention right which is independent of and distinct from copyright infringement. Unlike the Federal Circuit's view, there is no nexus that needs to be established between the two.

---

[16] *Lexmark Int'l, Inc. v. Static Control Components, Inc.* 387 F.3d 522 (6th Cir. 2004) (the decision was mainly based on the court's conclusion that the 'toner loading program' was not a copyrighted work since it was purely functional).
[17] Ibid, 75.   [18] *Chamberlain Group, Inc. v. Skyline Techs., Inc.* 381 F.3d1178 (Fed. Cir. 2004)
[19] Ibid, 1201.
[20] *Storage Tech. Corp. v. Custom Hardware,* Eng'g & Consulting Inc. 421 F.3d 1307 (Fed. Cir. 2005).
[21] *MDY Industries v. Blizzard Entertainment* 629 F.3d 928 (9th Cir. 2010) (14 December 2010) 2013.

It is suggested that the question of whether or not one may circumvent a TPM under Section 1201(c)(1) in order to engage in activities that do not involve copyright infringement is far from clear and may need to be settled by the Supreme Court. As things currently stand, the anti-circumvention provisions under the DMCA may have a chilling effect in cases where a party wishes to engage in reverse engineering and decompilation for fair-use purposes other than achieving interoperability. For example, where Benjamin Edelman, a computer researcher, wished to research the Internet blocking program N2H2, which was protected by TPMs, including an encryption system, he felt obliged to seek from a federal court a declaratory judgment that his research and its subsequent publication would not attract liability under the DMCA.[22] Mr Edelman's research objective was to establish that rather than merely filtering websites containing child pornography and other objectionable matter, the said program was also indiscriminately blocking sites with no objectionable content. The research would have involved decompilation of the N2H2 code and, for that purpose, decryption—which might constitute circumvention of a technological-protection measure. In court, the defendant's motion to dismiss was allowed, an appeal was not filed, and the research, most probably, never took place.[23]

Notwithstanding Section 1201(f), circumvention of TPMs in order to engage in decompilation for the purposes of achieving interoperability is not necessarily immuned from the effect of the anti-circumvention provisions of the DMCA. This effect can clearly be seen in the Eighth Circuit decision of *Blizzard v. BnetD*.[24] The case illustrates that even where the contested activity comprises decompilation designed to achieve interoperability, the DMCA has the potential of rendering such circumvention illegal. In this case, the defendants created an open source application (BnetD) that emulated Blizzard's Battle.Net, enabling owners of Blizzard title to connect to unofficial servers. Playing on non-Battle.Net servers enabled players to gain more control over channel names and account attributes, and to take action easily against undesirable players. In addition, it enabled players to play online for free, while avoiding Battle.Net burdensome administration. Before creating their open source application, the defendants agreed to Blizzard's End User Licensing Agreement and Term of Use notices. These explicitly prohibited reverse engineering and the hosting of Blizzard

---

[22] See *Edelman v. N2H2* 263 F.Supp.2d 137 (D. Mass. 2003).
[23] Although the judge in this case stated that he was not prepared to provide an 'advisory opinion' to a hypothetical situation, he nevertheless opined that Edelman's substantive arguments were unconvincing 'because there is no plausibly protected constitutional interest that Edelman can assert that outweighs N2H2's right to protect its copyrighted property from an invasive and destructive trespass'.
[24] *Davidson & Associates DBA Blizzard Entertainment, Inc.; Vivendi Universal Inc. v. Jung et al.* 422 F.3d 630 (8th Cir. 2005).

1.2 Restricting Licensees

games on other servers. Apart from the issue of breach of licence terms, the court also considered whether the defendants' actions amounted to a violation of the anti-circumvention provisions under the DMCA. In order to serve as a functional alternative to Battle.Net, BnetD had to be interoperable with Blizzard's software. In particular, interoperability required that BnetD speak the same protocol language as Battle.Net. In order to uncover the said protocol language, the defendants engaged in decompilation. Blizzard games, through Battle.Net, employed a technological measure, a 'secret handshake' (CD key) to control access to its copyrighted games. The emulator developed by the defendants allowed Blizzard games to access Battle.net mode features without a valid or unique CD key. As a result, unauthorized copies of the Blizzard games were played on bnetd.org servers. The court first ruled that the 'secret handshake' between Blizzard games and Battle.net effectively controlled access to Battle.net mode within its games. Thus, it constituted a TPM within the meaning of Section 1201(a)(1) DMCA. Next, the court surprisingly rejected the defendants' argument that the interoperability exception under Section 1201(f) applied to their prima facie violation of the DMCA. Unfortunately, the court did not engage in any meaningful discussion on this point. The court merely stated: 'the Appellants failed to establish a genuine issue of material fact as to the applicability of the interoperability exception'.[25] Irrespective of whether or not this case was correctly decided, the case clearly demonstrates that an act of decompilation, which prior to the enactment of the DMCA, would most probably have been held to constitute 'fair use', now resulted in an anti-circumvention violation under Section 1201(a)(1) DMCA.[26]

In this context, it may be noted that the practice of obfuscation may also have critical implications in the context of anti-circumvention regime. Obfuscation is the process of making code harder to understand in decompiled form, without changing the semantics; namely, it is about making the code look different so it will be more difficult to decompile and decipher.[27] Obfuscators are obfuscation programs that are designed to assist with code obfuscation and can easily be obtained from various sources.[28] Unsurprisingly, there are now tools that are designed to assist

---

[25] Ibid, 649.
[26] In essence, the case is not unlike *Sony v. Connectix*. It is noteworthy that the defendant in this case did not even attempt to argue that his actions constitute fair use and, therefore, that decompilation should be permissible under Section 1201(c)(1). Hence, the defendant was in the view that the only relevant exception that may apply to his case was the decompilation for achieving interoperability exception under Section 1201(f).
[27] Note that obfuscation can sometimes be counterproductive. It may change the code so drastically so that it does not work on certain platforms. On this point see discussion: 'What are the advantages of obfuscating release code?' <http://programmers.stackexchange.com/questions/17995/what-are-the-advantages-of-obfuscating-release-code> Accessed 30 January 2016.
[28] For example, see Skater, an obfuscator for NET platform, 'Main features of Skater.Net Obfuscator' <http://www.smrtx.com/RS/obfuscator_net.htm> Accessed 15 January 2016.

programmers to decompile obfuscated code.[29] The question of whether or not such tools amount to circumvention tools under the DMCA depends on whether obfuscation is considered a 'technological-protection measure' that 'effectively controls access' to a copyrighted work.

1.3 REVERSE ENGINEERING, REPRODUCING FUNCTIONAL ELEMENTS, AND CONTRACTUAL PROVISIONS

What is the position under US copyright law regarding a contractual provision that seeks to prohibit reverse engineering and reproduction of software's functional elements? As copyright-based limitations and defences, such as the idea-expression dichotomy and the fair-use doctrine, may potentially excuse a defendant only from copyright infringement and not from breach of contract, they are of little assistance in dealing with such contractual provisions. Furthermore, it should be noted that there is no US equivalent to Article 8 of the Software Directive.[30] Article 8 provides that 'Any contractual provisions contrary to Article 6 or to the exceptions provided for in Article 5(2) and (3) shall be null and void.' However, although a prohibition against reverse engineering will be considered as null and void under the Software Directive, a prohibition against copying functional features of a computer program, which are outside the scope of copyright protection altogether, will not necessarily be treated in a similar fashion.[31] Also, as we shall see, the Software Directive does not apply various software aspects such as to GUIs.[32] Rather, the latter is governed under the Information Society Directive, which does not address the relationship between copyright's exceptions and limitation and contracts.[33] Thus, a prohibition against the copying of functional elements of GUIs will not be examined under the Software Directive, but under the Information Society Directive—which is silent on this point.

---

[29] For example, 'Salamander', which is a.NET decompiler that converts executable files (.EXE or.DLL): it automatically removes string encryptions injected by obfuscators. See, 'Salmander.Net Decompiler' <http://www.remotesoft.com/salamander/index.html> Accessed 15 January 2016.

[30] Thus, Sections 102 and 106 of the US Copyright Act are waivable provisions and therefore may be overridden by contract.

[31] See the next chapter for a discussion on this point.

[32] *Bezpečnostní softwarová asociace - Svaz softwarové ochrany v. Ministerstvo kultury*, Case C-393/09.

[33] See, 'Study on the implementation and effect in member states' laws of directive 2001/29/EC on the harmonisation of certain aspects of copyright and related rights in the information society', Report to the European Commission, DG Internal Market, February 2007, Amsterdam Law School Research Paper No. 2012-28 (stating 'Since neither the Directive nor the relevant international instruments on copyright and related rights, such as the WCT and the WPPT, prescribe any rules on the subject, the specific regulation of licensing contracts has been left to the Member States.' p. 135).

As discussed below, contractual prohibitions against reverse engineering and reproduction of functional elements are customary with many right holders. It follows that where the relevant copyright exceptions and limitation are not granted a non-waivable status as in Article 8 of the Software Directive, a right holder may be able to override copyright law's checks and balances successfully using restrictive contractual provisions. Admittedly, the aforementioned scenario may sometimes be resolved against the right holder owing to the operation of other branches of law, but as the ensuing discussion demonstrates, the legal mechanisms available under the said branches of the law often fall short in dealing with such restrictive licensing provisions.

At first glance, it seems that the position in Europe is more favourable to public interest. As aforementioned, Article 8 of the Software Directive provides that any contractual provision that prohibits reverse engineering, carried out in accordance to Articles 5 and 6, is void. Thus, the EU approach on the matter is consistent. Namely, after identifying a policy-based objective according to which reverse engineering is regarded as beneficial under certain circumstances, EU legislators were not prepared to let such objective be overridden using contractual provisions. It follows that the use of restrictive contractual provisions has no effect on the legitimacy of permissible reverse engineering in the EU. As the next chapter demonstrates, the legal position in the European Union in relation to contractual prohibitions against reproduction of functional features in GUIs is much less straightforward.

1.3.1 Contractual prohibitions on reverse engineering and reproduction

Contractual prohibitions against reverse engineering and reproduction of any part of the licensed software are commonplace in software licence agreements. In the context of prohibitions against copying, it is clear that such restrictions are not meant to apply only to elements that are protected under copyright law. If that were the case, a contractual provision stating that the licensee would not engage in copyright infringement would have sufficed. Thus, restrictions that refer to copying of any part of the software, without any derogation,[34] are intended to cover reproduction of any part of the software—whether or not permitted under copyright law. Below are a number of examples of the language employed in such licences.

From Adobe's Adobe General Terms of Use:[35]

> You must not misuse the Services, Software, or content that we provide to you as part of the Services. For example, you must not:

---

[34] For example, in the cases of fair-use copying.
[35] Adobe General Terms of Use at <http://www.adobe.com/legal/terms.html>.

copy, modify, host, stream, sublicense, or resell the Services, Software, or content;[36]

From Intel:[37]

You may not copy, modify, rent, sell, distribute or transfer any part of the Software except as provided in this Agreement, and you agree to prevent unauthorized copying of the Software.
You may not reverse engineer, decompile, or disassemble the Software.

From Napster:[38]

You may not: . . . (iii) modify, translate, reverse engineer, decompile, disassemble (except to the extent that this restriction is expressly prohibited by law), tamper with, or create derivative works based upon the Application, including the Content, or any portion thereof (including without limitation any watermarks, security components and digital rights management); (iv) copy the Application or any portion thereof;

From Apple:[39]

You may not copy (except as expressly permitted by this license and the Usage Rules), decompile, reverse engineer, disassemble, attempt to derive the source code of, modify, or create derivative works of the Licensed Application, any updates, or any part thereof (except as and only to the extent any foregoing restriction is prohibited by applicable law or to the extent as may be permitted by the licensing terms governing use of any open sourced components included with the Licensed Application).

From Oracle's Oracle Cloud Services Agreement:[40]

You may not, or cause or permit others to: modify, make derivative works of, disassemble, decompile, or reverse engineer any part of the Services (the foregoing prohibition includes but is not limited to review of data structures or similar materials produced by programs), or access or use the Services in order to build or support, and/or assist a third party in building or supporting, products or Services competitive to Oracle;
  The rights granted to You under this Agreement are also conditioned on the following: except as expressly provided herein or in Your order, no part of the Services may be copied, reproduced, distributed, republished, downloaded, displayed,

---

[36] This provision is included in both Adobe's product and cloud-related licenses.
[37] See, Intel Software License Agreement http://www.intel.com/design/network/drivers/sla_ec.htm?
[38] Napster EULA <http://www.napster.com/eula.html.
[39] ITunes EULA <http://www.apple.com/legal/itunes/appstore/dev/stdeula/>.
[40] Oracle's Online Cloud Services Agreement <http://www.oracle.com/us/corporate/contracts/cloud-services/index.html>.

posted or transmitted in any form or by any means, including but not limited to electronic, mechanical, photocopying, recording, or other means;

1.3.2 Licence types

In general, the above contractual clauses can be found in licences that may be classified under three headings: shrink-wrap, click-wrap, and browse-wrap.

A shrink-wrap licence is a licence in a tangible form where the customer is informed (usually by terms wrapped on the packaging in a transparent film and visible to the customer) that by opening the seal of the package he is accepting the terms of the licence.[41]

A click-wrap licence is a type of licence that became popular when software vendors began distributing software by means other than disks, such as when the software is pre-installed on a computer for the user, or when the software is downloaded over the Internet. Upon downloading, installation, or first use of the application, a window containing the terms of the licence opens for the user to read. The user is asked to click either 'I agree' or 'I do not agree'. If the user does not agree, the process is terminated. Click-wrap licences give rise to many fact-based questions such as whether the user had adequate notice of the licence terms and clearly assented to them before the contract is concluded. With respect to software downloads, the click-wrap terms are regularly displayed at the very start of the contract formation process, although often the terms are contained in a scrollable window that requires the user to scroll down and assent.[42] In the present context, 'cloud computing agreements' and 'software as service agreements' should be treated equally to click-wrap licences.[43] In all those cases, the agreement is not concluded before the licensee manifests its consent to the terms of the agreement by clicking 'I agree'.

A browse-wrap licence is a licence that is used in an online environment such as in the case of software downloads. The licence does not appear on the screen, and the user is not compelled to accept or reject its terms as a condition for completing the download process. Instead, a reference to a browse-wrap agreement appears only as a hyperlink that is accessed by clicking on that link. It is optional, not compulsory. This makes browse-wrap agreements more susceptible to challenges on the grounds of lack of reasonable notice and bona fide consent to the browse-wrap terms.

---

[41] Sometimes the customer is only informed in a visible manner on the outside of the package as to the existence of license terms inside the package. The customer is informed that keeping the product rather than returning it for a full refund amounts to acceptance of the license terms. See M A Lemley et al., *Software and Internet Law* (3rd edn., Santa Monica, CA, Aspen 2009)324.

[42] Ibid, 341.

[43] This is particularly so in the context of the next chapter, where the validity of those agreements in terms of contract formation is examined.

1.3.3 Summation

We have seen that right holders often use of licensing provisions to 'work around' copyright's exceptions and limitations and obtain a greater degree of control over their product than that granted to them under copyright law. But does the principle of freedom of contract always prevail in such contexts? One of the principle arguments of proponents of mass-market standard form digital licences is that they do not unravel the balance within our intellectual property regime, since intellectual property rights are rights in rem while a right created under a licence is a right in personam. Namely, the principle of freedom of contract, representing a two-party deal, is not at odds with rights in rem as the latter amount to an initial entitlement which can later be modified according to the parties' will. As attractive as this argument may appear at first glance, it is suggested that its blanket application may prove problematic in cases of mass-market standard form digital licences for software products. In order to assess whether the enablement of right holders to derogate from the exceptions and limitation granted under copyright law has any notable merits, it is first necessary to briefly examine the core of one of the cornerstones of our legal system: the principle of freedom of contract.

1.4 THE CASE FOR FREEDOM OF CONTRACT

Apart from rights organized by legislation, contracts constitute society's main source of obligations between individuals. Contracts govern most areas of our life: the purchase of a DVD, the taking of driving lessons, subscribing to a gym, subscribing to an online service, etc. French law defines *a contract* as an 'agreement through which one or more persons commit themselves towards one or more other persons, to give, to do or not to do something'.[44] German law provides a similar definition to a valid contract.[45] The American Uniform Commercial Code defines a contract as the 'total obligations, which result from the parties' agreement'.[46] It follows that our legal systems, whether civil law or common law based, recognize a contract where two key conditions are satisfied: two or more persons manifest an intention to be bound by an agreement and that an agreement is in fact concluded to produce legal effect. The principle of freedom of contract is implicit to these conditions in that people are free to bind themselves to legal obligations. Such freedom to bind oneself is thought to have both theoretical and practical value. The theoretical component extols the enforcement of private agreement as an intrinsic virtue. The practical component is a result of both the

---

[44] French Civil Code, Art. 1101.   [45] Palandt (2000) Section 145, at 140.   [46] UCC, S 1-201(11).

practical economy in letting the parties to decide on their own terms, what suits them best and of the inefficiency in substituting government regulations for the parties' expectations.[47]

The classic contract model suggests an agreement that is a result of free and voluntary negotiation process, which is bona fide conducted between informed parties. The key element here is the existence of an 'agreement'. This is more than just a formal requirement for contractual validity. In Continental Europe modern contract law emerged in the nineteenth century as a natural derivative of the liberal and moral principle of autonomy of the will. Thus, without true contractual assent a contractual agreement cannot be regarded as valid and enforceable. Like its English ancestor, American contract law has somewhat different origins and it emerged out of notions of reliance, the protection of the parties' expectations, and consideration given in return to a promise. However, it is clear that under modern American contract law the principle of autonomy of will does play a key role. Hence, under American law, a contract is formed where one party manifests its intention to agree and the other party has reason to believe that this is the case.[48] It is clear that regardless of the historical origins of modern contract law, it is imperative that in order to have a valid contract, the parties need to manifest their actual or apparent consent and the intention to be bound by it. Enforcing such a contract limits the parties' autonomy in one sense, but in another sense, it reinforces it. Thus, persons are free to choose with whom they wish to deal and the terms of such dealings, but they are not free to undo their dealing without legal consequence. Contract enforcement also serves an economic purpose: it enhances the certainty in bargaining and therefore reduces transaction costs in agreements between individuals. Without confidence in having such agreements honoured and if necessary, enforced, economic development will be hampered. Moreover, economic theory supports an efficiency argument in enforcing the outcome of parties' bargaining in the market place. This principle can be found in the Coase theorem: putting aside transaction costs, bargaining will achieve optimal outcome.[49] In addition, enforcing such contracts has also a moral element: holding one to one's promise is considered morally justifiable. Hence, whether one supports utilitarianism or ethics as a justification for the legal set of rules that governs our commercial environment, enforcing freely negotiated contracts should come up high on his list.[50]

---

[47] See E A Farnsworth, *United States Contract Law: Revised Edition* (New York, Juris Publishing 1999) 32.
[48] Ibid, 116.
[49] R H Coase, 'The problem of social cost' (1960) 3 J. L. & Econ. 1.
[50] On the key role of 'consent' in modern contract theory, see R E Barnett, 'A consent theory of contract' (1986) 86 Colum. L. Rev. 2, and F Kessler, 'Contracts of adhesion-some thoughts about freedom of contract' (1943) 42 Colum. L. R.

It follows, though, that the effect of a contract is merely relative. Namely, it can only bind the contracting parties but not unrelated third parties. This principle of the relative effect of the contract is explicitly recognized under civil law systems as a logical derivative of the principle of the autonomy of the will.[51] Similarly, common law systems recognize the principle of the relative effect of the contract under what is known as the principle of privity of contract. That is why we refer to rights that are created under the contract as personal rights, or rights 'in personam'. These types of rights are to be distinguished from rights 'in rem', which are absolute rights or rights against the whole world.[52] Thus, I may have the prerogative to decide whether or not to be bound by a contractual agreement, but I do not get to decide to bind non-contracting third parties. Another outcome of our contract law being based on the principle of personal autonomy is that parties to a contract are free to determine the content and nature of their contractual obligations. Therefore, most general rules of contract law are considered as default options: namely, they have no application where the parties agreed to the contrary.

Modern contract law pursues three general aims:[53] first, it determines under which circumstances a valid contract has been formed; then, it stipulates a list of default rules, which are designed to fill in any gaps that may have been left out in the parties' agreement; finally, it prescribes rules for interpreting the parties' intentions under the contract.

In a system where unrestricted freedom of contract is paramount, the courts' role may be described as nothing more than uncovering the parties' intention and enforcing it. Thus, where the parties' intention is unequivocally clear, as a general rule, the courts should refrain from substituting the parties' intention with their own perception on efficiency and morality. However, where the parties' intention is unclear or ambiguous, the courts may step in and fill in such gaps according to the abovementioned default rules. Furthermore, as a general rule, the courts must refrain from intervening where they consider a contract to be disadvantageous to one of the parties; otherwise, the courts may damage the principle of legal certainty. Moreover, an examination of the fairness of the contract by the courts contradicts the utilitarian argument that is one of the tenets of our economic system; namely, that 'the invisible hand of the market' usually serves the public interest in the most optimal manner.[54] Thus, if prices are excessively high or contractual terms are too unfavourable, the principle of free competition in the marketplace is best suited to provide the necessary fix. Generally, modern contract law supports

---

[51] For example, see Art. 145 of the German Civil Code and Art. 1165 of the French Civil Code.
[52] Property rights are rights 'in rem'.
[53] E A Farnsworth, *United States Contract Law: Revised Edition* (New York, Juris Publishing 1999).
[54] A term used by Adam Smith to describe the self-regulating nature of markets; the term was used in *The Theory of Moral Sentiments* (London, A. Millar 1759).

the courts' intervention in rescinding what appears to be the parties' intention only where there is no 'real' consent or where an involuntary element is involved.[55]

Such arguments, however, may not be taken to the extreme. If one accepts that freedom of contracts should always prevail,[56] there would be little justification for some of our substantive laws. But, of course, substantive laws are an inherent part of our legal system. Substantive law serves at least three aims under our legal system:[57] first, it governs the behaviour of the parties where the mechanism of contract is inefficient;[58] second, where a contract is an inefficient means for distributing resources since an agreement between two parties may produce positive or negative 'externalities' affecting an uncompensated third party; third, it may be the case that under certain circumstances society is not prepared to accept the outcome of certain consensual arrangements.[59] It is suggested that the first two abovementioned aims are relevant in the context of intellectual property law and, in particular, copyright law. In part, intellectual property law has originally emerged because of the unsuitability of contract law in dealing with relevant works. Once an idea or an expression became public, its reproduction by third parties is easy. Thus, it was necessary to change the balance in favour of authors so that their works would attract legal protection irrespective of contractual obligations. These intellectual property laws, however, also limit the powers granted to the right holders and secure certain privileges for users. The allocation of such privileges under our intellectual property regime often reflects a balance of various interests that cannot always be represented in a contract. As discussed above, many contracts governing works protected by intellectual property rights often seek to change the aforementioned balance. In doing so such contracts may affect not only the contracting parties, but also third parties.[60] The social costs of these 'externalities' are not taken into account within the contractual framework.[61]

1.5 CONTRACTS OF ADHESION

Contracts of adhesion, which are sometimes referred to as standard form contracts, are contracts that do not allow for negotiation. This type of contract

---

[55] For example, where one of the parties does not have legal capacity or where fraud, duress, or undue influence is involved.

[56] Except for where, as aforementioned, there is no 'real' consent or where an involuntary element is involved.

[57] M A Lemley, 'Intellectual property and shrinkwrap licenses' (1995) 68 S. Cal. L. Rev. 1250.

[58] For example, owing to transaction costs.

[59] For example, a contract where a person is contracting himself into slavery or, in most jurisdictions, into prostitution, is not likely to be enforced.

[60] For example, other users, future authors and inventors, etc.

[61] M A Lemley, 'Intellectual property and shrinkwarp licenses' (1995) 68 S. Cal. L. Rev. 1250.

involves a simple 'take it or leave it' proposition. Namely, either one of the parties signs the contract 'as is' or abandons it altogether. The principle of supremacy of freedom of contract is most convincing when meaningful bargaining takes place. Take away the bargaining element and the aforementioned arguments lose some of their force. That is not to say that contracts of adhesion are not and should not be enforceable. Such contracts reduce transaction costs and enhance efficiency. It is beyond doubt that they play a critical role in the construction of a digitized information economy. Nevertheless, owing to their particular nature, one should examine such contracts with a number of caveats in mind.[62]

Contracts of adhesion often involve large entities on the one hand and consumers or end users on the other hand. The end user is in no position to negotiate or 'bargain' on the standard terms of such contracts, nor does the entity's salesperson have any authority to do so. In the case of mass-market software products, virtually all relevant licences are contracts of adhesion,[63] where no meaningful bargaining takes place. Generally speaking, such licences are more difficult to accommodate within the framework of classic contract law. All issues relating to applicable law, liability, warranties, etc. are usually predetermined by the right holder. The end user would be, if at all, free to decide on the date of delivery and no more. Such unilateral terms often derogate from the default rules available under contract law, most often in favour of the right holder. It is true that the preparations and negotiations of hundreds of thousands of similar contracts for similar transactions makes very little sense and is highly unpractical as transaction costs would be enormous. It is mainly for this reason that our framework of contract law recognizes contracts of adhesion as valid contracts notwithstanding their lack of meaningful 'meeting of the minds'. The Restatement (Second) of Contracts points out to the benefit that such contracts provide:

> Standardization of agreements serves many of the same functions as standardization of goods and services; both are essential for a system of mass production and distribution. Scarce and costly time and skill can be devoted to a class of transactions rather than to details of individual transactions. (. . .) Sales personal and customers are freed from attention to numberless variations and can focus on meaningful choice among a limited number of significant features: transaction type, style, quantity, price and the like. Operations are simplified and costs reduced to the advantage of all concerned.[64]

---

[62] For an authoritative discussion on the nature, role, and effect of contracts of adhesion, see F Kessler, 'Contracts of adhesion: some thoughts about freedom of contract' (1943) 42 Colum. L. R.

[63] Commonly known as EULA (End User License Agreement).

[64] See L M C R Guibault, *Copyright Limitations and Contracts* (The Hague, Kluwer Law 2002) at 120, citing from American Law Institute, Restatement (Second) of Contracts, Section 211, comm. at 120.

Freedom of contract is still considered as one of the main tenets of our legal systems and in many cases, contracts of adhesion are treated as any other contract. Nevertheless, different legal systems have developed different means for dealing with contacts of adhesion, usually in the form of additional basic safeguards to the benefit of the adhering party. Whether these safeguards can generally be regarded as sufficient for maintaining a desirable equilibrium within our commercial legal system is beyond the scope of this title. It is suggested that at least in the instance of contracts of adhesion for mass-market software products, there are cases where the principle of 'freedom of contracts' should not necessarily have the final say. This is so since in such instances, the concept of contractual assent is overstrtetched and, in combination with the application of TPMs, produces the equivalent of private legislation, practically effective against the world, which defeats public policies underlying our intellectual property regime.

Do the aforementioned safeguards amount to adequate regulatory tools for dealing with contracts of adhesion that prohibit reverse engineering, decompilation, and reproduction of non-literal and functional elements in the case of mass-market software products? Do our legal systems place appropriate and proportional limitations on the principle of 'freedom of contract' under such circumstances? Before examining these questions, we must conduct a general examination of the type of restrictions, relevant for works protected by intellectual property rights, that our legal systems place on the principle of freedom of contract, the circumstances in which such restrictions are imposed, and the rationale behind them.

1.6 REGULATING 'FREEDOM OF CONTRACTS'

1.6.1 Limitations based on public policy

What constitutes 'public policy'? In the nineteenth century, the notion of public policy was limited to aspects of state organization and public powers. This definition, however, did not remain static and has evolved through the years to encompass aspects relating to social and economic considerations. The significance of public policy considerations in the context of contract enforcement was well illustrated by the US Supreme Court, which stated: 'A promise will be found unenforceable if the interest in its enforcement is outweighed in the circumstances by a public policy harmed by enforcement of the agreement.'[65] Establishing whether public policy considerations outweigh the interest in enforcement in a specific

---

[65] *Newton v. Rumery* 480 U.S. 386, 392 (1987).

instance may prove tricky; the Restatement (Second) of Contracts provides some guidance, stipulating that:[66]

> In weighing the interest in the enforcement of a term, account is taken of
>
> (a) the parties' justified expectations,
> (b) any forfeiture that would result if enforcement were denied, and
> (c) any special public interest in the enforcement of the particular term.
>
> In weighing a public policy against enforcement of a term, account is taken of
>
> (a) the strength of that policy as manifested by legislation or judicial decisions,
> (b) the likelihood that a refusal to enforce the term will further that policy,
> (c) the seriousness of any misconduct involved and the extent to which it was deliberate, and
> (d) the directness of the connection between that misconduct and the term.

As mentioned, the notion of public policy in this context has developed through the years and now encompasses economic and market efficiency considerations, such as free competition. Modern Competition or Antitrust regimes are based, inter alia, on the premise that freedom of contract must give way to considerations such as prevention of restraint of trade, formation of monopolies and abuse of dominant position. The early libertarian view that unrestricted freedom of contract would promote societal welfare in all circumstances and result in contractual justice came to be viewed as naïve, as it proved to lead to exploitation, creation of monopolies and cartels, abuse of dominant position and, generally speaking, to the surrender of societal interest to an individual one.

The creation of the first substantive law for protecting society against the aforementioned contingencies took place in the United States with the enactment of the Sherman Act.[67] With time, most Western legal systems followed suit and adopted a competition law regime, designed, inter alia, to safeguard against the aforementioned negative by-products of freedom of contracts. For example, Section 1 of the Sherman Act prohibits agreements resulting in restraint of trade. Section 2 of the Sherman act concerns a scenario where an undertaking acquires a dominant position. A good example for public policy considerations embodied in intellectual property laws outweighing the interest in enforcing a contract that disturbs the balance within such laws can be seen in *Lear v. Adkins*.[68] There, the US Supreme Court held that a contractual term according to which a licensee waived his right to challenge the validity of a patent was unenforceable. The court explicitly held that an agreement that seeks to 'opt out' of the allocation of rights as established

---

[66] Reinstatement (Seconds) of Contracts, Art. 178(2) & (3).
[67] First enacted in 1890; U.S.C Title 15.
[68] 395 U.S. 653 (1969).

1.6 Regulating 'Freedom of Contracts'

by patent law is unenforceable since it defeats the public policy embodied in patent law. Similarly, agreements seeking to extend the term of a patent were often declared unenforceable in the United States.[69] The European Union, too, established a highly developed system designed to promote free competition. The said system imposes numerous restrictions on freedom of contracts. For example, Article 101 of the EC Treaty provides that agreements, which affect trade by preventing, restricting or distorting competition, are void unless they fall under a limited list of exemptions.

Another example for substantive law overriding freedom of contract can be found in EU Community trademarks legislation: an assignment of a Community Trademark with respect to only a part of EU territory is not effective.[70] Since one of the objectives of EU law is the creation of a functioning internal market, a contractual instrument that has the effect of partitioning the said market would be unenforceable.

1.6.2 Regulating the enforceability of contracts of adhesion

Recognizing that contracts of adhesion pose a conceptual dilemma regarding 'autonomy of will' and 'meeting of the minds', our contract law systems created numerous juridical tools designed to enable the courts to interpret, supplement and 'correct' such contractual arrangements. For example, in the EU, the Directive on Unfair Contract Terms in Consumer Contracts[71] seeks to deal with such contracts. Although the scope of the Directive is limited to transactions involving consumers,[72] it nevertheless illustrates an acknowledgement by EU law that contracts of adhesion should be handled with care by the courts. First, since limited to consumers, it recognizes that inequalities in economic power must be taken into consideration when enforcing contractual terms. Second, it provides that standard form contracts must comply with a standard of good faith and must not cause considerable imbalance in terms of consumer's rights and obligations,[73] in view of the goods and services concerned. There is no equivalent federal legislation in the United States. However, faced with a scenario involving contracts of adhesion, unequal

---

[69] For example, see *Meehan v. PGP Indus.* 802 F.2d 881 (7th Cir. 1986); *Boggild v. Kenner Prods.* 776 F.2d 1315 (6th Cir. 1985)

[70] See Art. 16(1) of Council Regulation (EC) 40/94 of 20 December 1993 on the Community trademark (referred to as 'CTM Regulation').

[71] Directive 93/13/EEC of the European Parliament and Council of 14 May 1991, on the legal protection of computer programs, [1991] OJ L122/42 (referred to as 'Directive 93/13/EEC').

[72] Thus, not directly applicable to reverse engineering and functionality copying scenarios as most parties engaged in such activities are most likely to be commercial entities.

[73] Ibid, Art. 3.

bargaining powers, and highly unfair terms, US courts sometimes resorted to juridical acrobatics in interpreting offensive contractual provisions. In doing so they often applied the doctrine of *'contra proferentem'*, according to which an ambiguous contractual term is interpreted against the party who drafted it and in favour of the adhering party. In addition and where applicable, Section 2-302 of the Uniform Commercial Code might serve as a useful judicial tool in this context. It states:

(1) If the court as a matter of law finds the contract or any clause of the contract to have been unconscionable at the time it was made the court may refuse to enforce the contract, or it may enforce the remainder of the contract without the unconscionable clause, or it may so limit the application of any unconscionable clause as to avoid any unconscionable result.
(2) When it is claimed or appears to the court that the contract or any clause thereof may be unconscionable the parties shall be afforded a reasonable opportunity to present evidence as to its commercial setting, purpose and effect to aid the court in making the determination.

The notion of *unconscionable contract or term* basically refers to an element of unfairness. Although the concept is not limited to transactions involving contracts of adhesion, the fact that the contract in question is non-negotiable plays an important role in the court's ruling, as Subsection 2 provides that the circumstances in which the contract was concluded are important to the court's determination on the unconscionability of the contested contract or term. It should be noted that the application of the doctrine of unconscionability by American courts is much more limited than that applied by their European counterparts, as the latter would examine not only the oppressive nature of a contested term but also whether the allocation of risks affected by such a term unfairly prejudices one of the parties.

Neither of these mechanisms is likely to be of much help to a commercial party to a standard form contract that prohibits reverse engineering and reproduction of any part of the software, copyright protected or not. Such clauses were never held to be unconscionable under US law owing to the limited scope of the unconscionability doctrine. As regards the European Union, the Directive on Unfair Contract Terms in Consumer Contracts does not apply to business-to-business contracts.

1.6.3 Misusing a legal right

The concept of misusing or abusing a legal right is a type of limitation that may be applicable to the manner in which a proprietor chooses to exercise its proprietary right.[74] Right holders who tend to license their rights often include in such licences

---

[74] Quite often the terms of use of a proprietary right are subject to an agreement. It is within this context that the said doctrine may regulate and determine the enforceability of such agreements.

contractual provisions that extend the right holder's legal monopoly beyond that which is granted to him under intellectual property law. When a software licensee does not comply with such a term, the right holder may bring an action for breach of contract, as well as claiming copyright infringement. Where a computer program is 'licensed' and a licensee fails to comply with a term, the right holder may argue that continued use of the said program not only constitutes breach of contract but also amounts to copyright infringement since the licence provides that the authorization given to the licensee to use the program is terminated under such circumstance.[75] Establishing copyright infringement has clear advantages for the right holder in terms of both available remedies and regulation of actions of third parties.[76]

In order to understand the basis of doctrines concerning abuse or misuse of rights, one must first distinguish between the existence and the exercise of a right. The fact that a right has been granted to a person automatically implies that certain restrictions are imposed on other persons. Exercised in a particular manner, the outcome may be considered as so prejudicial to other persons that the right holder's conduct is regarded abusive. Thus, under certain circumstances right holders may not be allowed by the courts to enforce their intellectual property rights in a particular manner. The concept of misuse or abuse of rights is discussed in detail below.[77]

1.7 THE COMBINED EFFECT OF CONTRACTS OF ADHESION AND TECHNOLOGICAL PROTECTION MEASURES

The growing use of digital contracts of adhesion in mass-market software products is closely related to the implementation of TMPs. It is mainly due to TPMs that one cannot gain access to and/or use a software product without consenting to such contracts. It is where some type of access control mechanism is being used that one has to 'assent' to standard contractual terms. Thus, without having a digital fence, people would not have to agree to enter by the gate, as set by the right owner.

TPMs provide right owners with a control mechanism over the terms of access and use of their works. These measures may not only help right holders by defining an authorized use, but might also actively enforce any deviation from the authorized scope. Coupled with a licensing provision prohibiting reverse engineering

---

[75] Thus the temporary copies created on the licensee's device every time the program is used become unauthorized infringing copies.
[76] Namely, downstream parties who do not have a contractual relationship with the right holder.
[77] See Chapter 5.

and reproduction of functional elements, the user may not only be obliged to assent to such a term in the first place in order to gain access to and/or use a software in question, but may also find out that he is technically barred from reverse engineering and reproducing functional elements in the said software owing to an effective protection measure applied to the software product.[78]

It is suggested that an unregulated use of non-negotiable contracts, coupled with application of effective TPMs, yields high social costs and may hamper rather than encourage growth in the software industry. Treating a click-wrap licence for a mass-market software product as a contractual mechanism that establishes nothing more than a mere personal right is at best naïve and at worst misleading. Let us illustrate this point with an example. A certain application program may be offered, both on- and offline. Being offered online, one is not allowed to download it without manifesting his 'assent' by scrolling down the licence terms and clicking 'I agree'. Please note that it is the TPMs that make sure that our licensee must always click as aforementioned, otherwise download could not be completed. In most cases this downloaded copy could not be legally assigned or sublicensed to a third party,[79] but even where that is possible, such third party would not be considered as 'authorized user'[80] without 'assenting' to the terms of the licence by clicking 'I agree'. Such 'assent' will have to take place owing to the operation of TPMs during the download process. A right holder that also offers his product in a cloud environment ends up in a similar position. Thus, cloud agreements or SAAS agreements lead to the same outcome in the sense that access and use of the software could not take place without first assenting to the terms of use. Let us now turn to the tangible offline copy. An offline copy (e.g. on a USB stick) purchased off the shelf leads to a similar outcome. First, the purchaser would often be bound by the terms of a shrink-wrap licence.[81] But even after unwrapping the software product and attempting to run it on his computer, our licensee would have to acknowledge his 'assent' to the full terms of the licence by clicking 'I agree'. Again, where our licensee wishes to assign or sublicense his rights to a third party, he will usually be prohibited from doing so by the licence terms. But even where such transfer is possible, it will usually be conditioned upon the new licensee 'consenting' to the same licence terms. Again, in order to run for the first time its newly acquired second hand computer program, our licensee in this instance would be obliged to

---

[78] For example, encryption, scrambling, and code obfuscation.
[79] Subject to the decision in *UsedSoft GmbH v. Oracle International Corp.* C-128/11; see the discussion in the next chapter.
[80] Not being an authorized user means you are in breach of the right owner's copyright, since the temporary reproduction taking place on your computer is without the right owner's authorization. If such authorization is to be given, the sublicensee is required to express its consent to the licence terms by clicking 'I agree'.
[81] The validity of such licenses is jurisdiction dependent and is discussed below.

click 'I agree' as a matter of technical necessity owing to the application of technological measures. Furthermore, even if our third party walks down a street and finds a copy of the program at the roadside, takes it home, and wishes to use it, he would be obliged to 'assent' to the terms of the licence, by clicking 'I agree', in order to run it for the first time. Although in this latter case, there may not be a binding contract as there is no mutual agreement between two parties and there is no consideration, the click-wrap licence might be treated as a bare licence that sets out the conditions under which the computer program in question may be used. Non-compliance with such terms might not necessarily result in breach of contract but may nevertheless result in copyright infringement.[82] Even in the unlikely eventuality that our alleged licensee manages to establish that the terms of the licence in question do not apply to him,[83] he might still find that he cannot proceed to reverse engineering or to reproduce functional elements of the program in question as copyright law permits him to do, since he will be compelled to circumvent TPMs in order to do so. In such a case, although safe from copyright infringement, as well as from breach of contract claims, he may nevertheless be liable for violating anti-circumvention provisions.

We have seen that a 'mere' right in personam, in the context of contracts of adhesion for mass-market software products, may be de facto effective against the whole world. Thus, the power to construct a 'two-party' deal in the digital world, coupled with the use of non-negotiable terms, effective TPMs, and anti-circumvention legislation, is so overwhelming in its impact that it is often practically equivalent to private legislation effective against the world. Viewed in this way, it appears that our delicately balanced copyright system of rights 'in rem' is under threat from an often-conflicting privately arranged system of obligations, designed naturally to best serve the interests of right holders. Should one give 'freedom of contracts' a free rein, important interests that are protected under our copyright regime are likely to be jeopardized.

But why focus only on software? After all, using standard form licences in respect of mass-market digital works is not unique to the software industry. Such licences can be found nowadays in relation to various informational goods, where right holders seek to derogate from rights and privileges as set out under copyright law. For example, one may seek to restrict, using a combination of contractual and technological measures, the number of times a user may read an electronic book, the platform on which a track in an MP3 format might be played, or the creation of

---

[82] Such bare licences are the legal mechanism on which the Open Source Software model is based. They are in essence a conditioned IP grant. Any use outside the terms of such a grant might constitute copyright infringement.

[83] For example, because in reality there was no license but a sale (on this point, see the discussion below).

a fair-use copy of a part of a film. One might argue that all of these practices should be safeguarded against encroachments by right owners, as such limitations on the type and scope of use of a work are not compatible with copyright law. Be that as it may, it is suggested that traditional copyright works in digital format pose less of a problem in this context. It may nevertheless be the case that certain privileges guaranteed under our copyright regime should be safeguarded against attempts to derogate from them,[84] but it is suggested that the software sphere presents a strong case for regulatory intervention where right holders seek to derogate from copyright law.

1.8 THE SPECIAL CASE OF SOFTWARE

Software must be the most peculiar subject matter protected under copyright law. In earlier times both courts and academics voiced their doubts as to whether object code is a proper subject matter for copyright law because it has a low expressive value.[85] Whatever merits such arguments originally held, this debate is no longer practically relevant these days as it is universally acknowledged that code, as well as other elements of computer programs, are protected under copyright law. This, however, should not obscure the fact that software is a highly unconventional subject matter for copyright protection and, therefore, poses a number of challenges in this context. Owing to its unique nature, it should be handled with care when evaluating the protective umbrella that it might enjoy due to the combined effect of copyright, contracts, and TPMs.[86]

1.8.1 The collapse of the copyright–patent dichotomy

Abstract ideas, discoveries, laws of nature, and natural phenomena are not eligible for intellectual property protection.[87] While copyright may protect expression of ideas, patent law protects the utilitarian embodiments of ideas. Thus, generally

---

[84] For example, the author of this book is in the view that right owners should be entitled to use the copyright in their work in a way that would enable them to engage in genuine price discrimination. Thus, licensing the right to read an electronic book only two times, three times, and four times does not necessarily appear objectionable. In contrast, denying the right to criticise and review a work does appear objectionable as it clashes with fundamental public policies underlying our legal system.

[85] For example, see P Samuelson et al., 'A manifesto concerning the legal protection of computer programs' (1994) 94 Colum. L. Rev. 2308, 2314.

[86] For a general discussion on the unique nature of software and the manner in which it may be used by right holders in order to circumvent public policy objectives that underlie our copyright law, see B Frischmann and D Moylan, 'The evolving Common Law doctrine of copyright misuse: a unified theory and its application to software' (2000) 15 Berkeley Tech. L. J. 865.

[87] This assertion does not consider trade secrets.

speaking, copyright law is not concerned with functional works. That is not to say that functional works cannot be protected under copyright law. One of the earliest examples for functional works protected under copyright law was geographical maps. Maps, however, are expressive in their nature. It is true that most people would use maps for functional rather than cultural or aesthetic purposes, but this is not to say they are not expressive. Maps, as all other functional works protected under copyright law, save software, can be 'experienced' by a user in a conventional manner; they are intended to be used by humans and, therefore, considered expressive. Code, on the other hand, is not aimed at humans at all.[88] The main reason people embark upon the costly and time-consuming practice of reverse engineering is exactly because, viewed in an object-code form, a computer program is unintelligible to a reader, viewer, or listener. Nevertheless, copyright law protects code.

1.8.2 Software's expressive core

One of the main objectives of our copyright regime is to encourage the creation, dissemination, and exchange of creative expressions.[89] Owing to the peculiar nature of software, this objective is not being fully realized in the case of software.

As mentioned, copyright law protects the expression of ideas rather than ideas themselves. As discussed in Chapter 4, the idea–expression dichotomy provides that ideas embodied in expressive works are not subject to protection and, therefore, may be viewed, studied, and used by the public. By granting authors exclusive rights in expressive works, it is hoped that it will encourage the creation and dissemination of more works, which, in turn, will promote the flow of ideas, as well as expressions, to the public. Unfortunately, the unique nature of software may frustrate some of these goals. Some of the logical building blocks underlying a computer program are concealed from the public eye because of software's peculiar technical nature. We have seen that since computer programs are intentionally released into the market only in object-code form, many of the ideas underlying them are not readily apparent.[90] In many cases, in order to pick into a program's internal organs and thereby examine such ideas, processes, methods of operation, and mathematical concepts embodied therein, it would be necessary to

---

[88] It should be noted that although object code may not be 'experienced' or comprehensible to humans, other functional aspects of programs might be. For example, GUIs could certainly be experienced in a similar fashion to geographical maps and are therefore of less relevance to the current discussion.

[89] See P Goldstein, *Goldstein on Copyright* (3rd edn., Santa Monica, CA, Aspen Publishers 2006).

[90] Software publishers can also release computer programs in source code form, but for obvious reasons prefer to keep these in-house as trade secrets.

reverse engineer the said program. This is not the case with other functional works protected under copyright law. As the *Sega* court observed:

> The unprotected aspects of most functional works are readily accessible to the human eye. The systems described in accounting textbooks or the basic structural concepts embodied in architectural plans, to give two examples, can be easily copied without also copying any of the protected, expressive aspects of the original works. Computer programs, however, are typically distributed for public use in object code form, embedded in a silicon chip or on a floppy disk. For that reason, humans often cannot gain access to the unprotected ideas and functional concepts contained in object code without disassembling that code—i.e., making copies.[91]

This phenomenon is further compounded in the case of SaaS, where the user has no access to the code to start with, whether in object or source code versions. There is no other example of a work protected by copyright where ideas and concepts that underlie such work are not discoverable upon an examination that does not involve copyright infringement.

1.8.3 Software as a vault

One of the side-effects of having some of the logical building blocks of software embedded in its internal organs and concealed from an observer's eye is that protected and unprotected elements of a program intertwined in such a way that one cannot be discerned from the other without infringement.[92] The fact that a software proprietor can enforce his copyright in a program as one piece, protected and unprotected elements included, means that he is acquiring de facto control over unprotected elements, as well as protected ones. An exception for reverse engineering and decompilation provides a partial means of neutralizing this problem by excusing the reverse engineer from potential infringement owing to the necessary copying taking place during the technical process. As argued elsewhere in this title, prohibiting the public from decompiling a computer program is akin to granting right holders a type of monopoly over unprotected elements of software. Moreover, unlike a book or a CD, a mere use of a computer program involves the creation of temporary copies, thus engaging copyright laws. Hence, where a licence stipulates a list of restrictions so that any violation of the said restrictions

---

[91] *Sega Enterprises Ltd v. Accolade, Inc.* 977 F.2d 1510, 1525 (1992).
[92] This refers to ideas and concepts that are concealed in the internal architectural layers of software products, rather than their GUIs. Nevertheless, it should be borne in mind that in the case of the latter, although the functionality of a GUI could be studied from observing the program in operation, repetitive observations involve repetitive creations of temporary copies of the GUI on one's screen. Where the authorization for creating such copies is conditioned upon adherence to licensing provisions, violation of these provisions may result in copyright infringement.

causes the termination of the licence, such violation may result not only in breach of contract, but also in copyright infringement.

To conclude, the vault-like nature of software and the fact that its use necessitates the creation of a temporary copy every time software is run, the prevalence of standard form licence terms and TPMs, together with anti-circumvention legislation, have a combined effect that runs contrary to some of the main public policy objectives that stand at the heart of our copyright regime.

1.8.4 Barriers to entry

As the software industry grew and matured, right holders became more successful in erecting a multilayered protective fence around their works. They rely on copyright for protecting source code, object code, and certain architectural features, as well as, indirectly, ideas and concepts embodied in their software. Copyright may also protect artistic and textual elements in GUIs. They rely on patents to protect their software related inventions, as far as they are able to do so. They may also rely on the law of designs and registered and unregistered trade-marks protecting their brand name and logos, as well as the 'look and feel' of their products. Our right holders may also fall back on trade secrecy. Regarding the latter, coupled with standard form licences and TPMs, trade secrecy can become quite effective for right holders. On top of this tapestry of legal means, software proprietors were at the forefront of using technological means for protecting their works, such as 'secret-handshake' devices, encryption techniques, scrambling, and code and data structure obfuscation. We have seen that such technical measures are often used in order to try to secure for the right holders that which copyright law itself does not grant. Technology may also be used to make two pieces of software dependent upon one another so that the two products are integrated in such manner as to obstruct any potentially competing entrant to the market.[93] Finally, right holders may apply TPMs as a means of detection, thus policing the activity of users against unauthorized forms of use and reacting to such conduct in numerous ways.[94] Any attempt to overcome such technological means may result in violation of anti-circumvention legislation. The combination of these mechanisms puts established right holders in a very powerful position.

In addition, innovation in software's ecosphere may also be affected by other surrounding circumstances. First is the speed of growth in the software industry. Dominance in the market place may be established at astonishing pace.[95] Second,

---

[93] See *United States v. Microsoft Corp.* 87 F.Supp.2d 30 (D.D.C 2000) 51.

[94] Technology may assist software proprietors to detect, prevent, and even penalize users they deem to behave in an objectionable manner.

[95] See, for example, Google: from a firm with eight employees in 1999 it grew to be worth $186 billion in 2008 and $367 as of May 2015, to become the dominant player in the search engine market (see, respectively, Google's Company History, *Wall Street Journal* (2010) and *Forbes* http://www.forbes.com/companies/google/.

the software market clearly exhibits lead-time effects, thus offering a window of opportunity in which right holders may enter the market and establish their position over their competitors. This may act as a barrier to new entrants and it is of significance because innovation in this area is often incremental, thus serving as a basis for innovation.[96] Such lead-time effects may be practical or legal. In the former case, it may be that a right holder is best placed to offer a compatible piece of software, as it has all the relevant information in place and the facilities and marketing tools to move quickly into production and distribution phases. A competitor would have to study the earlier program and probably to reverse engineer or decompile it in order to offer a compatible product. Furthermore, brand loyalty, if it can be established within a fairly short period of time, can also prove significant, thus having trade-mark law acting as another bull-bar against later competitors. Over all, such lead-time effects can act as a further barrier to later entrants, thus helping a dominant market player to establish further his dominance over his competitors.

Software also displays what may be described as 'application effects'.[97] This is the value in having users accustomed to using your product, usually associated with the program's GUI.[98] Such application affects, in turn, contribute to the aforementioned brand loyalty. Its overall effect is that users are less likely to switch to a substitute once 'locked-in' owing to their familiarity and the expertise they develop in respect of the earlier program interface and work environment.[99]

Finally, software often displays network effects. Thus, the value of many software products for users increases as the number of users increases. For example, the more people use FaceTime as a VOIP application, the more FaceTime is valuable for a new user, as he is able to make voice and video calls using Wi-Fi, or over 3G/4G network to more persons. As brilliant as FaceTime might be as a piece of technology, if only a small number of people use it, it is of general little value. Clearly, such network effects may reinforce an already existing dominant position held by software proprietor holder.[100]

---

[96] J H Reichman, 'Legal hybrids between patent and copyright paradigms' (1994) 94 Colum. L. Rev. 2432, 2439.

[97] B Frischmann and D Moylan, 'The evolving common law doctrine of copyright misuse: a unified theory and its application to software' (2000) 15 Berkeley Tech. L. J. 865.

[98] Such user interfaces may be protected under copyright, patent, trade marks, trade dress, and design laws.

[99] On the implications of such 'application effects' in terms of competition in the software market, see Judge Boudin concurring opinion at *Lotus Development Corporation v. Borland* 49 F.3d 807 (1st Circ. 1995) 819.

[100] See D S Karjala, 'Protecting innovation in computer software, biotechnology, and nanotechnology' (2011) 16 VA. J. L. & Tech. 42, and P Samuelson et al., 'A manifesto concerning the legal protection of computer programs' (1994) 94 Colum. L. Rev. 2308.

1.8.5 Summation

The unique nature of software's technical sphere, in combination with the specificities of the software market, lend towards the creation of dominant market actors.[101] Once entering the market first and establishing a leading position, a right holder is placed in a uniquely favourable position to fend off competing new entrants. Such an environment amplifies the effect of copyright protection, which, in combination with restrictive licensing terms, TPMs, and anti-circumvention legislation, risks unravelling key public policy objectives.

---

[101] See B Frischmann and D Moylan, 'The evolving Common Law Doctrine of Copyright Misuse: a unified theory and its application to software' (2000) 15 Berkeley Tech. L. J. 865, D S Karjala, 'Copyright protection of operating software copyright misuse and antitrust' (1999) 9 Cornell J. L. and Public Policy 161, M O'Rourke, 'Drawing the boundary between copyright and contract: copyright preemption of software license terms' (1995) 45 Duke L. J. 479.

2

LEGAL MECHANISMS FOR MITIGATING THE EFFECT OF RESTRICTIVE LICENSING PROVISIONS

2.1 Introduction	32
2.2 Contract Law–Based Mechanisms	34
2.2.1 Licence or sale?	34
2.2.1.1 *United States*	35
2.2.1.2 *European Union*	38
2.2.2 Contract formation and content	38
2.2.2.1 *Contract formation*	39
2.2.3 Contract content	46
2.2.3.1 *UCITA*	47
2.2.3.2 *Directive on unfair terms in consumer contracts*	47
2.2.3.3 *Directive for the protection of computer programs*	47
2.3 Pre-Emption-Based Mechanisms	51
2.3.1 Statutory pre-emption	51
2.3.2 Constitution pre-emption	54
2.4 Competition Law–Based Mechanisms	56
2.4.1 EU competition law and prohibitions on reproduction of functional software features	57
2.4.1.1 *Article 101*	57
2.4.1.2 *Article 102*	59
2.4.2 US antitrust law	65
2.4.2.1 *Section 1 of the Sherman Act—anticompetitive agreements*	65
2.4.2.2 *Section 2 of the Sherman Act: abuse of dominant position*	66

2.1 INTRODUCTION

The analysis in the following chapter relates to both negotiable and non-negotiable licences. In the previous chapter, we have seen that the software industry favours

2.1 Introduction

licensing over sales and that the licensing model is being used in order to regulate the manner in which licensees may use the licensed software. We have also seen that licences attempt to regulate the ability of licensees to utilize functional elements of the said software and to reverse engineer it.

Right owners wish to regulate the ability of licensees to copy elements of the licensed software stems, inter alia, from uncertainty in relation to the scope of protection of copyright to functional elements, and, even where the said scope is not ambiguous, right owners attempt to minimize competition. Thus, from the perspective of right owners, the rationale behind such licensing provisions is fairly straightforward: if the activity covered by the relevant restrictive provision is also prohibited under copyright law, there is no harm in having such 'double prohibition'. If, however, the said activity is permissible under copyright law since, for example, it concerns a subject matter that is excluded from copyright protection or may amount to fair use, then using such licensing provisions could have a significant impact on the licensee's scope of permissible use.

Under certain circumstances, software's functional elements are not eligible for copyright protection.[1] This chapter concerns the ability of right owners to place restrictions successfully on the utilization of functional elements of software and on reverse engineering, whether or not such elements are protected under copyright law.[2] In particular, the focus will be on judicial means for regulating licensors' use of such restrictive provisions.

Our copyright-law regime makes various choices in relation to its preferable scope of protection concerning software. As explained elsewhere in this title, courts and legislatures in the US and the EU fine-tuned the law during the last few decades so that certain elements of software remain outside the scope of copyright protection and thus open for emulation by third parties.[3] We have seen that right owners tend to employ licensing terms in order to circumvent the allocation of rights and privileges as set under copyright law. We have also seen that although the concept of freedom of contracts is one of the key elements of our legal system, it too has its limits and it is kept checked in relation to various public policy considerations. It therefore follows that in order to further public policy objectives in the context of the software industry, courts may seek an adequate mechanism for dealing with the specificities of software, for regulating the abovementioned use of licensing terms.[4] Thus, the remainder of this chapter

---

[1] See Chapters 3 and 4.
[2] It particularly focuses on licensing provisions that restrict activities that are arguably permissible under copyright law.
[3] See Chapters 3 and 4.
[4] See D E Phillips, *The Software License Unveiled: How Legislation by License Controls Software Access* (Oxford, Oxford University Press 2009), arguing that if software providers will not make changes on their own (to their End User License Agreements), consideration should be given to enacting legislation to that effect.

examines the extent to which existing judicial and statutory tools are effective in regulating restrictive licensing provisions used by the software industry.[5]

2.2 CONTRACT LAW–BASED MECHANISMS

Before examining whether and to what extent the provisions of a given licence are enforceable or not, it might be necessary to ascertain whether the item under consideration is a licence in the first place. Where a right owner wishes to define a given arrangement as a licence, the written document would usually refer to a 'licence', the consideration would often be described in terms of 'royalties' and all other relevant terminology would imply that the arrangement at issue is a licence. However, 'dressing up' a transaction in licence-related terminology should not affect its legal status.

2.2.1 Licence or sale?

As mentioned, the vast majority of right owners would prefer to license rather than sell copes of their software.[6] Licensing allows them to maintain control over their software in ways that a sale does not. Classifying a given transaction as a sale rather than a licence could have serious consequences on the right owners' ability to restrict third parties from reproducing or appropriating functional features in his software product. This is especially the case where the reproduction in question is permissible under copyright law. Thus, where the use in question is not restricted under copyright law, for example, reproduction of unprotectable functional features, an outright sale of a copy of the software in question is likely to result in any restriction on such use being ineffective, in particular against non-contracting parties. On the other hand, executing the transaction as a licence is more likely to lead to such restriction being effective, with a failure to abide by the terms of such licence leading to both copyright infringement and breach of contract. Obviously, parties to a transaction should be free to choose, in most cases, the type of transaction they wish to enter into and the relationship they wish to form. However, it may be the case that although the written document in question is using terminology that implies a licence, what the parties agreed upon, as a matter of law, is a sale. It is noteworthy that in the case of a service offered in a cloud environment,

---

[5] Even though the copyright misuse doctrine, the civil law doctrine of abuse of rights, and the English common law doctrine of restraint of trade are all potentially applicable in the context of restrictive licensing provisions, they will be examined in detail in Chapter 6.

[6] See M A Lemley et al., *Software and Internet Law* (3rd edn., Santa Monica, CA, Aspen 2009), Ch. 6.

the question of Sale versus Licence is of little relevance. Since a copy of the software at issue is never given to the licensee and remains with the service provider, it cannot be convincingly argued that the transaction at hand has the characteristics of a sale. In fact, a cloud contract is not even a software licence in a traditional sense, but a mere service contract. Thus, the ensuing discussion relates to transactions that involve the transfer of a copy of the software, either in physical or digital form, to the licensee.

Clearly, what constitutes a sale rather than a licence is a question that would be answered quite differently in different jurisdictions. Nevertheless, a brief examination of a number of US authorities and one EU decision concerning standard form licences for software products may illustrate the type of factors that courts may take into consideration when assessing the legal status of a given transaction.

2.2.1.1 *United States*

In *Microsoft v. Harmony*, the defendant was selling Microsoft products as 'stand-alone' rather than bundled with personal computer systems. Inter alia, the court had to decide whether an unauthorized party could legitimately sell Microsoft products.[7] The plaintiff in this case argued that since the defendant was not an authorized Microsoft licensee, it was not entitled to sell any Microsoft products, whether counterfeits or not. The plaintiff argued that the defendant violated the terms of licence under which Microsoft distributes its products and, therefore, was liable for copyright infringement. The defendant argued that since they bought their Microsoft products from authorized Microsoft licensees, the first sale doctrine applied and Microsoft could no longer control the manner of circulation of its products in the marketplace. It was clear that if the first sale doctrine was indeed applicable, there could be no infringement regarding the sale of genuine Microsoft products.[8] Without much analysis, the court found that the first sale doctrine did not apply to the facts of the case. As the defendants did not establish a chain of title going back to Microsoft, the court held that the doctrine was not applicable. The court maintained that in order for the doctrine to apply, there must be a first sale to start with. Since Microsoft presented evidence according to which it never seeks to sell its products but rather to license them, the court simply held that the first sale doctrine did not apply. Therefore, the defendant was bound by the licence terms and liable for copyright infringement. The court found that this was so irrespective of whether or not there was contractual relationship between the defendant and Microsoft.[9]

---

[7] *Microsoft Corp. v. Harmony Computers & Electronics, Inc.* 846 F.Supp.208 (E.D.N.Y 1994).
[8] The case also involved allegations concerning the sale of counterfeit products.
[9] This case illustrates the point discussed in the preceding chapter that a right created under a licence might be de facto effective against the whole world and thus in many respects akin to right in rem.

The above decision could be contrasted with *Softman v. Adobe*.[10] Here, the plaintiff argued that the defendant was selling, primarily through its website, unbundled versions of the plaintiff's products. The defendant did not dispute the fact that it was 'breaking down' Adobe software suites and selling its various components as stand-alone products. It was also not contested that the licence under which Adobe was distributing its software prohibited the 'unbundling' of its software. The defendant argued that since there was no contractual relationship between it and Adobe, it was not bound by the terms of the licence and was therefore entitled to 'unbundle' the software it legitimately acquired.[11] Again, one of the questions the court had to consider was whether the first sale doctrine applied. Similar to the argument submitted by Microsoft in the previous case, Adobe argued that the doctrine was not applicable as it never sells its products but merely licenses them. Here, however, the court took a different approach. The court stated that since copyright grants certain rights to owners of a particular copy, what Adobe itself purported to grant was irrelevant in this context. Thus, Adobe licence terms were in conflict with copyright law, which specifically provides for the first sale doctrine.[12] At that stage the court turned to discuss the nature and background of the prevailing licensing model in the software industry. The court noted that this licensing model had emerged at times, where it was far from clear that software was protected by copyright and even if it was there was uncertainty as to the scope of protection. With time, however, as copyright protection for software became established, the original need to categorize a transaction as a licence became obsolete. With that in mind, the court went on to stress that in order to determine whether a given transaction is a 'licence' or a 'sale', one has to examine the economic realities of that transaction. Where it appears that regardless of the terminology used, a transaction constitutes a sale as a matter of law, it should be treated as such by the courts. Examining the factual matrix of the case, the court opined that the transaction in question appeared to be more of a sale than a licence. For example, the purchaser obtained one copy of the software, paid at the time of the transaction a one off payment, the 'licence' run for an indefinite period without any need for renewal. Furthermore, the court was of the opinion that Adobe's arrangements with its distributors also supported a sale rather than a licensing model. Citing with approval from Nimmer's work *The Law of Computer Technology*, the court concluded that all the surrounding circumstances supported the conclusion that Adobe sold individual copies of its software rather than merely licensed that software.[13] The court found the following aspects in Adobe's transaction model to

---

[10] *Softman Products Company v. Adobe Systems Inc.* 171 F.Supp.2d 1075 (C.D. Cal. 2001).
[11] The defendant was not a licensee of Adobe but merely purchased its products from authorized licensees.
[12] Section 109(a) 17 UCD.
[13] R Nimmer, *The Law of Computer Technology* (Boston, Warren Gorham & Lamont 1999).

be of particular importance: unlimited possession, absence of time limit for the said possession, pricing, and payment schemes that are unitary rather than serial and licence terms under which subsequent transfer did not require the consent of Adobe. Moreover, the court went on to decide that in any event the licensing terms in question did not bind the defendant, as it was not a party to it. This was so since the defendant in this case did not manifest its assent to the said terms. Since the defendant never loaded the software onto a computer, it could not be bound by the terms of the click-wrap licence. If anyone at all was bound by it, it was the end user rather than the defendant. Finally, the court rejected Adobe's contention that placing a notice concerning the licence terms on the outer package binds the purchaser unless he returns it for a full refund according to the enclosed terms. Referring to the decision in *Microsoft v. Harmony*,[14] the court explicitly stated that to the extent that it purported to suggest that the placement of such notice would suffice to bind a purchaser to the enclosed licensing terms, it was not prepared to follow the same analysis.

To conclude, the court stated that in its view, a system of licensing whose sole justification is to enable the right owner to gain excessive power to control prices and channels of distribution was objectionable on public policy grounds. The court found in favour of the defendant.

The two decisions above are not easily reconcilable. It is quite clear that in the former the court's decision was influenced by the fact that the defendant also sold counterfeit products. However, even under the latter approach, a more careful draughtsmanship may result in classifying the transaction as a licence rather than a sale. For example, a right owner may require that any subsequent transfer of a specific copy should be subject to its prior approval. Recently, the Ninth Circuit clarified the issue. In *Vernon v. Autodesk* the court stated that a transaction will be classified as a licence 'where the copyright owner (1) specifies that the user is granted a license; (2) significantly restricts the user's ability to transfer the software; and (3) imposes notable use restrictions'.[15] Thus, it is clear that although, on occasions, the legal classification of a transaction may assist a court in maintaining copyright's checks and balances intact, more often than not a court would have little choice other than classifying a given transaction as a licence.[16] This conclusion holds whether or not the licence in question is negotiable.

---

[14] *Microsoft Corp. v. Harmony Computers & Electronics, Inc.* 846 F.Supp.208 (E.D.N.Y 1994).
[15] *Vernor v. Autodesk, Inc.* 621 F.3d 1102 (9th Cir. 2010), 1111.
[16] Although see B Carver, 'Why license agreements do not control copy ownership: first sates and essential copies' (2010) 25 Berkeley Tech. L. J. 1887 (disagreeing with Autodesk and arguing that on a proper analysis of this question, courts should focus on whether the customer is entitled to perpetual possession).

2.2.1.2 *European Union*

The question of whether a given transaction constitutes a licence or a sale has been examined by the CJEU in *UsedSoft*.[17] Similar to the cases discussed above, the decision hinged on the European Union's equivalent of the first sale doctrine: the principle of exhaustion.[18] Although the restrictive provision in question concerned the right to re-sell or re-licence, it is of relevance to any instance where a right holder attempts to prevent, through the use of licensing provisions, types of use that are otherwise allowed under copyright law. This is so since when a court finds that the transaction in question is not a licence but a sale, the effectiveness of such restrictive provisions may be called into question. It is noteworthy that this should be the case whether or not the licence in question is a standard form EULA or a licence that was properly negotiated between the parties. Similar to the court in *Vernon*, the CJEU chose to focus the transaction's substance rather than its form and essentially concluded that while the terminology used was of little consequence, it is the economic circumstances of the transaction that matter. Thus, the CJEU held where you 'dress up' what is effectively a sale of a copy of a software product as a license,[19] it is still going to be considered as a sale, and the exhaustion principle therefore applies.

But what is the significance in classifying a transaction as a sale rather than a licence in a case that involves a prohibition against emulating or copying functional aspects or against reverse engineering? After all, neither the first sale doctrine nor the exhaustion principle is directly applicable in such instances. It is suggested that the ramification of finding a transaction to be a sale rather than a licence are considerable. When one purchases a copy of software, he is effectively entitled to use it in a manner that does not infringe the copyright (or patent) in that software. In such a case, the seller cannot argue that a breach of a licensing term results in termination of the permission granted under the licence, where any subsequent use by the buyer results in copyright infringement. Therefore, in case of a sale rather a licence, any contractual prohibition against a type of use that is permissible under copyright law is much less effective and might be enforceable, if at all, under contract law only against a party to the contract.

2.2.2 Contract formation and content

Rather than focusing on the classification of a transaction as either a licence or a sale, some courts may opt for questioning the validity of the terms upon which a right

---

[17] *UsedSoft GmbH v. Oracle International Corp.* C-128/11.

[18] See Art. 4(2) of the Software Directive.

[19] The Oracle 'licence' granted the right to use a copy of a computer program for an unlimited period, in return for a one-off payment.

owner seeks to rely, querying whether these terms were actually incorporated into a contract. In this context, a distinction must be made between the different distribution and contractual models that right owners employ.

2.2.2.1 Contract formation

If I pick up an off-the-shelf software product, pay for it at the cash register, take it home and learn there and then that my product is actually licensed to me and is subject to certain terms, physically enclosed to or digitally embedded in the product, such terms are not necessarily incorporated into the purchase contract. This is so, since the contract was formed and concluded before such terms being brought to my attention and before any opportunity that I may have had to read them. This was the rationale behind the Third Circuit Court of Appeal in the *Step-Saver* decision.[20]

Box-top and shrink-wrap licences In this case the court held that the contract was concluded when the defendant agreed, on the telephone, to post a copy of the relevant program at the agreed price. The fact that each of the copies sent to the plaintiff had a box-top licence that contained several terms, one of which provided that opening the package indicates acceptance, while another provided that all expressed and implied warranties were excluded, was of little relevance. This was so, inter alia, since the contract between the parties was concluded over the telephone, while the terms were brought to the plaintiff's attention only subsequently. There was offer, acceptance, and intention to create legal relations, all present at the telephone conversation stage. The terms in the box-top licence could not amount to a conditional acceptance nor could they amount to a counter-offer since the contract was concluded over the phone when the price and other conditions relevant to the transaction were discussed and agreed upon.

What would be the position where one has an opportunity to view the package, and therefore the shrink-wrap or box-top licence, before the conclusion of the contract? This is a more common scenario to most of us when we pick an off-the-shelf software product and, in theory, have an opportunity to notice that the package contains a box-top licence before the contractual offer and acceptance that usually takes place at the cash register. The licence in this case may provide that opening the package indicates acceptance of the terms and that in case of non-acceptance the purchaser is entitled to return the product for a full refund. Putting licence terms on the outer package is not something many proprietors are interested in doing for practical reasons. Much more common would be to place a notice on the package, informing potential customers that the transaction would be subject to

---

[20] *Step-Saver Data Systems v. Wyse Technology* 939 F.2d 91 (3rd Cir. 1991).

licence terms that are to be found inside the package. Once the package is opened, should the user find the licence terms unacceptable, he is invited to return the product for a full refund. Obviously, such licence cannot become effective as soon as a customer tears the wrapping, as may be the case with box-top licence. Such licence terms will usually provide, inter alia, that keeping the product for more than a specified period indicates acceptance.

In a controversial decision, the Court of Appeal for the Seventh Circuit gave the shrink-wrap licensing model a clean bill of health.[21] In its decision, the court overturned the decision of the district court, which was based on two grounds: first, that the licence at stake was not part of the contract since it was positioned inside the box rather than on the outside and, second, even if it was part of the contract such contract was unenforceable due to the pre-emption doctrine. It is the former ground of this decision that is of interest in the present context.[22]

The plaintiff in *ProCD* compiled a vast database of phone directories. This was done at a great expense and effort though the court noted that such database was probably not copyrightable.[23] As the Court of Appeal noted, the plaintiff had two main options in terms of pricing its product. It could have set a unitary price policy, pricing the product evenly for all categories of customers. Alternatively, recognising that the product was worth much more to commercial users than to private ones, the plaintiff could set a different price level for each of these user categories. In order to price out as little customers as possible, the plaintiff opted for the second alternative. This, however, presented a problem: what was to prevent a commercial customer from buying a copy of the database priced for private use and use it to commercial ends? The plaintiff resorted to contract in a shrink-wrap form. Thus, a notice was placed on the outside of the box informing potential clients that the transaction was subject to terms that are to be found on the inside. Once opened, the terms provided that in case the customer did not accept the terms he is free to return the product for a full refund. On the other hand, keeping the product was deemed to constitute acceptance of the said terms. The defendant in this case purchased a copy designated for private use and offered an online service based on this copy at a price significantly lower than that charged by the plaintiff.[24] The defendant viewed the licence terms once he took the product home. The terms were not only available on the attached leaflet, but also digitally embedded in the product so that when the defendant tried to upload the database onto

---

[21] *ProCD, Inc. v. Zeidenberg* 86 F.3d 1447 (7th Cir. 1996).
[22] For discussion on the pre-emption doctrine, see below.
[23] Following the Supreme Court decision in *Feist Publications, Inc. v. Rural Telephone Services Co.* 499 US 340 (1991).
[24] Obviously, unlike the plaintiff, the defendant had no significant costs to recoup; at the relevant time, a private-use copy cost about $150, while the cost of compiling the database went over $10 million.

his server, he was not able to proceed without indicating his acceptance to terms which appeared on his screen.

As aforementioned, the court overturned the district court's decision according to which the contested licence terms did not form part of the contract since they were not available on the outside of the box but rather on the inside. The Court of Appeal stipulated that consent to a contract might be manifested by conduct under most legal systems. Where one accepts that terms on the outside of the box may be incorporated into the contract, one must also consider what is the status of a notice placed on the outer package according to which the transaction is subject to a licence that is to be found inside the package. The court noted that according to Wisconsin contract law, placing a priced product on a shop's shelf amounted to an offer (incorporating the terms attached) and that the customer accepts such offer upon payment at the cash register. Therefore, the court reasoned that by the time the defendant expressed his acceptance at the cash register, he was aware that the transaction was subject to licence terms, albeit not yet aware of their content. Once opening the package, the defendant was at liberty to return the database for a full refund in case the terms were unacceptable to him.

The court stressed that there was nothing exceptional or unique in transactions where money exchanges hands before the communication of detailed terms. Insurance policies will often be issued under such circumstances. The customer contacts the agent/broker, who explains the essentials of the policy and the customer pays. The complete policy with the full details is sent to the customer only days later. At that point he is at liberty to reject it and get his money back. Non-rejection indicates acceptance of the policy terms.

This part of the court's decision does not appear to be objectionable. We often carry out transactions, for example—over the phone, where money changes hands much before the full details of the transaction are communicated to us. In fact, there is a lot to be said in favour of conducting business in this fashion. It clearly reduces transaction costs and increases efficiency in supporting genuine price discrimination. Hence, a business model that consists of 'notice on the outside and terms on the inside' should not be, per se, objectionable.

Would the same rationale hold where a right owner does not place a notice on the outer box, but merely gives a party the right to return for a full refund at a later stage? It appears not, as the transaction is already concluded when the contested terms are brought to the attention of the customer. Thus, on this basis the ruling of the Seventh Circuit Court of Appeal in *Hill* is questionable.[25] In this case, which involved sale rather than licence and hardware rather than software, the

---

[25] *Hill v. Gateway 2000. Inc.* (1997) 105 F.3d 1147 (7th Cir.).

court held that whether or not there was a notice on a box was not crucial. The case involved a telephone order where there was no mentioning of the transaction being subject to additional terms. Nevertheless, the court held that the plaintiffs must have known that the computer cardboard box would include some important terms and did not seek to discover these in advance. Once they became aware of the terms, they had the opportunity to return for a full refund for a specified period. In the court's view, keeping the product for more than this period amounted to acceptance of the enclosed terms.

The enforceability of shrink-wrap licences has also been challenged in a number of European jurisdictions. Under English law, such transactions may sometimes prove problematic in relation to non-contracting parties owing to the concept of privity of contract. The validity of such a contract examined by the courts in the Scottish decision *Beta v. Adobe*.[26] Here the court upheld the terms of a shrink-wrap licence and concluded that the said terms were incorporated into the agreement. Based on Scottish law, the court got around the doctrine of privity by applying the Scottish doctrine of *ius quaesitum tertio*, which allows a party to a bilateral contract (i.e. the seller) to create rights in favour of a third party (i.e. the copyright owner).

The incorporation of shrink-wrap terms into a transaction is widely discussed under English case law, albeit not in the context of software. For example, there are different views regarding the point of time in which a contract is concluded in the case of an agreement between a carrier and a potential passenger. *Thornton v. Shoe Lane Parking* appears to suggest that the offer is made by the carrier when issuing the ticket, the terms being listed on the back of the ticket, while the passenger accepts the offer when he keeps the ticket without objection.[27] Other courts held that the contract is concluded at an even later stage, so that the offer is accepted when the passenger claims the accommodation offered under the ticket.[28] Yet another view appears to suggest that where a ticket is booked in advance, the contract is concluded when the carrier indicates that he accepts the booking,[29] or when he issues the ticket;[30] under this view, it is the passenger rather than the carrier who makes the offer. Treitel suggests that the authorities do not follow a single rule and the exact point of time in which a contract is concluded depends

---

[26] *Beta Computers (Europe) Ltd. v. Adobe Systems (Europe) Ltd* (1996) F.S.R. 367.
[27] *Thornton v. Shoe Lane Parking* [1971] 2 WLR 585.
[28] For example, see *MacRobertson Miller Airline Services v. Commissioner of State Taxation (WA)* (1975) 8 ALR 131 (High Court of Australia).
[29] For example, see *The Eagle* [1977] 2 Lloyd's Rep. 70; *The Dragon* [1979] 1 Lloyd's Rep 257 (affirmed [1980] 2 Lloyd's Rep. 2150.
[30] For example, see *The Mikhail Lermontov* [1991] 2 Lloyd's Rep 155.

on the document in question and the circumstances under which it was issued.[31] Whether or not a document containing contractual terms is incorporated into the contract chiefly depends on the type of notice given to the other party by the party seeking to rely on such terms. The key question in this context is not whether the terms were brought to the attention of the other party but whether the party seeking to rely on such terms took reasonable steps to bring them to the attention of the other party. As Treitel observes, the question of whether adequate notice was given turns on two main inquiries: the steps taken to give the notice and the nature of the terms at issue.[32]

An extreme example to the readiness of English courts to accept steps taken as adequate could be seen in *Thompson v. LM & S Ry*.[33] In this case the ticket had on its face the words *see back*, where it was further stated that the ticket was issued subject to conditions set out in the firm's timetable, which could be separately purchased. Notwithstanding the fact that the plaintiff was illiterate and that the timetable containing the term had to be purchased for money, the Court of Appeal held that since the notice at issue was clear and since it was common to incorporate terms using a ticket, the terms (in particular an exemption clause) were incorporated into the contract. This case is indeed an extreme example, but the principle of incorporation by reference appears to be sound. When it comes to the nature of the clause, the rule is that the more unexpected and draconian the clause is, the higher the degree of notice that will be required in order to have it incorporated into the contract.[34] Thus, in assessing the status of shrink-wrap licences under English law, it appears that if properly executed, such a licence should be enforceable. It is clear that English contract law recognizes a contractual arrangement whereby some of the terms of the contract are set out on a document that becomes available to the buyer only after money changes hands as long as clear notice is given in advance.

Indeed an English court acknowledged that this was the position under English law also in relation to software, and found a shrink-wrap licence to be enforceable.[35] It is noteworthy that the case did not involve any question of privity, as the defendant had direct contractual relationship with the plaintiff, Microsoft. In any event, it is now possible to get around the problem of privity in England and Wales under Section 1 of the Contracts (Rights of Third Parties) Act 1999. Accordingly, a person who is not a party to a contract may enforce, in his own right, a term of the contract if: (a) the contract expressly provides that he may, or (b) a term purports to confer a benefit on him. Thus, as long as the contract between the seller and the

---

[31] E Peel, *Treitel on the Law of Contract* (London, Sweet & Maxwell 2011).   [32] Ibid.
[33] *Thompson v. LM & S Ry* [1930] 1 KB 4.1.
[34] E Peel, *Treitel on the Law of Contract* (London, Sweet & Maxwell 2011).
[35] *Microsoft v. Electro-wide* (1997) F.S.R. 580.

customer makes it clear that the copyright holder has the right to enforce the terms of the contract and that these terms are to the copyright holder's benefit, the purchaser of a software product cannot hide behind the concept of privity and may be bound by the terms of such contract.

It appears that a top-box licence may also be enforceable in civil law jurisdictions. For example, in the Dutch case of *Coss HollandB.V. v. TM Data Nederland B.V.*, a distributor supplied software, produced by a third party, to a user.[36] According to the distributor the terms of the third party's shrink-wrap licence were enclosed to the software package and binding upon the purchaser/user. The users denied that the terms were so enclosed and sought to claim damages directly from the distributor, as the software was defective. The distributor refused to pay damages, claiming that it was not a party to the shrink-wrap licence as the said licence was concluded between the third party and the user. The Amsterdam court of first instance rejected this argument. It held that a licensing agreement cannot be formed by merely opening a package. In order to be incorporated into the agreement, the licence terms need to be brought to the attention of the user before the opening of the package, as well as the fact that opening the package will have the effect of making the user a party to the licensing agreement. Thus, it appears that under Dutch law a shrink-wrap licence may be enforceable as long as the user is aware of the presence of licence terms and their content before an agreement is concluded.[37]

Click-wrap and browse-wrap licences With the ever-growing increase of trade in software over the Internet, questions involving shrink-wrap and box-top licences become less relevant. A large quantity of software is licensed and distributed nowadays over the Internet. It is not only offered over the Internet but it is also delivered and downloaded over the Internet. Thus, there is no 'box' on the outside or inside of which one may place licence terms. Under these circumstances, the most common form of licence is 'click-wrap', and from a contract-formation perspective, it is clearly less controversial than the shrink-wrap, since the question of the detailed terms being brought to the attention of the parties before the conclusion of the contract is much more straightforward.

In *Specht*, the Court of Appeal for the Second Circuit was faced with a question concerning the enforceability of online licences with respect to software that was downloaded over the Internet.[38] From a contract-formation perspective, the case illustrates the difference between click-wrap and browse-wrap licences. The case involved the downloading of two interconnected programs, the Communicator

---

[36] *Computerrecht* 1997/2, 63–65.
[37] Namely, box-top licenses may be enforceable, while shrink-wrap licenses with nothing more than a notice on the outer package may not be.
[38] *Specht v. Netscape Communications Corp.* (2002) 306 F.3d 17 (2nd Cir.).

2.2 Contract Law–Based Mechanisms

and SmartDownload, offered free of charge on Netscape website. SmartDownload was a separate piece of software that was claimed by Netscape to enhance the browsing capabilities of its Internet browsing program, the Communicator. Although users could download the Communicator independently from SmartDownload, they were invited to download SmartDownload first so that their browsing capabilities while using the Communicator would be enhanced. Arriving at a Netscape's webpage with the caption SmartDownlaod, the prompt 'Start dowloading' was located at the bottom of the screen next to a tinted button labelled 'Download'. The plaintiffs argued that this is exactly what they did: they clicked the button and downloaded the SmartDownload program. This was in stark contrast to what the plaintiffs were required to do once they proceeded to download the Communicator program. In the case of the latter, the plaintiffs were presented with a scrollable text of the program's licence agreement and could not complete the downloading of the program unless they clicked the 'Yes' button to indicate their acceptance of all the licence terms. The court observed that the plaintiffs did not contest that this amounted to an express assent to all the licence terms. However, the court noted that in the case of SmartDownload no similar acceptance took place. The defendant in this case argued that the plaintiffs did not behave as a reasonably prudent offeree of downloadable software. It argued that had the plaintiffs scrolled down the webpage rather than immediately commence with the download, they would have encountered an invitation to view the licence terms of SmartDownload before downloading and using the software. Clicking on the said invitation, the plaintiffs would have been taken to a separate webpage containing the said licence terms. Hence, the defendant argued that placing the said invitation at the bottom of the download webpage puts the user on an 'inquiry notice'. The court rejected this argument, concluding that on the facts of the case a prudent offeree would have not necessarily known or learned about the SmartDownload licence terms prior to downloading the program.

The case illustrates the vulnerability of browse-wrap licences. The fact that the technical arrangement on the website did not compel the prospective licensee to view the licensing terms and 'assent' to them meant that the said terms were not incorporated into the contract. In contrast, the validity of a click-wrap licence, as was the case with the Communicator program, was clearly much more difficult to challenge.

In light of the position under English law on shrink-wrap licences, it appears that the enforceability of click-wrap licences is not likely to prove problematic. If anything, their enforceability is likely to prove more straightforward since the licensee is compelled to manifest its assent prior to conclusion of the contract.[39]

---

[39] Note that under English law, a person is bound by his or her signature on a contract whether or not he or she read it prior to signature. See *L'Estrange v. F Groucob Ltd* [1934] 2 K.B. 394.

The status of browse-wrap licences appears to be less straightforward under English law and is probably as precarious as it is under US law. The main problem with such licences is the notice given to the licensee about the existence of the terms. The key question is not whether the notice was given to the other party but whether the party seeking to rely on such terms took reasonable steps to bring it to the attention of the other party. This question turns on the nature of the steps taken to give such notice and the nature of the clause at issue. It is submitted that in the case of a browse-wrap licence it is the first of these inquiries that might prove problematic. Thus, in a scenario similar to the one at *Specht*, it is probable that an English court would have reached conclusions not unlike the US Court of Appeal for the Second Circuit. Where the licensee was invited to commence download and could have done so without scrolling down to the bottom of the page where the invitation to view the terms was presented, an English court is likely to find that a prudent offeree would not have been aware and could not have been reasonably expected to be aware of such terms before downloading the program.

We have seen that where the right holder wraps up its licence in a click-wrap format, there is little that a court may do on contract-formation grounds. Thus, if such terms are to be examined and their enforceability is to be evaluated, it should be under a different regulatory mechanism. The *Specht* decision serves as a reminder to right owners to keep away from browse-wrap licences and stick to the click-wrap model.

Negotiable licences   In the case of a licence that was properly negotiated between the parties, there could be little objection to incorporate the terms that were freely negotiated as a matter of principle. Of course, objections could be raised in a given instance where the contested term was not brought to the attention of the relevant party before the contract was concluded, but such objections may not be typical of the licensing model itself.

2.2.3 Contract content

When it comes to employing contract law-based mechanisms for scrutinizing the content of licensing provisions, three mains bodies of law may be borne in mind: UCITA in the United States,[40] and the Directive on Unfair Terms in Consumer Contracts[41] and the Directive on the Legal Protection of Computer Programs in the European Union.[42]

---

[40] Uniform Computer Information Transactions Act.
[41] Council Directive 93/13/EEC of 5 April 1993, on unfair terms in consumer contracts, [1993] OJ L95/29 (mentioned as 'Directive 93/13/EEC').
[42] Council Directive 2009/24/EC of 23 April 2009, on the legal protection of computer programs (codified version), [2009] OJ L111/16 (mentioned as 'Directive 2009/24/EC').

2.2.3.1 *UCITA*

In order to address the widespread availability of software in a large number of products and services and the growing use of software licences, the National Conference of Commissioners on Uniform State Laws promulgated UCITA. Being a model law, it is a proposed model of state contract law developed to regulate transactions in computer information products such as computer software, online databases, software access contracts, or e-books. UCITA renders standard form computer contracts, shrink-wrap contracts included, enforceable. However, owing to the high level of controversy UCITA generated during the eighteen years from the time the law has been introduced, only two states, Maryland and Virginia, adopted it. Thus, in practice UCITA has little effect in the present context on whether or not licensing provisions that prohibit the emulation of software functionality, reproduction of any part of the program, or reverse engineering are enforceable.[43]

2.2.3.2 *Directive on unfair terms in consumer contracts*

Similar to UCITA, this directive has little impact on the present context. Although it covers a wide variety of non-negotiable contractual terms, it applies only to contracts between businesses and consumers. Under Article 2(b) of the Directive, a 'consumer' means any natural person who, in contracts covered by this directive, is acting for purposes which are outside his trade, business, or profession. Thus for the present purpose, where a software developer seeks to emulate functional features of a given software product or to reverse engineer it, the directive is not likely to be applicable as such developers are not likely to fall within its definition of a consumer.

2.2.3.3 *Directive for the protection of computer programs*

The directive concerns, exclusively, the protection of computer programs under copyright law. The directive also addresses restrictive contractual provisions to the extent that it provides that any contractual provisions contrary to the provisions of the directive in respect of reverse engineering or to the exceptions provided in relation to the making of a back-up copy are null and void.[44] The non-waivable nature of these provisions holds whether or not the contract in question is of a standard form type. But Article 8 does not cover explicitly contractual provisions that prohibit the reproduction of functional features of a computer program.

---

[43] On the position in the United States in general, see R C Richards, 'Laws of licensing: U.S. computer information licensing under the common law, the Uniform Commercial Code, and the Uniform Computer Information Transactions Act', SSRN https://ssrn.com/abstract=1511643.

[44] See Art. 8 of the Directive 2009/24/EC.

Rather, it concerns the provisions that seek to prohibit the process of reverse engineering that is designed, inter alia, to uncover such functional features but not provisions that seek to restrict the actual reproduction of such features.[45] Could it therefore be argued that, by extension, the Article 8 also covers contractual provisions that seek to prohibit copying of functional features that are not eligible to copyright protection under the same directive?[46]

First, it is suggested that plain legal common sense supports this conclusion. As mentioned, the Directive and the interpretation given to it by the CJEU renders certain functional elements unprotectable under copyright law.[47] However, owing to the technical specificities of software, it is necessary to reproduce continuously the target program during a process known as reverse engineering in order to study and test the program and uncover the said features. The Directive therefore rightly stipulates that reproduction done for such purpose does not constitute copyright infringement. In order to make sure that the Directive's position on the non-protectability of such features is not rendered meaningless, the Directive further stipulates that contractual provisions that seek to prohibit such reverse engineering are null and void. The reason is that if functional elements are to be open for emulation by third parties, it must be provided that the means to access and uncover such features is not hindered by both copyright and contract. In the same vein, it could be convincingly argued that there is little point in declaring functional elements to be outside the scope of copyright law and making sure that the path to uncover them could not be blocked by contractual provisions, if contractual provisions could then be successfully employed in order to prohibit the actual emulation of such features. Thus, the public policy considerations that underpin the Directive suggest that licensing provisions that prohibit the copying of functional features, which are not protected under copyright law, should be unenforceable.

Second, it is suggested that the above conclusion is reinforced by the CJEU decision in *SAS*. One of the questions before the CJEU in *SAS* related to a person who obtained a copy of a computer program under licence, and carried out acts with a purpose that went beyond the framework established by the licence. It is noteworthy that the licence in this case restricted the use by the licensee to non-production purposes, but the defendant used the various copies of the Learning Edition of SAS Institute's program to perform acts that fell outside the scope of the

---

[45] Reverse engineering is referred to in a broad sense, covering black box reverse engineering and decompilation.

[46] Recital 11 and Art. 1(2) of the Directive suggest that certain functional elements are not eligible for copyright protection. In Chapters 4 and 5, it is maintained that various functional features are not eligible to copyright protection under the directive and the interpretation given to it by the CJEU in *SAS Institute Inc. v. World Programming, Ltd.* C-406/10.

[47] Ibid.

2.2 Contract Law–Based Mechanisms

licence. On the effect of such deviation from the purpose dictated by the licence, the CJEU opined:

> It must therefore be held that the copyright in a computer program cannot be infringed where, as in the present case, the lawful acquirer of the licence did not have access to the source code of the computer program to which that licence relates, but merely studied, observed and tested that program in order to reproduce its functionality in a second program.[48]

Thus, where a lawful acquirer was in possession of a program and was using it in accordance with the Directive, which in this case concerned studying and observing the program in operation, a licensing provision that prohibited use for production-related purposes was held to be ineffective. This was so, since the defendant did nothing more than that which it was permitted to do under the Directive. Holding otherwise would have rendered Article 8 meaningless in this context. Applying the same rationale to our present context, it is suggested that a licensing provision that seeks to prohibit the reproduction of non-protectable functional aspects of computer program should be met by a similar approach by the courts.

It should be noted that the above analysis is conducted under the provisions and interpretation of the Directive on the Legal Protection of Computer Programs. However, it should be borne in mind that certain functional elements in software products might not be covered by this directive but rather covered by the Information Society Directive. As we shall see, a prime example of such a feature is graphic user interface (GUI), which may enable a user to interact with a device.[49] In the *BSA* decision, the CJEU concluded that GUIs are not protected under the Software Directive but could be protected under the Information Society Directive, since they do not constitute a form of expression of a computer program.[50] On the protectability of GUIs under the Information Society Directive, the court explained that although possible, where the arrangement or configuration of the components which form part of the GUI is dictated by technical function, the criterion of originality is not met, and, therefore, the outcome of the intellectual effort invested by the author is not considered as 'intellectual creation' for the purpose of copyright law. Obviously, where that is the case, such features of GUIs could not be protected under the Information Society Directive.

The question in the present context is therefore whether a licensing provision that prohibits the reproduction of non-protectable functional elements of a GUI

---

[48] Ibid, para. 61.   [49] See Chapter 7.
[50] *Bezpecnostní softwarová asociace–Svaz softwarové ochrany v. Ministerstvo kultury* C-393/09.

will be enforceable before EU courts. As we have seen, GUIs are not protected under the Software Directive and, although potentially protectable under the Information Society Directive, are not so protected where their arrangement and configuration is dictated by technical considerations. It is therefore necessary to consider whether a subject matter that comes within the ambit of the Information Society Directive but in fact is not eligible to copyright protection, owing to its failure to meet the originality criterion under the Directive, could nevertheless be safeguarded against reproduction through the use of restrictive licensing provisions. Surprisingly, unlike the position under the Software Directive, the Information Society Directive is silent on the relationship between copyright exceptions and limitation and restrictive licensing provisions.[51] As the EU legislator refrained from adopting a unified position on the matter, it appears that the issue is to be resolved on a jurisdiction-by-jurisdiction basis. At present, only two jurisdictions within the EU addressed the issue explicitly: Belgium and Portugal.[52] The position in Belgium is somewhat odd: while Belgian law protects the beneficiaries of limitations on copyright in their off-line contractual relations against the effect of licensing provisions that seek to override such limitations, it fails to do so in relation to online relationships, where the need for protection against such practices probably greater.[53] The position is more straightforward in the case of Portugal. In Portugal, copyright law essentially provides that right holders may not contractually prohibit users from exercising copyright limitations.[54] As mentioned, except for the abovementioned jurisdictions, none of the other Member States sought to resolve this tension through legislation. Consequently, it will be up to the courts in each Member State to strike the balance between the principle of freedom of contracts on the one hand, and the ability to benefit from copyright limitations and exceptions on the other hand. This being so, it is worthwhile for right holders to attempt and extend the scope of their legal monopoly under the Information Society Directive through use of contractual restrictions that go beyond the scope of copyright law. It appears that if such extension of legal monopoly should be kept check in the European Union, the means for doing so should be sought outside the scope of the Information Society Directive.

---

[51] For a critique of this aspect of the directive, see B Hugenholtz, 'Why the Copyright Directive is unimportant, and possibly invalid', [2000] 11 EIPR 499–505.
[52] See L Guibault, G Westkamp, and T Rieber-Mohn, *Study on the Implementation and Effect in Member States' Laws of Directive 2001/29/EC on the Harmonisation of Certain Aspects of Copyright and Related Rights in the Information Society* (16 February 2012). Report to the European Commission, DG Internal Market, February 2007; Amsterdam Law School Research Paper No. 2012-28; Institute for Information Law Research Paper No. 2013.
[53] Supra, p. 161.   [54] Ibid.

2.3 PRE-EMPTION-BASED MECHANISMS

While unlike EU legislation, US federal copyright law does not have non-waivable provisions, US jurisprudence recognizes the concept of pre-emption. The concept of 'pre-emption' is unique to US jurisprudence. The idea is that federal law, such as copyright, prevails over any contravening state law or regulation. Any other outcome may result in state agenda interfering with federal policies. As contract law is state-based rather than federal, it may be argued that it should not be allowed to circumvent public policy considerations enshrined in federal copyright law.

There are two possible sources for pre-emption arguments relevant to our present discussion: (i) statutory pre-emption through Section 301 of the US Copyright Statute, and (ii) constitutional pre-emption which is derived from the Supremacy Clause of the Constitution, and asserts that state law is pre-empted when it conflicts with the objectives of Congress.[55]

2.3.1 Statutory pre-emption

This branch of pre-emption is sometimes referred to as direct-conflict pre-emption,[56] and may be applicable where state laws or court decisions are in direct conflict with the subject matter of copyright law, so it is impossible for one party to comply with both or where state laws create barriers to the accomplishment and execution of the goals that Congress had in mind upon creating the federal law.[57] In the case of contract law, there is no general principle according to which copyright law always pre-empts state contract law. Rather, there is an examination on a case-by-case basis to determine whether, in a given case, a right created under state law is equivalent to a right granted under copyright. Thus, in the present context, it may be argued that enforcing a contractual provision prohibiting the reproduction of software functionality has the effect of interfering with the policies underpinning Section 102(b), according to which certain functional features in a copyrighted work are not eligible to copyright protection and, as far as copyright law is concerned, belong to the public domain.

Section 301 of US Copyright Act provides that 'all legal or equitable rights that are equivalent to any of the exclusive rights within the general scope of copyright' are governed exclusively under federal copyright law. The difficulty had always

---

[55] U.S. Constitution. Art. VI, cl. 2.

[56] D Kwong, *The copyright-contract intersection: SoftMan Products Co. v. Adobe Systems, Inc. & Bowers v. Baystate Technologies, Inc.* (2003) 18 Berkeley Tech. L. J. 349, 359.

[57] *Davidson & Associates DBA Blizzard Entertainment, Inc.; Vivendi Universal, Inc. v. Jung et al.*, (2005) 422 F.3d 630, 638 (8th Cir.).

been in determining what may amount to 'equivalent' within the meaning of this provision. In order to assist themselves in determining what constitutes 'equivalence', the courts devised a method according to which in order to survive pre-emption argument, a claim must protect a right that is 'qualitatively different', with an 'extra element' that makes it distinct from a copyright action.[58]

The general consensus is that a right created under a freely negotiated contract to prohibit fair use in relation to a copyrighted work is not likely to be considered as 'equivalent' to any exclusive right granted under copyright law since the mutual assent and consideration elements present in a contractual claim constitute 'extra elements' and thus save such contract-based claim from pre-emption.[59] The same rationale should hold in the case of a freely negotiated prohibition on reproducing functional elements. Thus, parties should be free to negotiate a contract that prohibits acts permitted under copyright law. A tougher question for the courts in this context is whether shrink-wrap and click-wrap licences, which do not involve any meaningful form of bargaining and consent, are to be treated as consensual bargaining models for the purposes of pre-emption analysis?[60]

It was exactly this point that came before the court in *ProCD v. Zeidenberg*.[61] In this case, the district court held that since the State of Wisconsin, the relevant jurisdiction in that case, treats shrink-wrap licences as valid contracts, Section 301(a) of the Copyright Act prevents their enforcement. Section 301(a) pre-empts:

> legal or equitable rights [under state law] that are equivalent to any of the exclusive rights within the general scope of copyright as specified by section 106 in works of authorship that are fixed in a tangible medium of expression and come within the subject matter of copyright as specified by sections 102 and 103.

The district court observed that the Supreme Court held in *Feist* that information of the type to be found in the phone directory in question was not a copyrightable subject matter. Thus, such works should be in the public domain and should not be allowed to gain copyright-like protection via contract law. The appellant court in ProCD disagreed. The court rejected the district court's analysis that rights created by contract 'are equivalent to any of the exclusive rights within the general scope of copyright'. The court stated that rights in personam could not be said to be equivalent to rights in rem, as such rights were based on mutual assent and consideration—which were absent in case of a claim based on federal copyright law. The court illustrated its reasoning by opining that should someone find

---

[58] *Katz Dochtermann & Epstein, Inc. v. Home Box Office* (1999) 50 U.S.P.Q.2d 1957, 1959.   [59] Ibid.
[60] See M O'Rourke, 'Drawing the boundary between copyright and contract: copyright preemption of software license terms' (1995) 45 Duke L. J. 479, 528.
[61] *ProCD, Inc. v. Zeidenberg* 86 F.3d 1447 (7th Cir. 1996).

2.3 Pre-Emption-Based Mechanisms

a copy of the phone directory on the street, such person would not be affected by the licence.[62]

In *Bowers*, the Federal Circuit was faced with a similar question with respect to a contractual provision waiving the right to reverse engineer and decompile the purchased software.[63] Relying on the decision in *Pro CD*, the court found the said provision to be enforceable under Massachusetts contract law. The contract in question was a shrink-wrap licence, which included a prohibition on reverse engineering. Baystate obtained copies of Bower's software, decompiled it, and introduced a product that incorporated some of the features that were in Bowers' reverse engineered product. On the issue of conflict pre-emption of the shrink-wrap licence provision, citing with approval from Pro CD, the court held that the contractual claim involved 'an extra element' that was the parties' mutual assent and the contractual consideration. The court did not appear troubled by the fact that the licence in question was of a shrink-wrap type and was clearly not freely negotiated. The court acknowledged its decision in *Atari* according to which reverse engineering and decompilation are fair use.[64] Nevertheless, the court held that as long as there is a valid contract between the relevant parties, whether shrink-wrap or not, the 'extra element' necessary to overcome a pre-emption argument is present.

It is suggested that the above decisions lend excessive weight to the concept of freedom of contract, without differentiating between various types of contracts. According to this rationale, a licensing provision prohibiting reverse engineering or reproducing a program's functionality will never be pre-empted under Section 301 as there will always be extra elements present in the form of 'mutual assent' and contractual consideration. It is submitted that the court's rationale was flawed in that it failed to take into consideration the legislative history of the Copyright Act, according to which contractual provisions of the type approved of by the court in Bowers might be regarded as equivalent to those under the Copyright Act. Thus, the legislative history of the Copyright Act professed an intent that '[a]s long as a work fits within one of the general subject matter categories of sections 102 and 103, the bill prevents the States from protecting it even if it fails to achieve Federal statutory copyright [protection]'.[65] It is suggested that on the basis of the Congressional intent—since computer programs fall within the definition of a literary work under Section 102(a)(1), but functional features of it may nevertheless fail to achieve

---

[62] Though the court admitted that copyright law itself would limit the finder's ability to copy or transmit the application program that was necessary to access the said phone directory.
[63] *Bowers v. Baystate Techs, Inc.* 320 F.3d 1317 (Fed. Cir. 2003).
[64] *Atari Games Corp. v. Nintendo of America, Inc.* 975 F.2d 832 (Fed. Cir. 1992).
[65] Copyright Law Revision, H. R. Rep. No. 94-1476 (1976), 129-31.

copyright protection—state contract law that essentially enables protection of such functional features through non-negotiable standard form contracts should be preempted by federal copyright legislation. It is also suggested that the above decision was also lacking in that it failed to take into consideration the Supremacy Clause and examine the case under the principle of Constitution pre-emption.

2.3.2 Constitution pre-emption

Section 301 was meant to codify the Supremacy Clause of the Constitution, but since it did not do so in a complete and full manner, the Supremacy Clause can still be applied directly.[66] Hence, although a particular cause of action may survive a pre-emption examination under Section 301, it should still be assessed under the Supremacy Clause.[67] One ground for pre-emption under the Supremacy Clause, which is of particular relevance to a scenario involving a conflict between federal copyright law and rights created under shrink-wrap and click-wrap licences, is where state law conflicts with federal law to such an extent that it hinders congressional intentions and goals.[68] The difference between the two types of pre-emptions is that unlike statutory pre-emption, constitutional pre-emption requires a court not only to look at whether the rights at issue are equivalent but also to engage in an examination of the congressional objectives and the public policy considerations that underlie copyright law.[69] Thus, irrespective of the applicability of Section 301, it might be possible for a court to rescind the terms of a licence that is found to interfere with copyright law's overall objectives.[70]

In *Vault*, the Fifth Circuit was required to assess the enforceability of a shrink-wrap licence that prohibited decompilation.[71] The defendant purchased a copy of the plaintiff's software, and in violation of the shrink-wrap licence, decompiled it in order to create a program which unlocked Vault's software protection device. In this context the court had to determine whether the licence was enforceable or pre-empted. Being a contract of adhesion, the court held that the licence in question could only be enforced if the Louisiana Software Licensing Enforcement Act, which set out the requirements for shrink-wrap licences to be enforceable, was a

---

[66] U.S. Constitution. Art. VI, cl. 2. See, C Joyce, *Copyright Law* (7th edn., Newark, NJ, Matthew Bender 2008), 1032-5.
[67] M O'Rourke, 'Drawing the boundary between copyright and contract: copyright preemption of software license terms' (1995) 45 Duke L. J. 479, 534.
[68] *Calif. Fed. Sav. & Loan Ass'n v. Guerra* 479 U.S. 272, 278 (1987).
[69] D Kwong, 'The copyright-contract intersection: *SoftMan Products Co. v. Adobe Systems, Inc. & Bowers v. Baystate Technologies, Inc.*' (2003) 18 Berkeley Tech. L. J. 349, 360.
[70] M O'Rourke, 'Drawing the boundary between copyright and contract: copyright preemption of software license terms' (1995) 45 Duke L. J. 479, 535.
[71] *Vault Corp. v. Quaid Software Ltd.*, 847 F.2d 255 (5th Cir. 1988).

2.3 Pre-Emption-Based Mechanisms

valid statute. The court held that the Louisiana Act was pre-empted by the by federal law as it 'touched upon the area of Federal copyright law' and conflicted with the rights of a computer program's owner under the Copyright Act.[72] Hence, the anti-decompilation provisions, whose enforceability depended on the Louisiana Act, were held to be unenforceable.

Subsequently, however, the Eight Circuit rejected a defendant's argument, which was based on Vault, and held that Congress did not intend to take away parties' freedom to negotiate freely contractual terms that prohibit reverse engineering and decompilation.[73] The court quoted with approval from *Bowers* that 'private parties are free to contractually forego the limited ability to reverse engineer a software product under the exemptions of the Copyright Act....'[74] Although *Bowers* concerned statutory pre-emption, the court held that the same rationale applied to constitutional pre-emption as well. In effect, the court held that fair uses under copyright law could be contracted away and that such contractual claims do not conflict with copyright law. It is likely that the same type of rationale would be employed by the same court in a case of licensing provisions that prohibit the emulation of the functionality of a computer program. Thus, following the Eight Circuit's rationale, although US copyright legislation provides that functionality should not be the subject matter of copyright protection,[75] it is open to the parties to a contract to decide otherwise. The fact that they 'decide' to do so in a contract of adhesion is apparently of no relevance.

It is submitted that the courts' reasoning in both *Bowers* and *Davidson* is perplexing. Both cases suggest that pre-emption is not triggered in the case of freely negotiated contracts yet both cases clearly involved contracts of adhesion. Thus, the extra element of a meaningful 'mutual assent' was arguably absent.[76] Curiously, the court in *Davidson* distinguished *Vault* in that the latter involved a state law that rendered the contested licence enforceable, while the former involved nothing more than a private contractual arrangement. This rationale is baffling. As Judge Dyk stated in his dissenting opinion: 'From a pre-emption standpoint, there is no distinction between a state law that explicitly validates a contract that restricts reverse engineering (Vault) and general common law that permits such a restriction (as here)'.[77]

In conclusion, we have seen that although the pre-emption mechanism offers US courts a potential tool for regulating the use of contractual provisions in software

---

[72] Ibid, 269.
[73] *Davidson & Associates DBA Blizzard Entertainment, Inc.; Vivendi Universal Inc. v. Jung et al.* (2005) 422 F.3d 630 (8th Cir.).
[74] Ibid, 639. [75] As defined under Section 102(b).
[76] As in all cases of contracts of adhesion, it was a straightforward 'take it or leave it' proposition.
[77] *Davidson & Associates DBA Blizzard Entertainment, Inc.; Vivendi Universal Inc. v. Jung et al.* (2005) 422 F.3d 630 (8th Cir. 2005), para. 73.

licences that prohibit reproduction of functional features in software products, in most cases, US courts refrained from doing so under the pretext of uncertainty regarding Congressional intention in relation to the interface of contract law and federal copyright law.

2.4 COMPETITION LAW–BASED MECHANISMS

At first glance it might appear odd that competition law may even be considered suitable to remedy scenarios where the balance of interests maintained under copyright law is at risk due to licensing provisions. After all, it is often assumed that competition law and copyright law are locked into an inherent conflict, as competition law often addresses the abuse of monopolistic powers while copyright law may have the effect of strengthening legal monopolies.

Competitive markets depend, inter alia, on having the right balance between the ability to exploit existing works and encouraging the creation of new works. Such fresh creation is encouraged under copyright law by granting authors exclusive rights for their works. Since exclusivity stands at the core of copyright law, copyright holders are under no general duty to license the use of their work to third parties. However, a copyright holder's prerogative in deciding whether, under which terms and whom he wishes to deal with is not unqualified; thus, copyright holders may not use their exclusive right in a manner that hinders competition.[78] But could a contractual restriction that goes beyond the scope of the exclusive rights as defined by copyright law violate competition law principles? If so, under which circumstances might competition law be engaged?

Inter alia, competition law is designed to remedy market failures and further consumer welfare. Broadly speaking, copyright law is also designed to remedy certain market failures in the creative works' market and ultimately advance consumer welfare.[79] The relationship between the two regimes may be thus characterized as complementary rather than antagonistic, as they aim to maximize consumer welfare, though each takes a different path to achieve this goal.[80] Might it therefore be the case that since the two regimes share a similar goal, competition law principles could be used to inform the application of copyright law? In other words, can principles of competition law be used to maintain the balance of interests under copyright law, where this balance is challenged by licensing provisions?

---

[78] R S Vermut, 'A synthesis of the intellectual property and antitrust laws: a look at refusals to licence computer software' (1997) 22 Colum. J. L. and Arts 29.
[79] E Gellhorn et al., *Antitrust Law and Economics in a Nutshell* (St. Paul, MN, Thompson West 2004), 477.
[80] Ibid.

2.4 Competition Law–Based Mechanisms

Although both regimes may be designed to remedy market failures, it is different types of market failures that they seek to address. The goal of competition law is to 'protect the public interest in competition by prohibiting acts that exclude competitors from the market place or restrict output and raise prices as to harm consumer welfare',[81] while under a utilitarian school of thought copyright law seeks to promote consumer welfare by encouraging the creation and dissemination of new works.[82] Thus, the application of competition law to transactions involving copyright licensing may be of limited use in the present context. This is not to say that competition law has no role to play in cases involving copyrighted products. However, as discussed below, it is argued that the more a scenario requires construction of the nature, goals, and scope of a copyright grant, the less helpful it may be to refer to competition law. Thus, merely enforcing your copyright grant as a licensor and prohibiting licensees from engaging in reverse engineering and reproducing functional features may not necessarily have consequences under competition law.

2.4.1 EU competition law and prohibitions on reproduction of functional software features

The starting point for an examination of EU competition law in this context is whether and under which circumstances Article 101 TFEU might be applicable to a scenario that involves a right owner that licenses its software while prohibiting the licensee from reproducing functional elements of its software that are not protected under copyright law.

2.4.1.1 *Article 101*
Article 101 is concerned with anticompetitive agreements. The main scenario that should be considered in this context is one of a competitor who is purchasing a software product with a view to analyse it and potentially emulate its functional features.

For Article 101 to be engaged, the following points need to be considered:

a) Is there an agreement between two or more independent undertakings?
b) Is the license agreement capable of affecting trade between Member States to an appreciable extent?
c) Does the agreement (by its *object* or *effect*) prevent, restrict or distort competition to an appreciable extent in a relevant market within the EU?

---

[81] P Samuelson and K Opsahl, 'Licensing information in the global information market: freedom of contract meets public policy' (1999) 21 EIPR 385, 392.

[82] It is submitted that in the case of copyright protection for software, there is little point in looking beyond utilitarian reasoning for granting protection.

Commencing with the first point, it is necessary to establish whether the licensing agreement in question is concluded between two independent undertakings. The term *undertaking* has been interpreted in *Hofner and Elser v. Macrotron*,[83] where the CJEU stated: 'the concept of an undertaking encompasses every entity engaged in an economic activity, regardless of the legal status of the entity or the way in which it is financed.' In the present context, the question of what constitutes 'economic activity' is of utmost importance.

It is clear that the licensor in the scenario at hand is an undertaking engaged in an economic activity, but can the same be said about the licensee? It appears that this would be the case only where the goods or services purchased or licensed form an essential element of goods or services subsequently offered to the market place by the licensee.[84] This would clearly be the case where the licensee is a distributer or is licensing the software with a view to embed it in his own products. But where it is software that is intended to be used within the licensee's organization rather than being transferred downstream, the determination of whether there is an economic activity within the meaning of Section 101 is less straightforward. The difficulty in making this determination is that there are varying degrees to which the purchased good or service is a necessary input to a good or service subsequently offered.[85] The most obvious scenario involves a competitor that is acquiring a software product under a licence with a view to analyse it, so it may either develop or improve its own software product. Would a licensing agreement entered into under such circumstances relate to an economic activity on the side of the licensee? It is suggested that the answer to this question is probably yes.

Assuming that the scenario at hand satisfies the first precondition for the application of Article 101(1), it is suggested that the two other preconditions are also likely to be satisfied in the majority of cases. It is easily conceivable that some of those licensing agreements might have an effect on interstate trade and that the prohibition on copying functional elements might have either the object or the effect of preventing, restricting, or distorting competition. Where this is the case, the licence agreement in question is likely to trigger the application of Article 101. Consequently, the next question would be whether it also violates it. In order to make an assessment in this context it is necessary to examine the nature of the licence in question under Article 101(1). Article 101(1) provides:

---

[83] Case C-41/90, *Hofner and Elser v. Macrotron GmbH* [1991] ECR I-1979.
[84] See O Odudu, 'The meaning of undertaking within Article 81 EC' (2005) 7 *Cambridge Yearbook of European Legal Studies* 215.
[85] Ibid, 216.

2.4 Competition Law–Based Mechanisms

The following shall be prohibited as incompatible with the internal market: all agreements between undertakings, decisions by associations of undertakings and concerted practices which may affect trade between Member States and which have as their object or effect the prevention, restriction or distortion of competition within the internal market, and in particular those which:

(a) directly or indirectly fix purchase or selling prices or any other trading conditions;
(b) limit or control production, markets, technical development, or investment;
(c) share markets or sources of supply;
(d) apply dissimilar conditions to equivalent transactions with other trading parties, thereby placing them at a competitive disadvantage;
(e) make the conclusion of contracts subject to acceptance by the other parties of supplementary obligations which, by their nature or according to commercial usage, have no connection with the subject of such contracts.

It can be seen that the agreements described under Article 101(1)(b) and (e) are of particular relevance. The former could be argued to be applicable as a prohibition against copying functional elements that are not protected under copyright law, might be intended to restrict the development of competing products. As regards Article 101(1)(e), it could similarly be argued that an obligation not to copy functional elements that are not protected under copyright law has no connection with the subject matter of the licence in question—which is to grant permission to use a copyrighted work. Whether or not such arguments would prove successful is yet to be seen.[86] Should European courts be willing to accept such arguments, it is suggested that the derogation from Article 101(1) under Article 101(3) would be of little assistance to a licensor that wishes to enforce such anti-copying prohibition in the majority of cases. In addition, should a court decide that a licensing agreement that contains the said prohibition falls foul of Article 101, such an agreement is not likely to benefit from the Technology Transfer Block Exemption Regulation[87] and the Technology Transfer Guidelines.[88]

2.4.1.2 *Article 102*

Article 102 concerns in the present context the abuse by the licensor of its dominant position within the internal market. It provides that:

---

[86] To the best of this author's knowledge, such arguments have not yet been raised before EU courts.

[87] Commission Regulation (EU) No. 316/2014 Guidelines on the application of Art. 101 of the Treaty on the functioning of the European Union to technology transfer agreements (2014/C 89/03).

[88] This is so since in the case of the licensee and the licensor being competitors, the licence prohibition at stake might amount to a 'hardcore restriction' under Art. 4(1)(d) TTBER. Similarly, in the case of the licensee and licensor not being competing undertakings, the said prohibition might amount to an 'excluded restriction' under Art. 5(2) TTBER.

Any abuse by one or more undertakings of a dominant position within the internal market or in a substantial part of it shall be prohibited as incompatible with the internal market in so far as it may affect trade between Member States.
Such abuse may, in particular, consist in:

(a) ...;
(b) limiting production, markets or technical development to the prejudice of consumers;
(c) ...;
(d) making the conclusion of contracts subject to acceptance by the other parties of supplementary obligations which, by their nature or according to commercial usage, have no connection with the subject of such contracts.

Thus, similar to the analysis conducted above in relation to Article 101, the prohibition at issue might be considered as, both, restricting technical development and having no connection with the subject matter of the contract in question.[89]

European Competition law jurisprudence distinguishes between the existence and exercise of an IP right.[90] This doctrine was developed by the CJEU in order to use competition law in conjunction with Article 34 EC Treaty (ex-Article 28), which permits restrictions on the free movement of goods, which are intended to protect intellectual property as long as they do not hinder trade between Member States so as to fragment the internal market. Thus, the mere exercise of a copyright grant would not normally amount to abuse of dominant position. However, 'improper' exercise of such right may do so. After all, Article 8(2) of TRIPS provides: 'Appropriate measures, provided that they are consistent with the provisions of this Agreement, may be needed to prevent the abuse of intellectual property rights by right holders or the resort to practices which unreasonably restrain trade or adversely affect the international transfer of technology.' But under which circumstances may the exercise of copyright amount to 'abuse' under Article 102?

It is an established principle of EU competition law that where certain types of infrastructure are controlled by a dominant undertaking and where the said infrastructure is indispensable as a gateway to a market, the dominant undertaking may be required to make access to the said infrastructure available to competitors or it might be found liable for abuse of dominant position under Article 102.[91] This principle is commonly referred to as the essential facilities doctrine. The essential

---

[89] The contract in question concerns the licensing of copyrighted software, while the restriction covers non-copyrightable subject matter.
[90] The doctrine was established in the cases *Consten* and *Grundig v. Commission* (C-56 and 58/64) [1966] ECR 299.
[91] See T F Cotter, 'Intellectual property and the essential facilities doctrine' in R Towse and R Holzhauer, eds., *The Economics of Intellectual Property* (2002) (Vol. IV, Cheltenham, UK, Edward Elgar) 185.

2.4 Competition Law–Based Mechanisms

facilities doctrine was developed with respect to tangible resources and raw materials rather than intellectual property rights.[92]

Over time, the CJEU expanded the circumstances under which an abuse of dominant position may take place to include, under some limited circumstances, the exercise of intellectual property rights. Notwithstanding such expansion, the standard set for a successful claim under the essential facilities doctrine in the case of an intellectual property rights is higher than that set for cases involving access to assets of the type described above. In *Volvo v. Veng*, which concerned refusal of a car manufacturer to license the design of door panels to competitors, the CJEU made it clear that ordinary exercise of intellectual property rights, per se, did not amount to abuse of dominant position under the (then) Article 82; something additional, which amounts to exceptional circumstances, was needed.[93] According to the court, such additional exceptional circumstances may be present, for example, where a car manufacturer refuses to supply spare parts to independent repairers on an arbitrary basis, charges unreasonable prices for the spare parts, or decides not to provide spare parts for models that are still in circulation. Thus, according to *Volvo*, a mere refusal to provide certain information or the enforcement of intellectual property rights in a non-arbitrary manner against all competitors appears not to be in violation of Article 102.

In *Magill* the CJEU took a less orthodox approach.[94] The case concerned television listings in the United Kingdom and Ireland. Broadcasters licensed for free a list of their daily programs to newspapers for daily publishing. The broadcasters themselves published a weekly guide for their own programs, which was available for sale to the wide public. Magill wished to offer a comprehensive weekly guide where all broadcasters programs would be listed, but the broadcasters in question objected, relying on their copyright in the said listings. The question before the CJEU was whether or not the exercise of copyright by the broadcasters under these circumstances amounted to an abuse of dominant position under Article 82 (currently Article 102). Citing with approval from *Volvo*, the CJEU held that a mere refusal to license intellectual property rights does not amount to an abuse even where the undertaking concerned holds a dominant position. In this context the CJEU also pointed out that mere ownership of intellectual property rights does not confer a dominant position. However, the CJEU found that the broadcasters' conduct amounted to abuse of dominant position since the information withheld

---

[92] For example, see case C-6/72 *Europemballage Corp, Continental Can Co Inc. v. Commission* [1973] CMLR 199.

[93] *Volvo v. Eric Veng* (C-238/87), [1988] E.C.R. 6211.

[94] *RTE and ITP v. Commission*, Joint cases, (Magill) (C-241/91 and C-242/91), [1995] E.C.R. I-743.

by them was essential to Magill. There was no alternative to obtaining the said information, and the broadcasters' conduct prevented the emergence of a new product—a comprehensive TV guide for which there was potential consumer demand. The broadcasters' refusal to supply was not justified and was done with the view to reserve to themselves a secondary market in weekly television guides by excluding all competition. The case appeared to reflect an expansion of the principles set forth in *Volvo* and could be seen as an application of the essential facilities doctrine to intellectual property rights.[95] It was the first example in the present context for compulsory licensing under Article 82.[96]

In *Oscar Bronner* the CJEU elaborated on what were the exceptional circumstances it was referring to in *Magill*: (i) the information sought by Magill was indispensable; (ii) there was a proven consumer demand for a would-be product; (iii) there was no objective justification for refusal to supply; and (iv) the refusal would eliminate all competition in the secondary market for TV guides.[97]

In the subsequent *IMS* decision, the CJEU was again required to rule on whether or not the exercise of copyright, namely a refusal to license it, amounted to abuse of dominant position.[98] In this case the CJEU outlined the circumstances under which the exercise of copyright law may amount to abuse of dominant position, it stated:

> It is clear from that case-law that, in order for the refusal by an undertaking which owns a copyright to give access to a product or service indispensable for carrying on a particular business to be treated as abusive, it is sufficient that three cumulative conditions be satisfied, namely, that that refusal is preventing the emergence of a new product for which there is a potential consumer demand, that it is unjustified and such as to exclude any competition on a secondary market.[99]

Although it was not clear what exactly 'secondary market' and 'new product' meant, it appeared clear that there can be no right to a licence simply in order to duplicate what the owner of the IPR was already doing.

These principles were liberally applied by the CFI in its *Microsoft* decision.[100] This case was concerned, inter alia, with Microsoft's refusal to provide

---

[95] The case has been seen as an expansion of the 'arbitrary refusal to supply' requirement suggested in *Volvo*; see D Byrne, 'Compulsory licensing of IP rights: has the EC competition law reached a clear and rational analysis following the IMS and the Microsoft decision?' (2007) 2 J. Int. L. & Prac. 326.

[96] It is noteworthy that although not comprising a part of their reasoning for the decision in Magill, the Commission, Court of First Instance, and ECJ were probably influenced by the fact that the subject matter of the copyright in this case was something as mundane as TV listings, a subject matter that does not attract copyright protection under the majority of Member States' copyright regimes.

[97] *Oscar Bronner GmbH & Co. KG v. Mediaprint Zeitungs- und Zeitschriftenverlag GmbH & Co. KG, Mediaprint Zeitungsvertriebsgesellschaft mbH & Co. KG and Mediaprint Anzeigengesellschaft mbH & Co. KG.* C-7/97 [1998].

[98] *IMS Health GmbH & Co. OHG v. NDC Health GmbH & Co. KG.*, (C-418/01) [2004] E.C.R. I-503.

[99] Ibid, para 38.   [100] *Microsoft v. Commission* (T-201/04) [2007] E.C.R. II-1491.

2.4 Competition Law–Based Mechanisms

to its competitors its intellectual property protected interface specification for Windows work group servers operating systems so they may achieve interoperability with Microsoft's desktop Windows operating systems. Microsoft argued that it did not have to provide the requested information as information sufficient to achieve a satisfactory level of interoperability could be obtained by using alternative methods. In this context the court ruled that on the facts of the case information that could be obtained through such alternative methods did not enable an adequate level of interoperability to be achieved in an economically viable manner.[101] Hence, it was held that the only manner in which a competitor could achieve a satisfactory level of interoperability was by having access to specifically defined interoperability information, and the only feasible way to have access to such information was by Microsoft supplying it to its competitors.[102] Applying an 'incentives balancing test' (i.e. balancing the possible negative impact of a compulsory order on Microsoft's incentives to innovate against its positive impact on the level of innovation at an industry level), the court concluded that Microsoft's refusal to license the said interface information to its competitors amounted to abuse of dominant position under what was then Article 82. A notable feature of this judgment was the CFI's treatment of the 'new product' requirement. At first blush it appears that on the basis of earlier case-law, Microsoft's refusal should not amount to 'prevention of emergence of a new product'. However, the CFI stressed that the 'new product' requirement should be read in the context of Article 82(2)(b), which provided that abusive conduct may consist of 'limiting production, markets or technical development to the prejudice of consumers'. Thus, the CFI did not have to reach a positive finding that the emergence of a specific new product was withheld from the market; it was sufficient that there was a 'restriction of technical development' in that competitors were prevented from developing operating systems different from the Windows systems that were already on the market.[103] The court rejected Microsoft's claim that its conduct was objectively justified.

Although the Microsoft case was a landmark decision regarding the application of Article 82 to exclusionary behaviour of intellectual property holders by

---

[101] This illustrates the point made under Chapter 3 that decompilation may be a highly expensive and time-consuming activity.

[102] For technical reasons, obtaining the necessary information through reverse engineering was considered impractical by the court.

[103] This approach has been heavily criticized as it would be easy to make trivial changes to a protected product in order to make a new product. It has been referred to as a doctrine of 'convenient facilities'; see, D. Ridyard, 'Compulsory access under EC competition law: a new doctrine of "convenient facilities" and the case for price regulation' (2004) ECLR 670.

virtue of exercising their intellectual property rights,[104] the judgment focused on the exceptional specific factual findings made by the Commission. Thus, it is safe to assume that the application of the rationale of the *Microsoft* decision might take place in the rarest of circumstances. As with the *Magill* and *IMS* decisions, it is clear that these decisions can offer very little assistance to the vast majority of licensees that are compelled to 'consent' to a contractual provision according to which they are prohibited from reproducing the functionality of their licensor's proprietary software. First, a precondition for the application of Article 102 is that the intellectual property right holder must have a dominant position in the relevant market. As the CJEU pointed out in *Magill*, ownership of intellectual property is not to be confused with having a dominant position in the relevant market. Dominant position was described by the CJEU as 'a position of economic strength enjoyed by an undertaking which enables it to prevent effective competition [from] being maintained on the relevant market by giving it the power to behave to an appreciable extent independently of its competitors, customers and ultimately of its consumers'.[105] Unless the intellectual property right holder in question is in a monopolistic or quasi-monopolistic position in the relevant market, no dominant position may be established. Therefore, in the majority of cases, software proprietors who impose prohibitions on their licensees according to which they are prohibited from reproducing the functionality of the licensed software have nothing to fear from the application of Article 102, as they are not likely to be regarded as having a dominant position in the relevant market.

In conclusion, in most cases where licensees will attempt to argue that a licensors' conduct in enforcing against them a contractual provision that prohibits the reproduction of functional features amounts to an abusive behaviour under Article 102, they are likely to fail at the first hurdle of Article 102: establishing a dominant position in the relevant market.

Only where such dominant position is established one may proceed to examine whether the licensor's actions are 'abusive' within the meaning of Article 102. Even where such dominant position is established, we have seen that in the case of refusal to license aspects of one's intellectual property, violation of competition law might be found in exceptional circumstances.

---

[104] Most controversial was the CFI ruling that it was not necessary to show that refusal to provide the interface information would eliminate 'all competition' in the downstream market. It was sufficient that the refusal would eliminate effective competition in that market. Similarly, regarding the requirement for unmet consumer need, the CFI held that this did not necessarily imply blocking the emergence of a 'new product', as Magill and IMS appear to suggest, but rather that showing 'limitation of technical progress' sufficed in this context.

[105] See *La Roche & Co AG and Hoffmann-la Roche AG v. Centrafarm Vertriebsgesellschaft Pharmazeutischer Erzeugnisse mbH* (Case 102/77) 274.

2.4.2 US antitrust law

2.4.2.1 *Section 1 of the Sherman Act—anticompetitive agreements*

Section 1 of the Sherman Act provides that 'Every contract, combination in the form of trust or otherwise, or conspiracy, in restraint of trade or commerce among the several States, or with foreign nations, is declared to be illegal . . ..' Licensing arrangements may raise concerns under antitrust laws where they are likely to affect adversely the prices, quantities, qualities, or varieties of goods and services either currently or potentially available. Two types of tests might be applied in order to determine whether licensing restriction are anticompetitive under Section 1: the 'per se' and the 'rule of reason' tests. Most licensing arrangements are likely to be analysed under the rule of reason test. This test involves an inquiry as to whether the licence in question is likely to have anticompetitive effects and, if so, whether the restraint at issue is reasonably necessary in order to achieve pro-competitive benefits that outweigh the anticompetitive effects. In certain limited cases, the 'per se' analysis will be applied, where the licensing arrangement will be declared as per se unlawful without an inquiry into its competitive effects. The per se analysis is reserved to behaviour that is so plainly anticompetitive that no inquiry into its effect is necessary (e.g. certain types of tying arrangements). The Antitrust Guidelines for licensing Intellectual Property Law[106] state that '[t]o determine whether a particular restraint in a licensing arrangement is given per se or rule of reason treatment, the Agencies will assess whether the restraint in question can be expected to contribute to an efficiency-enhancing integration of economic activity'.[107] In addition, the Guidelines state that 'if there is no efficiency enhancing integration of economic activity and if the type of restraint is one that has been accorded per se treatment, the Agencies will challenge the restraint under the per se rule. Otherwise, the Agencies will apply a rule of reason analysis'.[108] After examining the relevant statutory and regulatory framework, it is next necessary to establish how an analysis of a licensing restriction, which prohibits the copying of non-copyrightable features of the licensed software, would fare under Section 101? In essence, such a restriction might be considered as adversely affecting competition, in that it hinders the development of new or improved goods or processes. At the end of the day, the object of a licence containing such a provision is, inter alia, to restrict the ability of competitors to copy functional features that are not protected under copyright law. Such features are likely to be sought by competitors

---

[106] Department of Justice and Federal Trade Commission Antitrust Guidelines for the Licensing of Intellectual Property (April 6, 1995), reprinted in 4 Trade Reg. Rep. (CCH) 13,132 (1995) (referred to as 'DOJ and FTC Antitrust Guidelines for Licensing IP').

[107] Art. 3.4.   [108] Ibid.

with one main goal in mind: developing a competing product or improving one's existing product. Restricting such pro-competitive conduct might amount to anticompetitive effect. It follows that the question in this context should be whether such anticompetitive effect is reasonably necessary in order to achieve pro-competitive benefits that outweigh the anticompetitive effect. This determination would depend on the factual matrix of each given instance.

2.4.2.2 *Section 2 of the Sherman Act: abuse of dominant position*

This provision makes it illegal to 'monopolize, or attempt to monopolize, or combine or conspire with any other person or persons, to monopolize any part of the trade or commerce among the several States, or with foreign nations'. Owning the copyright in a software product, could licensing it under restrictive terms attract liability under Section 2 of the Sherman Act? As the Microsoft litigation illustrated, software licensing is an activity that can constitute an exclusionary behaviour under antitrust law.[109] When a licensing practice is challenged in this context, liability could depend, inter alia, on whether the practice is considered a legitimate exercise of rights granted under federal copyright law. Two conditions need to be satisfied under Section 2: first, it must be established that the defendant has monopoly power, and second, that this monopolistic power has been acquired or maintained by improper means. Thus, it concerns the creation or misuse of monopolistic powers through exclusionary means. It is not the existence of monopolistic power on its own that is objectionable under this provision of the Sherman Act, but how the monopoly has been created or sustained. Could a restriction on the reproduction of functional features of software lead to a violation under Section 2 of the Sherman Act on the grounds of it being an objectionable exclusionary behaviour? Could the enforcement of copyright, consequent to the termination of the licence as a result of the breach of the said restriction, amount to a violation under Section 2 of the Sherman Act? First, it must be borne in mind that similar to the case with Article 102 TFEU, a precondition for the application of Section 2 is monopolistic power held by the defendant. As in the case of the European Union, the American position is that mere ownership of intellectual property rights does not confer the necessary market power on its owner.[110]

Where the defendant holds monopolistic power, refusal to deal or license may amount to violation of Section 2. Such cases may be examined by the courts under one of two following doctrines: the intent test or the essential facilities doctrine.[111]

---

[109] *United States of America, Appellee v. Microsoft Corporation* 253 F.3d 34 (D.C. Cir. 2001).
[110] DOJ and FTC Antitrust Guidelines for Licensing IP, § 5.3: 'the Agencies will not presume that a patent, copyright, or trade secret necessarily confers market power on its owner when assessing tying agreements'.
[111] See R Pitofsky, 'Antitrust and intellectual property: unresolved issues at the heart of the new economy' (2001) 16 Berkeley Tech. L. J. 535.

2.4 Competition Law–Based Mechanisms

According to the intent doctrine, the maintenance of monopolistic power is considered as wilful within the meaning of Section 2 of the Sherman Act where it is designed to eliminate competition by gaining a competitive advantage or destroying a competitor. Since all commercial entities would be interested in gaining a competitive advantage, whether or not enjoying a monopolistic position, a mere intention to gain a competitive edge over one's competitors is not sufficient and a wilful intention to eliminate competition should therefore be established. Because such a subjective state of mind is difficult to prove, the courts look at the effects that the contested monopolistic behaviour may have on the market.[112] Prohibiting others from reproducing the functionality of one's software, even where such functionality is fair game under copyright law, is not likely to be considered as a wilful intention to eliminate competition; the same conclusion holds in relation to a prohibition on reverse engineering permissible under copyright law. However, even where such conduct may amount to anticompetitive behaviour, a monopoly may still avoid liability by establishing legitimate business reasons for its behaviour.[113]

Under the essential facilities doctrine, a refusal to license or deal may amount to violation of Section 2 of the Sherman Act, where a monopoly controls an essential facility without access to which a competitor may not be able to compete in the market. Thus, excluding competitors from having access to such essential facility may result in eliminating all competition in the market. In order to establish liability under the essential facility doctrine four elements need to be assessed: (i) the defendant is a monopoly; (ii) the competitors may not reasonably be expected to duplicate the said essential facility; (iii) the defendant denies competitors access to the essential facility; and (iv) the viability of providing the essential facility to the competitor.[114] A facility is considered essential where access to it is necessary in order to compete in the market with the entity that controls it. Although the essential facility doctrine has been applied in relation to various facilities such as sky lifts tickets[115] and railroads terminals,[116] it has never been successfully applied to refusal to license or deal with respect to intellectual property rights.[117] Thus, although it is theoretically possible, it is it is highly unlikely for such a claim to prove successful. Moreover, in the present context claiming a violation of Section 2 in relation to a prohibition on the reproduction of functional features other than interoperability data makes it even more unlikely that such arguments will prove successful.

---

[112] Ibid.   [113] *Data general Corp. v. Grumman System Support Corp.* (1994) 36 F.3d 1147 (1st Cir.).
[114] See *Aspen Skiing Corp v. Aspen Highland Skiing Corp.* (1985) 472 U.S. 585.
[115] Ibid.   [116] *United States v. Terminal Railroad Ass'n.* (1912) 224 U.S. 383.
[117] Although see the court's opinion on this issue in *BellSouth Advertising v. Donnelley Information* 719 F.Supp.1551 (S.D. Fla. 1988), (stating that although the doctrine was always applied to tangible assets, the is no reason why it should not be applied to information wrongfully withheld).

It has been suggested that the essential facilities doctrine may render a contractual prohibition on reverse engineering unenforceable, where such reverse engineering is taken with a view of gaining access to interoperability information;[118] it follows that a prohibition on putting such interoperability information into use should be treated equally. Of course, such interoperability information must be considered as 'essential facility' for the essential facilities doctrine to apply in this manner. For example, if one hypothetically takes Microsoft's Windows operating system, its interoperability information may be considered as 'essential facility' and thus may satisfy the *Aspen* conditions: (i) Microsoft is a monopoly in the market for operating systems and owing to its copyright, it controls an essential facility (i.e. the interface specification necessary for competitors in order to create programs compatible with Windows); (ii) the competitor cannot reasonably be expected to duplicate the essential facility since it is actually prevented from trying to do so by contractual prohibitions in the licensing agreement; (iii) Microsoft denies such access as is manifested by its licence terms; and (iv) Microsoft can enable such access to the essential facility by, at the very least, removing the said prohibitive licensing terms.

However, in the antitrust *Microsoft* litigation,[119] the essential facilities doctrine was not applied by the court and was hardly mentioned by the Department of Justice in its complaint. It may be that the Department of Justice did not believe that an operating system's interface information could amount to an essential facility. Nevertheless, the court stated, *obiter dictum*, 'to require one company to provide its intellectual property to a competitor would significantly chill innovation.'[120] In any event, as part of the proposed judgment that was submitted by Microsoft and most of the plaintiffs, and as approved by the Federal District Court of the District of Columbia, it is quite clear that the disclosure obligation imposed on Microsoft implicitly prevents Microsoft from contractually prohibiting the use of such interoperability information by its licensees. But even more than in the case the CJEU Microsoft decision, the broader legal significance of this judgment is limited. First, it was an agreed judgment that was approved by a district court. Second, as mentioned, the factual circumstances in the case of Microsoft were exceptional in the light of Microsoft's monopolistic position in the market for operating systems. Moreover, the actual validity of the essential facilities doctrine had been called to question by the Supreme Court in the Trinko decision, where the court stated: 'we have never recognized such a doctrine . . . , and we find no need either to recognize it or to repudiate it here'.[121]

---

[118] M O'Rourke, 'Drawing the boundary between copyright and contract: copyright preemption of software license terms' (1995) 45 Duke L. J. 479, 548.
[119] *Re Microsoft Corp. Antitrust Litigation* 274 F.Supp.2d 743 (D. Md. 2003).   [120] Ibid, 745.
[121] *Verizon Communications Inc., Petitioner v. Law Offices of Curtis V. Trinko, LLP* (2004) 540 U.S. 398, 411.

Thus, it appears that the position of the essential facilities doctrine under US antitrust law is highly precarious. Moreover, even if it does survive Trinko, the application of the doctrine to intellectual property rights is arguable. The other route for establishing antitrust liability, namely the intent test, appears to be equally questionable in the context of enforcement of intellectual property and contractual rights owing to the Noerr-Pennington doctrine. Thus, the circumstances under which an undertaking may be obliged to refrain from enforcing its copyright or contractual right in this context are narrow.

3

ON REVERSE ENGINEERING AND DECOMPILATION

3.1 Reverse Engineering and Decompilation of Software:
   A Practical Overview — 71
   3.1.1 On reverse engineering — 71
   3.1.2 On software and black box reverse engineering — 71
   3.1.3 On software, reverse engineering, and decompilation — 72
   3.1.4 The various stages of reverse engineering — 73
   3.1.5 Motivation and methods for reverse engineering — 75
   3.1.6 Reasons for and benefits of decompilation — 78
   3.1.7 Interoperability — 79
      3.1.7.1 *Free and Open Source Software (FOSS)* — 80
3.2 Decompilation and Copyright Law — 83
   3.2.1 Idea-expression dichotomy and decompilation — 84
   3.2.2 The decompilation exception under the EU computer programs copyright regime — 85
   3.2.3 Decompilation under the US copyright regime — 85
      3.2.3.1 *Atari Games Corp. v. Nintendo of America, Inc.* — 86
      3.2.3.2 *Sega Enterprises v. Accolade* — 87
      3.2.3.3 *Sony Computer Entertainment v. Connectix* — 90
3.3 An Entitlement to Exclude Access to Ideas — 93
3.4 Entitlements in the Case of Decompilation of Computer Programs — 94
   3.4.1 An anomaly? — 95
3.5 A Critical Overview of Article 6 as a Means to Enable Decompilation to Achieve Interoperability — 96
3.6 A Note on Reverse Engineering in a Cloud Environment — 101

The US Supreme Court has observed that reverse engineering is 'an essential part of innovation', which 'could lead to significant advances in technology', and that 'the competitive reality of reverse engineering may act as a spur to the inventor'.[1] However, reverse engineering and, in particular, decompilation are highly

[1] *Bonito Boats, Inc. v. Thunder Craft Boats, Inc.* (1989) 141 US 489.

Beyond the Code: Protection of Non-Textual Features of Software. First Edition. Noam Shemtov.
© Noam Shemtov 2017. Published 2017 by Oxford University Press.

regulated under our copyright regime. We have also seen in Chapter 1 of this title that right holders seek to restrict this practice contractually. Chapter 2 demonstrated that outside copyright law, courts' ability to regulate the use of such prohibitive licensing provisions is limited. The present chapter, however, is concerned with the practice of reverse engineering, being one of the main means to uncover literal and non-literal building blocks in software products. It examines reverse engineering vis-à-vis copyright law and the extent to which it is permitted in relation thereto. Owing to the technological environment in which software and hardware interrelate, copyright law sets barriers to the practice of reverse engineering and, as a result, the public's ability to access certain ideas and concepts that are embodied in computer programs' architecture is restricted. As we shall see, the current legal position regarding decompilation is not easily reconcilable with the public policy considerations that underpin the idea-expression dichotomy and copyright law in general.[2]

3.1 REVERSE ENGINEERING AND DECOMPILATION OF SOFTWARE: A PRACTICAL OVERVIEW

3.1.1 On reverse engineering

Reverse engineering is a technique whereby a product is being analysed in order to understand how it was designed and how it operates. In order to do so, the article at issue is being worked 'backwards': in other words, starting with a final product, it is being analysed backwards so as to ascertain the methods, components, and logic that were used when the said article was designed and put together.[3] 'Black box' reverse engineering often refers to a process where systems are observed without examining their internal 'organs', whereas 'white box' reverse engineering involves an inspection of the systems' internal components as expressed in source code format.

3.1.2 On software and black box reverse engineering

As mentioned above, *black box reverse engineering* is a term that refers to testing a program by subjecting it to various inputs. Thus, the tester provides the program at issue with various inputs and observes the program's output in response. Testing a program in this fashion only requires the running of the program and

---

[2] In the subsequent chapter, the principle of idea-expression dichotomy under copyright law will be analysed in detail.

[3] For an excellent technical overview of reverse engineering of computer programs, see A Johnson-Laird, 'Software reverse engineering in the real world' (1993-4) 19 U. Dayton L. Rev. 843.

does not necessitate access to the program in its source code version. It does not even require access to the program in an object code form and it could be carried out remotely over a network. Consequently, copyright law could potentially be engaged only in relation to the intermediary copies that are created whenever a program is being used. Thus, the question in the current context is whether the creation of such intermediary copies requires the right holder's authorization.

The position under EU law is straightforward. Article 5(3) of the Software Directive provides that the

> person having a right to use a copy of a computer program shall be entitled, without the authorisation of the right holder, to observe, study or test the functioning of the program in order to determine the ideas and principles which underlie any element of the program if he does so while performing any of the acts of loading, displaying, running, transmitting or storing the program which he is entitled to do.

Furthermore, Article 8 provides that contractual provisions to the contrary shall be null and void. US copyright law similarly exempts black box reverse engineering from copyright infringement. Although US law does not provide an explicit exception for the practice of reverse engineering as EU law does, its fair-use defence under Section 107 may excuse reproduction for study and research related objectives. The appellant courts' rulings in *Sega*, *Atari*, and *Sony*, all discussed below also, stand for the proposition that when reproduction is carried out with a view to access unprotected, both literal and non-literal aspects of software products, it may constitute fair use.[4] Essentially, although an exemption for black box reverse engineering is provided in both jurisdictions via different routes, its effect is similar: running and loading a computer program with a view to observe it in operation so as to uncover and study ideas and principles that are embodied therein should not constitute copyright infringement. However, unlike Article 8 of the Software Directive, US copyright law does not safeguard this exception against conflicting contractual provisions. As discussed in Chapters 1 and 2, the effect of such contractual provisions may circumvent the effect of the exception under copyright law.

3.1.3 On software, reverse engineering, and decompilation

A computer ultimately manipulates binary digits in order to perform its functions and the instructions for the performance of these functions are 'read' by the machine (i.e. the hardware) in binary form before being translated into two

---

[4] *Sega Enterprises v. Accolade* 977 F.2d 1510 (9th Cir. 1992); *Nintendo v. Atari* 975 F.2d 832 (Fed Cir. 1992); *Sony Computer Entertainment, Inc. v. Connectix Corp.* 203 F.3d 596 (9th Cir. 2000), cert. denied

different levels of electrical current. In the very early days of computer programming, programs were written by programmers in binary form (i.e. as a set of instructions represented by ones and zeros) and could be understood by humans in their binary form. Nowadays, the average program contains hundreds of thousands if not millions of binary code lines, which are, as a whole, incomprehensible to humans. A program in its binary form is often referred to as written in *object code*. Object code is considered a low-level language. *Low* refers to the hierarchical position of object code, which is low in terms of its proximity to the computer's hardware. Since modern programs are complex and contain a large amount of binary code lines, the programs today are written in a human-readable format (i.e. alphabetical codes and symbols). A special purpose program, also known as a 'compiler' or 'assembler' (depending on the language used) will then convert these alphabetical codes to object code format. A program so written in a human-readable format is usually referred to as being in a *source code* format. Most computer languages prevalent nowadays, such as C++, JAVA, and Pascal, are expressed in source code but are all translated at the end of the day to object code, before being executed by a computer.

As mentioned, for reasons that will become apparent as the discussion progresses, the vast majority of computer programs[5] are released into the market in object code format, or a format that is incomprehensible to the human reader. Thus, such software is available in the marketplace in a low-level language that is of little use to a developer who wishes to learn about the subject system for various purposes. Therefore, in order to study a subject system, a reverse engineer may engage in a process of analysing a subject system in order to create representations of that system at a higher level computer language, while going backwards through the development cycle. As discussed below, the main method of practising such a process and recreating the source code that was used by the original developer, to the extent that this is possible,[6] is known as *decompilation* or *disassembly*.

3.1.4 The various stages of reverse engineering

Competitive reverse engineering may be part of the following process: Stage 1, analysis of the product; Stage 2, generation of an intermediate product

---

[5] This assertion refers to proprietary software. Software released under the Open Source model is released with its source code version.

[6] As discussed below, the original source code can never be recovered in full. Since a great deal of the original programmer's instructions, including commentary, notations, and specifications, are not included in the translation from source to object code, such information cannot be recovered through decompilation. Because the re-created source code forms only an approximation of the original source code, it is sometimes referred to as pseudo source code.

description; Stage 3, human analysis of product description to produce specification; and Stage 4, generation of a new product using the specification.[7] This chapter mainly concerns Stages 1 and 2. This is not to say that Stages 3 and 4 have no repercussions with respect to intellectual property laws. On the contrary, once a system is analysed under Stages 1 and 2, by using one of the prevalent methods,[8] the information extracted is usually put into some kind of use (e.g. implementation in a new product). Whether or not such use constitutes an infringement of an intellectual property right may be of paramount importance to a reverse engineer. This issue, however, is addressed in the next chapter, where infringement with respect to reproduction of various software elements is assessed under the idea–expression dichotomy. Furthermore, scope of protection with respect to software elements that were uncovered through reverse engineering may also be affected by one of defences that are available under our copyright regime.[9]

The discussion regarding the idea–expression dichotomy and copyrightable subject matter in software is of significant relevance to the question of infringement in the context of Stages 3 and 4. It is for this reason that parties that are engaged in reverse engineering often employ a technique known as 'clean room' or 'Chinese wall'. For example, if a party wishes to reverse engineer a computer program while accessing its code in order to create a competing program that emulates it, it may run a risk that the code in its newly created program may infringe the copyright in the emulated program's code. Thus, our reverse engineer may employ a clean-room technique in the following fashion.[10] First, a team of engineers will study and analyse the code of the emulated program; if the program is available only in object code format, it may be decompiled and converted into source code format.[11] Studying the program in its comprehensible format, our first team of engineers will then describe everything the program does, as completely as possible, without using or referencing any actual code.[12] At this stage a second team of programmers takes over. This second team should have no prior knowledge of the reverse engineered system and should have had no access to its code. Working only from the first team's functional specifications, the second team would then write a new program that operates as specified.[13] In this way, the resulting program will be different from the emulated program in terms of its code and software architecture, although for

---

[7] A Johnson-Laird 'Software reverse engineering in the real world' (1994) 19 U. Dayton L. Rev. 843.
[8] For example, decompilation or black box reverse engineering.
[9] For example, the fair-use copyright defence in the United States.
[10] For a review of clean-room procedure, see A Singh and B Gupta, 'Reverse engineering: a swiftly growing technology in the software world' (2009) 2 Int. J. of Recent Trends in Engineering 4.
[11] This broadly corresponds to Stages 1 and 2, above.   [12] Corresponding to Stage 3.
[13] This being Stage 4.

3.1 Reverse Engineering and Decompilation of Software

most intents and purposes, it may operate identically. Using the clean-room approach, even if some sections of code do happen to be identical, there may be no copyright infringement in relation to the newly created program, as software functionality is not easily protected under copyright law.[14] However, the actual process of reverse engineering, rather than the software developed on the basis of such process, may lead to copyright infringement. It is the potential infringement in relation to the process of reverse engineering that stands at the centre of this chapter.

3.1.5 Motivation and methods for reverse engineering

A person may wish to engage in reverse engineering of computer programs for two main reasons: (i) understanding the internal working of computer programs and (ii) understanding performance failures of computer programs. Understanding the internal working of a computer program may have four[15] primary objectives: (i) to produce a functionally equivalent or a better program (i.e. competition[16]); (ii) to produce a program that operates with the studied program or with programs that work with the studied program (i.e. compatibility or interoperability); (iii) to analyse solutions adopted by the studied program for research and educative purposes;[17] (iv) security auditing.[18] Understanding performance failures of a computer program is done for diagnostic purposes whereby the programmer attempts to understand why a program fails to perform in a desired manner.[19]

Thus, the ability to 'pick' into to a program's internal organs, beyond the object code in which it has been circulated in the marketplace, serves objectives that stand in the heart of the wellbeing of the software industry. But what practical methods are open to a programmer to employ while trying to understand the internal working of a computer program? Opponents of decompilation point out that there are three basic methods for understanding aspects such as

---

[14] Of course, where the system in question is protected by a patent, emulating its functionality may result in infringement. However, under such circumstances, reverse engineering is most likely to be redundant, as the patent's specifications should disclose the program's functionality: see Chapter 7.

[15] There may be some additional reasons; see the discussion below on reasons for decompilation.

[16] You may wish to create a functionally equivalent program for non-competitive purposes. The most common reason in this context is where you have an application written long back for a legacy system, the source code is not available, and you may need to port it to a new platform. Under these circumstances, the application may need to be written from scratch or, alternatively, decompilation may be used in order to understand the internal working of the program, and then write it again.

[17] Which may be done either with commercial or non-commercial objectives in mind.

[18] For example, identifying backdoors, viruses, malware, or spyware code in an installed program.

[19] For the various rationales for practising reverse engineering see, generally, G Davis III, 'Scope of protection of computer-based works: reverse engineering, clean rooms and decompilation' (1993) 370 Computer L. Inst. 115 (PLI Patents, Copyrights, Trademarks and Literary Property Practice Handbook Series No. G-370).

ideas, concepts, methods, and processes, which are embodied in a computer programs: (i) reading the program documentation, (ii) observing the program in operation, and (iii) disassembly and decompilation.[20] Therefore, the argument goes, it is not necessary to practice decompilation, an intrusive method that involves copyright infringement, when it is possible to achieve the same objectives while engaging in non-infringing activities. However, it is submitted that in various contexts it is only the practice of decompilation which provides effective means of accessing certain ideas and concepts embodied in a computer program.[21] As regards reading the program's documentation, although it may provide some useful information, at best, it does not enable a programmer to discern anything more than the most basic elements underling the studied program. For a start, the program's documentation is usually incomplete, out of date, and inaccurate compared with the actual software itself. In addition, the documentation is portraying a picture of what the software should have been like, rather than what the software actually is.[22] Moreover, the documentation is useless in the case of an attempt to understand why a program fails to perform. Black box testing done through observing the program in operation as a means of accessing the totality of ideas embodied in a computer program does not provide a suitable means in all cases.[23] It consists of no more than an educated guess as to how the program's coding is structured, and it fails to ascertain information as fact. In addition, similar to reading the program's documentation, it is not particularly effective in revealing the precise cause of a program's failure.

That leaves us with the third and final method for reverse engineering a computer program: disassembly and decompilation of the program's code.[24] Decompilation is a long and complex technical process. In non-technical language, it may be described as '. . . a species of reverse engineering that involves translating the object code into human-readable form, or "pseudo source code", largely through trial and error'.[25] It differs from traditional mechanical reverse engineering in that it potentially involves infringement of copyright in the code

---

[20] A Johnson-Laird (1994), 845–6, cited in fn. 6.

[21] Ibid. It is noteworthy that decompilation may be the most effective method for doing so, but it is nevertheless far from perfect, as the original source code can never be recovered in full. Since a great deal of the original programmer's instructions, including commentary, notations, and specifications, are not included in the compilation process from source to object code, such information cannot be recovered through decompilation.

[22] A Johnson-Laird (1994), 846, cited in fn. 6.

[23] It is, however, a fairly effective method in studying a program's functionality in terms of its behavioural aspects.

[24] Disassembly is used when the source code program is written in assembly language. It too involves the translation of object code to source code format. The term *decompilation* is henceforth used in a loose sense so as to encompass also disassembly.

[25] See J Litman 'Copyright and information policy' (1992) 55 Law Contemp. Probl. 185, 197–8.

3.1 Reverse Engineering and Decompilation of Software

of the reverse engineered program. This is the case since in the process of reverse engineering the program reproduces the code of the target program, converts the code, and saves the converted source code.

A number of myths surround the practice of decompilation. Those myths are often used by opponents of decompilation, and, therefore, deserve scrutiny. First, it should be recognized that decompilation of a computer program is a demanding, expensive, and time-consuming process.[26] It is not a cheap and parasitical method for appropriating a computer program's secrets. Second, decompilation does not lay bare the program's inner secrets. As one technologist puts it: 'the inner secrets of the program, the real crown jewels, are embodied in higher level abstraction materials, such as the source code commentary and specification. This never survives the process of being converted into object code'.[27] Finally, decompilation does not enable a programmer to determine the original design rationale. The reverse engineer can discern what the program is doing, but not the underlying reason for why it is doing it the way it does. Some of the missing information may be supplemented by a tedious process of trial and error, accompanied by educated guesses based on the reverse engineer's competence and expertise.[28] Finally, it should be noted that decompilation constitutes only one stage in what is typically a four-stage development process: (i) awareness and recognition that another company introduced a product into the market that is worth the cost and effort of reverse engineering; (ii) reverse engineering and decompilation; (iii) implementation of the know-how obtained through the reverse engineering process into the design and development of a new product; and finally; (iv) introducing the said product into the market.[29]

In comparison to other available methods of reverse engineering, there is little doubt that under certain circumstances, decompilation provides the most, and often the only, effective means, albeit far from perfect, of reverse engineering a computer program in order to gain access to some of its underlying building blocks.[30] Decompilation, however, is a practice that is heavily restricted under copyright law.[31] It is submitted that these restrictions have a considerable effect on the software market.

---

[26] See Johnson-Laird and A Lewis 'Reverse engineering of software: an assessment of the legality of intermediate copying' (2000) 20 Loy. L. A. Ent. Rev. 561.

[27] A Johnson-Laird (1994), cited in fn. 6. It can therefore never be 'resurrected' by decompiling the object code.

[28] Ibid. Also, see Chilling Effects, Professor Samuelson's Law Technology and Public Policy Clinic, http://www.chillingeffects.org/question.cgi?QuestionID=191 (last accessed in December 2015).

[29] P Samuelson and S Scotchmer, 'The law & economics of reverse engineering' (2002) 111 Yale L. J. 1757, 1584.

[30] A Johnson-Laird (1994), cited in fn. 6.

[31] As regards the position under patent law, see below.

It should be noted that arguments against a prohibition on decompilation should not be equated with arguing in favour of unrestricted copying of every computer programs' architectural design aspect uncovered through deocompilation. Decompilation is a process by which one may gain access to the ideas, concepts, procedures, and methods of operation that are embodied in a computer program. Whether or not and to what extent one chooses to reproduce such features in its product is a wholly different question.[32] After all, one may choose to develop its architecture 'around' the decompiled program's architecture, similar to the process of inventing around a patent. Alternatively, one may copy algorithms, data structures, or any other elements that may be considered to be an unprotectable idea, system, procedure, or method of operation. It is therefore the actual ability or entitlement[33] of right owners to block public access to, rather than block utilization off, ideas and concepts embodied in computer programs that this chapter is primarily concerned with.

After considering the motivation behind reverse engineering as a whole, it may be beneficial to highlight the importance of decompilation to the wellbeing of the software market and technological progress.

3.1.6 Reasons for and benefits of decompilation

A party may decide to engage in decompilation for a variety of reasons.[34] The output of such exercise may be used for multiple objectives, ranging from a comprehension aid[35] to creating compliable code.[36] Hardly anyone would argue that some of the potential objectives of a reverse engineer should be pursued without the authorization of the right owner. For example, optimization for a new platform: say you have an old program written for the 80286 processor, but you currently operate a sixth generation Intel Core processor. You may wish to recompile the decompiled code with optimizations appropriate for your actual hardware. In this case decompilation is being practised in order to produce an end product that is nothing more than an optimized version of the target program. In most cases it can be convincingly argued that this interferes with the legitimate interest of the copyright holder of the target

---

[32] As mentioned, this would be determined on the basis of the copyright ability of the part that was taken and the applicability of relevant defences.

[33] For a discussion on the concept of entitlements, see below.

[34] From Program-transformation: Program-transformation.org is a website dedicated to collecting, organizing, and disseminating information about all aspects of program transformation in order to share results across programming communities.

[35] Such resulting pseudo source code may be useful for identifying bugs, malware and other vulnerabilities, interoperability purposes, and learning about algorithms for educational ends.

[36] This might be useful in producing maintainable code for reasons such as fixing bugs and adding features and enabling optimization for a new platform where originally created for a legacy platform or for cross-platform use.

3.1 Reverse Engineering and Decompilation of Software

program and constitutes infringement of the copyright in the target program. This, however, may be contrasted with, for example, objectives such as finding bugs, identifying vulnerabilities,[37] and finding malware,[38] which can hardly be regarded as objectionable. Furthermore, it is submitted that learning about the algorithms used and the overall architectural design cannot and should not be regarded as objectionable under copyright law. This should be distinguished from reproducing such elements in the resulting product, an activity that is separately assessed under copyright rules. It is similar to examining the specification of a valid patent. The exercise may be highly beneficial for research purposes and honing one's skills in a given area in terms of ways of approaching and overcoming typical problems in a given field of technology. Of course, one must take care not to infringe such patent when implementing the lessons learned under such examination. In addition, and as discussed in the next chapter various aspects of a computer program such as algorithms and data structures often do not amount to copyrightable subject matter and may therefore be reproduced.[39] As discussed above, often the only effective way to gain access to such elements is through decompilation.

3.1.7 Interoperability

The most important reason for carrying out decompilation is interoperability.

Interoperability may be defined as 'the logical and, where appropriate, physical interconnection . . . to permit all elements of software and hardware to work with other software and hardware and with users'.[40] For example, in order to make application software to interact with an operation system, a developer must get access to the application programming interfaces. As earlier observed, if such information is not made available by a right owner, the only effective method for obtaining it is through decompilation. There are two types of interoperability scenarios, both of significant importance to the software market.[41] The first is horizontal interoperability. In the case of operating systems, it refers to the requisite information that enables the reverse engineer to develop his own operating system that would be compatible with already existing application software, which, in turn, is compatible with the target operation system. This type of interoperability usually leads to the creation of a competing operation system that is compatible with other application software but not necessarily with the target software itself. The second

---

[37] Scanning the program and looking for code that could be exploited. [38] Ibid.
[39] See the next chapter.
[40] Council Directive 2009/24/EC of 23 April 2009 on the Legal Protection of Computer Programs [2009] OJ L 111/16 (hereinafter referred to as the Software Directive), recital 10.
[41] As discussed in the latter parts of this chapter, decompilation is not legally feasible in a cloud environment.

type of interoperability is vertical interoperability. Here decompilation of an operating system may take place in order to enable the creation of compatible application software. For obvious reasons, most right holders will be more reluctant to disclose horizontal interoperability information than vertical interoperability information.[42] Whichever type of interoperability is concerned, it is clear that having access to interfaces information is crucial for a competitive software market. Otherwise, there is a clear risk that a publisher of a successful software platform will dominate the market and could make it practically impossible for late entrants to compete both in the provision of operation and application software. As a representative of the US government stated, 'To control the interface specifications is to control the industry.'[43] It is for this reason that the Software Directive provides for a limited exception[44] to copyright infringement in the case of decompilation done in order to achieve interoperability. Thus, as discussed elsewhere in this title—although the Directive is not as flexible as US copyright law with respect to decompilation as a whole—it nevertheless provides a limited exception in respect of obtaining information necessary for achieving interoperability.

Although interoperability is of paramount importance to the software market, and, therefore, exceptions to copyright infringement permitting decompilation in order to achieve interoperability are vital, there is a variety of other reasons that support a fair practice of decompilation. As discussed below, such additional justifications for decompilation are not reflected in a broader exception for decompilation in the European Union, while in the United States, the position is ultimately akin to what may be described as 'the Lord giveth, the Lord taketh away', where although copyright law may allow for decompilation in a broader set of circumstances, contract law often ensures that decompilation is illegal irrespective of its end goal.[45]

3.1.7.1 *Free and Open Source Software (FOSS)*
One of the reactions of actors in the programming communities to the locking away of source code behind proprietary walls and denying the public the right to gain access to it was the emergence of the FOSS movement.[46] Although,

---

[42] Some right holders of operation systems may actually publish their APIs and license them for free, or for a payment, so as to promote the creation of application software compatible with their operation system. The more application software is created for such an operation system, the more popular the operation system may turn out to be. On the other hand, some firms may choose to keep their APIs as trade secrets as a means for capturing the market in application software; this is sometimes referred to as walled-garden software ecosystem.

[43] *United State v. Microsoft Corp.* 87 F.Supp.2d 30 (D.D.C 2000).

[44] The Software Directive 2009/24/EC, Article 6.   [45] See Chapters 1 and 2.

[46] Although detailed discussion of the FOSS movement is beyond the scope of this work, it is nevertheless important to recognize that the promotion of access and use of source code is one of its key objectives; for a detailed understanding of the legal issues that surround the FOSS ecosystem, see N Shemtov and I Walden, eds., *Free and Open Source Software: Policy, Law, and Practice* (Oxford, OUP 2013).

3.1 Reverse Engineering and Decompilation of Software

admittedly, the objectives of leading organizations promoting the FOSS agenda are wider and go beyond enabling mere access to software source code, having access to the source code is nevertheless a key element in such organizations' manifesto. Thus, Freedom 1 of the Free Software Foundation (FSF) is the freedom 'to study how the software works and adapt it'; this Freedom encompasses access to a program's source code.[47] In the same vein, the second criterion of the Open Source Initiative (OSI) definition reads, 'Source code: the software to be distributed with the source code or well-publicised access to it'.[48] Thus, the ability, inter alia, to access software source code was recognized to be of paramount importance by people within the programming community as early as the early 1980s,[49] and the emergence of the FOSS movement as a parallel model was partially a reaction to the difficulties in gaining access to a computer program's source code.

Of course, if all software was FSF- or OSI-approved software, access to source code would be a non-issue as source code will always be available to members of the public and there would be no need for decompilation. However, irrespective of the proliferation of open source software, a significant amount of the software that is currently used in the marketplace is proprietary software. Therefore, it is necessary to examine whether the level at which the current restrictions to reverse engineering are set under our IP regime addresses the needs of our software market. Should that not be the case, one may query whether it would be justified for copyright law to carve out a broader exception that enables fair decompilation. In fact, that is exactly what the IEEE (Institute of Electrical and Electronics Engineers) USA has maintained for the last two decades. In its Board of Directors Position Statement on reverse engineering from June 2008 and after acknowledging the importance of granting copyright protection to expressive elements in a computer program, the IEEE emphasizes the importance of learning and studying non-protectable elements:

> Congress did not, under the Copyright Act, protect the ideas contained in that expression. Rather, Congress desired that the ideas contained in works, including computer programs, should be available for use by and to reach others. Accordingly, we consider it appropriate to perceive and learn those ideas by lawful means of reverse engineering.[50]

---

[47] See Free Software Foundation, 'The Free Software Foundation is nonprofit with a worldwide mission to promote computer user freedom and to defend the rights of all free software users' (2016) http://www.fsf.org/about/.
[48] See the Open Source Initiative definition.
[49] The FSF was established by Richard Stallman in 1985.
[50] IEEE-US (2008) 1.This statement was developed by the IEEE-USA's Intellectual Property Committee. IEEE-USA promotes the careers and public policy interests of more than 215,000 engineers, scientists, and allied professionals who are US members of the IEEE.

More than appropriate, the IEEE makes it clear that the ability to study the program through reverse engineering is of paramount importance; they state, 'We further believe that lawful reverse engineering of computer programs is fundamental to the development of programs and software-related technology'.[51] It is of such fundamental importance since it may assist engineers in 'designing competing products that are not substantially similar in expression, as well as to discover patentable subject matter and ideas not otherwise disclosed in the literature provided with the product by the originator'.[52] In explaining what the term legitimate reverse engineering, inter alia, encompasses, the IEEE expresses its support for 'the fair-use rulings in the *Sega Enterprises v. Accolade*, 977 F.2d 1510 (9th Cir. 1992) and *Nintendo v. Atari*, 975 F.2d 832 (Fed Cir. 1992) – decisions pertaining to disassembly of computer code'.[53] Regarding right owners' attempts to prevent such fair use through contractual mechanisms, the IEEE's view on the matter is also clear: 'Additionally, when the object code of a program is widely distributed, so that the object code is no longer a trade secret, contractual provisions accompanying the object code, which purport to limit the engineer's fair-use privileges to reverse engineer the object code, should not be enforceable'.[54] Thus, the position of the largest professional body of software engineers worldwide is clear, both on the importance of legitimate decompilation to the wellbeing of the software industry and technological progress, as well as on the extent to which right owners should be able to regulate and restrict such decompilation. This work illustrates that the legal position at present is quite different from that envisaged by the IEEE.

It is noteworthy that a number of economic studies conducted on the optimal scope of permissible decompilation indicate that current restrictions on decompilation are setting the level of protection too high and result in over-rewarding right owners, and that the software industry as a whole would benefit from easing current restrictions.[55] Such studies suggest that decompilation for reasons other than interoperability might also be desirable. For example, after using a market-oriented perspective for examining the impact of reverse engineering on societal welfare, refining the cost-benefit model to focus on monopoly length, breadth, and invention height, Graham and Zerbe concluded that copyright provides an excessive amount of protection for software.[56] Their conclusion is based on four

---

[51] Ibid.   [52] Ibid, 2.   [53] Ibid.   [54] Ibid.
[55] For example see F Monardo, 'Software reverse engineering and open source software: do we need more FUD to be satisfied' (2008) http://www.epip.eu/conferences/epip03/papers/Morando_EPIP-F_Morando-DEF.pdf. 46; L D Graham and R O Zerbe, 'Economically efficient treatment of software: reverse engineering, protection and disclosure' (1996) Rutgers Computer and Tech. L. J. 61.
[56] Ibid.

main arguments. First, they maintain that a prohibition against reverse engineering and decompilation grants a broader protection to right holders than originally intended under copyright law. As copyright law protects expressions rather than ideas and since it is not based on prohibiting access to, both, protectable and non-protectable elements of a work, right holders are currently excessively protected. Their second argument centres on protection levels in case the prohibition on decompilation is removed. They contend that since decompilation is about access rather than use, removing the prohibition on access will still leave right owners with an adequate level of protection since any infringing use of the information gained through decompilation will be actionable under copyright law. The third argument focuses on the inadequacy of copyright law for protecting software.[57] Thus, tracing the misclassification of software as a literary work protectable under copyright law as the reason for the present unjustifiable restrictions on decompilation, they argue that such misclassification might in part be corrected by allowing reverse engineering and decompilation in a broader set of instances. Finally, in their fourth argument they establish that a disclosure requirement is an essential ingredient in an economically efficient system of intellectual property rules. Thus, allowing reverse engineering and decompilation where no alternative means are available furthers, albeit indirectly, such disclosure. As mentioned, Graham and Zebre conclude that the current level of protection in this context is excessive.

3.2 DECOMPILATION AND COPYRIGHT LAW

The idea-expression dichotomy principle is one of the main tenets of copyright law. It provides that ideas and concepts are not a copyrightable subject matter and should therefore lie in the public domain, open to the public to view, study, and use. As we have seen, the only effective method by which one can achieve these goals with respect to some software features is decompilation. Owing to the particular nature of software and hardware environment, the process of decompilation involves, by definition, copyright infringement. In this respect copyright law contains an inherent contradiction that needs to be addressed. Thus, on one hand, decompilation is essential for accessing certain ideas and concepts that are embodied in a computer program, while on the other hand, decompilation may amount to copyright infringement. Consequently, the public's ability to view, study, and possibly use such ideas and concepts, in a manner compatible with the

---

[57] In this context they argue that the policy reasons for software protection do not support a prohibition on decompilation; see ibid., 23.

idea–expression dichotomy, is seriously compromised.[58] This leads to de facto protection granted to right owners in relation to ideas and concepts, notwithstanding the fact that the latter items lie explicitly outside the ambit of copyright protection. One may therefore have expected copyright law to permit decompilation of computer programs when the latter is conducted with a view to achieve one of the aforementioned objectives. This, however, is not the case.

As discussed below, the decompilation exception provided under EU law is a narrow one. As regards the legal position in the United States, although initially more relaxed and therefore in tune with the spirit of the idea–expression dichotomy principle, the introduction of anti-circumvention measures under the DMCA[59] and the ever-growing tendency to use licensing conditions in order to regulate the terms of use of software products have the effect of greatly restricting decompilation.

3.2.1 Idea–expression dichotomy and decompilation

Although the idea–expression dichotomy principle is widely accepted as a fundamental principle of copyright law, the real difficulty lies in its application, as the borderline between ideas and expressions in relation to computer programs is far from clear.[60]

It is suggested that irrespective of where one may choose to draw such borderline, decompilation of computer programs in order to gain access to ideas and concepts is nevertheless justified. Thus, one may concur with the extreme view expressed by the court in *Whelan v. Jaslow*,[61] according to which the purpose or function of a utilitarian work is the copyright ineligible idea, while everything else is the protected expression. Alternatively, one may support the expansive view expressed by the court in *Lotus v. Borland*,[62] according to which a lot of the literal and non-literal building blocks of a software product are not eligible for copyright protection under Section 102(b). Be that as it may, the question of protectability of architectural elements of computer programs should be distinguished from that of initial accessibility to such elements. Thus, wherever the line between protectable expression and non-protectable idea is drawn, the question of access is a separate one.

Accessibility has been traditionally regulated by trade secrets law, rather than copyright law. The position under trade secrets law is discussed in Chapter 8.

---

[58] The role of the idea–expression dichotomy under copyright law and the rationale in holding such non-literal aspects as copyright-ineligible is discussed in detail in the next chapter.
[59] The Digital Millennium Copyright Act 1998.   [60] See the next chapter.
[61] *Whelan Associates, Inc. v. Jaslow Dental Laboratory, Inc.* 797 F.2d 1222 (3rd Circ. 1986) (as mentioned, this decision has been widely criticized and it is not likely to be followed).
[62] *Lotus Development Corp. v. Borland Int'l, Inc.* 49 F.3d 807 (1st Cir. 1995).

3.2.2 The decompilation exception under the EU computer programs copyright regime

As mentioned, the legal position in the EU regarding decompilation of computer programs is codified under Article 6 of the Software Directive. It provides that translation from machine-readable code to human-readable code does not require the authorization of the right holder where such translation is 'indispensable to obtain the information necessary to achieve interoperability of an independently created computer program with other programs'. Thus, it is only decompilation with a view to achieving interoperability that might be excused under Article 6.

Three additional conditions must be fulfilled for decompilation to be legitimate under Article 6. First, the act must be performed by a licensee or a lawful user of the program. Second, the information sought must not be available to the party carrying out the act through any other source. Finally, the act of decompilation must be confined to the parts of the program necessary to achieve interoperability. This state of affairs should be contrasted with the rest of the language of the Software Directive. The Directive explicitly states that ideas embodied in a computer program are outside the ambit of copyright protection.[63] As discussed below, this legal position has the effect of denying public access to software architectural design concepts,[64] which might not be eligible to copyright protection. Consequently, decompilation carried out for any other purpose, while nevertheless done with a view to gain access to non-protectable software features, will amount to copyright infringement. Although limited in its application to cases involving interoperability, it should be noted that Article 6 is a non-waivable provision.[65] Namely, it cannot be overridden by contract.

3.2.3 Decompilation under the US copyright regime

Unlike Europe, the position in the United States is governed by case-law rather than statute. In three separate decisions discussed below,[66] different US circuit courts of appeal have ruled that decompilation done for the purpose of gaining access to unprotectable elements of computer program may amount to fair use under US copyright law as this trilogy of cases makes up the main part of US jurisprudence on the legal position of decompilation under copyright law, it is worthwhile examining these decisions in some detail.

---

[63] See Art. 1(2) and Recital 11 of The Software Directive 2009/24/EC.
[64] Being the only effective method of reverse engineering for doing so.
[65] See Art. 8, The Software Directive 2009/24/EC.
[66] *Atari Games Corp. v. Nintendo of America, Inc.* 975 F.2d 832; *Sega Enterprises Ltd v. Accolade, Inc.* 977 F.2d 1510 (1992); *Sony Computer Entertainment, Inc. v. Connectix Corp.* 203 F.3d 596 (9th Cir. 2000), cert. denied.

3.2.3.1 *Atari Games Corp. v. Nintendo of America, Inc.*

In *Atari Games Corp. v. Nintendo of America, Inc.*, the plaintiff, Nintendo, alleged that the defendant, Atari, infringed its copyright in the 10NES computer program by, inter alia, decompiling that program.[67] Thus, Nintendo claimed that by creating intermediary copies of the 10NES program during the process of decompilation, Atari had infringed the copyright in the said program. Nintendo's video game system included a monitor, console, and controls. The console was a base unit into which the user inserted game cartridges. Nintendo designed it 10NES program with a view to prevent the console accepting unauthorized game cartridges. The console contained a 'master chip' or a 'lock', while authorized game cartridges contained a 'slave chip' or a 'key'. Atari decompiled Nintendo's program with a view to gaining access to the 10NES lock in order to design the necessary data stream to 'unlock' the console and, thus, enable it to accept unauthorized game cartridges produced by Atari.

The court began its examination by reminding itself of the nature of the Congressional mandate to legislate on copyright.[68] Next, the court paid tribute to the idea-expression dichotomy concept, stressing that 'Section 102(b) is intended, among other things, to make clear that the expression adopted by the programmer is the copyrightable element in a computer program, and the actual processes or methods embodied in the program are not within the scope of copyright law'.[69] The court then expanded on the societal objective behind copyright law and the proper boundaries within which copyright law should be contained: 'The copyright holder has a property interest in preventing others from reaping the fruits of his labour, not in preventing the authors and thinkers of the future from making use of, or building upon, his advances. The process of creation is often an incremental one, and advances building on past developments are far more common than radical new concepts.'[70] Thus, the court expressed its view on the proper boundaries of copyright law in the light of copyright law's objective. Subsequently, finding that activities that fell outside those boundaries were 'fair use' was merely for the protocol. Thus, the court did not even bother to engage in a meaningful discussion of the four factors of fair use under Section 107 in order to reach its conclusion. Looking at the list contained in the preamble to Section 107, the court stated: '. . . the Act exempts from copyright protection reproductions for "criticism, comment . . . or research." These activities permit

---

[67] *Atari Games Corp. v. Nintendo of America, Inc.* 975 F.2d 832.

[68] Referring to the public policy objective behind copyright law as stated in Art. 1, Section 8, Clause 8 of the US Constitution.

[69] *Atari Games Corp. v. Nintendo of America Inc.* 975 F.2d 832, 838.   [70] Ibid.

public understanding and dissemination of the ideas, processes, and methods of operation in a work.'[71]

The court continued by paying a lip service to the second factor of the Section 107 and discharged the matter in two sentences by stating:

> Section 107 also requires examination of the nature of the work when determining if a reproduction is a fair use. When the nature of a work requires intermediate copying to understand the ideas and processes in a copyrighted work, that nature supports a fair use for intermediate copying. Thus, reverse engineering object code to discern the unprotectable ideas in a computer program is a fair use.[72]

Although the court occasionally referred to the text of Section 107, it appears that no detailed examination thereof actually took place. The court merely used the said text in order to justify a conclusion made on a different basis: the proper boundaries of copyright law. This was evaluated by reference to one of the main goals of copyright law itself: furthering creativity and dissemination of information, which depends on the free-flow of ideas. The court's subsequent finding that decompilation in order to get access to such ideas and concepts constitute 'fair use' was therefore hardly surprising.

It is noteworthy that although the decision concerned decompilation for the purpose of achieving interoperability, the court's conclusion was not limited to this scenario. Thus, the decision makes it clear that decompilation practised in order to gain access to unprotectable elements embodied in a computer program, whether with a view to achieving interoperability or not, may constitute 'fair use'.

3.2.3.2 *Sega Enterprises v. Accolade*

The facts in *Sega Enterprises v. Accolade*[73] were similar to those in *Atari Games v. Nintendo*. Again, the defendant was seeking to uncover the activation code used by the plaintiff in order to prevent unauthorized video games being played on its video game console. Again, the defendant decompiled the plaintiff software in order to uncover the said activation code, so it may be incorporated into video game cartridges produced by defendant. The plaintiff claimed, inter alia, copyright infringement, while the defendant argued that decompilation amounted to 'fair use'.

Unlike the court in *Atari*, the Court of Appeal for the Ninth Circuit did carry out a detailed examination of the four statutory factors under Section 107. The outcome, however, was exactly the same. Quoting with approval from *Harper & Row*,[74] the court commenced its fair-use examination by reminding itself that the list of

---

[71] Ibid, 842-3. [72] Ibid. [73] *Sega Enterprises Ltd v. Accolade, Inc.* 977 F.2d 1510 (1992).
[74] *Harper & Row, Publishers, Inc. v. Nation Enterprises* 471 U.S. 539 (1985).

statutory factors is not exhaustive. Rather, the court emphasised, the doctrine of fair use is in essence 'an equitable rule of reason'.[75] Next, the court turned to the examination of the four statutory factors, in the light of 'the policies underlying the copyright Act'.[76]

Looking at the first factor, the court surprisingly rejected Sega's contention that the code was reproduced in order to produce a competing product, the copying was carried out for a commercial purpose, and, therefore, that finding on the first factor weighed against fair use. Similar to the decision in *Atari*, the court was in the view that owing to the intermediary nature of the copies made in the process of decompilation, any commercial objective was 'indirect' and 'derivative'. The court supported its view by stating: '... there is no evidence in the record that Accolade sought to avoid performing its own creative work. Indeed, most of the games that Accolade released for use with the Genesis console were originally developed for other hardware systems'.[77] One may enquire what does the fact that Accolade was able to demonstrate a substantial creative input have to do with the finding that no commercial exploitation of the copies was made. In order to find the complained use 'fair', the court in Sega chose to focus on the intermediary nature of the copies and the creative input added by Accolade, as though these factors negated the overall commercial nature of Accolade activities. To be on the safe side, the court added, 'We further note that we are free to consider the public benefit resulting from a particular use notwithstanding the fact that the alleged infringer may gain commercially.'[78]

As regards the fourth statutory factor, the court completed its examination expeditiously by stating from the outset that it 'bears a close relationship to the "purpose and character" inquiry in that it, too, accommodates the distinction between the copying of works in order to make independent creative expression possible and the simple exploitation of another's creative efforts'.[79] Although the court proceeded to examine the potential effect of Accolade's reproduction on Sega's market, the tone was set in its aforementioned opening statement and it was hardly surprising that the examination of the fourth factor ended up with the same conclusion as the one reached under the first factor.

Assessing the second factor, the court observed that the nature of the copyright work rendered its scope of protection 'thin'. Thus, since being a computer program the work had clear functional nature, its scope of protection was 'thinner' in comparison to works of high authorship. Sega's argument that even if its work did contain a lot of functional elements, Accolade's action cannot amount to fair

[75] *Sega Enterprises Ltd v. Accolade, Inc.* 977 F.2d 1510 (1992), 1521.   [76] Ibid, 1517.
[77] Ibid, 1522.   [78] Ibid, 1522-3.   [79] Ibid, 1523.

use since it reproduced its code in its entirety and not just the functional bits, was rejected by the court owing to the unique technical nature of computer programs. The court explained:

> The unprotected aspects of most functional works are readily accessible to the human eye. The systems described in accounting textbooks or the basic structural concepts embodied in architectural plans, to give two examples, can be easily copied without also copying any of the protected, expressive aspects of the original works. Computer programs, however, are typically distributed for public use in object code form, embedded in a silicon chip or on a floppy disk. For that reason, humans often cannot gain access to the unprotected ideas and functional concepts contained in object code without disassembling that code—i.e., making copies.[80]

Thus, the court reverted to the ultimate public policy rationale that underlined its decision: it would be wrong to enable copyright proprietors to take advantage of the unique nature of software's technological environment in order to block access to unprotectable elements of copyrighted works.

Finally, the court found that it is only the third factor that weighed against fair use at the present case, since Accolade decompiled the entire program written by Sega, but was quick to note that this does not, necessarily, preclude a finding of 'fair use'. Overall, the court held that the first, second, and fourth statutory factors weighed in favour of Accolade, while only the third factor weighed in favour of Sega. The public interest element in the court's decision was highlighted in its conclusion, the court stated:

> In determining whether a challenged use of copyrighted material is fair, a court must keep in mind the public policy underlying the Copyright Act. The immediate effect of our copyright law is to secure a fair return for an 'author's' creative labor. But the ultimate aim is, by this incentive, to stimulate artistic creativity for the general public good.[81]

Although unlike the Atari court the Sega court went through the four statutory factors in some details, both decisions manifest one predominant intrinsic judicial motif: setting the limit on copyright protection at a point that is compatible with the principle embodied in the idea–expression dichotomy. In doing that, the court noted, 'if disassembly of copyrighted object code is per se an unfair use, the owner of the copyright gains a de facto monopoly over the functional aspects of his work – aspects that were expressly denied copyright protection by Congress'.[82]

[80] Ibid, 1525.   [81] Ibid, 1527.   [82] Ibid, 1526.

3.2.3.3 *Sony Computer Entertainment v. Connectix*

In *Sony Computer Entertainment v. Connectix*, the Ninth Circuit was called to decide on the issue of decompilation of computer program code found in a video game console in order to gain access to functional elements that underpinned it.[83] This case concerned horizontal interoperability and the court went one step further than its predecessors. The defendant in *Sony* did not seek to gain access in order to produce games that would be compatible with the said console, but rather in order to develop his own software that 'emulated' the functionality of Sony's PlayStation console, so that Sony PlayStation games could be played on the general purpose computer. Rather surprisingly, the court found that the production of an emulator, which was functionally identical to the original, amounted to fair use.

The court began its fair-use analysis by stating that in the context of computer programs, one of the fair-use doctrine's objectives was 'to preserve public access to ideas and functional elements embedded in copyrighted computer software programs'.[84] Following its earlier footsteps in *Sega*, the Ninth Circuit addressed the first statutory factor by observing that computer programs are eligible to a 'lower degree of protection than more traditional literary works'.[85] Interestingly, the court commented that because of the particular nature of software's technological environment, Connectix copying was necessary. The court did not examine necessity in the context of Connectix's ability to develop independently a competing product, but rather focused on the necessity to engage in intermediary copying once a party decided it wishes to access the unprotected elements embedded in a computer program. Thus, considering accessibility to such elements as a legitimate expectation, the court found that it was technically necessary to produce intermediary copies for that purpose. Under this approach, even if it is established that a competitor may be technically able to develop a similar product by independent creation, it may not weigh against it for the purposes of a fair-use assessment. This is so since regardless of the plausibility of such an alternative, a competitor's endeavour to gain access to unprotectable elements of a copyright work is likely to be seen as legitimate and, therefore, 'fair'.

Next, the court rejected Sony's contention that Sega's fair use in copying the code lines was limited to the number of instances strictly necessary to access its functional elements. The court observed that it was the necessity of the method used rather than necessity of the number of times the method was applied, which was decisive. Hence, the court concluded that the first factor weighed in favour of Connectix. While examining Connectix's actions under the first statutory

---

[83] *Sony Computer Entertainment, Inc. v. Connectix Corp.* 203 F.3d 596 (9th Cir. 2000), cert. denied.
[84] Ibid, 603.   [85] Ibid.

3.2 Decompilation and Copyright Law

factor, the court stated that the legal landscape had changed since its Sega decision. Sony argued that while enquiring about the purpose and the character of the use, the court must take into account Connectix's commercial purpose in copying Sony's program. However, the court stated that such consideration had no place while assessing the first statutory factor. Referring to the Supreme Court's decision in *Cambell v. Acuff-Rose*, the court stated that it was now clear that the defendant's commercial purpose should be assessed separately only under the fourth statutory factor and was not relevant for an examination under the first factor.[86] According to the court, the only relevant thing was Connectix's creative input in its final product. Since the 'emulator' was a wholly new product, notwithstanding the functional similarity between it and Sony's PlayStation console, Connectix's use was held to be transformative. The court stated, 'Sony does not claim that the Virtual Game Solution itself contained object code that infringes Sony's copyright. We are therefore at loss to see how Connectix's drafting of an entirely new object code for its VGS program could not be transformative.'[87] To be on the safe side, the court reiterated the rationale applied by the Sega court and held that, in any event, Conectix's commercial use of the copyright material was intermediary and therefore was only 'indirect and derivative'.

As regards the third statutory factor, reiterating its ruling in Sega, the court found that since Connectix copied Sony's program in its entirety, that factor weighed against it.

The most interesting part of the court's decision concerned its analysis of the fourth statutory factor. The court rejected the District Court's finding that since the emulator could substitute Sony's console, Sony was likely to lose sales and profits and, therefore, the fourth factor must weigh against Connectix. Since the court previously found that Connectix's use was transformative, it held that Connectix's product was less likely to affect adversely the market for the PlayStation! But to the extent that it did do so, the court asserted that it was the result of legitimate competition. According to the court, the outcome of such legitimate competition, even if it means lost sales and profits, does not compel a finding against fair use. In the court's view, it was the transformative nature of the VGS which made it a legitimate competitor in the market for platforms, and the prevention of such competition runs contrary to the statutory purpose of copyright law; namely, promoting creative expression.

Assessed on the basis of the textual scope of Section 107, such a finding is, at best, arguable. Where the allegedly infringing product is used for the same purpose

---

[86] *Campbell v. Acuff-Rose Music, Inc.* 510 U.S. 569 (1994), 579.
[87] *Sony Computer Entertainment, Inc. v. Connectix Corp.* 203 F.3d 596 (9th Cir. 2000), 607.

and may substitute the original, the conclusion of the court is somewhat surprising if the language of the fourth factor is to be taken at face value. If, however, it is not the text of Section 107 that is given prominence but rather the public policy considerations that underlie it, the Connectix decision rests on solid grounds. At the end of the day, it is about promoting creative expression while guaranteeing right holders' legitimate interests. The functional elements that were reproduced in the emulator were clearly not protected by copyright[88] and decompilation was carried out in order to gain access to such elements. This being so, the court was clearly of the view that any other finding than fair use would run contrary to the said public policy considerations.

It appears that the court used the 'fair-use' route in order to justify what is ultimately a public policy-based decision: which types of conduct are and are not permissible in view of the overall objective of copyright law. As Beebe's comprehensive study of fair-use opinions concludes in this context:

> In practice, judges appear to apply section 107 in the form of a cognitively more familiar two-sided balancing test in which they weigh the strength of the defendant's justification for its use, as that justification has been developed in the first three factors, against the impact of that use on the incentives of the plaintiff. Factor four provides the analytical space for this balancing test to occur, and the various doctrinal propositions under factor four are merely there to tilt the scales one way or the other. In essence, like the four factors themselves, they are not legal propositions, but policy propositions.[89]

The aforementioned decisions highlight one repetitive motif in the context of decompilation: one should not be able to take advantage of the unique technological specificity of software in order to block access to unprotectable elements of copyright works. As much as any competitor may examine and analyse ideas and concepts that are used in the creation of other, more traditional, types of copyright works, so should competitors in the software industry be entitled to do.[90] The courts were convinced that holding otherwise may result in a de facto broadening of the scope of the subject matter of copyright protection to ideas, schemes, and functional processes.

To conclude, at the end of the day the courts were employing a straightforward public interest type of analysis: first, reminding themselves of the underlying goals of copyright law; second, assessing whether the complained use furthers

---

[88] Sony did not even try to argue otherwise.
[89] B Beebe, 'An empirical study of U.S. copyright fair use opinions, 1978-2005' (2008) 16 U. of Penn. L. R. 549, 621.
[90] For more on the courts' ultimate rationale in decompilation fair-use cases, see P Samuelson 'Computer programs and copyright's fair use doctrine' (1993) 39(9) *Communications of the AMC* 19–25.

such goals or hinders them, while factoring into this assessment the harm that is likely to be suffered by the plaintiff; finally, to the extent that the use in question was found to further such purposes it was classified as 'fair'. These decisions were issued on a clear public policy basis, according to which the costs of granting software proprietors a de facto monopoly over such intellectual spaces will be too high and is more likely to stifle creativity in the software industry than promote it. Thus, unlike the position under EU law, under US copyright law decompilation carried out with a variety of objectives in mind, and not merely in order to achieve interoperability, may amount to fair use as long as it was done in order to gain access to unprotectable elements of a computer program. It is suggested that this more relaxed attitude towards decompilation is attuned with the idea-expression dichotomy principle and the language of Section 102(b).[91]

3.3 AN ENTITLEMENT TO EXCLUDE ACCESS TO IDEAS

In their seminal paper *Property Rules, Liability Rules and Inalienability: One View from the Cathedral*,[92] Calabresi and Melamed articulated the concept of entitlements, protected by property, liability, and inalienability rules. The elaboration of this particular concept was undertaken in the context of the broader objective of their paper: analysing the topics of property and torts with a framework of a unified, as opposed to disparate, approach. Calabresi and Melamed commenced their paper by outlining the problem of entitlement. Simply put, the problem of entitlement is that whenever the state is presented with conflicting interests, it must decide whom to favour, or 'entitle'. Entitlements thus represent preferences made by the state whenever there are parties with conflicting interests. The state's preference as to which party is 'entitled' to prevail constitutes an entitlement.

Another problem that Calabresi and Melamed illustrate is that after an entitlement is issued, the state then has to decide on the manner in which the entitlement is enforced. That is, subsequent to the resolution of the question of who wins, the state must decide on the type of protection to be granted to ensure that its decision is continually accepted. The present discussion is concerned with entitlements enforced in two particular ways: entitlements enforced by property rules and entitlements enforced by liability rules. As Calabresi and Melamed state:

---

[91] Please note that, to a large extent, the ability to engage in fair-use reverse engineering could be compromised owing to use of technological protection measures and restrictive contractual provisions; see Chapter 4.
[92] G Calabresi and A D Melamed, 'Property rules, liability rules and inalienability: one view from the cathedral' (1971) 85 Harvard L. R. 1089.

An entitlement is protected by a property rule to the extent that someone who wishes to remove the entitlement from its holder must buy it from him in a voluntary transaction in which the value of the entitlement is agreed upon by the seller ... Whenever someone may destroy an initial entitlement if he is willing to pay an objectively determined value for it, an entitlement is protected by a liability rule.[93]

In the case of intellectual property rules, entitlements to exploit exclusively a work or an invention are clear examples of entitlements protected by property rules. However, while copyright law makes it clear as to what aspects of computer programs are eligible to property rights, it is the de facto protection given to a program's internal architecture that is at issue here. Clearly, ideas, concepts, processes, procedures, and methods of operation that are embodied in a computer program's internal architecture may not be the subject of property rules under copyright law[94] (i.e. it is not the subject of an entitlement protected by property rules). Nevertheless, the current situation suggests that right owners are given a de facto entitlement, protected by liability rules, to exclude all others from accessing certain ideas and concepts embodied in their computer programs.

3.4 ENTITLEMENTS IN THE CASE OF DECOMPILATION OF COMPUTER PROGRAMS

As discussed above, in the EU decompilation of a computer program constitutes prima facie copyright infringement, unless done for the purpose of achieving interoperability. Where such infringement takes place, one may be required to pay an objectively determined price.[95] Thus, as a consequence of the current legal position, a party who wishes to access ideas that are embodied in a computer program, and decompiles a computer program in order to do so, may incur liability for 'trespassing' onto the right owner's exclusive property. In this respect, it is both property rules and liability rules that the present discussion is concerned with: a first glance at our copyright regime may lead one to think that ideas and concepts that are embodied in a computer program are not the subject of any entitlement. That, however, is true only in respect of an entitlement protected by property rules per se.[96] As we have seen, the prohibition against decompilation, which is the only

---

[93] Ibid, 1092.
[94] See the discussion in the subsequent chapter on the idea-expression dichotomy principle.
[95] Objectively determined by an organ of the state, e.g. the courts.
[96] In the case of copyright law, it is explicitly stated that the exclusive property right of the proprietor does not extend to ideas, procedures, systems, and methods of operation embodied in a computer program.

3.4 Entitlements in the Case of Decompilation

effective method for gaining access to some ideas and concepts embodied in a computer program has the effect of granting software proprietors an entitlement, protected by liability rules, to block public access to such ideas and concepts. It does not appear that this position is supported by a convincing public welfare-based justification.

3.4.1 An anomaly?

As mentioned above, the practice of decompilation is undertaken to allow access to certain underlying ideas and concepts that are embodied in the internal architecture of computer programs; such ideas may form the logical building blocks that were used in the program's development process. As we have seen, although far from perfect, decompilation is often the only effective method to gain such access. Notwithstanding the legal principle of the idea/expression dichotomy, in practice, the current legal position in the EU entails a de facto prohibition on decompilation under copyright law, except when done for the limited purpose of interoperability. Such prohibitions enable software proprietors to lock away certain 'intellectual spaces', which are ultimately not the subject matter of any proprietary right.

It is suggested that the current position under our copyright regimes regarding decompilation is self-contradictory: while one part of this regime provides that ideas and concepts are open for the public to study and use, another part effectively provides that where computer programs are at issue, the only effective manner for gaining access to certain ideas and concepts constitutes copyright infringement unless done for the limited purpose of achieving interoperability. Thus, one branch of our copyright regime appears to defeat an explicit objective of another branch of the same regime. It might be helpful to elaborate further on this inherent contradiction by reference to an analogy with the world of real property.

Let us assume, for example, that there is a country where private ownership of land is permissible and encouraged owing to the government's recognition of the advantages of such a system over common management of land. Now, let us also assume that owing to a policy-based decision, the property laws in such a country do not enable private ownership over natural resources such as ports, riverbanks, and roads and requires that such resources would be kept open for use by the public.[97] On the basis of these given circumstances, it would make little sense for the government to grant farmer X exclusive ownership over a plot of land, which is

---

Similarly, in the case of patent law, it is only the claimed invention, which is fully disclosed in the patent specification, that is the subject of the proprietor's property right.

[97] For example, owing to efficiency arguments related to the significance of such resources in the development of commerce, trade, and, thus, its general contribution to public welfare.

adjacent, for example, to a natural sea port, so that the only way to access such a port overland would be by trespassing onto farmer X's private property. Such grant of exclusive ownership would give farmer X a de facto monopoly over a resource to which open access is considered to be essential for the efficient functioning of the market and therefore for general public welfare.[98] A system that wishes to promote efficiency by ensuring that such essential resources are open for public use must provide that such an exclusive grant of land is subject to some form of public 'right of way' which enables the public to access the aforementioned natural port, albeit with as minimal interference as possible to farmer X's exclusive ownership. This analogy reflects the anomaly present in copyright laws concerning decompilation of computer programs. On the one hand, our copyright law regime explicitly recognizes the significance of ideas as building blocks of our society, and the role that allowing open access to ideas plays in promoting competitiveness and market efficiency. On the other hand, in the case of certain computer program's architectural elements, ideas, and concepts are essentially blocked from public access as a result of bad legal planning.

A peculiarity of the technical specificity of software dictates that, unlike other types of literary works, uncovering the ideas and concepts that are embodied in computer programs requires the creation of intermediary copies of the said program and, sometimes, a source code adaptation of the object code version. A more balanced copyright regime could have provided for an adequate 'right of way' in order to enable such practice.

As mentioned below, with the provision of software increasingly moving to cloud environment, the question of decompilation as a means to uncover non-copyrightable software elements is becoming less relevant.

3.5 A CRITICAL OVERVIEW OF ARTICLE 6 AS A MEANS TO ENABLE DECOMPILATION TO ACHIEVE INTEROPERABILITY

Even where examining Article 6 in light of the limited objective it is set to achieve, it is arguable whether it delivers on its promise in an optimal manner.

Various commentators have been critical of Article 6 as a means to enable and encourage interoperability.[99] Such criticism tends to focus on a number of perceived key deficiencies of Article 6.

---

[98] Accessing ideas and concepts that are by definition outside the monopoly scope of a copyright holder is of significant importance. See the discussion above on the merits of the idea-expression dichotomy in general and of decompilation in particular.

[99] See e.g. C Meyer and M Colombe, 'Inoperability still threatened by EC Software Directive: a status directive' (1990) 12 EIPR 325; T Dreier, 'The Council Directive of 14 May 1991 on the legal protection of computer programs' (1991) 13 *European Intellectual Property Review* 319; A K Palmer and T C Vinje, 'The EC Directive on

3.5 A Critical Overview of Article 6

First, it should be observed that Article 6 does not impose an obligation to disclose interoperability information. Since decompilation is a technically challenging process, there is no guarantee that the decompilation process will yield the sought-after interface-specification information. This being so, it could be argued that the objective of encouraging open access to interoperability information is not fully achieved through Article 6 and that an active duty to disclose such information might be sometimes appropriate. In fact, this was the Commission's conclusion in the *Microsoft* decision, where it essentially stated that the complexity of the target programs made decompilation practically non-viable[100] and that under the circumstances of the case, an active duty to disclose was consistent with the objective of Article 6.[101] The problem of technical feasibility of decompilation also applies to the practice of some right owners to constantly change interface specifications.[102] But is there a practical way to alleviate this technical burden of reverse engineers seeking interoperability? This author does not support an overreaching active duty to disclose interface-specification information as a means of addressing a potential technical difficulty in decompilation techniques.[103] It is submitted that where, as in the *Microsoft* case, an extraordinary set of circumstances is present and the copyright owner enjoys exceptionally strong market dominance, competition law rather than copyright law might step in and impose such a duty.[104] However, where this is not the case and where refusal to disclose and licence does not constitute competition law violation, no active duty to disclose should be imposed under copyright law.[105] van Rooijen argues that such ex post intervention would be better conducted by a specially created regulatory authority rather than by a court. He contends that such an authority could consider whether the ex ante approach of copyright to interoperability is sufficient in light of a given state of the art of computer programming and decompilation techniques and, potentially, loosen the conditions

---

the Legal Protection of Computer Software: new law governing software development' (1992) 2 Duke J. Comp. & Int'l. L. 65; P Samuelson, 'Comparing U.S. and E.C. copyright protection for computer programs: are they more different than they seem?' (1994) 13 J. L. and Com. 279; A van Rooijen, *The Software Interface between Copyright and Competition Law: A Legal Analysis of Inoperability in* (Dordrecht, The Netherlands, Kluwer Law International, 2010); U Mylly, 'An evolutionary economic perspective on computer program inoperability and copyright' (2010) 41 IIC 284.

[100] Microsoft (Case COMP/C-3/37.792) Commission Decision C(2004)900 final, Section 685.
[101] Ibid, Section 747.   [102] See van Rooijen (2010), 89, cited in fn. 100.
[103] See van Rooijen (2010), 239, cited in fn. 100, arguing against a mandatory disclosure of interface information rule, but proposing a regulatory authority that will review such cases ex post and impose adequate terms of disclosure in appropriate cases.
[104] A detailed examination of competition law principles that might play a part in such a decision is beyond the scope of this work; for a detailed discussion on this point see A Ezrachi and S Anderman, eds, *Intellectual Property Law and Competition Law: New Frontiers* (Oxford, OUP, 2011).
[105] The same conclusion was reached in a Commission Staff Working Document: Analysis of measures that could lead significant market players in the ICT sector to license interoperability information, ec.europa.eu/information_society/newsroom/cf/dae/document.cfm?doc_id=2290.

on decompilation, if not impose an active duty to disclose, in appropriate cases.[106] Thus, he essentially argues that where technological difficulties that are obstructing decompilation intended to achieve interoperability could be said to be anticipated by ex ante copyright rules, no further intervention is required. However, where such a regulatory authority will judge a given scenario to involved technical difficulties not anticipated by ex ante copyright rules, such invention becomes an option. He further maintains that such a regulatory authority, having the necessary rule making, dispute resolution and monitoring powers, would be preferable to a court in that it will have the necessary technical expertise and will be cheaper and quicker to deal with.[107] Although a detailed discussion in van Rooijen's suggestions in this respect is beyond the scope of this title, the issues highlighted by him illustrate the somewhat limited effectiveness of Article 6 under a given set of circumstances. It is noteworthy that the only empirical study to date on the possibility of introducing legislative measures that impose a duty to disclose interoperability information concludes that such measures may not prove successful or desirable.[108]

Another critique often levelled at Article 6 is that although it addresses the question of access to interface-specification information, it says nothing about the use of such information once it is obtained through legitimate decompilation.[109] Thus, interoperability will not be achieved if reverse engineers are prevented from using original copyright protected interface information. As mentioned, it is true that Article 6 and the Software Directive in general are silent about the copyright-eligibility of such information. As argued earlier, although interface-specification information is not expressly excluded from copyright protection, treating such information, whether or not original in the sense of being its author's own intellectual creation, in any way other than reproducible for the purpose of achieving interoperability, would render Article 6 meaningless.[110] Admittedly, an expressed statement to this effect, similar to the one under Section 47D(1)(d) of the Australian Copyright Act 1968, which explicitly allow the use of such information once obtained through legitimate decompilation, would have been welcomed. However, it is submitted that an EU court faced with such a question is likely to interpret the Software Directive with its legislative intent in mind; namely, enabling and encouraging interoperability and, therefore, permitting the reproduction of interoperability information for such an end.

---

[106] Seevan Rooijen (2010), 232, cited in fn. 100.   [107] Ibid, 233, cited in fn. 100.

[108] See, Commission Staff Working Document: analysis of measures that could lead significant market players in the ICT sector to license interoperability information; available at: ec.europa.eu/information_society/newsroom/cf/dae/document.cfm?doc_id=2290.

[109] Ibid, 88.

[110] Pamela Samuelson is of the opinion that the Software Directive permits reproducing interface information in another program in order to achieve interoperability; see P Samuelson (1994), 283, cited in fn. 100. Similarly Vinje is of the view that the Directive implicitly authorizes the use of interface-specification

van Rooijen also notes that Article 6 sanctions interoperability with other programs but is silent about software-to-hardware interoperability. Samuelson, on the other hand, believes that the Software Directive *'can fairly be read as regarding requirements for program-to-hardware interoperability as equally unprotectable under copyright law'*.[111] Samuelson bases her view on the Directive's recitals, which make a direct reference to instances where physical interconnectors might be required. The Commission has previously acknowledged that the exclusion of hardware from the interoperability definition of Article 6 might be an issue, but noted that to date it did not receive any evidence that this restrictive definition is causing problems.[112] If the options for achieving interoperability under the Software Directive are too narrow, it may be the time to address it, especially in the light of the Commission's initiative regarding the 'Internet of Things', which is, inter alia, about developing inter-connections between computers, software, and physical devices.[113] But are those options indeed narrow as a result of defining interoperability as a program-to-program arrangement only? It is submitted that this is not necessarily the case. In addition to Samuelson's above interpretation of the Software Directive in light of its Recitals, it should be noted that the Software Directive considers firmware as software. This being so, and since most relevant hardware in this context includes firmware, it can be convincingly argued that the program-to-program formula used by the Directive is sufficient to enable interoperability between software and physical devices in the vast majority of cases. In case of a future revision of the Software Directive and for the avoidance of any doubt, it might be beneficial to clarify that interoperability comprise both software-to-software and software-to-hardware relationship, in a similar manner to Section 47D(1)(b) of the Australian Copyright Act 1968.[114]

A number of commentators highlighted the fact that Article 6(2)(b) prevents competitors from sharing the effort and cost of decompilation.[115] Where certain interfaces have emerged as a de facto standard, it might be the case that

---

information in order to create a program interoperable with another program; see, T C Vinje, 'The legislative history of the EC Software Directive' in M Lehmann and C Tapper, *A Handbook And European Software Law* (Oxford, OUP, 1993) 39.

[111] P Samuelson (1994), 286, cited in fn. 100.

[112] Commission, 'Staff Working Paper on Review of the EC Legal Framework in the Field of Copyrights and Related Rights' 995 SEC (2004) 9.

[113] Communication of 18 June 2009 from the Commission to the European Parliament, The Council, the European Economic and Social Committee and the Committee of the Regions: Internet of Things: an action plan for Europe, COM (2009) 0278 Final.

[114] Which refers to interoperability with another program or article.

[115] See e.g. B Czarnota and R J Hart, *Legal Protection of Computer Programs and Europe: A Guide to the EC Directives* (London, Butterworths, 1991), 81; P Samuelson and S Scotchmer 'The law & economics of reverse engineering' (2002) 111 Yale L. J. 1757, 1586; A van Rooijen, *The Software Interface between Copyright and*

numerous parties will be interested in the interface-specification information. In light of the cost and effort involved in decompilation, it appears wasteful to require each of those parties to decompile independently the same target program. van Rooijen's solution is, again, a regulatory authority that might permit a joint effort in decompilation, where the circumstances are adequate.

It has also been noted that Article 6 does not appear to sanction explicitly decompilation with a view to assist future compatibility. As Samuelson observed,[116] the Software Directive does not contain an express authorization to decompile one program in order to create future compatible programs.[117] This could prove to be an issue where competitors might have the need to decompile a certain program since they expect it to emerge as a de facto standard even before they have a concrete program of their own intended to be compatible with that standard.[118] Samuelson appears to be in the view that EU experience in this context might make a difference. She points to EU history of litigation with IBM concerning changes to IBM's interfaces that rendered competitive peripheral equipment incompatible. Since such problems could potentially be avoided by competitors decompiling a relevant program with an eye to future compatibility, courts in the EU might prove sympathetic to the argument that the Software Directive and Article 6 apply to future compatibility scenarios as well as present ones.[119] Again, this issue could be easily addressed with a simple amendment to Article 6, which may clarify that decompilation might be permitted with respect to programs existing at present or created in the future.

Finally, it has been suggested that the fact that decompilation is limited to the parts which are required to achieve interoperability might be problematic as on occasions reverse engineers might not know in advance in which parts of the program the interoperability information is located.[120] It is submitted that under such circumstances, decompilation of parts that do not contain interoperability information might be excused, as the relevant point of time for assessing the legitimacy of the decompilation at issue should be the time when decompilation was contemplated. Thus, if at that point of time it was not clear where exactly the sought-after information is located, and as a result parts of the program that do not contain such information were also decompiled, such decompilation should

---

Competition Law: A Legal Analysis of Inoperability in Computer Programs (Dordrecht, The Netherlands, Kluwer Law International, 2010), 90; P Heindl, 'A status report from the software decompilation battle: a source of sores for software copyright owners in the United States and the European Union' (2008) Transatlantic Technology Law Forum Working Paper, 79.

[116] P Samuelson (1994), 283, cited in fn. 100.
[117] Neither does it use explicit language to the contrary.
[118] See A van Rooijen (2010), 90, cited in fn. 100.   [119] P Samuelson (1994), 284, cited in fn. 100.
[120] See A van Rooijen (2010), 90, cited in fn. 100.

nevertheless be excused if the decision to target such parts appears to be reasonable under the circumstances.

3.6 A NOTE ON REVERSE ENGINEERING IN A CLOUD ENVIRONMENT

As mentioned above, black box reverse engineering could be carried out remotely, even without access to the target program's object code. Thus, a reverse engineer may feed a program with various inputs and observe it in operation while running remotely in a cloud environment. All that is required is for the program to accept inputs. Therefore, overall a cloud environment does not pose a particular challenge to black box reverse engineering as far as copyright law is concerned.[121]

It is the practice of white box reverse engineering or decompilation that is hampered by a cloud environment. This, however, is not a result of copyright law's shortcomings, but of the service provider's ability to control and restrict access to the program's object code. We have seen that decompilation involves a process where the program's object code is being 'converted' as close as possible to its original source code version. Needless to say, this requires access to the program's object code. Such access is hardly an issue in a conventional environment as software is being distributed in an object code format. However, no such distribution takes place in a cloud environment, as the program is being accessed remotely while residing in the cloud, rather than on the user's hard drive. Any attempt to overcome the relevant technical barriers from afar and access such software remotely in order to reverse engineer and decompile it would trigger laws restricting computer interference and circumvention of technological protection measures. As Determann and Nimmer observe, 'The move to cloud models has the potential for less interoperability and adverse effects on innovation. Whether this potential will materialize remains to be seen.'[122]

---

[121] Furthermore, unlike black box reverse engineering in a conventional environment, in a cloud environment, no intermediary copies of the program are being created on the reverse engineer's computer as the program is being run remotely and not on the said computer. Of course, such black box reverse engineering could be restricted by contractual website-access restrictions and technological-protection measures; these are discussed in Chapters 1 and 2.

[122] L Determann and D Nimmer, 'Software copyright in the cloud', in C S Yoo and J Blanchette, *Regulating the Cloud: Policy for Computing Infrastructure* (1st edn., Cambridge, MA, MIT Press 2015)

4

THE IDEA–EXPRESSION DICHOTOMY AND ITS ROLE IN SOFTWARE-RELATED DISPUTES

4.1 Introduction	102
4.2 The Idea-Expression Dichotomy: Critique and Justifications	104
4.2.1 A brief note regarding critiques of the idea-expression dichotomy principle	104
4.2.2 Economic and efficiency-based justifications of the idea-expression dichotomy	105
4.2.3 The idea-expression dichotomy and natural laws systems	106
4.3 Idea-Expression Dichotomy: Emergence and Development	108
4.3.1 The emergence of the idea-expression dichotomy on both sides of the Atlantic	109
4.3.2 The development of the idea-expression dichotomy in the United Kingdom	112
4.3.3 The application of the idea-expression dichotomy in recent UK software-related disputes	120
4.3.4 The application of the idea-expression dichotomy in EU software-related disputes	121
4.3.5 The development of the idea-expression dichotomy in the United States	124
4.3.6 The application of the idea-expression dichotomy in US software-related disputes	127

4.1 INTRODUCTION

In *Nova v. Mazooma*, a case concerned with copyright infringement of a video game, Jacob LJ stated, 'The well-known dichotomy between an idea and its individual expression is intended to apply and does to copyright in computer software. When I say "well-known" I mean not just known to copyright lawyers of one

Beyond the Code: Protection of Non-Textual Features of Software. First Edition. Noam Shemtov.
© Noam Shemtov 2017. Published 2017 by Oxford University Press.

4.1 Introduction

country but well-known all over the world.'[1] It is a position that is universally held, be it under TRIPS, WIPO Copyright Treaty, US Copyright Act, or the EU Software Directive.[2] The dichotomy had been described as follows:

> Copyright does not preclude others from using the ideas or information revealed by the author's work. It pertains to the literary, musical, graphic, or artistic form in which the author expresses intellectual concepts. It enables him to prevent others from reproducing his individual expression without his consent. But anyone is free to create his own expression of the same concepts, or to make practical use of them, as long as he does not copy the author's form of expression.[3]

The operation of the doctrine requires no objective assessment of the merits of ideas as it is the case under patent law.[4] Hence, copyright law may allow the appropriation of ingenious and highly creative ideas and concepts. Appropriation of such ideas by other creators is seen as a desirable feature of a society that encourages the maximization of knowledge, and the dichotomy serves as a safety valve, preventing the monopolization of ideas and excessive rewards to authors under copyright law.[5]

For one to be able to study and possibly utilize such ideas in a non-infringing manner, practical access to such ideas and concepts must first be available. We have already seen that such access is of great importance to the efficient functioning of the software industry. This chapter, however, focuses on the idea–expression dichotomy in order to demonstrate that access to such ideas, as well as the freedom to utilize them, is also justified as a matter of copyright law. Hence, this chapter traces back the idea–expression dichotomy to its origins, and surveys the key milestones in its development. In doing so, it examines the public policy considerations that stand at its heart. This is done in order to enable the reader to assess better its current boundaries and the manner in which those may be applied to disputes involving copyright eligibility of various aspects of software and the application of the idea–expression dichotomy thereto.

---

[1] *Nova Productions Limited v. Mazooma Games Limited & Others* [2007] EWCA Civ. 219, para. 31.
[2] See TRIPS Art. 9(2), WCT Art. 2, Section 102(b) of US Copyright Act and Art. 1(2) of Directive 2009/24/EC.
[3] Report of the Register of Copyrights on the General Revision of the United States Copyright Law (1961), reprinted in G Grossman, Omnibus Copyright Revision Legislative History, at 5.
[4] For example, the requirements of novelty and inventive step under patent law.
[5] E Samuels, 'The idea-expression dichotomy in copyright law' (1989) 56 Tenn. L. Rev. 321.

4.2 THE IDEA–EXPRESSION DICHOTOMY: CRITIQUE AND JUSTIFICATIONS

As Jacob LJ's abovementioned dicta states, the dichotomy is a worldwide known principle. Nevertheless, over time, doubts have been raised as to its actual role in infringement cases and as to whether or not it has any coherent meaning.[6]

4.2.1 A brief note regarding critiques of the idea–expression dichotomy principle

The critique on the dichotomy usually focuses on its imprecise boundaries and its ability, through reinterpretation, to acquire new meanings as times and needs may demand.[7]

It is true, as Jones suggests, that in some respects, an idea cannot really exist apart from some expression.[8] This being so, one may not refer to a distinction between ideas and expressions in a meaningful way as no expressionless ideas may exist. Thus, according to Jones, one may only refer to protectable and non-protectable expressions. But how does one differentiate between protectable and non-protectable elements if reference to ideas and expressions is indeed meaningless? This is the main allegation against the idea–expression dichotomy as an operative limitation on the scope of copyright law.[9] After all, how can it be useful when there is no certainty about its scope and limits?

First, it is submitted that Jones's argument on the dichotomy's literal meaning being meaningless has some merit. The author of the US Treatise on copyright, Paul Goldstein, maintains that the dichotomy is used as a mere metaphor for aspects of protected works that are either within or outside the scope of copyright protection. This, however, does not render the dichotomy useless or without merit.[10] It is submitted that as long as there are fairly clear and reasonable standards for the application of the dichotomy as a judicial tool for balancing competing interests

---

[6] For example, see A Rosen, 'Reconsidering the idea/expression dichotomy' (1992) University of British Colombia L. R. 263 and R H Jones, 'The myth of the idea/expression dichotomy in copyright law' (1990) 10 Pace L. R. 551.

[7] See S Ang, 'The idea expression dichotomy and merger doctrine in copyright laws of the U.S. and the U.K.' [1994] 2 IJL & IT 111.

[8] R H Jones, 'The myth of the idea/expression dichotomy in copyright law' (1990) 10 Pace L. R. 551.

[9] See, also, A Rosen, 'Reconsidering the idea/expression dichotomy' (1992) University of British Colombia L. R. 263; S Ang, 'The idea expression dichotomy and merger doctrine in copyright laws of the U.S. and the U.K.' [1994] 2 IJL & IT 111; M J Spence and T A O Endicott, 'Vagueness in the scope of copyright' (2005) 121 Law Quarterly Rev 657-80; Oxford Legal Studies Research Paper.

[10] P Goldstein, *Goldstein on Copyright* (3rd edn., Santa Monica, CA, Aspen Publishers 2006), S 2.3.1.

in copyright law, whether one refers to such doctrine by one term or another is of little consequence. Thus, as discussed below, the flexible nature of the dichotomy should not be seen as a shortcoming but rather as an advantage. Spence and Endicott argue: '. . . the vagueness of the idea-expression dichotomy enables the law to achieve its purposes, where the formulation of precise standards would be impossible'; they convincingly maintain that setting such precise and effective standards in the case of the idea-expression dichotomy would be impossible.[11] It is submitted that when applied in combination with statutory language such as that of Section 102(b) of the US Copyright Act or Article 9(2) of TRIPS and when given an expansive rather than literal meaning, it can play a vital role in maintaining the internal equilibrium within our copyright regime. In contrast, when given a narrow and literal interpretation, coupled with excessive vagueness regarding the standards employed when applying the dichotomy, it may be reduced to little more than a lip service a court pays when deciding on copyright infringement.

4.2.2 Economic and efficiency-based justifications of the idea-expression dichotomy

It is economic and efficiency-related justifications to the dichotomy that are the focal point of the present discussion since, at least in the case of software, protection is justified mainly by reference to utilitarian objectives.

The traditional justification for protecting only expressions of ideas rather than ideas themselves concerns welfare losses associated with higher monopolistic prices for works. Simply put, if ideas in a copyrighted work are to be protected against copying, the scope of competition that such a work may face will be more limited, which, in turn, may lead to higher prices being charged for such a work. Furthermore, protecting ideas under copyright law is most likely to lead to a reduction in the number of new works created. That, by itself, is a clear welfare loss even without considering the effect that it may have on the price of existing works. Since every first generation author is also a second-generation author: in other words, every author utilizes old ideas when generating new works, allowing monopolization of ideas will have the effect of dramatically reducing the overall numbers of new works.[12]

The costs of coming up with un-patented ideas is usually negligible in comparison to the costs of expressing them.[13] An originator of a new idea will usually

---

[11] M J Spence and T A O Endicott, 'Vagueness in the scope of copyright' (2005) 121 *Law Quarterly Review*; Oxford Legal Studies Research Paper, 263.

[12] R Brown, 'Eligibility for copyright protection: a search for principled standards' (1985) 70 Minn. L. Rev. 579.

[13] See R Posner and W Landes, 'An economic analysis of copyright law' (1989) 17 J. Legal Stud. 325, 348.

obtain sufficient returns from being the first in the market, even without copyright protection for the said idea. In addition, he will be able to obtain returns for the costs of his effort in expressing such ideas through copyright law. Therefore, the majority of authors will probably agree to a rule that, unlike expressions, ideas should not be protected.[14]

Another potential problem associated with protecting ideas under copyright law is that of rent seeking. Once ideas become protectable under copyright law, keeping in mind the low cost of creating such un-patentable ideas in comparison to the potential licensing fee one may be able to extract from a prospective author, we may face a rush of creators to develop and 'bank' new ideas, with minimal expression, in the hope of future authors negotiating for their use. Hence, while the creation of new ideas may be speeded-up, their dissemination is likely to suffer from an opposite effect.[15]

In conclusion, it appears that there is a clear economic case against the protection of ideas under copyright law.

4.2.3 The idea–expression dichotomy and natural laws systems

Except for Ireland, Cyprus, and the United Kingdom, all other countries in the European Union follow the civil law model. Similarly on global level, the majority of legal systems worldwide are based on the civil law model. It is therefore necessary to examine how a doctrine such as the idea–expression dichotomy fares under such a model. After all, the ensuing discussion mainly focuses on the utilitarian nature of the dichotomy, its role as a judicial tool in maintaining the balance between the competing interests in software products' ecosystem under copyright law, and its function in furthering public welfare in this context. As most of these justifications may be considered somewhat alien to the underlying philosophy in natural rights based legal systems, the position of the dichotomy under natural right theory would be briefly discussed. Be that as it may, one must not lose sight of the fact that whether a country has a civil law or common law system, in the end of the day all EU Member States are bound by the Software Directive, which gives effect to the dichotomy and is primarily based on utilitarian objectives.[16]

Under the utilitarian theory, copyright law is mainly about incentives designed to encourage further creativity and its dissemination. The author's exclusive right

---

[14] No survey on the position of authors has been done in the context of computer programs. However, the Institute of Electrical and Electronics Engineers (IEEA-USA), the biggest professional organization of its kind in the world, comprising over 230,000 electronics and computer engineers, has clearly stated its view on the issue in a Position Statement on Reverse Engineering (June 2008): 'reverse engineering of computer programs is fundamental to the development of programs and software-related technology'; see IEEE-US (2008).

[15] R Posner and W Landes, 'An economic analysis of copyright law' (1989) 17 J. Legal Stud. 325, 349.

[16] Furthermore, the Directive's preamble refers exclusively to utilitarian considerations as justification to the exclusive rights granted therein.

and legal entitlement is thus a means to an end rather than the end itself. Natural law based theories put at their centre the author's natural right to the fruits of his labour and his inherent dignity as an author. Thus, rather than being a means to an end, the authorial right is often considered as an end in itself.

It is therefore not surprising that various commentators raised the question of whether curtailing the author's monopoly under the pretext of the idea-expression dichotomy in order to achieve objectives that are independent from the author's personal interest is objectionable under natural rights theory. For example, David Vaver argues: 'the logic flowing from the concepts of natural rights, that ideas should be protected in perpetuity and throughout the world, has never been accepted by even the most ardent promoters of a strict intellectual property regime'.[17] In the same vein, David Fewer maintains, 'the natural rights approach fails to account for copyright law's fundamental division between ideas and expression'.[18]

It is suggested that natural law theory does not necessitate an abandonment of public interest and should not be read as aiming at unmitigated authorial monopoly. Whether one examines Lockean or Kantian property-based theories, it appears that these are flexible enough to allow for accommodation of the idea-expression dichotomy.

In the case of Locke's labour theory, the position is more straightforward. Public interest is a recognized external factor that informs the scope of the labourer's right. Thus, the theory refers not only to the rights of a labourer in the products of his labour but also explicitly to the public's right to limit the labourer's entitlement. This right of the public arises through Locke's famous dicta that the labourer is entitled to the fruits of his labour as long as 'there is enough and as good left in common for others'.[19] As W. Gordon argues, the above dicta 'prohibits a creator from owning abstract ideas because such ownership harms later creators . . . to give ownership in general ideas would have a restrictive impact on the amount of the physical world open to later comers'.[20]

Drassinower articulates an interesting viewpoint regarding the accommodation of the dichotomy within a Kantian-based authorial-right system.[21] He argues that the public domain is not an external factor imposed upon the author, as is the case under the Lockean theory, but internal to the author's very right. He states, 'The

---

[17] D Vaver, 'Intellectual property today: of myths and paradoxes' (1990) Can. Bar. Rev. 98-100.

[18] D Fewer, 'Constitutionalizing copyright: freedom of expression and limits of copyright in Canada' (1997) 55(2) U.T. Fac. L. Rev. 175, 188.

[19] J Locke, *Two Treatises of Government*, (Peter Laslett, ed., Cambridge, Cambridge University Press 1690), 19.

[20] W J Gordon, 'A property right in self-expression: equality and individualism in the natural law of intellectual property' (1993) 102 Yale L. J. 153.

[21] A Drassinower, 'A rights based view of the idea/expression dichotomy in copyright law' (2003) 16 Can. J. Law Jurisprud.

category "product of the author's labour" is overall wider in scope than the category "author's entitlement to copyright".' The latter is a selection drawn from the former. From this point of view, the fundamental question of copyright is a question about the logic, if any, of this selection. He convincingly argues that under a natural right theory, a plaintiff's assertion of his dignity as an author is perceivable only as long as such assertion may be consistent with the defendant's dignity as an author. Thus, the plaintiff may have a right to his expression only to the extent that such right does not interfere with the defendant's equally significant right to his expression. It follows that:

> a plaintiff seeking to enjoin a defendant from using or adopting in the defendant's own work ideas expressed in the plaintiff's work is a plaintiff seeking to interfere with the defendant's own original expression. Where the defendant expresses an idea in his own words, the plaintiff cannot complain of a violation of her copyright because her own claim to copyright is but an affirmation that persons have a right to their expression . . . .The proposition that only expression is copyrightable, and not ideas, is thus necessarily rooted in the equality of the parties as authors.[22]

Thus, rather than an externally imposed limitation, the idea–expression dichotomy not only can be accommodated but in fact plays an important role in regulating the space between authors (and their authorial dignity).

To conclude, similar to the position under the utilitarian view of copyright law, natural right based copyright systems lend support to the view that not everything that originated from the author, every aspect of the author's effort and creativity, is protected under copyright law.

4.3 IDEA–EXPRESSION DICHOTOMY: EMERGENCE AND DEVELOPMENT

The idea-expression doctrine emerged, as we know it nowadays, in the second half of the nineteen century. Up until that point, there was no real need for protection against the appropriation of ideas under copyright law. The application of copyright law, even in the case of expressive elements of a work, was limited to the extent that the risk of monopolization of ideas was insignificant. For example, early English copyright law gave authors the exclusive right to 'print, reprint or import' their works.[23] Thus, for example, literal translations of works were kept outside the ambit of authors' exclusive rights.[24] Early American copyright law

---

[22] Ibid, at 14.   [23] Statute of Anne c. 19.
[24] For example, see *Burnett v. Chetwood* 2 Mer. 441, 35 Eng. Rep. 1008 (Ch. 1720).

followed the same path. Authors were given the exclusive right '. . . of printing, reprinting, publishing and vending' their works.[25] Under both jurisdictions, the fundamental rationale for their restrictive approach towards copyright protection was recognition of the main goal of copyright law: the encouragement of new creative works while bearing in mind that derivative works, such as translations, may well be as important as the initial work. It is clear that as long as copyright law was narrow in its application, no real need for a mechanism that prevents monopolization of ideas was present. It is with the broadening of the boundaries of copyright protection that the idea-expression dichotomy doctrine has emerged.[26]

4.3.1 The emergence of the idea–expression dichotomy on both sides of the Atlantic

As early as the nineteenth century, courts started to draw the line between ideas and expressions. This was followed by judicial recognition that certain ideas had to be expressed in a certain way and that in this case their expression, too, should not be protected under copyright law.[27] In one case, *Hollinrake v. Truswell*, an English Court of Appeal found that the plaintiff's 'Sleeve Chart' was in fact an apparatus or a mechanism, rather than a literary work.[28] The 'Sleeve Chart' was used for the purpose of accurately measuring the inner part of a sleeve and incorporating, for that purpose, certain lines, figures and text printed on a piece of cardboard. The fact that the 'Sleeve Chart' was a combination of words, curved lines, and figures[29] did not stop the court from finding that the work in question was not a

---

[25] US Copyright Law 1790, Section 1. Also, see for judicial approach on literal translations, *Stowe v. Thomas* 23 Fed. Cas. 201 (C.C.E.D. Pa. 1853).

[26] Some commentators traced the origins of the dichotomy to Lucius Annaeus Seneca in the first century AD, the UK origins of the concept to the famous cases of *Millar v. Taylor* 98 Eng. Rep. 201 (KB 1769) (Yates, J., dissenting) and *Donaldson v. Beckett* 1 Eng. Rep.837 (H.L. 1774). The US Drone's treatises on copyright law, which were published a year before *Baker v. Selden*, stated that copyright does not protect ideas but only authorial expression of them. See e.g. R Y Libott, 'Round the prickly pear: the idea-expression fallacy in a mass communication world' (1967) 14 UCLA L. Rev. 735, and for a summary of British law on this point, see B Kaplan, *An Unhurried View of Copyright* (New York, Columbia University Press 1967). I opted for the mid-to-late nineteenth century as a starting point since it was then when, for the first time, the concept was clearly articulated in its present form.

[27] This later become known as the 'merger' doctrine under American copyright law; it refers to a situation where an idea can only be expressed in a limited number of ways and is therefore considered as 'merged' with its expression, rendering such expression unprotectable. Although there are statements in *Baker v. Selden* that support this proposition, scholars such as Pamela Samuelson argue that the merger doctrine did not begin to emerge until the late 1950s, reaching its peak in the 1980s. See P Samuelson, '*Baker v. Selden*: sharpening the distinction between authorship and invention' in R C Dreyfuss and J C Ginsburg, eds., *Intellectual Property Stories* (Mineola, NY, Foundation Press 2005), 215.

[28] *Hollinrake v. Truswell* [1894] 3 Ch. D 420.

[29] These are conventional components of a literary work.

proper subject matter for copyright protection and, if at all, may only be protected under patent law. Thus, the court refused to grant protection to a functional apparatus, irrespective of the fact that this apparatus was 'expressed' in a manner usually found in literary works. It should be noted that the court's reluctance to grant protection in this case was not a result of the work being functional in nature. In fact, the court acknowledged that copyright protection is granted to utilitarian works and compilations, such as maps and Post Office directories. However, in this case the court felt that protection was sought for an actual apparatus or a system. In a statement that is surprisingly similar in substance and form to the present language of Section 102(b) US Copyright Act, the court explained: 'Copyright, however, does not extend to ideas, or schemes, or systems, or methods; it is confined to their expression'. [30]

American courts faced with similar scenarios adopted a similar line of analysis. The development of the idea–expression dichotomy doctrine, as we know it today, is widely attributed to the Supreme Court decision in *Baker v. Selden*.[31] It should be noted that some commentators argue that the case should be understood as standing for a proposition that goes much further than a mere idea/expression distinction; thus, they argue that it should be seen to point to a distinction between protectable and non-protectable subject matter, of which an idea/expression distinction is just one facet.[32]

The plaintiff in this case, Selden, developed a system of bookkeeping that used forms also developed by him, which contained lines and columns illustrating how the system is to be employed. Selden published his system in a book. The book consisted of pages of bookkeeping forms with sample entries, a short preface, and introduction. Most of the 650 words of text in the book highlighted the merits of the system rather than explained how to use it.[33] Subsequently, Baker published his own book, using the system developed by Selden, as well as the forms included in Selden's book, subject to some minor variations.[34] Selden sued Baker for copyright infringement. There was no copying of the textual explanation in Selden's book and the parties agreed that the question before the court should be whether Selden's system constituted a copyrightable subject matter; namely, whether the 'functionality' of the book was protected under copyright law. Selden argued 'the ruled lines and headings, given to illustrate the system, are part of the book and, as

---

[30] *Hollinrake v. Truswell* [1894] 3 Ch. D 420, per Lindsey LJ, 427.
[31] *Baker v. Selden* 101 U.S. 99 (1879).
[32] See, e.g., P Samuelson, 'Frontiers of intellectual property: why copyright law excludes systems and process from scope of its protection' (2007) 85 Tex. L. Rev. 1921, 1922.
[33] See P Samuelson, '*Baker v. Selden*: sharpening the distinction between authorship and invention' in R C Dreyfuss and J C Ginsburg eds., *Intellectual Property Stories* (Mineola, NY, Foundation Press 2005) 181.
[34] The organization of columns on his forms was different and different headings where used.

such, are secured by the copyright; and that no one can make or use similar ruled lines and headings . . . without violating the copyright'.[35] Delivering the court's opinion, Justice Bradley stated: '. . . there is a clear distinction between the book, as such, and the art which it is intended to illustrate'.[36] In describing Selden's ruled lines forms, he stated, 'It is a mechanical device, by which a skilled person may accomplish certain results and avoid errors in book-keeping . . . .. Its ingenuity as a mechanical device may entitle it to entry at the Patent Office, but copyright is intended for authors, not inventors.' Justice Bradley concluded that 'to give the author of the book an exclusive property in the art described therein, when no examination of its novelty has ever been officially made, would be a surprise and a fraud upon the public. That is the province of letters-patent not of copyright.'[37]

The significance of *Baker v. Selden* lies in its being the first articulated judicial manifestation of, both, the idea-expression dichotomy and, more broadly, the protectable/unprotectable distinction in copyright law. Some scholars, as Professor Melville Nimmer has argued,[38] maintain that the underlying reason for the decision in *Baker v. Selden* was that the Selden's 'blank' forms were not copyrightable since they 'expressed' the system in such a way as to 'merge' with it. Thus, there was no other way to describe the system and therefore the expression of the idea embodied in Selden's work (i.e. the forms organized in a particular manner) was deemed to be non-copyrightable as the idea itself. It is suggested that Nimmer's interpretation of Justice Bradley's opinion is questionable, as it over emphasizes the significance of any merger doctrine-based argument in that decision. Examining *Baker v. Selden*, it appears that the court was not too concerned with the question of whether there was another way to 'express' the system. Admittedly, the court stated that where an idea may only be expressed in one way, that expression becomes necessary for using the idea and is therefore unprotectable. However, while referring to the facts of the case, the court simply found that the 'ruled lines' and 'headings', incorporated into the 'blank' forms, were not part of an expression of the system, but that they were in fact part of the system itself. Thus, the 'blank' forms were found to be non-protectable on the basis of being part of a system. On this view, it appears that even if Selden's bookkeeping system could have been employed using other sets of forms,[39] Selden's forms would still be non-copyrightable since they would still constitute part of a bookkeeping system. The case is often regarded as setting the basis for the present Section 102(b) of the US Copyright Act.[40]

---

[35] *Baker v. Selden* 101 U.S. 99 (1879) 101.   [36] Ibid, 102.   [37] Ibid.
[38] See M B Nimmer, *Nimmer on Copyright* (New York, Matthew Bender Publishing 1978) § 13.03 [F].
[39] Thus, not giving rise to the 'merger' doctrine.
[40] See, e.g., 'Brief amicus curiae of the copyright law professors in support of respondent, *Lotus Dev. Corp v. Borland Int'l, Inc.* 516 U.S. 233 (1996) 4; P Goldstein, *Goldstein on Copyright* (3rd edn., Santa Monica, CA, Aspen

4.3.2 The development of the idea–expression dichotomy in the United Kingdom

English courts continued throughout the early part of the twentieth century and onwards to reiterate the idea–expression dichotomy doctrine as one of the main tenets of copyright law and to apply it in appropriate cases. In *McCrum v. Eisner*,[41] Peterson J reiterated with approval Lindsey LJ statements from in *Hollinrake v. Truswell* to the effect that copyright law does not protect ideas but rather protects their expressions. Similarly, in *Harman v. Osborne* Goff J (as he then was) stated that it was a long established principle of copyright law that 'there is no copyright in ideas or schemes or systems or methods—it is confined to their expression'.[42]

The idea–expression dichotomy has thus become one of the underlying principles of UK copyright law.[43] However, although every English court dealing with the subject paid the obligatory tribute to the idea–expression dichotomy, one could identify a growing tendency to decide relevant cases by reference to the rules on originality and substantial taking rather than by reference to the dichotomy principle. Effectively, UK courts have been collapsing the dichotomy principle into the rule on originality rather than deciding appropriate cases on the basis of the dichotomy, which implies a different type of judicial inquiry. Fortunately, as discussed below, this approach is no longer popular at least in the case of software.

The House of Lords decision of *L.B. (Plastics) Limited v. Swish Products Limited* provides a good starting point to examine the emergence of the said approach.[44] In this case the plaintiffs were designers and manufacturers of a plastic 'knock-down' drawer system. The system was mainly sold to furniture manufacturers, who fitted it into carcases of their own manufacture. One of these manufacturers, G.P., who owned the defendant, suggested to the defendant that it would design and manufacture its own plastic 'knock-down' drawer system that would fit to furniture carcases produced by G.P. G.P. required that such a system would be interchangeable with the plaintiff's system in any of G.P.'s range of carcases. After a number of attempts, the defendant managed to manufacture successfully its own version of a plastic 'knock-down' drawer system that fitted into furniture carcases produced by G.P. The plaintiff sued for infringement of artistic

---

Publishers 2006), Infringement, 112; P Samuelson, *'Baker v. Selden*: sharpening the distinction between authorship and invention' in R C Dreyfuss and J C Ginsburg, eds., *Intellectual Property Stories* (Mineola, NY, Foundation Press 2005), 205.

[41] *McCrum v. Eisner* [1917] 87 L.J. Ch. 99, 102.

[42] *Harman v. Osborne* [1967] 2 All ER 324, [1967] 1 WLR 723, at 728.

[43] For other examples of English Courts application of the idea–expression dichotomy, see *Poznanski v. London Film Production, Ltd.* (1937), MacG. Cop. Cas. (1936–45) 107; *Rees v. Melville*, (1914) MacG. Cop. Cas. (1911–16) 168; *Kenrick v. Lawrence* (1890) 25 QBD 99.

[44] *L.B. (Plastics) Limited v. Swish Products Limited* [1979] RPC 551.

4.3 Emergence and Development

copyright in its drawer system. The defendant denied copying in the first place, but more importantly for the present discussion, also argued that his system incorporated nothing more than the idea behind the plaintiff's system, referring to the idea–expression dichotomy principle. Their Lordships overturned the Court of Appeal decision, which was based, inter alia, on the dichotomy principle, and rejected the Court of Appeal's finding that as a functional concept, the copied elements from the plaintiff's work should be protected, if at all, under patent law but not under copyright law.

It is suggested that the House of Lords erred in its application of the dichotomy principle, as well as in its findings in relation to the role that the dichotomy plays in copyright infringement cases. For example, the court stated, 'concept leads to design. You need a concept in order to put it down on paper. There is no copyright in a concept but once it is put down on paper there is copyright in what is on the paper.'[45] It is an overly simplistic approach that overlooks the possibility that what is put down on paper may constitute 'ideas, or schemes, or systems, or methods' and it conflates elements of the requirement of fixation with the dichotomy.[46] Thus, on this rationale, Selden forms as well as Hollinrake 'sleeve chart', since expressed 'on paper', merit copyright protection.

Indeed, a careful reading of the House of Lords decision leaves the reader with a strong impression that the court had failed in its analysis of the dichotomy's role in balancing conflicting interests under copyright law. The House of Lords was clearly of the opinion that a defendant may not use a concept of a copyright work, unless that concept does not constitute a substantial part of the author's effort. This reasoning is clearly flawed. Copying of a substantial part of the author's skill labour and judgement is a prerequisite to a successful infringement action in any event, regardless of whether the part taken may be described as an idea, concept or system. Thus, the House of Lords' approach simply reiterated the general position concerning copyright infringement.

However, if one acknowledges the role of the dichotomy as a limitation on the scope of copyright protection, as the House of Lords clearly did, then surely one must also accept that it has a certain part to play whereby it may come to the rescue of a defendant that may otherwise be found to be an infringer. The plaintiff in a copyright infringement action in the United Kingdom must show substantial taking in order to establish prima facie infringement.[47] If the defendant can show

---

[45] Ibid, 558.

[46] See *Hollinrake v. Truswell* [1894] 3 Ch. D 420. In that case copyright protection was denied for elements of the work, which were put down on paper since they constituted a system or a scheme.

[47] Although, following the CJEU decisions in Case C-5/08 *Danish Infopaq v. Danske Dagblades Forening* and Case C-145/10 *Painer* case, as well as the A-G opinion in Case C-604/10 *Football Dataco Ltd and others*

that no such substantial taking has occurred then the plaintiff's action would inevitably fail. It would make little sense to have a legal doctrine that requires the defendant to show affirmatively that the plaintiff cannot succeed in proving an essential element of an infringement action (i.e. substantial taking) as such doctrine will not make any difference to the final outcome of a case. Thus, it is suggested that the operation of the dichotomy principle necessitates the examination of the nature of the parts taken, in terms of whether or not they are protectable, rather than simply evaluating whether they form a substantial part of the overall effort the author has invested in the work and whether that which was taken was 'put down on paper'. If all that was taken represents a concept, process, system, or method, then even where the development of such aspects involved a substantial amount of skill, labour, and judgement, it should nevertheless lie outside the ambit of copyright protection.

This problematic approach was followed in *Ibcos*, where one may easily identify the same flawed analysis employed by the House of Lords in *L.B. (Plastics)*.[48] One of the questions that Jacob J (as he then was) had to consider in that case concerned the subsistence of copyright in the general architecture of the computer program in question. Responding to the defendant's invitation to examine the nature of the parts taken, and whether or not such functional elements merit copyright protection in the first place, Jacob J stated:

> For myself I do not find the route of going via US case law particularly helpful. As I have said UK copyright cannot prevent the copying of a mere general idea but can protect the copyright of a detailed 'idea'. It is a question of degree where a good guide is the notion of *overborrowing* (emphasis added) of the skill, labour and judgement which went into the copyright work. Going via the complication of the concept of a 'core of protectable expression' merely complicates the matter so far as our law is concerned. It is likely to lead to overcitation of US authority based on a statute different from ours.[49]

Thus, again, the focus turned to the amount of the skill and labour of the original author that was taken, rather than first establishing whether the parts taken merit copyright protection from a public policy based perspective. As was illustrated above, the notion of unprotectable subject matter is not exclusively American and has deep roots in English copyright jurisprudence. There were plenty of English decisions to be cited in support of the proposition that copyright does not protect systems, methods, concepts, etc. Although it is the view of the author of this title

---

v. Yahoo! UK Limited, the test for infringement in the United Kingdom appears to be the taking of a part that represents the author's own intellectual creation.
[48] *Ibcos Computers v. Barclays Mercantile Highland Finance* [1994] FSR 275. [49] Ibid, 32–3.

that the application of the idea-expression dichotomy, as a general principle under English copyright law, should have found its way to the *Ibcos* analysis, it is worth noting that the acts examined in that case were carried out prior to the coming into force of the Software Directive.[50] While bearing in mind that the Software Directive has not been discussed in *Ibcos*, it is suggested that the decision may and should have been different, had the Software Directive been applicable to the case.[51] As we shall see while examining subsequent decisions, the Software Directive is crucial to the analysis of non-literal copying scenarios in the European Union, in particular to the policy considerations that the court may factor into such decisions. However, where the Software Directive did not apply, more recent English courts' approach to the application of the idea-expression dichotomy had been overly restrictive. It is argued that properly applied, the dichotomy should function independently of the 'substantial taking' infringement test. Thus, whether or not one takes a substantial part of the author's skill, labour, and judgement or takes a part that represents the author's own intellectual creation, it should be assessed independently from the evaluation of the nature of the part taken.[52]

In light of the United Kingdom's likely departure from the European Union, and the potential subsequent abandonment of the jurisprudence of the CJEU in that respect, one may wonder whether UK courts are likely to pivot back to their pre-Software Directive days and apply the dichotomy restrictively to software-related scenarios. It might therefore be useful to examine the position under UK law in non-software-related scenarios, as an indication to what might be the legal position in the United Kingdom once it leaves the European Union.

Any hope that the aforementioned restrictive approach would be put right by a higher court was discarded after the House of Lords decision in *Designers Guild*.[53] The claimant, DGL, commenced proceedings against the defendant, RWT, alleging that a fabric design produced by the latter infringed the copyright in one of its own designs. Overturning the trial judge decision, the Court of Appeal first confirmed the trial judge findings on similarities between the two works: the fact that both fabric designs had flowers and stripes, as well as similarities arising from such matters as the brushwork, the resist effect, and the loose arrangement

---

[50] Council Directive 2009/24/EC of April 23 2009 on the Legal Protection of Computer Programs (Codified Version) [2009] OJ L111/16 (previously, Directive 91/450) (mentioned as 'Directive 2009/24/EC').

[51] See Arnold J in *SAS Institute, Inc. v. World Programming Ltd* [2010] EWHC 1829 (Ch.), at para. 205 (indicating that Jacob J's decision in *Ibcos* may have been right under the then legal position but would not be so at present).

[52] Or, in the light of Infopaq, whether or not one takes a part that encapsulates the author's own intellectual creation; see, *Infopaq International A/S v. Danske Dagblades Forening*, Case C-5/08. After all, an innovative algorithm might reflect the author's own intellectual creation, while such algorithm, as much as Einstein's $E = mc^2$, should lie outside a copyright owner's scope of monopoly.

[53] *Designers Guild Ltd v. Russell Williams (Textiles) Ltd* [2001] 1 WLR 2416; [2001] FSR 11; [2001] ECDR 10 (HL).

of freely drawn leaves and flowers. However, as regards to the flowers and stripes, the court held that these were non-original ideas, whilst the rest of the similarities were dismissed as being mere techniques. The court also found that no visual similarity between the two works existed. Therefore, the Court of Appeal found that there was no substantial taking of *protectable* elements and thus no infringement. When the case came before the House of Lords, after paying the now usual lip service to the idea-expression dichotomy, their Lordships overturned the Court of Appeal decision. Delivering the leading opinion, Lord Hoffmann first stated that the operation of the dichotomy principle largely depends on what one means by 'ideas'. Lord Hoffmann then proceeded to find that since every expression in an artistic work is a result of the author's idea, these expressions are protectable to the extent that a substantial part of them is copied by the defendant. Although at first blush Lord Hoffmann's reasoning seems unobjectionable, it is suggested that it is unhelpful since no guidelines were given as to what type of nexus is required in order to render an idea a part of a protectable expression.

The decision in *Designers Guild* simply states that every expression results from an idea and that copyright infringement may take place where a substantial part of the skill, labour, and judgement of the author in making his choices is copied by the defendant. Lord Hoffmann maintained that the central question is where the skill, labour and judgement been expended. He appears to suggest that substantial amount of such skill and labour can be expended only on detailed (i.e. protectable) ideas rather than general (i.e. non-protectable) ideas. The decision makes no reference to the copyright eligibility of styles, techniques, systems, or methods, all of which may be the result of a significant amount of effort and skill.[54] However, Lord Hoffmann did acknowledge that where a literary work expresses a system or an invention, the author is not entitled to claim protection for the system or invention as such. Thus, his Lordship stated:

> a literary work which describes a system or invention does not entitle the author to claim protection for his system or invention as such. The same is true of an inventive concept expressed in an artistic work. However striking or original it may be, others are (in the absence of patent protection) free to express it in works of their own....[55]

Overall, the approach adopted by the House of Lords in *Designers Guild* is problematic. What the House of Lords did was to conflate its enquiries into copying and

---

[54] On this point, see the discussion below on Arnold J's deviation from Hoffmann's approach in the *SAS* referral.

[55] *Designers Guild Ltd v Russell Williams (Textiles) Ltd* [2001] 1 WLR 2416; [2001] FSR 11; [2001] ECDR 10 (HL), at 707.

4.3 Emergence and Development

substantial taking and second, treat the idea–expression dichotomy as a subset of the substantiality enquiry.

Thus, the court first addressed the question of copying by inference. Since in most cases there is no direct evidence to the defendant copying from the claimant's work, the court is prepared to infer that prima facie copying took place where the defendant had access to the claimant's work and where there is a sufficient degree of similarity between the two works. Once prima facie copying is established, the court has to establish whether the part copied forms a substantial part of the claimant's work. It was on this point that the court conflated the two separate enquiries. The House of Lords held that where the court answers the copying by inference question affirmatively, the answer to the subsequent question of substantial taking will be inevitable. That is so since where there is sufficient similarity between the works in order to infer copying, this level of similarity will be sufficient to satisfy the substantiality requirement. It is noteworthy that in deciding on the issue of substantiality, the House of Lords referred to and relied upon the House of Lords decision in *Ladbroke (Football)*,[56] which in turn cited with approval on this matter the decision of Peterson J in *University of London Press* that 'what is worth copying is prima facie worth protecting'.[57]

As argued by Spence and Endicott,[58] this approach to substantiality effectively makes any copying a breach and has been too influential in UK jurisprudence. Furthermore, conflating the idea-expression distinction with the assessments for substantial taking and originality ties the dichotomy to the said assessments and therefore to the initial inference of copying. Hence, according to the House of Lords in *Designers Guild*, a finding of inferred copying inevitably leads to a finding of substantial taking. Since Lord Hoffmann treated the idea-expression question as part of the substantiality enquiry,[59] it follows that a decision in relation to the inference of copying may ultimately decide the question of whether the part taken is a protectable expression or an unprotectable idea.

It is suggested that this approach is misguided and reduces the dichotomy to little more than a judicial lip service. The question of whether the alleged infringer copied a substantial part of the author's skill and labour is a question that should be assessed independently from the application of the idea-expression distinction. Irrespective of the amount of labour and effort that went into the part that was taken by an alleged infringer, it may be that owing to public policy considerations,

---

[56] *Ladbroke (Football) Ltd v. William Hill (Football) Ltd* [1964] 1 WLR 273.
[57] *University of London Press v. University Tutorial Press* [1916] 2 Ch. 601, 610.
[58] M J Spence and T A O Endicott, 'Vagueness in the scope of copyright' (2005) 121 *Law Quarterly Review*; Oxford Legal Studies Research Paper.
[59] By stating that the more abstract and simple an idea is, the less likely it is to constitute a substantial part, and vice versa.

such aspect of the work should lie outside the scope of copyright law altogether. It is suggested that here lays another problem concerning the treatment of the idea–expression dichotomy in UK courts. As discussed above, Lord Hoffmann suggested that once an idea is sufficiently specific in order to be fixed,[60] it may be protected by copyright law (provided that it forms a substantial part of the author's skill labour and judgement). Thus, it is only the very abstract that lays outside the scope of what constitutes protectable subject matter. As in the case of *L.B. (Plastics)*, this form of analysis is overly simplistic. It would have been preferable for the House of Lords to treat the dichotomy, as suggested by the US Treatise author Paul Goldstein, as a metaphor for aspects of protected works that are either within or outside the scope of copyright protection owing to public policy considerations.[61] As discussed above, previously UK courts in cases such as *Hollinrake v. Truswell* and *Harman v. Osborn* have held that it is not merely abstract ideas that are unprotectable but also elements such as schemes, systems, and methods of operation. These lie outside the scope of copyright protection, owing to public policy reasons, and not because they cannot be expressed on paper or are lacking in detail.

An equally restrictive interpretation of the idea–expression dichotomy, if not its practical abandonment, could also be seen in the more recent decision in *Temple Island Collections Ltd v. New English Teas*.[62] In this case the court found that a general layout and composition of a photograph of public buildings and a red bus passing by constituted a protectable subject matter. Judge Birss QC decided that the defendant infringed the claimant's copyright in the said layout by recreating a similar public scene, which was therefore substantially similar to the claimant's. Essentially, the defendant's photograph reproduced a substantial amount of the 'look and feel' of the claimant's photograph, but without using the claimant's photograph in terms of its manipulation. This decision appears to be excessively based on the similarity between the two photographs and the fact that the defendant set out from the beginning to create a similar image by, inter alia, capturing a similar scene. It is suggested that under adequate application of the idea–expression dichotomy, none of these factors should have made a difference. The entire scope of the intellectual effort of an author is not necessarily eligible for protection under copyright law, but only the aspects that go into the expression-related phase of creating a work. Thus, elements such as item and angle selection in relation to a public scene could be convincingly argued to reside on the idea side of the idea–expression divide. This being so, they should not be taken into account when comparing the two works. Similarly, the fact that the defendant intentionally set out to

---

[60] As discussed above, this argument was also made by the House of Lords in *L.B. (Plastics)*.
[61] P Goldstein, *Goldstein on Copyright* (3rd edn., Santa Monica, CA, Aspen Publishers 2006), S 2.3.1.
[62] *Temple Island Collections Ltd v. New English Teas* [2012] EWPCC 1.

4.3 Emergence and Development

create a similar image should be of little consequence. Ultimately, if the defendant managed to achieve such similarity by replicating non-protectable elements of the claimant's work, the court must find in his favour. Fortunately, this line of rationale was lately discarded in software copyright disputes. Furthermore, as discussed below, UK courts now recognize that the idea-expression dichotomy also applies to subject matter protected under the Information Society Directive, notwithstanding the fact that the dichotomy is not explicitly mentioned therein.

Turning back to software copyright disputes, in *Ibcos*, Jacob J maintained that the question of whether copyright subsists in functional elements of a computer program is an unhelpful analytical avenue, which is based on American copyright principles, which, in turn, are based on a different legislative framework. It is suggested that Jacob J's approach does not represent the present legal position in the United Kingdom in software cases. As mentioned, the facts in *Ibcos* took place prior to implementation of the 1991 version of the Software Directive. Article 1(2) and Recital 11 of the Software Directive read as follows:[63]

> Article 1(2) - Protection in accordance with this Directive shall apply to the expression in any form of a computer program. Ideas and principles which underlie any element of a computer program, including those which underlie its interfaces, are not protected by copyright under this Directive.

> Recital 11 - For the avoidance of doubt, it has to be made clear that only the expression of a computer program is protected and that ideas and principles which underlie any element of a program, including those which underlie its interfaces, are not protected by copyright under this Directive. In accordance with this principle of copyright, to the extent that logic, algorithms and programming languages comprise ideas and principles, those ideas and principles are not protected under this Directive. In accordance with the legislation and case-law of the Member States and the international copyright conventions, the expression of those ideas and principles is to be protected by copyright.

Thus, the Recital, elaborating on Article 1(2), suggests that, irrespective of whether or not they are put on paper and irrespective of whether such elements represent a substantial part of the author's skill and labour, or a part that represents the author's own intellectual creation, where such elements are classified as an 'idea', they are not protected under the Directive.

It is a known feature of copyright law that protection does not only extend to the text of a work, but also covers non-textual elements. Much has been said about the similarity between software's non-literal elements and a plot of a play or a book in

---

[63] Council Directive 2009/24/EC of April 23 2009 on the Legal Protection of Computer Programs (Codified Version) [2009] OJ L111/16 (previously, Directive 91/450) (mentioned as 'Directive 2009/24/EC').

the context of the idea-expression dichotomy. Thus, it is often argued that as much as copyright not only protects textual elements of traditional literary works but may also protect non-textual elements such as a book's plot, it may also protect the 'plot' of a computer program (i.e. its internal architecture).

However, this line of argument is unhelpful. There is little in common between a book and a computer program in that a program does not have anything like a plot, even metaphorically speaking. In this context, Pumfery J's statement in *Navitaire* should be borne in mind: 'To say these programs possess a plot is precisely like saying that the book of instructions for a booking clerk acting manually has a plot: but a book of instructions has no theme, no events, and does not have a narrative flow. Nor does a computer program....'[64] Applying Pumfery J's suggested analogy may thus be more constructive for our purpose:[65] while verbatim reproduction of the aforementioned instructions themselves may constitute copyright infringement, following such instructions in the sense of implementing them in a new product in terms of sequence and scope should not.

4.3.3 The application of the idea–expression dichotomy in recent UK software-related disputes

The *Navitaire* decision involved an assessment of the role of idea-expression dichotomy in software copyright cases in the United Kingdom. The case concerned an action for copyright infringement in computer software. The case is both factually and technically complex, and a detailed discussion of the factual matrix of the case would be of little benefit to the current discussion. It suffices to say that in *Navitaire*, a part of the claimant's action was based on 'non-textual' copying or, in other words, the copying of functional ideas and logic. It was not contested that the defendant in this case had no access to the claimant's code and the main issue before the court was whether the claimant enjoyed copyright protection over 'look and feel' aspects of his program. Citing earlier authorities, Pumfrey J acknowledged that copyright is designed to prevent a defendant from taking a substantial part of the claimant skill and labour. That, however, may not be enough, and the court should not stop its inquiry at this stage. Pumfrey J proceeded to point out that the nature of the part taken must also be an equally relevant factor.[66] Hence, the copied element in question must be eligible for copyright protection in the first place. For example, where in the *Exxon* case there was plenty of skill and labour invested in the creation of the word Exxon, copyright

---

[64] See *Navitaire Inc. v. Easyjet Airline Company and Bulletproof Technologies Inc.* [2004] EWHC 1725 (Ch), para 125.
[65] That is, between a book of instructions and a computer program.
[66] Thus, departing from Jacob J's line of reasoning in *Ibcos*.

4.3 Emergence and Development

protection was nevertheless denied since the relevant work, owing to its nature, was held to be ineligible for copyright protection.[67] Pumfrey J emphasized that although it is the 'skill, labour and judgment' that are protected under copyright law, it must to be the 'right' type of 'skill, labour and judgment' in order to attract protection.[68] On that basis Pumfrey J proceeded to conclude that merely because two completely different computer programs produce an identical result in terms of their functionality, it does not automatically follow that the defendant is liable for copyright infringement. This is so notwithstanding the fact that the defendant deliberately set out to create a program that replicated the functionality of the claimant's program. In the later case of *Nova Productions Limited v. Mazooma Games Ltd*, Jacob LJ echoed Pumfrey J's aforementioned view in Navitaire, stating: 'Not all of the skill which goes into a copyright work is protected [...]'[69]

4.3.4 The application of the idea–expression dichotomy in EU software-related disputes

The first decision by the CJEU on the copyright eligibility of different elements of computer programs appeared to be encouraging in the context of the idea–expression dichotomy. Although the *BSA* decision was mainly concerned with the question of whether or not a user interface screen-display was a form of expression of a computer program and should therefore be protected as a part of a computer program, part of the court's reasoning is of relevance to the current discussion.[70] In *BSA* the CJEU articulated for the first time a concept not unlike the American merger doctrine. Referring to the originality of components of the graphic user interface, the court stated: 'where the expression of those components is dictated by their technical function, the criterion of originality is not met, *since the different methods of implementing an idea are so limited that the idea and the expression become indissociable* [emphasis added]'.[71] Thus, the court appears to suggest that where functionality-related constrains may lead to a limited number of choices available to a software engineer, even elements that reside on the expression side of the idea-expression divide will be rendered unprotectable. Although the court's rationale for this conclusion was that such expressive elements are not original

---

[67] *Exxon Corp. v. Exxon Insurance Consultants International Ltd* [1981] 3 All E.R. 241.
[68] *Navitaire, Inc. v. Easyjet Airline Company and Bulletproof Technologies, Inc.* [2004] EWHC 1725 (Ch.), para. 127.
[69] See *Nova Productions Limited v. Mazooma Games Limited & Others* [2007] EWCA Civ 219, para. 35.
[70] *Bezpečnostní softwarová asociace – Svaz softwarové ochrany v. Ministry of Culture of the Czech Republic*, C-393/09.
[71] Ibid, para. 49.

because they do not spawn from the author's intellectual creation,[72] which is somewhat different from the American rationale to the merger doctrine,[73] it nevertheless leaves room for reasoning that where an element of a software product is created or expressed with a functional objective in mind (as is often the case) and where an adoption of such expression is one of a limited number of ways for achieving such functionality with any reasonable degree of success, such expression does not constitute copyrightable subject matter.

Unlike the *BSA* decision, the decision in *SAS v. WPL* concerned the application of the idea-expression dichotomy in relation to non-literal elements of computer programs.[74] In this case WPL sought to and succeeded in creating rivalling software that emulated the functionality of the SAS program. In order to create the said rivalling program, WPL obtained and studies a version of the SAS software known as 'learning edition', which was subject to a licence. It is also noteworthy that it was not in dispute that WPL did not have access to SAS source code. SAS claimed copyright infringement on three levels: (i) in SAS software, by creating the WPL software ('program-to-program' claim); (ii) in SAS user manuals, by creating WPL software ('manual-to-program' claim); (iii) in SAS user manuals, by creating WPL user manuals ('manual-to-manual' claim). Arnold J referred a number of questions to the CJEU. The CJEU acknowledged that functionality, programming language and data file formats were not protectable expressions of computer programs. However, somewhat confusingly, the court then suggested that while programing languages and data file formats were not protected under the Software Directive, they may nevertheless be eligible for copyright protection under the Information Society Directive if they constitute the author's own intellectual creation. Thus, while it is clear that reproducing the functionality of a program will not result in copyright infringement, reproducing programming language or data file formats might do, albeit under the Information Society directive.

The CJEU further maintained that ideas and principles, which underlie any element of a computer program, could not be protected through the operation of a licence agreement.[75] Regarding manuals, the CJEU commented that those could be protected provided that the part taken thereof contains elements that are the expression of

---

[72] This is an awkward reasoning. Of course it all hinges on what one means by *dictated*; an element may be 'dictated' by functional constrains in the sense of it being the only effective way for overcoming a functional problem. Designing such an element may clearly involve creativity.

[73] According to which protecting an expression under such circumstances would result in de facto protecting an idea, which, in turn, is contrary to the idea-expression dichotomy.

[74] *SAS Institute, Inc. v. World Programming Ltd* [2010] EWHC 1829 (Ch).

[75] In this case the restrictive licensing provision limited the use of the learning edition copy to 'non production purposes'. Arnold J found the WPL used the SAS copy for purposes that fell outside the scope of the licence.

4.3 Emergence and Development

the intellectual creation of the author. In the court's view, the keywords, syntax, commands, and combinations of commands, options, defaults, and iterations consist of words, figures, or mathematical concepts, when considered in isolation, are not, as such, an intellectual creation of the author. However, through the choice, sequence, and combination of those words, figures, or mathematical concepts, the author may express his creativity in an original manner and such creativity may be eligible for copyright protection under the Information Society Directive. It is for the national court to evaluate whether the reproduction of parts of user manuals constitutes the reproduction of the expression of the intellectual creation of the author of the user manual.

After the case was remitted back to the UK courts, Arnold J found in favour of the defendant on all accounts except for some limited literal copying in the 'manual-to-manual' claim. SAS appealed on all points except the lower court's finding in relation to the program-to-program claim. On appeal, the Court of Appeal upheld Arnold J judgement, in the course of which it made a number of interesting observations.[76]

One of the more interesting points was made in relation to the CJEU's conclusion that the manuals could be protected as literary works to the extent that they expressed the author's own intellectual creation. In this context, the Court of Appeal concluded that the Information Society Directive and the Software Directive have the same policy goals. Therefore, the CJEU's conclusions regarding the operation of the idea–expression dichotomy under the Software Directive hold equally in the context of the Information Society Directive, irrespective of the fact the latter does not refer explicitly to the dichotomy. Since WPL took and implemented elements from the manuals such as statistical operations and mathematical formulas, rather than the description of such elements, the parts taken did not represent the expression of the intellectual creation that went into the development of the said manuals. Thus, such taking did not constitute copyright infringement. It is suggested that on the basis of this interpretation of the CJEU decision, one might be able to argue that the same rationale applies to elements such as programming languages, data file formats and algorithms. Although SAS did not appeal against the High Court findings regarding the program-to-program claim, if they would have done so, the Court of Appeal might have found that programming languages and data file formats, irrespective of the creative effort that went into developing them, constitute an unprotectable idea under the Information Society Directive. This being so, their reproduction would not constitute copyright infringement.

---

[76] Although the court agreed with Arnold J's conclusion, on occasions, it departed from its reasoning.

What drives UK courts to prefer, at present, its narrow approach to the idea-expression distinction in cases that do not involve software and to refuse to engage in a broader balancing exercise? Why does Peterson J's dictum that *what is worth copying is worth protecting* still hovers in UK courtrooms in infringement cases?

In his examination of the application of the idea-expression dichotomy Masiyakurima argues that this approach is ultimately driven by a desire to minimize misappropriation of copyright works.[77] He maintains that this desire to minimize misappropriation cuts across most aspects of UK copyright law and has a debilitating effect on most copyright exceptions and limitations including the idea-expression dichotomy. Thus, it is the absence of a general law on misappropriation or unfair competition in the United Kingdom that drives the courts to stretch the boundaries of copyright law. He argues that introducing such a general law of unfair competition in the United Kingdom may enable the courts to use copyright doctrines, including the idea-expression dichotomy, in order to limit the scope of copyright monopolies effectively. In the meantime, and as long as the prevailing approach in UK courts follows the House of Lords in *Designers Guild*, the idea-expression dichotomy will fail to function in a manner that furthers the public policy considerations that underlie our copyright regime. As mentioned, in the case of software, the Software Directive acts as a bullbar against the continuing erosion of the dichotomy in UK courts and enables the courts to side step the simplistic analysis applied in *Designers Guild*.[78] Whether or not this will continue to be the case once the United Kingdom leaves the European Union is anyone's guess.

4.3.5 The development of the idea–expression dichotomy in the United States

Following *Baker v. Selden*,[79] one of the subsequent significant American decisions on the issue of non-literal copying and the operation of the idea-expression dichotomy was *Nichols v. Universal Pictures Corp*.[80] In fact Pamela Samuelson argues that more than any other judge, it was Judge Learned Hand who was responsible for focusing copyright infringement analysis on the idea-expression distinction.[81] The case concerned an allegation by the plaintiff that the defendant has infringed his copyright in a play by copying elements of the plot of that play and incorporating

---

[77] P Masiyakurima, 'The futility of the idea/expression dichotomy in UK copyright law' (2007) 38 IIC 548.
[78] It might be that such an approach could not have been applied by UK courts in a copyright case not involving computer programs.
[79] *Baker v. Selden* 101 U.S. 99 (1879).
[80] *Nichols v. Universal Pictures Corp.* 45 F.2d 119 (2nd Cir. 1930).
[81] Interestingly, Samuelson also argues that in her entire judicial career, Hand cited *Baker v. Selden* only once. This observation was brought by Samuelson in support to her argument that *Baker v. Selden* was not a case about the idea-expression dichotomy distinction but rather about a broader concept of protectable

4.3 Emergence and Development

them into his film. The court commenced by stating that copyright protection cannot be limited to the text, or else a plagiarist would be able to evade infringement by making insignificant variations. In one of the more famous passages in his decision, Judge Hand explained that:

> Upon any work, and especially upon a play, a great number of patterns of increasing generality will fit equally well, as more and more of the incident is left out. The last may perhaps be no more than the most general statement of what the play is about, and at times might consist only of its title; but there is a point in this series of abstractions where they are no longer protected, since otherwise the playwright could prevent the use of his 'ideas,' to which, apart from their expression, his property is never extended.[82]

In *Nichols* the court found that even where the defendant did borrow elements from the plaintiff's plot, it was permissible since these elements consisted of nothing more than non-protectable ideas rather than protectable expressions. However, a key question necessary to the application of Judge Hand's test was left unanswered: When exactly does one step out of the realm of expression and enter that of mere idea? According to Judge Hand, '[n]obody has ever been able to fix that boundary, and nobody ever can.'[83] Fixing the boundary must therefore 'inevitably be adhoc'.[84]

Although concerned with a play, Judge Hand's abstraction approach of starting with the literal text and successively progressing to the more abstract elements of the work found favour with copyright scholars and subsequently courts in relation to copyright protection of computer programs.[85]

As illuminating as they are in relation of American courts' approach to non-literal copying, 'plot-borrowing' cases do not share much in common with software copyright infringement scenarios. A more appropriate analogy can be drawn with what may be described as 'systems cases'.[86]

Thus, cases such as *Baker v. Selden*, which were concerned with the protection of a system, method, or process, are the closest non-digital relatives of software non-literal infringement cases. In both types of cases, the contested subject matter of a copyrighted work concerns a manner of carrying out a series of steps in order

---

and non-protectable distinction. See P Samuelson, 'Baker v. Selden: sharpening the distinction between authorship and invention' in R C Dreyfuss and J C Ginsburg, eds., *Intellectual Property Stories* (Mineola, NY, Foundation Press 2005) 210.

[82] Ibid, 121.   [83] Ibid.
[84] *Peter Pan Fabrics, Inc. v. Martin Weiner Corp*, 274 F.2d (2nd Cir. 1960), 276 (per Hand J).
[85] See below Nimmer's Abtraction-Filteration-Comparison test.
[86] For a detailed survey of these 'system cases', see P Samuelson, 'Why copyright law excludes systems and processes from the scope of its protection'(2007) 85(1) Texas L. R., 1921; UC Berkeley Public Law Research Paper No. 1002666. Available at SSRN: https://ssrn.com/abstract=1002666.

to achieve a requisite result. Thus, the question of whether or not one can protect via copyright functional design elements of computer programs, or whether or not one may claim copyright in a certain bookkeeping system, calls upon similar considerations.

A helpful and more modern example than *Baker v. Selden* to such 'system cases' is *Aldrich v. Remington Rand*.[87] Here the plaintiff developed a system called the 'Tax Record System'. The system was designed for the use of counties, cities and other taxing districts of Texas, and was described as 'the most modern and efficient system of property revaluation for tax purposes'.[88] For the purpose of efficient use of the tax system, the plaintiff devised a bookkeeping system, which comprised, partially, many forms illustrative of the system. Both the Tax Record System and the bookkeeping system were described in a book issued by the plaintiff. The plaintiff argued that the defendant, while installing the Tax Records system for a local municipality, copied his forms and therefore infringed the copyright subsisting in them. The trial judge's factual finding confirmed the plaintiff allegations as to the defendant's copying. Thus, the question before the court was whether the said forms were eligible to copyright protection. Applying *Baker v. Selden*, the court had no hesitation in finding that the said forms were not a proper subject matter of copyright law: 'Plaintiff is asserting rights here he could only assert successfully if he had a patent on his tax bookkeeping system. But he has no patent. That and that only could protect him as against a use by the public of the system he describes in his book and *illustrates by his forms*' (emphasis added).[89] The court also tackled the plaintiff's claim that his forms, which illustrated his tax bookkeeping system, became a component part of his book and were therefore covered by the very same copyright that protected the book. The following passage from the court's decision is particularly telling of the considerations behind the exclusion of methods, systems, and procedures from copyright protection, even if expressed 'on paper':

> The forms in question *embody the mechanics* [emphasis added] of the tax bookkeeping system taught by plaintiff . . . They embody in practice what plaintiff taught, all the public can use, after their use is explained or understood. The public can use the forms as plaintiff makes them, or modify them, change, improve them, or make them worse, without committing any piracy. Those forms belong to the public, the plaintiff himself merely being a constituent part of it. *How could the public appropriate the system identically, if it could not use the forms*? [emphasis added] That is all the defendants did, for which they are sued.[90]

---

[87] *Aldrich v. Remington Rand, Inc.* 52 F.Supp.732 (N.D. Tex. 1942).   [88] Ibid, 732.   [89] Ibid, 734.
[90] Ibid, 735 (interestingly, the court is prepared to take into account the needs of the defendant in deciding whether to copied part is protectable. As discussed below, this line of reasoning was explicitly rejected in *Oracle Am., Inc. v. Google, Inc.* 750 F.3d 1339, 1364 (Fed. Cir. 2014)).

4.3 Emergence and Development

Hence, following this rationale, it may be argued that where forms, algorithms, data file formats, or any other manifestation of a system embodied in a copyright work are required for the proper use of the said system, process, or method,[91] the public may copy them with impunity; they are in the public domain.

The approach that we have witnessed in the 'system cases', as well as the approach advocated by Judge Hand found its way to the 1976 Copyright Act. At first, the Copyright Revision Bill that was brought before the US Senate Sub-Committee did not pay any heed to the idea–expression dichotomy.[92] However, that was met with a strong resistance at the Senate Sub-Committee hearings stage, in particular by representatives of educational organizations, who argued that the broad language of the Bill could be interpreted as covering functional elements of computer programs.[93] As a result, the Sub-Committee came up with the language of what is presently known as 17 U.S.C. § 102(b) on copyrightable subject matter, which makes it clear that copyright protection does not extend to idea, procedure, process, system, or method of operation; thus resurrecting the wording of *Baker v. Selden*. In addition, the Sub-Committee added to the Committee Report its own explanatory comment on the objective of 17 U.S.C. § 102(b), which was to 'make clear that the expression adopted by the programmer is the copyrightable element in a computer program, and that the actual processes or methods embodied in the program are not within the scope of the copyright law'.[94]

4.3.6 The application of the idea–expression dichotomy in US software-related disputes

In the light of the aforementioned decisions and taking into consideration the legislative intent behind the 1976 Act, the issue of copyright protection for functional elements of a computer program might appear at first glance to be straightforward. For example, the Court of Appeal for the Federal Circuit has made it clear that functionality of a computer program per se is not eligible to copyright

---

[91] Obviously, such an assessment would hinge on how one defines *system, method, process*, etc.
[92] Maybe not surprisingly so, since the Bill was essentially put together by different interest groups with the blessing of the US Copyright Office; in the case of the distinction between idea and expression, there was no interest group with the relevant vested interest represented in the process of the drafting of the bill.
[93] See Copyright Law Revised Bill (1967): Hearings on S. 597 Before the Subcomm. on Patents, Trademarks and Copyrights of the Senate Comm. on the Judiciary, 196–200 (testimony of Arthur Miller, Ad Hoc Committee of Educ. Insts. and Orgs. on Copyright Law Revision); (testimony of Edison Montgomery, Interuniversity Communications Council); ibid. at 1058-9 (testimony of W. Brown Morton, Interuniversity Communications Council).
[94] Senate Sub-Committee Rep. 1974, S. Rep. No. 983, 93d Cong., 2d Sess. 107. See also Register of Copyright Revision Report 1975, 10.

protection under Section 102(b).[95] In *Hutchins* the Federal Circuit was faced with a question not unlike the one faced by Pumfrey J in *Navitaire*. Namely, does copyright law protect behavioural aspects of software, where the defendant's program performed the same task, in the same way, and in response to the same input as the plaintiff's program? Could the defendant replicate the plaintiff's 'system of logic' and incorporate it into his own program? The Federal Circuit had little difficulty in finding that under Section102(b), all of the above was not protected under copyright law and that a defendant that engaged in such activities was not liable for copyright infringement. In another decision, algorithms were treated similarly and were held to constitute a 'process' under Section 102(b).[96]

As we have seen, the legislative intent behind Section 102(b) points in the same direction as *Baker v. Selden*. After a series of decisions scaling from virtually full copyright protection for software architecture[97] to a more limited degree of protection on the basis of the application of Nimmer's complex 'successive filtration' test,[98] it was the Court of Appeal for the First Circuit in *Lotus v. Borland* that adopted the most liberal approach to the application of the dichotomy in software cases.[99] However, before we embark on an examination of the decision in *Lotus*, it is necessary to examine the so-called abstraction-filtration-comparison (AFC) test, as developed by Professor Melville Nimmer.[100] Nimmer's approach deserves special attention since it proved highly influential in software non-literal infringement cases. In a decision that is still considered as a leading authority on non-literal copying in the context of computer programs, the Court of Appeal for the Second Circuit explicitly endorsed it.[101] In the *Atlai* decision, the court stated, 'Professor Nimmer suggested, and we endorsed, a "successive filtering method" for separating protectable expressions from non-protectable materials.'[102] Based upon Hand's successive filtration test, Nimmer's test has three steps.

---

[95] *Hutchins v. Zoll Medical Corp.* 492 F.3d 1377 (Fed. Cir. 2007).
[96] '[. . .] processes can be found at any level, except perhaps the main purpose level of abstraction. Most commonly, processes will be found as part of the system architecture, as operations within modules, or as algorithms. *Gates Rubber Co. v. Bando Chemical Indus., Ltd.* 9 F.3d 823, 844-45 (10th Cir. 1993).
[97] See e.g. *Whelan Associates, Inc. v. Jaslow Dental Laboratory, Inc.* 797 F.2d 1222 (3d Circ.1986), where the court stated that: 'the purpose or function of a utilitarian work would be the work's idea, and everything that is not necessary to that purpose or function would be part of the expression of the idea'. Just as the idea behind Selden's work was 'a peculiar system of bookkeeping, the idea in Whelan's computer program is 'to run a dental laboratory in an efficient way'. Thus the court adopted a simplistic approach whereby everything beside the general idea of the program, i.e. 'to run a dental laboratory in an efficient way', constitutes protectable expression.
[98] See *Computer Associates International, Inc. v. Altai, Inc.* (1992) 982 F.2d 693, 704 (2nd Circ.).
[99] *Lotus Development Corporation v. Borland* (1995) 49 F3d 807 (1st Circ.).
[100] See M B Nimmer, *Nimmer on Copyright* (New York, Matthew Bender Publishing 1978), § 13.03 [F].
[101] It was recently hailed as the predominant test for adjudicating non-literal copying cases in the United States. See *Oracle Am., Inc. v. Google, Inc.* (2014) 750 F.3d 1339 (Fed. Cir.)
[102] *Computer Associates International, Inc. v. Altai, Inc.* (1992)982 F.2d 693, 704 (2nd Circ.).

First, the court is required to construct a hierarchy of abstractions for the allegedly infringed program, scaling from the most abstract to the most detailed. Second, the court sifts out all non-protectable material, such as features that are (i) constrained by external factors such as the relevant hardware or software environment in which the program was to operate; (ii) dictated by efficiency considerations; and (iii) constrained by standard programming techniques or public domain elements. Third, the court compares the 'core of protectable expression' of the original program with the allegedly infringing program and looks for substantial similarities.

It is suggested that Nimmer's AFC test is problematic on a number of grounds. It is likely that it results from Nimmer's misinterpretation of *Baker v. Selden* as an essentially merger doctrine–based decision.[103] Moreover, it is arguable whether the successive filtration test, as developed by Judge Hand, is suitable for application to computer programs. As mentioned above, program's internal architecture and a play's plot are two very different things. There is nothing expressive in data file formats or programming algorithms, while a play's plot may be as expressive as the actual play's dialog. As Pumfrey J explained in Navitaire, unlike a novel a computer program has no theme, no events, and does not have a narrative flow; an analogy between the two is therefore misguided.[104] Software's architecture is a purely functional mechanism, which has more in common with an industrial manufacturing process than with the plot of Shakespeare's Othello.

Nimmer argued that the reason for the decision in *Baker v. Selden* is that the Selden's 'blank' forms were not copyrightable since they represented the system in such a way as to merge with it. In other words, there was no other way to describe the system. However, as discussed above, it appears that the court's main concern was not whether there was another way to 'express' the system. The court simply decided that the 'blank' forms were themselves part of a system, owing to their functional role in enabling the system. They did not 'express' the system in any meaningful way. Therefore, the 'blank' forms were found to be non-protectable on the basis of them being a system, or a method, and thus being the subject matter of patent law rather than that of copyright law. This reading of *Baker v. Selden* was explicitly endorsed in *Taylor v. Fawley-Brost*, where the Court of Appeal for the Seventh Circuit found that the plaintiff's charts, which were designed as components of his temperature recording systems, were not protected under copyright

---

[103] For a comprehensive review of Nimmer's erroneous interpretation of *Baker v. Selden*, his reliance on a strained reading of *Mazer v. Stein*, and the reasons for the highly influential status of Nimmer's test during the 1980s and 1990s, see Samuelson (2007), cited in fn. 32.

[104] See *Navitaire, Inc. v. Easyjet Airline Company and Bulletproof Technologies, Inc.* [2004] EWHC 1725 (Ch.), para. 125.

law since they were a mechanical elements of the temperature recording systems of which they were an integral part. Thus, the charts were excluded from copyright protection on the grounds of them being a system or part thereof. It is with this analytical approach in mind that we may examine to the First Circuit seminal decision in *Lotus v. Borland*.[105]

Lotus involved a series of claims and counter-claims in the District Court of Massachusetts. In the first instance, a judgment was given in favour of Lotus determining, inter alia, that Borland has copied Lotus's menu command hierarchy and that the menu constituted a copyrightable expression. On appeal, the court had to determine whether Lotus menu command hierarchy was a copyrightable subject matter. Borland admitted that it had copied Lotus's menu command hierarchy. However, Borland contended that the menu did not constitute a copyrightable subject matter since it fell within the list of excluded subject matter of Section 102(b), which includes, inter alia, a system, process, method of operation, or procedure. The court dealt with the primary question in the following order: first, the court rejected the applicability of Nimmer's AFC test to the Lotus scenario since the case involved literal copying. Next, the court turned to determine whether the menu command hierarchy was within the list of the excluded subject matter of Section 102(b).[106]

The court found the menu to be 'a method of operation' and hence not copyrightable; that is, it was held that Lotus's menu command hierarchy was an unprotectable method of instructing a computer to perform spreadsheet functions. In doing so the court stated, 'We think that "method of operation", as that term is used in Section 102(b), refers to the means by which a person operates something, whether it be a car, a food processor, or a computer.'[107] Since the court's finding resolved the case, it did not find it necessary to opine on whether the menu command hierarchy also constituted a system or a process. The court, however, did stress that the fact that the menu was expressive and that the menu was not dictated by functionality and could have been designed differently was immaterial. Thus, once it had established that the copied feature was a method of operation, the court enquired no further into the expressiveness of the menu, neither did it engage in the application of the merger doctrine.

It is submitted that this type of approach suits cases which involve both literal and non-literal copying as it captures the real essence of the idea-expression distinction in a manner that accommodates public policy considerations that are at the heart of the dichotomy. For example, data file formats are no less 'a procedure'

---

[105] *Lotus Development Corporation v. Borland* (1995) 49 F.3d 807 (1st Circ.).
[106] Which, as we have seen, stems out and originates from the Supreme Court's decision in *Baker v. Selden*.
[107] *Lotus Development Corporation v. Borland* (1995) 49 F.3d 807 (1st Circ.) 815.

4.3 Emergence and Development

than a menu command hierarchy is 'a method of operation'. The same can be said about routines, operations, and numerous other non-literal elements of a computer program. Indeed, the court in *Lotus* stated obiter, 'We think that the *Altai* test should contemplate this being the initial inquiry.'[108] Hence, where the 'initial inquiry' results in an element being excluded from copyright protection under Section 102 (b), the 'successive filtration' test becomes redundant. Moreover, the court suggested that its proposition is supported by the Supreme Court decision in *Baker v. Selden*. This author finds the approach convincing.[109]

The *Lotus* analysis was explicitly rejected recently in the *Oracle v. Google* dispute.[110] The case involved, inter alia, Java's application programming interfaces (APIs), thirty-seven of which Oracle accused Google of replicating, including the declaring code and structure, sequence, and organization (SSO) of these thirty-seven API packages. The district court found in this context in favour of Google on copyright-eligibility grounds; namely, the court concluded that the above elements were not subject to copyright protection, endorsing the *Lotus* analysis. It held that the declaring code was not protectable since, inter alia, there was only one way to write it and, therefore, the merger doctrine barred Oracle from claiming copyright in this expression. As regards the SSO, the court found that although it was creative and original, it was nevertheless a command structure and therefore a system or method of operation under Section 102(b). On appeal, the Court of Appeal for the Federal Circuit reversed and found in favour of Oracle. The appellant court found that both elements of Oracle claim, the literal copying claim in relation to the 7000 lines of declaring source code and the non-literal copying claim in relation to the SSO of the thirty-seven API packages were eligible to copyright protection.

Regarding the declaring code, the appellant court explained that the district court erred in focusing its investigation on the options that were available to Google at the time when the decision to replicate the code was taken. The appellant court did not

---

[108] Ibid, 817.

[109] A similar view was expressed in the Borland Brief (1995) by thirty-four copyright professors who argued that Lotus's menu command hierarchy was unprotectable under Section 102(b) since it was a fundamental part of the functionality of the Lotus program. In Samuelson's view:

> developing a more robust toolkit for limiting the scope of copyright protection that includes S.102(b) is important for many reasons, including preserving the public domain, promoting the ongoing creation and dissemination of knowledge, stimulating competition and innovation in the market place and maintain the proper balance between the rights of the authors and the rights of the public in intellectual property law.

(see P Samuelson, 'Frontiers of intellectual property: why copyright law excludes systems and processes from scope of its protection' (2007) 85 Tex. L. Rev. 1921, 1940. It is noteworthy that a Certiorari was granted by the Supreme Court but the First Circuit decision was affirmed by an equally divided vote.

[110] *Oracle Am., Inc. v. Google, Inc.* (2014) 750 F.3d 1339, 1364 (Fed. Cir.).

disagree that once Sun/Oracle created a package and then named it with a particular header, programmers who wished to use that particular package had to call it by its header's name. This, however, was of little consequence to the copyright-eligibility investigation. The appellant court explained that rather than focusing on the options available to Google at the time of copying, the district court should have focused on the options available to Sun/Oracle at the time it created the API packages. At that point of time, the options open to Sun/Oracle were numerous. Therefore, the chosen expression did not merge with the idea. It appears that the appellant court did not give sufficient weight to the need of the programmers that Google was catering for in developing its Android APIs, as it is their professional needs that may render the declaring code unprotectable under Section 102(b). Thus, the court opined that Google replicated 'Oracle's declaring code and SSO to capitalize on the pre-existing community of programmers who were accustomed to using the Java API packages.'[111] But is it not its very own observation that renders the appellant court's findings questionable? As the Computer & Communication Industry Association explained in its Amicus Curiea, 'What could be better proof that something is a procedure, system, or method of operation than if a person can become 'trained,' 'experienced,' or 'accustomed' to using it in the course of developing new works?'[112]

On the issue of copyright eligibility of the SSO, the appellant court rejected the district court's conclusion that it was not eligible to copyright protection since it was a system or method of operation. Citing with approval from *Mitel*,[113] the appellant court stated: 'Section 102(b) does not extinguish the protection accorded a particular expression of an idea merely because that expression is embodied in a method of operation.'[114] This should be contrasted with the view of the *Lotus* court that the 'fact that Lotus developers could have designed the Lotus menu command hierarchy differently was immaterial to the question of whether it is a 'method of operation' and that '[i]f specific words are essential to operating something, then they are part of a 'method of operation' and, as such, are unprotectable.'[115] Thus, explicitly rejecting *Lotus* and following *Mitel*, the appellant court was of the view that once it was established that an element of a program is expressive and original, the fact that it was necessary in order to carry out a method or a process does not render it ineligible to copyright protection. The appellant court stressed that the correct manner to evaluate infringement under these circumstances was by

---

[111] *Oracle America, Inc. v. Google Inc.* (2012) in the US District Court for the Northern District of California at 53.
[112] Amicus Curiae of the Computer & Communications Industry Association, *Oracle Am., Inc. v. Google, Inc.* (No. 14-410) (7 November 2014).
[113] *Mitel, Inc. v. Iqtel, Inc.* (1997) 124 F.3d 1366, 1372 (10th Cir.).
[114] *Oracle Am., Inc. v. Google, Inc.* (2014) 750 F.3d 1339, 1364 (Fed. Cir.), 22.
[115] *Lotus Development Corporation v. Borland* (1995) 49 F.3d 807, 816 (1st Circ.).

4.3 Emergence and Development

reference to the AFC test. Applying this test, the court concluded that the SSO of the 37 API packages was eligible for copyright protection.

The court's approach raises a number of questions. It essentially treats the 'procedure, process, system or method of operation' part of Section 102(b) as a subset of 'idea'. The court explained that if a part of the program, such as a command structure, is original, it should not be regarded as an 'idea'. This suggests that the divide is between ideas and expression and that the reference to 'procedure, process, system or method of operation' is nothing more than listing classes of 'ideas'. It is suggested that neither the text of Section 102(b) nor its legislative history supports this conclusion. This provision could equally be read, as the *Lotus* court understood it. Thus, the reference to 'procedure, process, system or method of operation' identifies a list of independent non-copyrightable subject matter—whether or not the members of this list constitute an idea. It is suggested that the court's analysis illustrates that a strict textual reference to the idea-expression dichotomy is not helpful. As mentioned above, the reference to the idea-expression dichotomy is best understood if seen as a metaphor to a public policy-derived distinction between protectable and non-protectable subject matter. It is suggested that looked at in this way, the part of Section 102(b) referring to 'procedure, process, system or method of operation' should be assessed differently. Namely, as a list of subject matter residing on the non-protectable side of the divide between protectable and non-protectable, rather than as types of 'idea' (as opposed to expression). Hence, the fact that a feature of a program is creative, original, or expressed in a textual format does not necessarily render it a protectable expression.

Finally, it is suggested that the court erred in finding that compatibility arguments are relevant only to a fair-use analysis but not to copyright ability. The district court based its conclusion on this point on the trilogy of decompilation cases that was discussed in the previous chapter.[116] The appellant court in *Oracle v. Google* criticized the lower instance's decision since it found Oracle's APIs to be analogous to the interface protocols and procedures that were at issue in *Atari, Sega*, and *Sony*. According to the appellant court, these cases were primarily about fair use and not about copyright eligibility. Hence, if there was a compatibility justification to use the replicated APIs, or parts thereof, such consideration may be relevant for a fair-use analysis but cannot render those parts per se non-protectable. However, although it is correct that the trilogy decisions focused on fair use, the copyright eligibility of the interface procedures of the decompiled programs played a key part in those decisions. It was mainly because the said interface protocols and

---

[116] *Atari Games Corp. v. Nintendo of America, Inc.* 975 F.2d 832; *Sega Enterprises Ltd v. Accolade, Inc.* (1992) 977 F.2d 1510; *Sony Computer Entertainment, Inc. v. Connectix Corp.* (2000) 203 F.3d 596 (9th Cir.).

procedures were not eligible to copyright protection that the copying which took place as part of the decompiling process was excused from infringement under the fair-use doctrine. Thus, once the court was convinced that decompilation, and the copying it entailed, were necessary in order to gain access to non-protectable interface protocols and procedures, it was prepared to find that such copying constitutes fair use. Those decisions make it abundantly clear that but for the non-protectability of the program's interface, reproducing the code as part of a decompilation process would not have been excused.

The practical implications of this part of the court's decision are also problematic. Rather than following the up-to-then settled view that interface elements are non-protectable under copyright law, the court chose to treat them as prima facie protectable but ultimately subject to a fair-use analysis. Essentially, this implies that before developing an interoperable program, a programmer should engage in a complex fair-use analysis, which is an exercise that even an experienced jurist may find daunting.[117] In general, treating APIs as eligible to copyright protection is likely to have a negative impact on interoperability. This, in turn, could have a chilling effect on innovation. IT companies usually take a relaxed approach towards their API with a view to drive growth of their platforms. But of course, this could change under certain circumstances if copyright protectability of API becomes an option. The cloud environment is a good example to an ecosystem where such development could have significant implications. For example, Amazon APIs are widely used by start-up companies, as well as by veteran cloud services. Up to date, Amazon took an overall hands-off approach in relation to its APIs. This, however, could change. Should Amazon decide to repel competition from open technologies, such as the OpenStack platform, it may opt to go after OpenStack users.[118] As OpenStack emulates Amazon's API's, treating such APIs as copyrightable would enable Amazon to enforce it and, in doing so, stifle innovation.[119]

Regrettably, the Supreme Court refused to hear Google's appeal in this case, and the opportunity to bring much needed clarity to this area of the law had been missed.[120] The case has been remitted back to the district court by the Court of Appeal. Successfully claiming fair use in relation to the thirty-seven API packages was thought to be tricky in light of Google's commercial use, the portion taken by Google from these API packages and the alleged impact on Oracle's potential

---

[117] The fair use doctrine has been referred to as 'the most troublesome in the whole law of copyright.'; see *Monge v. Maya Magazines, Inc.* (2012) 688 F.3d 1164, 1170 (9th Cir.).

[118] For example, Hewlett-Packard.

[119] For a detailed discussion on the effect that having copyright-protectable APIs might have on the cloud environment, and, in particular, in relation to Amazon, see Amici Curiae Computer Scientists *Oracle Am., Inc. v. Google, Inc.* (No. 14-410) (7 November 2014), 16.

[120] 29 June 2015. http://www.supremecourt.gov/search.aspx?filename=/docketfiles/14-410.htm.

Java-based smartphone platform.[121] Google's best chances under the fair-use defence resided in its arguments in relation to interoperability under fair use second and third indents; as the appellant court stated:

> while we have concluded that it was error for the trial court to focus unduly on the functional aspects of the packages, and on Google's competitive desire to achieve commercial 'interoperability' when deciding whether Oracle's API packages are entitled to copyright protection, we expressly noted that these factors may be relevant to a fair use analysis.[122]

Referring to the said factors, the appellant court observed, 'reasonable jurors might find that they are relevant to Google's fair use defense under the second and third factors of the inquiry'.[123] On 26 May 2016, a jury did exactly that. Thus, after the case was remanded to the District Court for Northern California, a jury returned a unanimous verdict according to which Google has shown that its use in Android of the declaring lines of code and their structure sequence and organization of the Java program constituted fair use under the Copyright Act.[124] Oracle filed its appeal on 16 October 2016.

---

[121] Sun/Oracle has never successfully developed its own smartphone platform using Java; see *Oracle Am., Inc. v. Google, Inc.* (2014) 750 F.3d 1339, 1364 (Fed. Cir.) 9.
[122] Ibid, 1.   [123] Ibid.
[124] US District Court of the Northern Circuit of California, Case 3:10-cv-03561-WHA Document 1982, Filed 26 May 16, https://www.dropbox.com/s/7qpfd67lglltoi1/Jury%20Verdict%20Form.pdf?dl=0.

5

THE COMBINED EFFECT OF COPYRIGHT AND RESTRICTIVE LICENSING PROVISIONS

5.1 Exercising a Right in a Manner that Runs Contrary to its Objectives and Social Function	138
5.2 The US Copyright-Misuse Doctrine	140
5.3 The 'Function' of Intellectual Property Rights as a Means to Regulate the Manner of their Exercise	149
5.3.1 The essential function of a patent	150
5.3.2 The essential function of a copyright	151
5.3.3 The functions of a trade-mark as a curb on the manner of its exercise: the CJEU setting internal limitation on the circumstances in which a trade mark could be enforced	152
5.3.4 Applying the 'protectable functions' rationale to software-related scenarios	156
5.4 A Brief Note on the Prohibition of Abuse of Law in the European Union	158

We have seen that licensing terms may sometime be used in order to restrict the ability of a third party to use software's non-literal elements. Where such licences amount to valid contracts, use that does not comply with the said licence terms may constitute breach of contract.[1] However, notwithstanding any breach of contract claim that a third party may face, using a software product outside the scope of a licence may also result in copyright infringement. In essence, a licence in this context is conditional permission to use a work, where the licensor retains the legal title. Any use outside the scope of the said permission may result in the termination of authorization to use the work. In the context of software, every instance where the said software is used necessitates the creation of intermediary copies on the user's machine.

---

[1] See Chapter 3.

Beyond the Code: Protection of Non-Textual Features of Software. First Edition. Noam Shemtov.
© Noam Shemtov 2017. Published 2017 by Oxford University Press.

Where the creation of such copies is done without the authorization of the licensor, the user/licensor may become liable for copyright infringement. Hence, conduct that may be initially permissible under copyright law might nevertheless lead to copyright infringement where it is in violation of the terms of a licence.

It follows that the combined operation of copyright law and restrictive licensing terms may effectively enable right holders to extend the monopoly originally grated under copyright law. Before we turn to examine juridical mechanisms that may enable courts in the United States and European Union to mitigate this combined effect, it is first necessary to highlight the circumstances under which the scope of copyright law could be extended in this manner.

As discussed in Chapter 3, US copyright legislation does not contain non-waivable provisions. In principle, the ability to act within exceptions and limitations to US copyright law could potentially be waived by licensees. The position in the European Union is somewhat more complex. We have seen that while the relevant provisions under the Software Directive are non-waivable,[2] no similar arrangement exists in relation to the Information Society Directive. Since the protection of various elements of computer programs, such as GUIs, are not governed by the Software Directive but rather by the Information Society Directive,[3] extending the protection given to such elements under copyright law by using restrictive licensing terms may be possible. Thus, while the CJEU decided that licensing terms which seek to restrict the ability of a licensor to utilize aspects that were found to be non-protectable under the Software Directive are not enforceable, owing to the non-waivable nature of the privileges given under Articles 5(3) and 6,[4] no such conclusion has been reached in relation to elements of software covered by the Information Society Directive,[5] as exceptions and limitations granted under the latter might be contractually waivable.[6]

---

[2] Directive 2009/24/EC of the European Parliament and of the Council of 23 April 2009 on the legal protection of computer programs, i.e. Arts 5(3) and 6.

[3] *Bezpecnostní softwarová asociace – Svaz softwarové ochrany v. Ministerstvo kultury* C-393/09.

[4] *SAS Institute Inc. v. World Programming Ltd* [2010] EWCH 1892 (Ch.), C-406/10.

[5] It is noteworthy that the Information Society directive does not refer explicitly to the idea expression divide. But there is little doubt that it is an operative concept under the directive in relation to aspect of software products governed therein (e.g. see the decision of the Court of Appeal in *SAS Institute Inc. v. World Programming Ltd.* [2013] EWCA Civ 1482, para. 76).

[6] We have seen in Chapter 3 that the Information Society Directive is silent on the relationship between copyright exceptions and limitation and restrictive licensing provisions and effectively leaves it for Member State to decide.

5.1 EXERCISING A RIGHT IN A MANNER THAT RUNS CONTRARY TO ITS OBJECTIVES AND SOCIAL FUNCTION

We have seen that together with adequately drafted restrictive licensing provisions, copyright law may effectively be used to prevent licensees from making use of software features, which are initially non-protectable under copyright law. Thus, in combination with restrictive licensing provisions, copyright law may be used for purposes that stand in contradiction to some of the main public policy considerations that underlie copyright law itself. This is possible simply owing to the technical manner in which software interacts with hardware, rather than stemming from legal planning.

Any judicial tool that may enable courts to mitigate the use of copyright law in this manner should be copyright centred; the maintenance and fine-tuning of the delicate balance existing under copyright law should ideally be at its heart. While such a tool is in existence in most circuits in the United States, it is suggested that the doctrinal infrastructure for having such a mechanism in the European Union might also be present.

The concept that using a right within the limits prescribed for it by the law may nevertheless amount to abuse or misuse was not widely accepted until the twentieth century. Nineteenth-century legal scholars such as Planiol claimed that such argument contains an irreconcilable oxymoron: how can exercise of a right within the limits prescribed by law amount to abuse?[7] It is only where exercising a right outside the boundaries permitted by the law that abuse may take place. Scholars did not contest the notion that subjective rights had limits, but they argued that it was the legislature that placed those limits by defining the scope of the said rights. Where the boundaries of such rights were defined by the legislature, any exercise of these rights within these defined limits was legitimate and could not be considered as abusive.

However, from the beginning of the twentieth century onwards, the concept of abuse of rights started to gain wide acceptance. This change resulted from the movement of socialization of the law that also prompted the adoption of competition rules and endorsed judicial intervention in contractual relationship in order to protect 'weaker' parties.[8] Unlike the more simplistic nineteenth-century approach, jurists nowadays recognize that there are external and internal limits to a right. External limits may be set by the legislature and they define the powers granted under the right in question; these are set according to the purpose and

---

[7] See L M C R Guibault, *Copyright Limitations and Contracts* (Kluwer Law, 2002), 185.   [8] Ibid.

nature of the right in question. Internal limits may put restrictions, under certain circumstances, on the manner of exercise of that right. But what are these circumstances? When does exercising one's right stop being legitimate, crossing the line into the realm of abuse? Although there is no unanimity on the relevant criteria for assessing abuse,[9] this author is of the view that the most convincing criterion originates from the writing of Josserand. Josserand's argument is based on the notion that every right performs a social function.[10] It follows that the exercise of a given right must be done in accordance to its said social function. By granting an individual a subjective right, society seeks to further the social interest that stands at the basis of that right. Thus, exercising a right in a manner that is not compatible with its objective is objectionable from a public interest perspective and may therefore be curbed by the courts. It is submitted that this rationale stands at the basis of copyright-misuse doctrine in the United States, the essential function of the right doctrine as developed under EU jurisprudence, and the abuse of right concept as recognized by some EU Member States.

While the US doctrine of copyright misuse is consistently gaining acceptance amongst various circuit courts, the position in the European Union is somewhat more complex as there is no clear harmonized position on the issue of misuse or abuse. First, several Member States recognize the principle of abuse of right. As discussed below, this principle rests on the theory that the grant of a right to one person implies the imposition of certain limitations on other persons. However, it is also recognized that, although such limitations may have some tolerable negative implications, at a certain point, the exercise of the said right may lead to excessively high social costs and, therefore, may be regarded as abusive. Such abuse is to be assessed with reference to public policy considerations that underpin the right in question.

Second, EU courts have developed their own juridical tool for dealing with what they deem to be an excessive exercise of an intellectual property right. As early as the 1970s, EU courts have placed limits on the exercise of intellectual property rights by referring to the functions and, in particular, the essential function of the right in question. Thus, where a defendant's actions do not interfere with the functions of the claimant's intellectual property right and, as a result, do not adversely affect the claimant's interests as a proprietor, a court may refuse to enforce the intellectual property right in question. It is suggested that this legal

---

[9] For example, according to some writers, an abuse of right should be based on the concept of fault in civil liability in terms of behaving in a manner that may not be expected from a reasonable man in his position; another possible criterion may be intent: whether, by exercising the right, there was an intention to harm. In my view, both criteria are too narrow and, therefore, unsatisfactory.

[10] See H C Gutteridge, 'Abuse of rights' (1933) 5 The Cambridge L. J. 242, 24.

principle shares a similar rationale with an abuse—a based doctrine that rests on Josserand's theory that could be developed further in a similar fashion to the misuse doctrine in the United States, in order to address the combined negative effect of prohibitive licensing provisions together with copyright's exclusive rights.

5.2 THE US COPYRIGHT-MISUSE DOCTRINE

In US jurisprudence, misuse is a common law defence that has its roots in the equitable doctrine of unclean hands.[11] Interestingly, the defendant itself does not have to be affected by the un-equitable conduct,[12] although according to certain circuit courts the defendant itself must not come to the court with unclean hands when seeking shelter under the misuse defence.[13] Once the misuse is 'purged', the plaintiff may return to the court and seek the enforcement of his right.[14]

The copyright-misuse doctrine is only a couple of decades old and is therefore not yet fully established across the jurisdictions of all US circuit courts. This is because, to date, there is still no United States Supreme Court decision that firmly establishes the copyright-misuse defence in a manner similar to the establishment of the patent misuse defence in *Morton Salt*.[15] The Court of Appeal for the Fourth Circuit in *Lasercomb*[16] was first to recognize formally copyright misuse as an affirmative defence. It did so by reference to the rationale outlined by the Supreme Court in *Morton Salt*. Therefore, before embarking upon an examination of the copyright-misuse doctrine, it is necessary to familiarize oneself with its parent: the patent misuse doctrine and the Supreme Court decision in *Morton Salt*.

In *Morton Salt* the Supreme Court established the patent misuse defence. Before 1942, the legal position regarding patent misuse resembled the current state of copyright misuse with respect to both its uncertain boundaries and future potential application.[17] In this case, the plaintiff, Morton Salt, was the proprietor of a patent in a salt-depositing machine. Morton's patent licence required

---

[11] For a comprehensive discussion on the Copyright Misuse Doctrine in the context of software, see B Frischmann and D Moylan, 'The evolving common law doctrine of copyright misuse: A unified theory and its application to software' (2000) 15 Berkley Tech. L. J. 865.

[12] *Lasercomb Am., Inc. v. Reynolds* 911 F.2d 970 (4th Cir. 1990), 979.

[13] For example, see the Ninth Circuit in *Atari Games Corp. v. Nintendo of America Inc.* 975 F.2d 832 (Fed. Cir. 1992) at 846; compare and contrast with the Fifth Circuit in *Alcatel USA v DGI Techs.* 166 F. 3d 772 (5th Cir. 1999), 794–5 (stating that it is the inequitable conduct of the plaintiff that matters regardless of that of the defendant).

[14] *Lasercomb Am., Inc. v. Reynolds* 911 F. 2d 970 (4th Cir. 1990), 979.

[15] *Morton Salt Co. v. G.S. Suppiger Co.* 314 U.S. 488 (1942).

[16] *Lasercomb Am., Inc. v. Reynolds* 911 F.2d 970 (4th Cir. 1990).

[17] M Leaffer, 'Engineering competitive policy and copyright misuse' (1994) 19 Dayton L. Rev. 1250.

5.2 The US Copyright-Misuse Doctrine

that licensees use only salt tablets produced by Morton; the tablets themselves were not covered by any patent. Morton brought an action against the defendant for infringing its patent in the salt-depositing machine. The Supreme Court found that by using the said licensing provision, Morton was using its patent in order to gain an advantage and restrain competition in an area that was outside the ambit of its patent grant; namely, the unpatented salt tablets. This, the Supreme Court emphasized, was contrary to the public policy embodied in the grant of a patent. The court stated:

> The grant to the inventor of the special privilege of a patent monopoly carries out a public policy adopted by the Constitution and laws of the United States . . . But the public policy that includes inventions within the granted monopoly excludes from it all that is not embraced in the invention. It equally forbids the use of the patent to secure an exclusive right or limited monopoly not granted by the Patent Office and which it is contrary to public policy to grant.[18]

Thus, the court concluded that the courts of equity 'may rightly withhold assistance from such use of a patent by declining to entertain a suit for infringement, and should do so at least until it is made to appear that the improper practice has been abandoned and that the consequences of the [patent misuse] have been dissipated'.[19]

The doctrine was clearly based on equity and not on antitrust law. Thus, the court stressed that the defence is independent of any antitrust examination and reversed the Seventh Circuit decision, which was based on its finding that the patent proprietor did not substantially restrain competition in the salt tablet market. The Supreme Court made it clear that patent misuse may take place in instances that fall short of antitrust violation. It is noteworthy that the Supreme Court, obiter, touched upon copyright misuse by referring to two copyright cases where an equitable defence prevailed on similar grounds. The validity of the patent misuse defence was subsequently affirmed and refined by the Supreme Court in later cases.[20] In 1988, Congress limited the scope of the defence by passing the Patent Misuse Reform Act 1988, which provided, inter alia, that a patent proprietor is not barred from enforcing its patent for the reason of refusing to license it. Nevertheless, it remains that using a patent to gain control over a market of unpatented goods may still amount to patent misuse.

As discussed above, *Morton Salt* laid the foundations for the emergence of the copyright-misuse defence. In *Lasercomb* the plaintiff was a manufacturer of steel

---

[18] *Morton Salt Co. v. G.S. Suppiger Co.* 314 U.S. (1942) 488, 492–3.   [19] Ibid, 493.

[20] For example, see *United States Gypsum Co. v. National Gypsum Co.* 352 U.S. 465; *Zenith radio Corp v Hazeltine Research, Inc.* 395 U.S. 100 (1969).

rule dies that were used to cut and score paper and cardboard for folding into boxes and cartons.[21] *Lasercomb* developed a computer program, Interact. Using this program, a designer created a template of a cardboard cut-out on a computer screen, and the software directed the mechanized creation of the conforming steel rule die. *Lasercomb* brought an action against the defendant, a competitor, and a licensee, claiming that it had made unauthorized copies of Interact and, in addition, had created a computer program of their own, the PSD-1000, that was almost entirely a direct copy of Interact.

The court commenced by stating that it has no doubt that the defendant was engaged in unauthorized copying and that it had done so by employing deceptive practices. Nevertheless, allowing the defendant's appeal, the court reversed the district court decision and stated that Lasercomb anticompetitive clauses in its standard licensing agreement constituted misuse of copyright. The offending clauses in *Lasercomb*'s standard licensing agreement provided that licensees are prohibited from writing, developing, producing, or selling computer-assisted dye-making software.

The court arrived at the above conclusion notwithstanding the fact that the defendant did not sign the contested licensing agreement and, therefore, was not affected by it. Acknowledging that there was little case-law on the subject of copyright misuse, the court emphasized that it had little doubt that copyright misuse was part of copyright law as much as patent misuse was part of patent law. This was so since 'similarity of rationales underlying the law of patents and the law of copyrights argues for a defence to an infringement of copyright based on misuse of the copyright'.[22] This similarity was based on both patent law and copyright law seeking to increase human knowledge and the arts by rewarding inventors and authors with exclusive rights to their works for a limited time. However, this granted monopoly power does not and should not extend to subject matter that is not covered by the grant. Citing the abovementioned passage from *Morton Salt* the court noted that the phraseology could be adapted easily to the copyright context. The court stated:

> The grant to the [author] of the special privilege of a [copyright] monopoly carries out a public policy adopted by the Constitution and laws of the United States . . . But the public policy which includes [original works] within the granted monopoly excludes from it all that is not embraced in the [the original expression]. It equally forbids the use of the [copyright] to secure an exclusive right or limited monopoly not granted by the [Copyright] Office and which it is contrary to public policy to grant.[23]

---

[21] *Lasercomb Am., Inc. v. Reynolds* 911 F.2d 970 (4th Cir. 1990).   [22] Ibid, 971.   [23] Ibid, 975.

5.2 The US Copyright-Misuse Doctrine

Having established copyright misuse as an affirmative defence analogous to patent misuse, the court observed that Lasercomb's prohibition on developing a competing program constituted an anticompetitive restraint and an affront on copyright's objective of encouraging creation. Thus, the court concluded that similar to patent misuse, copyright-misuse defence would be available where 'the copyright is being used in a manner violative of the public policy embodied in the grant of a copyright'.[24]

It should be noted that when referring to 'anticompetitive restraint' the court was not implying that it was necessary to prove an antitrust violation.[25] In this context, the court clarified:

> So while it is true that the attempted use of a copyright to violate antitrust law probably would give rise to a misuse of copyright defense, the converse is not necessarily true—a misuse need not be a violation of antitrust law in order to comprise an equitable defense to an infringement action. The question is not whether the copyright is being used in a manner violative of antitrust law (such as whether the licensing agreement is 'reasonable'), *but whether the copyright is being used in a manner violative of the public policy embodied in the grant of a copyright* [emphasis added].[26]

Thus, in the court's view, it was not the actual effects on competition or the market dominance of the plaintiff that was central to an examination under the copyright-misuse doctrine, but the attempt by the plaintiff to use copyright 'to control competition in an area outside copyright'.[27] Using copyright for objectives contrary to the public policy embodied in copyright law amounted to misuse of the copyright grant; the court simply refused to entertain an attempt to exercise one's copyright in that manner.

The potential of the copyright-misuse doctrine to curb attempts by right holders to gain control over software features that lie on the idea side of the idea–expression divide is obvious. As mentioned above, the court in *Lasercomb* stressed that the public policy embodied in a copyright grant includes original works within the granted monopoly but excludes from it, all that is not covered by the original expression. As discussed below, this type of rationale may be used by the courts in scrutinizing the combined use of copyright and standard form licences, where the effect is violative of the public policy embodied in a copyright grant under: the idea–expression dichotomy.

---

[24] Ibid, 978.

[25] This makes sense because, otherwise, there would be no need for an independent copyright-misuse defence.

[26] *Lasercomb Am., Inc. v. Reynolds* 911 F.2d 970 (4th Cir. 1990), 978.   [27] Ibid, 979.

It took a number of years for the copyright-misuse doctrine to gain approval amongst other circuit courts, and it appears that after some deliberation, such courts adopted the model suggested by the Fourth Circuit in *Lasercomb*.

For example, in *Practice Management* the Ninth Circuit followed suit and recognized copyright misuse as an affirmative defence.[28] The case concerned a comprehensive list of medical procedures, which were updated every year by the defendant, the American Medical Association. The defendant licensed this list to the Federal Government Healthcare Financing Administration for use with certain billing codes. Once the latter started to use the list, the plaintiff sued for a declaratory judgment, with a view to clearing the ground for the publication of its own medical procedure code list, claiming that the defendant's copyright was unenforceable since its licensing terms amounted to copyright misuse as they prohibited the Federal Government Healthcare Financing Administration to use any list other than the list licensed to it by the defendant. Although coming short of finding that the defendant's list now forms part of the public domain, the Ninth Circuit nevertheless held that the contested terms did amount to copyright misuse, which rendered the defendant's copyright unenforceable unless and until the said misuse was purged; namely, the offensive terms removed from the defendant's licensing agreement. The court dismissed various arguments raised by the defendant that were based on antitrust analysis and emphasized that it was the language of the said licensing terms which was crucial to the case. Thus, an analysis under the copyright-misuse doctrine was different from and independent of any examination of antitrust violation. It concluded that the terms gave the defendant a substantial and unfair advantage in the market place, securing for it 'an exclusive right or limited monopoly not granted by the Copyright Office . . . in a manner violative of the public policy embodied in the grant of a copyright'.[29]

In *Alcatel* it was again mainly the language of the licence terms that proved decisive to the Fifth Circuit's decision that the plaintiff engaged in copyright misuse.[30] The Plaintiff, Alcatel, produced switching equipment to route long-distance telephone calls. It was also the proprietor of an operating system used to control the switching equipment. The licensing agreement of the said software included terms that provided that the licensee was prohibited from using the software with any equipment other than that produced by the plaintiff. In order to keep up with the growing demand for long-distance calls, customers often used 'cards' in order to expand the capacity of the switching equipment. The defendant was one manufacturer of such expansion cards. Since these cards needed to be compatible with

---

[28] *Practice Management Information Corporation v The American Medical Association* 121 F.3d 516, 520 (9th Cir. 1997).
[29] Ibid, 520–1.   [30] *Alcatel USA, Inc. v. DGI Technologies Inc.* 116 F.3d 772 (5th Cir. 1999).

the plaintiff's operation system, the defendant had no choice but to download the plaintiff's operation system on several occasions in order to test and develop its cards.[31] The plaintiff brought an action against the defendant claiming, inter alia, copyright infringement owing to the intermediary copies created when the defendant downloaded the plaintiff's operating system. Unlike *Lasercomb* and *Practice Management*, where the copyright proprietor endeavoured to restrain competition with its copyrighted work, here the plaintiff was trying to gain an advantage in a market in which he neither had a copyrighted product nor a patented one; namely, the market for expansion cards. Thus, the contested licensing terms in effect prevented competing card manufacturers from developing expansion cards compatible with the plaintiff's operating system and thus reserved the market in the said non-copyrightable and unpatented expansion cards for the plaintiff. As in *Lasercomb* and *Practice Management*, the court did not engage in an antitrust analysis and was not concerned with the plaintiff's market power in the expansion card market or the actual effect that its conduct had on competition. The court found that the said licensing terms mucked the plaintiff's hands so that relief could be withheld with respect to the copyright infringement claim.

The Seventh Circuit Court of Appeal approached the subject of copyright misuse more hesitantly. In the *Saturday Evening Post*, the court made a distinction between two possible approaches to copyright misuse.[32] The first was the antitrust approach, requiring the establishment of antitrust violation for the court to find that the plaintiff engaged in copyright misuse. The second approach was the public policy approach, merely requiring, as the Fourth, Fifth, and Ninth Circuits found previously, to establish that the plaintiff was engaged in a practice that was 'violative' of the public policy embodied in copyright law. Unlike the other circuits, in *Saturday Evening Post*, the court appeared to favour the antitrust approach. It was only in the subsequent case of *Assessment Technologies* that the Seventh Circuit came around and endorsed the public policy approach.[33] In this case, the plaintiff was the copyright proprietor in a form of a database used by municipalities to maintain real estate records. The defendant wished to use the real estate records for his own purposes and approached certain municipalities accordingly. The plaintiff, presumably with a view to extracting licensing fee from the defendant, objected to any transfer of the real estate records from the municipalities to the defendant, arguing that its copyright prevented the municipalities from making a copy of the real estate records in their database form. The Seventh Circuit refused to enforce the plaintiff's copyright and held that its behaviour amounted

---

[31] Namely, engaging in reverse engineering in order to achieve interoperability.
[32] *Saturday Evening Post Co. v. Rumbleseat Press, Inc.* 816 F.2d 1191, 1200 (7th Cir. 1987).
[33] *Assessment Technologies of Wi, Inc. v. WIREdata, Inc.* 350 F.3d 640 (7th Cir. 2003).

to copyright misuse. Departing from its earlier view, the court held that, first, if confined to a finding of antitrust violation, the doctrine would have little use. Importantly, the court stressed that an attempt by a copyright proprietor to use its copyright in order to gain control over a subject matter that is outside the ambit of a copyright grant amounted to a misuse. Such a misuse may render the exclusive right that was being misused unenforceable. The Seventh Circuit issued another decision in the same year and found copyright misuse where a plaintiff used its copyright 'to suppress the underlying facts of his copyrighted work rather than to safeguard its creative expression'.[34]

The doctrine has also been recognized by the Third Circuit.[35] At present, although there are various district court decisions to this effect, there were no other circuit courts of appeal that explicitly endorsed and applied the copyright misuse defence in its public policy-based form. It may be that unless the Supreme Court is presented with the right opportunity and rises up to the challenge, thus acknowledging copyright misuse as an affirmative defence as it did in *Morton Salt*, such pan-circuit endorsement will be slow to take place. However, it is evident that the doctrine is consistently gaining support among different circuit courts and may be characterized as follows.[36] It prevents a copyright holder who has misused its copyright from enforcing it; it does not invalidate copyright altogether but rather prevents its enforcement until the misuse is purged; it is independent of any finding of antitrust violation; the defence is also available to parties that had not themselves been affected by the misuse. Most importantly, the defence is rooted in the principle that a copyright holder may not use its copyright in order to gain control over subject matter not covered by copyright law since doing so violates the public policy embodied in the grant of copyright.

As discussed above,[37] the idea-expression dichotomy embodies one of the key public policies underpinning copy-right law.[38] Thus, the copyright-misuse doctrine may prevent a right holder who, through the combined use of his copyright grant together with restrictive licensing terms, seeks to prohibit a licensee from studying, analysing, and utilizing non-copyrightable features in the

---

[34] *Bond v. Blum* 317 F.3d 385 (7th Cir. 2003), 397–8.
[35] *Video Pipeline, Inc. v. Buena Vista Home Entm't, Inc.* 342 F.3d 191 (3d. Cir. 2003).
[36] See P Goldstein, 'Fair use in context' (2008) 31 Colum. J. L. & Arts 433 11.6, 11:40 (arguing that the doctrine is becoming widely accepted, both in dicta and in holding).
[37] See Chapter 4.
[38] Interestingly, in *Bateman v. Mnemonic, Inc.* 79 F.3d 1532 (11th Cir. 1996) the Eleventh Circuit suggested that copyright misuse may be appropriate to prevent a copyright owner from obtaining protection for an idea in violation of S.102(b) of US Copyright Act). This observation seemed to be limited to software compatibility scenarios. Similarly, in *Bond v. Blum* 317 F.3d 385 (7th Cir. 2003), the Seventh Circuit found copyright misuse where a copyright owner attempted to use its statutory rights to prohibit what the fair-use defence clearly allowed.

5.2 The US Copyright-Misuse Doctrine

licensed software, such as ideas, systems, processes, methods of operation, and procedures.

However, even if it was to win wide approval across the various circuits, it should be noted that copyright misuse does not provide a comprehensive solution to the abovementioned licensing pattern. This is so since reliance on the contracts themselves may not amount to a misuse of a statutory right. Thus, the doctrine might prove effective against right owners enforcing their copyright in a given case, but it does not currently prevent a licensor from enforcing his contractual rights. For example, in *Davidson & Assocs. v. Internet Gateway*, the court did not allow the copyright-misuse defence against a breach of contract claim, since 'the Court is reluctant to apply the copyright-misuse defence as a defence to a contract claim because the defence is normally used in copyright infringement actions and the copyright claim has been dismissed in this case'.[39] Similarly, in *PRC Realty Sys* the court did not allow the doctrine to apply to breach of contract, which resulted in the defendant being excused from copyright infringement on the grounds of copyright misuse while being found liable for breach of contract.[40] Thus, although potentially effective against liability for copyright infringement, it appears to be ineffective against potential liability for breach of contract.

Several commentators criticized the application of the misuse doctrine to copyright cases. On a broad principle-based level, Leslie Wharton[41] argued that unlike patent law, copyright law provides a broader but thinner layer of protection and thus its enforcement is less likely to result in an anticompetitive outcome. According to Wharton, while patent protection is narrow but runs deep, enabling the patentee to exclude all types of exploitation and use of its invention, copyright does not. For example, copyright does not exclude the use of ideas, facts, etc., all contained in the copyrighted work. This being so, the risk that a particular manner in which the copyright holder chooses to enforce its copyright will lead to an anticompetitive outcome is much lower than in the case of patents. It is submitted that Wharton's argument was perhaps justifiable at the very early days of copyright misuse, but it carries much less weight nowadays. We have seen that coupled with non-negotiable licences and accompanied by technological protection measures, a copyright grant has the potential to yield a very powerful legal monopoly. Finally, it has been demonstrated that the copyright-misuse doctrine has evolved beyond the mere examination of anticompetitive effects and is mainly concerned with effects injurious to the public policy embodied in a copyright grant. Hence,

---

[39] *Davidson & Assocs. v. Internet Gateway* 334 F.Supp.2d 1164 (E.D. Mo. 2004), 1182–3.
[40] *PRC Realty Sys., Inc. v. Nat'l. Ass'n. of Realtors*, Nos 91-1125, 91-1143, 1992 U.S. App. LEXIS 18017, at 38 (4th Cir. 4 Aug. 1992).
[41] L Wharton, 'Misuse and copyright: a legal mismatch' (1991) 8(3) *Computer Law* 5.

the question of whether or not enforcing one's copyright might lead to an anticompetitive outcome is not decisive in this context.

Leaffer appears to be particularly critical where the doctrine is applied to scenarios involving computer programs.[42] He argues that the misuse doctrine is ill suited to copyright law and will play havoc with commercial licensing practices in the software industry. He maintains that since software licences are often drafted with a view to protect both copyright and trade secrets embodied in the same program, and that such licences will therefore often prohibit the licensee from copying the program and from reverse engineering it, applying the misuse doctrine might result in disclosing the trade secret—protected portion of the code.[43] He observes in this context that software licences do not distinguish between protectable and non-protectable code and that this is so for a practical reason: it is impossible to gain access to the unprotectable elements without reproducing protectable ones.

It is suggested that it is exactly this peculiar aspect of software that may make intervention via a misuse doctrine desirable.[44] It has been demonstrated that allowing a copyright holder to leverage its copyright to take advantage of this peculiar technical reality, in order to gain control over non-protectable elements, interferes with the public policy embodied in copyright law. The fact that a right holder in this instance claims that its unprotected elements constitute trade secrets should not change this conclusion, as the application of the doctrine should not alter the position under trade-secrets law. As we have seen, the copyright-misuse doctrine in its current form might regulate the enforcement of a copyright grant. It does not prevent a licensor from relying on its contractual right. A right holder may use a licence to identify certain non-copyrighted bits of the licensed software as trade secrets and place limits on their use. It should not be copyright law that the right holder relies on in case of non-compliance with the said terms, but contract law and trade-secrets law.

A further line of criticism levelled at the misuse doctrine relates to its equitable element where a licensee can raise the doctrine as a defence irrespective of whether or not he was personally affected. As Dolan puts it, a licensee who decides that the terms of the licence are not acceptable to him anymore and does not wish to abide by them, only needs to look for an offensive term in his licence or even in a licence signed between the licensor and others.[45] Should he be fortunate enough

---

[42] M Leaffer, 'Engineering competitive policy and copyright misuse' (1994) 19 Dayton L. Rev. 1250.
[43] He views this as an undesirable outcome.
[44] See B Frischmann and D Moylan, 'The evolving common law doctrine of copyright misuse: a unified theory and its application to software' (2000) 15 Berkley Tech. L. J. 865, at 879, arguing that it is this very unique nature of software as a copyright-protected literary work that lends further support to regulation through the copyright misuse doctrine.
[45] M Dolan, 'Misusing misuse: Why copyright misuse is unnecessary' (2007) 17 DePaul-LCA J. Art. & Ent. L. 207.

to identify such a clause, he could rest assured that the licensor would not be able to enforce his copyright against him. This author is of the view that this argument has merit. Such retributive justice does little to address the balance of competing interests under copyright law in a given dispute. Ideally, the misuse doctrine should come into play only where the offending clause it being enforced.

We have seen that although the copyright-misuse doctrine is slowly gaining a hold amongst various circuits, it is yet to become a part of a judicial toolkit that is workable throughout all circuits. For this to happen the US Supreme Court may need to step in and endorse it.

5.3 THE 'FUNCTION' OF INTELLECTUAL PROPERTY RIGHTS AS A MEANS TO REGULATE THE MANNER OF THEIR EXERCISE

There is no equivalent to the copyright-misuse doctrine in EU jurisprudence. Available defences are prescribed in either the Software Directive or the Information Society Directive. Thus, there is no effective EU doctrine that may address a scenario where a right holder seeks to use and enforce its intellectual property right in a manner that gives it control over an area that is outside the ambit of the said intellectual property grant. Of course, as discussed above, such a scenario may be actionable where it constitutes a violation of the EU competition rules. But where the necessary market power cannot be established or where one of the other criteria necessary for breach of competition rules cannot be met, there is little that can be done in terms of curbing an abusive use of an intellectual property right. However, if one seeks to identify an existing jurisprudential basis for such legal mechanism, one could look to the EU's established concept of the 'function' of intellectual property rights. This concept has the potential of being judicially developed into a tool that could restrain the manner in which an intellectual property right might be exercised, where the manner of exercise contravenes a key public policy objective that underpins that right. Such restrictions may be placed independently of any competition law-related finding. The principle works by implicitly defining the scope of the rights given to a right owner under the relevant grant in terms of their objective, with reference to their impact when enforced in the marketplace. This, however, should be read with a caveat: where the rights in question are copyright, patents, or designs, the concept of the essential function of these rights has been used to date only in cases involving violations of competition rules and free movement of goods.[46] In principle, however, there is no reason to limit its operation to such instances. Finally, one should note that

---

[46] For the definition of the *essential function of designs*, see Case C-238/87 *Volvo v. Veng* [1988] ECR 6211.

unlike the misuse doctrine, distinguishing between existence and exercise of an intellectual property right as a means to curb forms of exercise that contravenes key public policy objectives is not a defence per se, but a limitation placed on the scope of the relevant right.

The discussion below examines the concept of functions of intellectual property rights under EU law, with a view to investigate its origin and current application, in order to explore its potential application in software cases involving copyright law.

5.3.1 The essential function of a patent

In the case of patent rights, the concept of the essential function of the right has been limited to situations involving questions concerning free movement of goods. Thus, in the early case of *Centrafarm v. Sterling Drug* the CJEU was required to decide whether a patent proprietor in one member state had the right to object to the importation of goods covered by its patent from another member state, by relying on its national patent right.[47]

What is now Article 34 of the EC Treaty states: 'Quantitative restrictions on imports and all measures having equivalent effect shall . . . be prohibited between Member States.'[48] Differences in patent protection between the various Member States can prevent goods from moving across national borders and as such, could be classified as measures having an equivalent effect to quantitative restrictions. However, Article 36 of the TFEU states that: 'The provisions of Articles 30 to 34 shall not preclude prohibitions or restrictions on imports, exports or goods in transit justified on grounds of . . . the protection of industrial and commercial property. Such prohibitions or restrictions shall not, however, constitute a means of arbitrary discrimination or a disguised restriction on trade between Member States.' Thus, under certain circumstances, rights granted under patent law may prevail over the principle of free movement of goods.

In this context, however, the court in *Centrafarm* stated:

> In as much as it provides an exception to one of the fundamental principles of the common market, Article 36 in fact only allows of derogations from the free movement of goods where such derogations are justified for the purpose of safeguarding rights which constitute the specific subject matter of this property.[49]

The court went on to define that the scope of the essential function of:

> [. . .] the patent is to guarantee that the patentee, to reward the creative effort of the inventor, has the exclusive right to use an invention with a view to manufacturing

---

[47] Case C-15/74, *Centrafarm v. Sterling Drug* [1974] ECR 1147.   [48] Then Art. 30.
[49] Case C-15/74, *Centrafarm v. Sterling Drug* [1974] ECR 1147, para. 7.

industrial products and putting them into circulation for the first time, either directly or by the grant of licences to third parties, as well as the right to oppose infringements.[50]

Admittedly, the essential function of the right in this case was defined in fairly loose terms and with reference to one of the core objectives of the EC Treaty, free movement of goods. This may be understandable as patent law was not harmonized on EU level, and in principle, there may be variations between different Member States in relation to the public policy considerations embodied in the grant of a patent.

Nevertheless, the court in this case distinguished between the existence and exercise of intellectual property rights and maintained that although Article 30 has no effect on the existence of intellectual property rights it may have an effect on the manner of their exercise. The court recognized that at least in the case of national grants of patents, limits may be put on the exercise of such right where it conflicts with what is viewed as a paramount public policy objective.

5.3.2 The essential function of a copyright

Similar to the *Centrafarm* decision, the CJEU in *Deutche Grammophon* held that derogations from the free movement of goods principle were allowed only in so far as the exercise of copyright was compatible with its specific subject matter and its essential function.[51] However, in this case the CJEU did not proceed to define what is the essential function of a copyright grant. It was only many years later in *Coditel I* that the court for the first time made a reference to what constitutes the essential function of a copyright grant.[52]

The court explained: 'the right of a copyright owner and his assigns to require fee is part of the essential function of copyright in this type of literary and artistic work'.[53] Again it took years for the concept of the essential function of copyright to make another appearance and this time the definition given to it was more elaborate. In *Magill* the CFI stated: 'the essential function [of copyright] . . . is to protect the moral rights in a work and ensure a reward for the creative effort of the [author]'.[54] The CJEU referred to this passage with approval in subsequent cases.[55] Thus, in *Magill* the CJEU referred to the objective of copyright law and the

---

[50] Ibid, para. 9.
[51] *Case* C-78/70 *Deutsche Grammophon Gesellschaft mbH v. Metro-SB-Grossmärkte GmbH & Co. KG* [1971] ECR.
[52] Case C-62/79 *Coditel v. Cine Vog Films* [1980] E.C.R 881.   [53] Ibid, para. 14.
[54] Case T-69/89 *RTE v. Commission* 1991 E.C.R. II-485 [1991], para. 71.
[55] Joined Cases C-24 and C-242/91 *RTE and ITP v. Commission,* (Magill) [1995] E.C.R. I-743, 28.

justifications for granting it, in order to set a limit on the manner in which the proprietor may exercise its right. As mentioned above, the case was ultimately concerned with violation of EU competition rules and the court ruled that the mere exercise of copyright might, under exceptional circumstances, constitute breach of what was then Article 82. In this context it was held, inter alia, that since a copyright proprietor sought to exercise his right in a manner that gave him an advantage and control in a sphere that was outside the ambit of what the court considered the essential function of copyright, a violation of community competition rules could be established.

The court made a similar use of the concept of the essential function of copyright in the *Microsoft* decision.[56] Here the court explained that the appropriate test for assessing abuse of dominant position in the context of exercise of a copyright was whether the right is no longer being exercised according to its essential function but is being used instead to achieve an anticompetitive purpose.

As illustrated above, although the CJEU gradually defined aspects of what it considered to be the essential function of copyright and used this definition in order to place limits on the manner in which a proprietor may exercise its copyright, these limits were placed with reference to European competition rules rather than with reference to the public policy considerations that underpin the intellectual property right in question. Thus, at present, the courts do not yet take the extra step to hold that under certain circumstances exercising one's copyright may be contrary to the essential function of copyright in that it clashes with key objectives of the copyright grant itself.

5.3.3 The functions of a trade-mark as a curb on the manner of its exercise: the CJEU setting internal limitation on the circumstances in which a trade mark could be enforced

From all of the intellectual property rights, trade-marks and designs are the only ones to be fully harmonized at the EU level. It is possible that it is partially for this reason that the CJEU finds itself most often compelled to interpret, refine, and perfect the way trade mark rights are used and enforced in the European market. It is therefore likely that owing to this fact, it is in trade-mark law that the CJEU made the biggest strides in using the concept of the function of the right as a means to regulate the manner in which it is exercised. Namely, by identifying the functions of the trade mark, in particular its essential function, the CJEU was able to restrict the exercise of trade marks in situations where it considered the defendant's actions not to interfere with these functions. Allowing a right

---

[56] Case T-201/04 *Microsoft v. Commission* [2007] E.C.R. II-1491.

5.3 'Function' of Intellectual Property Rights

owner to exert its legal monopoly in instances where the functions of the trade-mark are not jeopardized runs contrary to the objective for which the said trade mark was granted in the first place.

Similar to the aforementioned copyright and patent cases, the first time the CJEU described the essential function of a trade-mark was in a case involving a question of parallel importation and free movement of goods. In *Hoffmann-La Roche* the CJEU stated: 'Regard must be had to the essential function of the trade mark, which is to guarantee the identity of the origin of the trade-marked product to the consumer or ultimate user, by enabling him without any possibility of confusion to distinguish that product from products which have another origin.'[57] Similar to its holdings in *Deutche Grammophon* and *Centrafarm*, the CJEU held that although what is now Article 36 of the EC Treaty allows for derogating from the principle of free movement of goods, such derogation is possible only where a proprietor exercises its right in a manner compatible with the essential function of trade marks.

The *Hoffmann-La Roche* decision dates back to the days when EU trade mark law was not yet harmonized. As trade-marks law became fully harmonized in the early 1990s, so did the CJEU feel more confident to use the essential-function doctrine in order to define the scope of a trade-mark monopoly with reference to public policy objectives embodied in trade-mark law itself rather than policies rooted in competition law and the exhaustion of rights principle.

Under Article 10(2)(a) of the Trade-marks Directive,[58] often referred to as the double-identity provision, prima facie trademark infringement occurs where the defendant is using the mark in the course of trade and the parties' marks and goods or services are identical. In *Arsenal*,[59] while construing the above provision, the court could have taken one of the following two approaches: it could have ruled that any use by the defendant in trade-related context where the parties' marks are identical and their goods are identical constitutes infringement. One might argue that on a plain literal interpretation of the provision, this was the correct approach to adopt. The second possible approach was to hold that, even where the parties' marks and goods are identical and where the contested use is commercial in nature, it is only use that puts the proprietor's legitimate interests at risk, by affecting the functions of the trade-mark, that may constitute infringement. The CJEU opted for the latter approach. Although, on the facts of the case, the CJEU implicitly suggested that the defendant's conduct was jeopardizing the

---

[57] Case C-02/77 *Hoffmann-La Roche & Co AG and Hoffmann-la Roche AG v. Centrafarm Vertriebsgesellschaft Pharmazeutischer Erzeugnisse mbH* 1978 E.C.R. 1139, 3 CMLR 217 [1978], para. 7.

[58] Formally, Art. 5(1)(a), under the previous version directive.

[59] Case C-206/01 *Arsenal Football Club v. Reed* [2002] E.C.R. I-10273.

essential function of trade marks (which is to guarantee origin), it suggested that contested uses must be assessed in the light of the objectives of and justification to our trade-marks regime.

This judicial mechanism of defining the scope of protection under trade-mark law with reference to its legitimate functions was used in the subsequent case of *Adam OPEL*.[60] It is submitted that the case is a good example to the manner in which the CJEU uses the concept of the functions of the trade mark in order to regulate the manner in which trade marks are enforced and to mould EU trade-mark law in accordance with what it considers as its public policy objectives rather than objectives routed in competition law. Therefore this decision is discussed below in some detail.

Opel was the proprietor of a national figurative mark registered in Germany for, inter alia, motor vehicles and toys (hereinafter 'the blitz logo'). Autec manufactured remote-controlled scale-model cars, which it marketed under the trade mark 'cartronic'. Opel found out that Autec manufactured and marketed in Germany a remote-controlled scale-model toy car of a certain Opel car model, bearing the blitz logo on its radiator grille as found on the original vehicle. Autec's 'cartronic' trade mark, as well as the indication 'AUTEC AG', was clearly visible on the user's instructions accompanying each scale model, and on the remote-control transmitter. Opel argued that since its trade mark was used on toys, the double-identity provision applies and infringement should follow automatically. Thus, one of the questions that the German court had to address was whether the complained use was use in the course of trade within the meaning of Article 5(1)(a).

Autec argued that the complained use did not amount to infringement because such use was made in order to replicate the features of the original car on a toy replica. It was therefore obvious to the relevant public in Germany that the scale model did not come from Opel but was a mere replica. Autec's argument was supported by the German Toy Industry Association, which opined that the German public was used to the fact that for more than 100 years, the toy industry has been reproducing faithfully (i.e. right down to the affixing of the trade-mark) replicas of full-size vehicles.

Before considering the CJEU ruling, it may be helpful to flesh out the basic factual matrix in this case. The case was referred to the CJEU. Opel had its mark registered for toys; Autec was using the blitz mark on toys. It should also be borne in mind that the double-identity provision does not contain any requirement for consumer confusion. Autec essentially argued that since the public was not

[60] Case C-48/05 *Adam Opel AG v. Autec AG* [2007] E.C.R. I-1017.

5.3 'Function' of Intellectual Property Rights

likely to be confused as to the true origin of its toy cars, the interest of Opel as the trade-mark proprietor was not put under threat. The CJEU held that if the German national court concludes that Autec assertions were correct in fact, such use did not jeopardize the essential function of the trade-mark and, therefore, should not amount to infringement under the double-identity provision. The court stated:

> If, by those explanations, the referring court intended to emphasize that the relevant public does not perceive the sign identical to the Opel logo appearing on the scale models marketed by Autec as an indication that those products come from Adam Opel or an undertaking economically linked to it, it would have to conclude that the use at issue in the main proceedings does not affect the essential function of the Opel logo as a trade-mark registered for toys.[61]

As mentioned, although there is no requirement for likelihood of confusion under the double-identity provision, the CJEU, in effect, imported such requirement through the back door by reference to the 'essential function' of the trade mark. It is clear that it had done so since, otherwise, the exclusive right granted under trade-marks law may be exercised in an excessive manner that would run contrary to the objectives and public policies embodied in trade-marks law. By referring to the essential function of the trade mark, the CJEU was defining the scope of trade-mark protection with reference to its objectives in order to keep it within its desirable boundaries. As the CJEU stated in *Arsenal*:

> The exclusive right under Article 5(1)(a) of the Directive was conferred in order to enable the trade-mark proprietor to protect his specific interests as proprietor, that is, to ensure that the trade mark can fulfil its functions. The exercise of that right must therefore be reserved to cases in which a third party's use of the sign affects or is liable to affect the functions of the trade-mark, in particular its essential function of guaranteeing to consumers the origin of the goods.[62]

Thus, the CJEU appeared to have established in these cases that there are internal limitations on the exercise of a right, as opposed to external ones that are defined by legislation. These limitations are derived from the objective or function of a trade-mark grant. The court internalized this recognition into its construction on the proper scope of the trade-mark grant, rather than via the route of developing a defence as US courts have done in the case of the misuse doctrine.

It should be noted that recently the CJEU has broadened the internal limits of a trade-mark grant by explicitly recognizing other legitimate functions that, if adversely affected by the defendant's actions, may lead to infringement. Thus, in L'Oreal[63]

---

[61] Ibid, para. 24.   [62] Case C-206/01 *Arsenal Football Club v. Reed* [2002] E.C.R. I-10273, para. 51.
[63] Case C-487/07 *L'Oréal SA v. Bellure NV* [2009] ECR I-5185, para. 58.

and in Google France and Google,[64] the CJEU stated that in addition to the essential function of the trade-mark, which is to guarantee origin, other functions must also be taken in to account, such as guaranteeing quality and those of communication, investment, or advertising. These functions should now form the internal limits of a trade-mark grant. If the defendant's use does not affect any of these functions, it will not amount to infringement.

5.3.4 Applying the 'protectable functions' rationale to software-related scenarios

Unlike the copyright misuse in the United States, the concept of the functions of intellectual property rights is not a defence per se but rather used as a preliminary assessment of the legitimate scope of protection. This may be so, since in the case of such rights, the list of available defences under European legislation appears exhaustive, and it may therefore be less complicated to internalize these factors into the scope of protection assessment.

The above discussion suggests that a spurt of judicial activism from the CJEU may equip courts in the European Union with a juridical mechanism for curbing the exercise of copyright in instances where it is being enforced in a manner that is contrary to the public policy considerations embodied in copyright grant for software. At least in the case of software, the objectives and public policy considerations that underpin protection are harmonized across the European Union and are prescribed in the Recitals of the Software Directive. As mentioned, in case of the Software Directive, some of the key provisions therein are not waivable by contract and therefore enable the courts to curb licensors' attempts to gain control over spaces that lie outside of their copyright grant. Where software features that are not covered by the Software Directive but rather under the Information Society Directive are at issue, the position across the EU also appears to be harmonized owing to the CJEU decisions in *BSA*[65] and *Infopaq*.[66] Namely, while the former decision explains which software features may or may not be covered by the Information Society Directive, the latter defines the scope of protection granted to literary works under this Directive and its objectives. Hence, the Information Society Directive is concerned with protecting expressions of the

---

[64] Joined Cases C-236/08, C-237/08, and C-238/08 *Google France SARL and Google Inc. v. Louis Vuitton Malletier SA, Google France and Google Inc. v. Viaticum SA and another,* and *Google France and Google Inc. v. CNRRH and others,* para. 77.

[65] Case C-393/09 *Bezpečnostní softwarová asociace – Svaz softwarové ochrany v. Ministerstvo kultury* [2010] I-13971.

[66] Case C-508 *Infopaq International A/S v. Danske Dagblades Forening* [2009] E.C.R. I-6569; [2009] E.C.D.R. 16

5.3 'Function' of Intellectual Property Rights

author's own intellectual creation. The Directive's Recitals refer to copyright's utilitarian objectives, stating that copyright and related rights 'protect and stimulate the development and marketing of new products and services and the creation and exploitation of their creative content'.[67] Hence, preventing the use of software features that do not constitute protectable expression of intellectual creation within the meaning of copyright law seems to run contrary to the aforementioned Directive's objective.

It is submitted that in principle there is a harmonized EU view on the public policy objectives and the desired scope of protecting various aspects of software products under copyright law. This being so, an activist CJEU should find it feasible to regulate the manner of exercise of copyright in relation to a software product by reference to the objectives for which the said copyright was granted in the first place—even where the said exercise appears to be in accordance with the outer limits of the copyright grant. We have seen that some right owners employ restrictive contractual provisions that prohibit the utilization of features that lie on the idea side of the idea–expression divide. Where the Information Society Directive governs such features, none of the relevant exceptions and limitations enjoys a non-waivable status. Thus, in principle, such exceptions and limitations, including the idea–expression dichotomy, might be contractually waived. In such circumstances, a court could find that a right owner should not be able to enforce its copyright even though a licensee used the software outside the scope of its licence. The reasoning would be that allowing a party to enforce a copyright against a defendant that utilized elements that are outside the scope of copyright protection, violates one of the key public policy principles that underpin our copyright law: the idea–expression dichotomy.

It is suggested that the rationale of Josserand's theory, implicitly, has gained some acceptance with EU courts via the functions of the right doctrine. Thus, the concept of limiting the scope of exercise of an intellectual property right, when such exercise is regarded excessive in light of the public policy objectives that underpin the said right, is not alien to European legal jurisprudence.

It is submitted that as a judicial corrective tool, the concept of the legitimate functions of the right may not be that dissimilar to that of copyright misuse; both define the internal limitations of a right and the scope of the legitimate exercise of such right by reference to the public policy objectives and legitimate functions that stand at the heart of such right. Under both principles, irrespective of the external explicit legislative limits, the courts may curb the exercise of an IPR

---

[67] See Recital 2 of the Directive.

where such exercise contravenes the public policy objectives and functions of such right.

At last, it should be borne in mind that even if the above rationale successfully migrates to the sphere of copyright protection for software, it would not be effective against potential liability for breach of contract. Thus, similar to the US copyright-misuse doctrine, it is an IPR-centred concept that has no effect on potential liability stemming from other branches of law.

5.4 A BRIEF NOTE ON THE PROHIBITION OF ABUSE OF LAW IN THE EUROPEAN UNION

'The concept of abuse of rights refers to situations in which a right is formally exercised in conformity with the conditions laid down in the rule granting the right, but where the legal outcome is against the objective of that rule.'[68] In civil law tradition, the concept of *abuse of rights* originates in Roman law. *Exceptio doli generalis* is a term coined by later jurists evaluating a situation where a party would seek a relief when the plaintiff's action was inequitable. These concepts have been adopted both in French and German jurisprudence as a reaction to legal formalism. They are based on the principle that laws should not be applied in a way that is inconsistent with their purpose.[69] The doctrine of abuse of rights has been recognized in a number of EU Member States,[70] but not in all of them.[71] It is however mainly, although not exclusively, in France and the Netherlands[72] that the

---

[68] A Lenaerts, 'The general principle of the prohibition of abuse rights: A critical position on its role in a codified European contract law' (2010) 6 European Rev. of Private L. 1121.

[69] J Gordley, 'The abuse of rights in the civil law tradition', Ch. 4 in R de la Feria and S Vogenauer (eds) *Prohibition of Abuse of Law: A New Principle of EU Law?* (Vol. 13 Studies of the Oxford Institute of European and Comparative Law 2011).

[70] A Lenaerts, 'The general principle of the prohibition of abuse rights: A critical position on its role in a codified European contract law' (2010) 6 European Review of Private Law 1121, at 1127 (maintaining that it had been recognized in Germany, Greece, Luxembourg, Netherlands, Portugal, Spain, Italy, Austria, Belgium, and France).

[71] See A G Tesauro in Case C-367-96 *Kefalas and Others v. Greek State and OAE* [1998] ECR 1-2843, para. 22; L N Brown, 'Is there a general principle of abuse of rights in European community law? In D Curtn and T Heukels (eds), *Institutional Dynamics of European Integration: Essays in Honour of Henry G Schermers*, (Vol. ii Dordrech, Martnius Nijhof 1994) 511, 513-15; R de la Feria, 'Prohibition of abuse of (community) law: the creation of a new general principle of EC law through tax' (2008) 45 Common Market L. Rev. 395, 437.

[72] It is noteworthy that other EU jurisdictions adhere to this interpretation of the concept of abuse of rights; for example, under Art. 281 of the Greek Civil Code, the exercise of right is prohibited if it manifestly exceeds the bounds provided by good faith, public morals, or the *social* or *economic purpose* of the right [emphasis added].

doctrine has endorsed the social function of a given right as a criterion for determining abuse.[73]

How significant is this principle in the present context? Does the fact that a few Member States have recognized the concept of prohibition against abuse of rights in a manner that is broadly compatible with Josserand's theory have an impact on EU law as a whole? If so, could it be applicable to copyright scenarios?

The answer to both questions appears to be affirmative, although no copyright-related decision was given by the CJEU in this context to date. As Professor de la Feria points out, while the CJEU has been alluding to abuse and abusive practices in its rulings for more than 30 years, it is only recent developments in the court's jurisprudence that made it clear that references by the court to abuse amounted to the development of a general community principle of abuse of rights (or abuse of law).[74] Although the most recent developments took place almost exclusively within the area of tax law, once the 'prohibition of abuse of law' becomes a general principle of community law, its potential application need not necessarily be limited to one area of community law.

The discussion above does not purport to suggest that, at present, an EU court is likely to endorse an abuse-of-rights type of argument where a right owner relies on his copyright for a purpose that ultimately runs contrary to the public policy considerations that underlie copyright law. Professor de la Feria argues that there is still much to be explained about the prohibition on abuse of rights as a general principle of community law. She contends that 'further clarification is likely to be requested from the CJEU, not only as regards the more theoretical aspects of the principle, such as the Community's concept of abuse of law, but also its more practical consequences and/or implications, such as the principle's scope of application, onus of proof, available remedies, etc.'.[75] However, it is submitted that in principle, once the air is cleared and should the CJEU provide the aforementioned clarifications in a manner that corresponds to Josserand's formula of the prohibition of abuse of rights, there is nothing to stop the court from applying the concept to the type of copyright cases discussed in the previous chapters.

---

[73] See, H C Gutteridge, 'Abuse of rights' (1933) 5 Cambridge L. J. 24. (Although the concept of abuse is recognized under German law, Art. 226 of the BGB on Schikaneverbot, focuses, inter alia, on the intent behind the contested exercise rather than on its compatibility with the social function of the right.)

[74] R de la Feria, 'Prohibition of abuse of (community) law: the creation of a new general principle of EC law through tax' (2008) 45 Common Market L. Rev.395.

[75] Ibid, at 441

6

PATENTING SOFTWARE

6.1 Computer-Implemented Inventions in the United States	161
6.1.1 Background	161
6.1.2 Policy trends and judicial interpretation	162
6.1.2.1 *Policy trends*	162
6.1.2.2 *The development of case-law*	163
6.2 Computer-Implemented Inventions at the European Patent Office	178
6.2.1 Background	178
6.2.2 Trends and case-law development	179
6.2.2.1 *The contribution approach*	179
6.2.2.2 *The 'any-hardware' approach*	180
6.3 Convergence of the Present Approaches in the United States and European Patent Office	184

The availability of patent protection for computer-implemented inventions is an attractive option for right holders. On the face of it, it offers advantages that other forms of intellectual property rights cannot compete with. For example, unlike copyright, which, inter alia, protects against copying, or trade secrets law, which protects against misappropriation, infringement under patent law may take place whether or not the defendant copied from or had access to the claimant's product. In other words, independent creation is no defence to a patent infringement action. Furthermore, patent law may protect ideas or concepts that may be placed on the idea side of the idea–expression divide under copyright law.[1] In essence, the notorious 'functionality' label under which various aspects of a software product may be rendered un-protectable under copyright law is not necessarily terminal where patent law is concerned, since

---

[1] For example, in both the United States and the United Kingdom, court decisions that are widely considered to be the birthplace of the idea-expression dichotomy refer to patent law as a potentially more suitable vehicle for protection where the subject matter was considered to be on the idea side of the idea–expression divide: *Hollinrake v. Truswell* [1894] 3 Ch. 420; *Baker v. Selden* 101 US 99 (1879).

Beyond the Code: Protection of Non-Textual Features of Software. First Edition. Noam Shemtov.
© Noam Shemtov 2017. Published 2017 by Oxford University Press.

functional aspects of a product may be subject to patent protection.[2] In light of the breadth and depth of the monopoly offered under patent law, it is hardly surprising that software developers sought patent protection for their innovations throughout the last few decades. In doing so, they repeatedly tested the boundaries of patent law, contributing to the emergence of a hospitable software patent regime.

Patent protection is discussed in this title in various contexts. First, patent protection for GUIs is discussed in Chapter 7. In the same chapter, design patent protection for GUIs (as opposed to utility patents) is also discussed. Thus, while the present chapter examines some key elements of patent protection for computer-implemented inventions, it does not discuss the patentability of their GUIs. In addition, the present chapter does not aim to cover claim construction and infringement of software-related patents. While the latter is an area of immense importance to patent enforcement, it would require an extensive and technically detailed analysis that goes beyond the scope of this title. Hence, the ensuing discussion will focus on the patent eligibility of software-implemented inventions in the United States and the European Patent Office (EPO).

6.1 COMPUTER-IMPLEMENTED INVENTIONS IN THE UNITED STATES

6.1.1 Background

As in the case of copyright, Article 1, Section 8, of the United States Constitution provides the mandate for Congress to make laws for the protection of inventions. Pursuant to this provision, Congress enacted Title 35 of the United States Code under which the Patent Act of 1952 was passed. Section 101 of the Patent Act defines subject matter eligibility. It reads: 'Whoever invents or discovers any new and useful process, machine, manufacture, or composition of matter, or any new and useful improvement thereof, may obtain a patent therefor, subject to the conditions and requirements of this title.' Under this provision, subject matter eligibility is determined according to two criteria: (i) the claimed invention must be directed to one of the four statutory categories: process, machine, manufacture, or composition of matter; (ii) it must not be wholly directed to subject

---

[2] Although pure functional claiming is problematic; see, M A Lemley, 'Software patents and the return of functional claiming' (2013) 905 Wis. L. Rev. 925.

matter comprising a judicially recognized exception, comprising laws of nature, natural phenomena and abstract ideas.[3]

In the past opponents of patent protection for software argued that in order for computer programs to become patentable subject matter, Congress rather than the courts needs to intervene and create the appropriate statutory platform for it.[4] It is suggested that this argument is not convincing. Since the enactment of the first Patent Act, about 250 years ago, the textual form of the statute has hardly led the way with regard to new emerging technologies.[5]

6.1.2 Policy trends and judicial interpretation

6.1.2.1 *Policy trends*

In the mid-1960s, digital computers started to emerge as commercial tools. At first glance it may look peculiar that the very branch of government that was in charge of issuing patents and rewarding inventors for their innovation (i.e. the Patent and Trademark Office (PTO)), was the very one that fought vigorously against patent protection for computer-implemented inventions.

The PTO's attitude stemmed from two main factors. The first was that at the time the government viewed patents as a tool used by big corporations to crumple competition. Generally speaking, the government had an 'anti' big corporations approach, as was reflected in a rigorous and expansive application of antitrust policies, rather than encouraging innovation. Second, in light of that attitude it was unlikely for the PTO to get more funding for adapting itself to deal with a new fast developing area of industry.[6] The PTO desperately needed examiners that were experienced in that area and those were scarce in those days. Moreover, hiring such people involved resources that the PTO did not have and in the light of the governmental approach to patents, was not likely to get. In addition, in order to assess patent applications relating to computer-implemented inventions, the PTO needed to put together an adequate database of prior art. That also involved resources that the PTO lacked, which resulted in the PTO adopting an approach under which examiners were instructed to reject claims directed to software.[7]

---

[3] See, e.g. *Bilski v. Kappos*, 561 U.S.593, 601, 130 S. Ct. 3218, 3225, 95 USPQ2d 1001, 1005–6 (2010) (stating, 'The Court's precedents provide three specific exceptions to Section 101's broad patent-eligibility principles: "laws of nature, physical phenomena, and abstract ideas."') (quoting *Diamond v. Chakrabarty*, 447 U.S. 303, 309, 206 USPQ 193, 197 (1980)).

[4] For example, see Justice Douglas opinion in *Gottschalk v. Benson* 409 U.S. 63, 175 USPQ (BNA) 673 (1972).

[5] See E Kitch and H Perlman, *Legal Regulation of the Competitive Process* (Mineola, NY, Foundation Press, 1972) 642.

[6] See G J Maier and R C Mattson, 'State Street Bank in the context of the software patent saga' (1999) 8 GMLR 307.

[7] Ibid.

The PTO abandoned its 'anti' software approach only after a long and persistent fight against the Court of Custom and Patent Appeal (CCPA), in which three times the PTO took the costly and unusual step of appealing all the way to the Supreme Court. Furthermore, by the early 1980s, a fundamental shift took place in governmental attitude towards big corporations and innovation. Enter the Regan's era, when attitudes changed and patents were perceived as a useful mechanism to encourage innovation. Consequently, the PTO at last received the necessary funding for suitably equipping itself to deal with an increased load of computer-implemented patent applications, while at the same time a revamp of the PTO fee structure enabled it to be fully self-funded regardless of its workload.[8]

6.1.2.2 The development of case-law
In a series of decisions, the first of which is dated back to 1968, the CCPA confronted the PTO Board of Appeal (hereinafter the Board) with regard to patentability of software-related inventions under Section 101 and rejected its main reasoning for dismissing applications for software-related inventions (i.e. the 'mental-step' doctrine).[9] Under this doctrine, where a method claim defines nothing more than that which could be performed as a human mental exercise, the claim lies outside the statutory boundaries of patentable subject matter under Section 101 and thus is not allowable. The CCPA was of the view that in order for a process claim to lie within the statutory boundaries of Section 101, it was sufficient for a process to be in the field of 'technological art' and to have a useful application so as to satisfy the constitutional purpose of promoting the progress of useful art. According to this view, the question of whether or not some or all of the steps defined in a process claim can be carried by humans was of no relevance. Eventually, the PTO decided to take the battle to the Supreme Court: the right opportunity arrived in the case of *Gottschalk v. Benson*.[10]

Early Supreme Court trilogy   In *Benson*, while expressly stating that it does not hold that software-related inventions are un-patentable per se, the Supreme Court apparently accepted the PTO's position that such inventions constitute a new category and that there is a need for Congressional clarification on the patentability of the said category.[11] The court further opined that where a claim wholly

---

[8] Ibid.
[9] See *re Partet*, 415 F.2d 1393, 162 USPQ (BNA) 541 (CCPA 1969); *re Bernhart*, 417 F.2d 1395, 163 USPQ (BNA) 611 (CCPA 1969); *re Mahony*, 421 F.2d 742, 164 USPQ (BNA) 572 (CCPA 1970); *re Musgrave* 431 F.2d 882, 167 USPQ (BNA) 280 (CCPA 1970); *re Foster* 438 F.2d 1011, 169 USPQ (BNA) 99 (CCPA 1971).
[10] Supra footnote 63.
[11] *Gottschalk, Acting Commissioner of Patents v. Benson et al.*, 409 U.S. 63 (1972).

pre-empts the use of an algorithm, granting a patent will amount to patenting the algorithm itself, which was deemed un-statutory. It was in *Benson* that the PTO proposed the 'machine or transformation' test as a tool for assessing patent eligibility for software-related inventions. According to this test, a claimed subject matter is patent eligible where: (i) it is implemented by a particular machine in a non-conventional and non-trivial manner or (ii) it transforms an article from one state to another. The Supreme Court however was reluctant to endorse this test as the sole benchmark for assessing patent eligibility. It maintained that the test could be useful in some cases, but was not necessarily suitable for assessing patent eligibility under all sets of circumstances.

Essentially, the Supreme Court reaffirmed its position in *Benson* in its subsequent decision in *Parker v. Flook*.[12] Here, again, the PTO challenged a decision of the CCPA to allow an appeal against a decision of the Board in relation to what the Board considered an un-patentable algorithm. Allowing the appeal, the Supreme Court held that while the fact that an algorithm or a law of nature serves as one of the claim's components did not render the claim un-statutory, and although a claim should be considered as a whole, the algorithm (since in itself is a non-patentable subject matter) was considered as a part of the prior art, whether or not that was indeed the case. Where such an algorithm constituted the invention's innovative concept, considering it as part of the prior art dealt a deathblow to the application.

The last Supreme Court's decision during that era was in *Diamond v. Diehr*.[13] In a five-to-four vote, the court decided that an industrial process, involving in one of its steps the use of a mathematical algorithm, constituted a patentable subject matter under Section 101. It abandoned its prior proposition in Flook, according to which one should look into the novelty aspects of the claim while excluding the mathematical algorithm in order to determine whether the claim is directed at a patentable subject matter. A key part of the court's reasoning was that the applicant did not seek to exclude the use of the mathematical algorithm per se, but merely used it to affect the transformation of an article into a different state of thing; in that instance, the said industrial process concerned the transformation of uncured rubber into cured rubber. The court pointed to the Committee Report on the 1952 Patent Act[14] and especially to the statement: 'Congress intended statutory subject matter to include anything under the sun that is made by man.'

Springtime for software-related inventions After *Diehr* the PTO contested the CCPA decisions no more. Furthermore, the new attitude of the Reagan

---

[12] See 437 U.S 584, 198 USPQ (BNA) 193 (1978).   [13] See 450 U.S. 175, 209 USPQ 1 (1981).
[14] S. Rep. No. 1979, 82d Cong., 2nd Sess., 5 (1952).

administration enabled the PTO to get the necessary funding to deal with a fresh load of computer-implemented patent applications that followed the *Diehr* decision.

During the period in which the Supreme Court delivered the decisions of *Benson*, *Flook*, and *Deihr*, the CCPA responded in a trilogy of cases of its own, where a twofold test was introduced in order to assess patent eligibility of computer-implemented inventions; the test became known as the *Freeman*[15]-*Walter*[16]-*Abele*[17] test.[18] According to this test, the court should commence its examination by assessing whether a claim directly or indirectly recites a mathematical algorithm, and if the answer was affirmative, the court had to continue to the second phase and assess whether the claim was otherwise statutory; where that was the case, patent eligibility was established notwithstanding the mathematical algorithm.

In 1982 after the *Abele* decision, the Court of Appeal for the Federal Circuit (CAFC) was established as the sole national appellate court on patent issues. The objective was to have one source of judicial decisions on patent issues and over time to develop a coherent and clear body of case-law. Up to 1994 the CAFC mainly applied the Freeman-Walter-Abele test on questions of patent eligibility. However, during that period, the court's approach often depended on the composition of the CAFC panel rather than merely on the factual matrix of a case.[19] For example, CAFC's decisions such as *re Grams*[20] and *re Iwahashi*,[21] which were decided at the same year by different panels, had different outcomes where similar relevant facts were involved.

In 1994 the CAFC delivered a landmark patent-eligibility decision while sitting 'en banc'. In *re Alappat*,[22] the claim at issue dealt with means for creating a smooth waveform display in a digital oscilloscope. The invention involved means for measuring and altering the intensity of pixels on the oscilloscope screen so that the result was a clearer picture. It was an apparatus claim drafted in a 'means for' form. It should be noted that the disclosed apparatus was nothing more than a known type of a general-purpose computer. Reciting *Deihr*, the court stated that the claims should be read as a whole and the question of whether or not the claim included a mathematical algorithm was not relevant. The court also took the

---

[15] *re Freeman* 573, D.2d 1237, 197 USPQ (BNA) 464 (CCPA 1978).
[16] *re Walter* 618, F.2d 758, 205 USPQ (BNA) 397 (CCPA 1980).
[17] *re Abele* 684, F.2d 902, 214 USPQ (BNA) 682 (CCPA 1982).
[18] This test was subsequently discarded in the CAFC's decision in *re Alappat*, 33 F.3d 1526 (Fed. Cir. 1994) (en banc).
[19] See Richard H Stern, 'Solving the algorithm conundrum: after 1994 in the Federal Circuit Patent Law needs a radical algorithmectomy' (1994), 22 AIPLA Q. J. 167, 213 (1994).
[20] See 888 F.2d 835 (Fed. Cir. 1989). [21] Ibid 1370 (Fed. Cir. 1989).
[22] *re Alappat*, 33 F.3d 1526 (Fed. Cir. 1994).

opportunity to discard the then long-standing *Freeman-Walter-Abele* test. Since the claim at issue was not directed to a disembodied mathematical algorithm but rather to a combination of interconnected electronic circuits, each performing a mathematical operation resulting in the conversion of data samples of waveforms to pixels on a screen, it was held that the claim was directed to a statutory subject matter. The court simply treated the invention as any other invention rather than one that belongs to a special category, and thus requiring a special analysis. The court further asserted that the fact that a claim was directed to a general-purpose computer did not render the claim non-statutory. Such a 'general-purpose' computer, once programmed, was turned into a 'new machine' because it essentially became a special purpose machine programmed to perform a particular task. In conclusion, writing for the majority Judge Rich somewhat simplistically stated that it was clear that 'in any case, a computer, like a rasterizer, is apparatus, not mathematics'.[23] Following *re Alappat*, where a patent attorney could realize the claimed invention in 'machine' form (e.g. a programmed general-purpose computer), the invention was deemed to constitute a patentable subject matter under Section 101.

In the light of *re Alappat* and subsequent case-law, the PTO was compelled to reconsider its examination guideline for software-related inventions and as a result new guidelines were published, consistent with the new case-law.[24] In essence, the examiners were instructed that like any other type of invention, for a software-related invention to be patent eligible, inter alia, it simply had to be useful, novel, and non-obvious. Laws of nature, natural phenomena, and abstract ideas were still treated as un-patentable.

The *re Alappat* rationale was applied even more expansively in two notable decisions that concerned computer-implemented business methods inventions in the late nineties: *State Street Bank*[25] and *AT & T*,[26] both concerning patent infringement actions but essentially revolving around the validity of the plaintiff's patent.

The rise of business methods patents In *State Street Bank*, the patent opposed covered a software-implemented financial process. This invention was quite different from the inventions in the cases that formed the bulk of the CAFC case-law up to that point. In this case, there were no physical aspects such as pixels, electromagnetic waves, or temperatures of moulded rubber. The invention was simply

---

[23] Ibid (per Rich J).
[24] Examination Guidelines for Computer-related Inventions, 61 Fed. Reg. 7,478 (1996), (hereinafter 'PTO guidelines').
[25] *State Street Bank & Trust Co v. Signature Financial Group Inc.*, 149 F.3d 1368 (Fed. Cir. 1998).
[26] *AT&T Corp v. Excel Communication Inc.*, 172 F.3d 1352 (Fed. Cir. 1999).

a computerized method of doing business. As such, the CAFC also had to defuse another long-standing judicial exception to patentability, known as the 'method-of-doing-business' exception.[27]

The court asserted that the question of patentability does not depend on the court identifying a special subject matter category in the claim. The important factors to be considered were the characteristics of the subject matter and especially its utility. The court stated:

> Today, we hold that the transformation of data, representing discrete dollar amounts, by a machine through a series of mathematical calculations into a final share price, constitutes a practical application of a mathematical algorithm, formula, or calculation, because it produces 'a useful, concrete and tangible result'—a final share price momentarily fixed for recording or reporting purposes and even accepted and relied upon by regulatory authorities and in subsequent trades.[28]

Thus, the court rejected the long established 'physical limitation' requirement and determined that lack of physical transformation of some sort does not render the subject matter ineligible. The essential characteristic required in order to render the subject matter patentable was 'a useful, concrete, and tangible result' as opposed to an abstract idea.

The effect of the *State Street Bank* decision was further buttressed in the subsequent decision of *AT&T*.[29] Moreover, the fact that the *AT&T* decision was delivered by a different CAFC panel suggested that these decisions were not a panel-specific but rather represented the then-present approach of the court as a whole, sending corresponding signals to the district courts. Unlike *State Street Bank*, the court in *AT&T* was required to address process claims. The invention related to a computer-implemented method for improving the technology used to calculate the price of direct-dial long distance telephone calls. Addressing the 'physical transformation' requirement, the court stated that it was simply one example of a useful application of a mathematical algorithm and not a precondition for patent eligibility. The decision was justified on the grounds that patent law must 'adapt to new and innovative concepts, while remaining true to basic principles'.[30] The court reasoned that the principles established in the Supreme Court's trilogy, which concerned process claims, were relied upon by the CAFC in *re Alappat*, which concerned machine claims. On that basis, the court felt emboldened to apply the

---

[27] For a detailed analysis of the 'method of doing business' exception in the context of the *State Street Bank* decision, see T R Makin, 'Hotel checking: you can checkout any time you want, but can you ever leave? The patenting of business methods' (2000) 24 Colum-VLA J. L. & Arts 93.
[28] *State Street Bank & Trust Co v. Signature Financial Group Inc.* 149 F.3d 1368 (Fed. Cir. 1998), at 1373.
[29] *AT & T Corp v. Excel Communication Inc.* 172 F.3d 1352 (Fed. Cir. 1999).   [30] Ibid, 1356.

'no-physical-limitation' rule established in *re Alappat* to the process claims in *AT&T*.[31] As in *State Street Bank*, the Supreme Court denied certiorari.

The Supreme Court reins in One of the consequences of the approach taken by the CAFC during the 1980s and 90s, and most of the noughties, was that functional or result oriented claiming became prevalent. In essence, functional claiming takes place where the application or patent claims the end that is to be achieved, rather than the means for achieving it. Thus, it is the goal itself rather than the steps taken to achieve that goal that is being claimed. Where granted, such patents may exclude all possible processes or machines for achieving the said goal. Interestingly, such broad functional claiming was initially a reaction by applicants to early judicial doubts as to the patentability of computer algorithms themselves. During this early period, applicants attempted to describe inventions and what was happening in plain English terms, rather than by references to mathematical algorithms or programming approaches. Namely, such inventions were claimed on a more abstract level.[32] The consequences of this trend, however, were problematic, as Robin Feldman explains:

> Most troubling, the incentive to describe what is happening in linguistic rather than mathematical terms could also provide a tremendously wide footprint for each patent. For example, consider the applicant who would now simply use the claims language 'applying a statistical model' rather than providing the notation of the actual statistical model or formula that is used. The general term 'statistical model' will have very broad coverage if it is not strictly defined.[33]

After two decades of allowing such manner of claiming,[34] and after almost three decades since the Supreme Court last visited the subject of software-related patents, the Supreme Court finally stepped-in in *Bilski*, where it found that a business method patent was not patentable, inter alia, since it sought to monopolize an abstract idea.

The Supreme Court's second trilogy: Bilski,[35] *Mayo,*[36] *and Alice*[37] Almost thirty years after *Diehr* was decided, the Supreme Court finally granted certiorari in a case relating to patent eligibility of a software-related invention. In *re Bilski*,[38] it

---

[31] Previously the CAFC rejected process claims involving algorithms unless the claim at issue involved physical transformation.
[32] See R Feldman, *Rethinking Patent Law*, (Cambridge, MA, Harvard University Press, 2012) 109.
[33] Ibid, 111-12.
[34] M A Lemley, 'Software patents and the return of functional claiming', (2013) 905 Wis. L. Rev. 925.
[35] *Bilski v Kappos* 561 U.S. 593 (2010).
[36] *Mayo Collaborative Services v Prometheus Laboratories, Inc.* 132 S. Ct. 1289 (2012).
[37] *Alice Corp. Pty. V CLS Bank Int'l* 134 S. Ct. 2347 (2014).
[38] *In re* Bilski 545 F.3d 943 (Fed. Cir. 2008).

was the en banc CAFC that decided it was time to paddle back on its previously established jurisprudence and limit the flow of overly broad and functional patents that were previously successfully granted. In doing so, the court rejected its aforementioned test for patent eligibility, according to which the court enquires whether the invention produced a 'useful, concrete, and tangible result'. Instead, the CAFC held that a claimed process was patent eligible if: (i) it was tied to a particular machine or apparatus or (ii) it transformed a particular article into a different state or thing. The court held that this 'machine or transformation test' was the sole test for patent eligibility of a 'process' under Section 101, and concluded that Bilski's application was therefore not patent eligible.

The patent in *Bilski* related to a method for hedging risk in the field of commodities and commodity options trading, without being limited to a practical application or a specific apparatus. The Supreme Court concluded that the patent was directed to an 'abstract idea'.[39] Referring to its previous holding in *Benson, Flook,* and *Diehr*, the court reiterated the three judicially recognized exceptions to patentability: abstract ideas, laws of nature, and natural phenomena. The court further held that granting a patent for Bilski's method for hedging risk, would pre-empt the use of this method in all possible fields and effectively grant Bilski a monopoly over this concept in abstract; in other words, over an abstract idea. Rejecting the CAFC recently resurrected 'machine or transformation' test as the sole filter for determining patent eligibility in such cases, the Supreme Court contended that this test was nevertheless 'a useful and important clue... for determining whether some claimed inventions are processes under § 101'. Although the patent at issue also included a number of narrower dependent claims, the Supreme Court nevertheless held that these were nothing more than mere examples to implementations of the claimed abstract idea. The Supreme Court did not provide, however, satisfactory guidelines to distinguish between un-patentable abstract idea and patent-eligible subject matter.

Two years after *Bilski* the Supreme Court was faced with another patent-eligibility case, this time the patent at issue was not software-related. Nevertheless, this decision sought to clarify the court's position regarding the judicially recognized exceptions to patentability. In *Mayo*[40] the patent at stake was directed to a method consisting of the steps: (i) 'measuring' the levels of 6-Thioguanine in patients who had received a particular drug; (ii) 'analysing' whether the level fell within one of three ranges; and (iii) increasing, decreasing, or maintaining the dosage level based on that analysis.[41] The Supreme Court held that the claims at issue, which

---

[39] *Bilski v. Kappos* 561 U.S. 593 (2010).
[40] *Mayo Collaborative Services v. Prometheus Laboratories, Inc.* 132 S. Ct. 1289 (2012).
[41] Ibid, 1295.

were essentially directed to methods for optimizing the efficacy of a drug, were directed to laws of nature and, therefore, were not patent eligible. The court held that the relationship between metabolite level and drug efficacy was nothing more than a law of nature and thus not patent eligible. Expanding on its views in *Bilski*, the court maintained: 'to transform an unpatentable law of nature into a patent-eligible application of such a law, one must do more than simply state the law of nature while adding the words "apply it" '.[42] Turning to the facts of the case, the court concluded that the claims at issue were mere 'instructions' that 'add nothing specific to the laws of nature other than what is well-understood, routine, conventional activity, previously engaged in by those in the field'.[43] The court held that the steps of 'administering' and 'determining' were not sufficient to satisfy the 'transformation' limb of the 'machine or transformation' test, since they were nothing more than 'insignificant post-solution activity'.

What the court did not clarify was what 'extra' element was needed in order to turn a claim that relates to a law of nature into a patent-eligible subject matter. After all, all electrical circuits, chemical and mechanical processes, at their heart, are based on laws of nature, such as Maxwell's, Schrodinger's, and Newton's physics equations, and are ultimately applications of such rules of nature. Furthermore, the court did not provide clear guidelines on how one distinguishes between significant and insignificant post-solution activity. For example, assuming that the therapeutic range for the metabolite constituted a rule of nature, how much further does one need to travel in order to identify a patentable subject matter?

A careful examination of the court's opinion in *Mayo* suggests that in establishing whether the claims manifest a patentable subject matter, a court should enquire, in this order, as follows: (a) whether or not the claim recites or involves one or more judicial exception and, if yes, (b) whether or not the claim as a whole recites something significantly more than the judicial exception/s. Thus, claims may be considered to involve a patentable subject matter where the subject matter is significantly different from that which exists in nature, or where the claims practically apply the judicial exception/s in a significant way, for instance where they add significantly more to the said rule of nature.

The Supreme Court's third decision in its second trilogy was in *Alice Corp. v. CLS Bank*.[44] Unlike *Mayo*, the patent in *Alice* was software related. It related to a computerized trading platform designed to eliminate the risk in financial transactions between two parties by using a natural third party. The latter, essentially an escrow, safeguards that both parties meet their respective obligations before any of the obligations were in fact exchanged. An en banc CAFC concluded that the

---

[42] Ibid, 1294.   [43] Ibid, 1296.   [44] *Alice Corp. Pty. v. CLS Bank Int'l* 134 S. Ct. 2347 (2014).

6.1 Computer-Implemented Inventions

claims involved a patent-ineligible subject matter but the different judges could not agree on why that was the case.

Affirming the CAFC's decision the Supreme Court held that the claims were ineligible since they 'are drawn to the abstract idea of intermediated settlement'[45] and 'merely require [a] generic computer implementation [that] fails to transform that abstract idea into a patent-eligible invention'.[46] Relying on its holding in *Mayo*, the Supreme Court maintained that in determining whether or not the claims involve nothing more than an abstract idea or any other judicial exception, it is necessary to ask three interconnected questions. First, as a preliminary question, is the claim directed to one of the four statutory categories (i.e. process, machine, manufacture, or composition of matter)? If no, the claim does not involve an eligible subject matter under Section 101. If yes, the second question, which is the first part of the *Mayo* test, is whether the claim is directed to a law of nature, natural phenomenon or an abstract idea? If no, the claim is patent eligible under Section 101. If yes, the final question in this context, which constitutes part two of the *Mayo* test, is, does the claim recite some additional elements that amount to significantly more than the judicial exceptions? If yes, the claim involves a patent—eligible subject matter. If no, the claim fails under Section 101.

Asking the above questions in relation to Alice's claims, the court was of the view that the claims satisfactorily passed the first preliminary question. However, it was the *Mayo* test that the claims failed to satisfy. When the court examined Alice's claims, it found them indistinguishable from the business method claims in *Bilski*. Starting with the first part of the Mayo test, the court found that the use of a third party to mitigate risk settlement 'Like the risk hedging in Bilski, the concept of intermediated settlement is "a fundamental economic practice long prevalent in our system of commerce." '[47] Consequently, the court found that Alice's claims were directed to an abstract idea. Turning to the second part of the *Mayo* test, the court queried whether the claims contain something significantly more than the said abstract idea, namely an inventive concept that transforms the claimed abstract idea into a patentable subject matter? Applying the *Mayo* rationale, the court explained that merely providing steps known in the art, specified at a high level of generality, was not sufficient to constitute an 'inventive concept' for that purpose.

The court's conclusion regarding the failure of Alice's claims to satisfy the second part of the Mayo test was also supported by its finding that the claims did not solve any technological problem[48] or improve the internal working of a computer.

---

[45] Ibid, 2355.   [46] Ibid.   [47] Ibid.
[48] As was the case in *Diamond v. Diehr* 450 U.S. 175, 209 USPQ 1 (1981)

Rather, the court noted that the claims recited nothing more than a generic computer implementation of the covered abstract idea. This was so whether or not the said steps were considered separately or as a combination.

Post Alice: the current position It is clear that the effect of *Alice* on the landscape of software-related patents, and in particular business methods patents, was gargantuan. In fact, when *Alice* was before CAFC and before it was heard by the Supreme Court, Justice Moore predicted dire consequences to portfolios of such patents if Alice's patents would be invalidated on the grounds of the abstract idea exclusion. He stated: 'And let's be clear: if all of these claims, including the system claims, are not patent-eligible, this case is the death of hundreds of thousands of patents, including all business method, financial system, and software patents as well as many computer-implemented and telecommunications patents.'[49]

It became clear immediately after the Supreme Court decision in *Alice* that the legal position on software and business methods patents changed markedly. For example, in the immediate period after the Supreme Court's decision, between 1 July and 15 August 2014, 830 software-related patent applications were withdrawn from the US PTO.[50] Jasper Tran conducted an empirical analysis of the post-*Alice* landscape two years after the decision. He noted:

> As of June 19, 2016, courts have examined 568 challenged patents brought under § 101 motions citing Alice, resulting in 190 valid patents and 378 patents invalidated with an average invalidation rate of 66.5%. Specifically, the Federal Circuit upheld 3 patents and invalidated 34 patents—an average invalidation rate of 91.9%. Also, courts have decided a total of 500 motions brought under § 101 citing Alice, resulting in 109 validation holdings and 391 invalidation holdings with an average invalidation rate of 78.2%. Specifically, the Federal Circuit has decided 26 motions, resulting in 2 validation holdings and 24 invalidation holdings with an average invalidation rate of 92.3%. The district courts have decided 251 motions, resulting in 84 validation holdings and 167 invalidation holdings with an average invalidation rate of 66.5%. The PTAB has decided 209 motions, resulting in 23 validation holdings and 186 invalidation holdings with an average invalidation rate of 89.7%.[51]

---

[49] *CLS Bank Int'l v. Alice Corp. Pty. Ltd* 717 F.3d 1269 (Fed. Cir. 2013), 1313.
[50] T Le Coz and C Duan, 'Apply it to the USPTO: review of the implementation of *Alice v. CLS Bank* in patent examination' (2014) 1 Patently-O Patent L. J. 3.
[51] J L Tran, 'Two years after *Alice v. CLS Bank*' (20 June 2016) 98 *Journal of the Patent and Trademark Office Society* 354.

6.1 Computer-Implemented Inventions

At the time of writing, the CAFC issued only three post-Alice opinions upholding patent eligibility of software-related inventions.[52]

The patent at stake in DDR Holdings related to 'systems and methods of generating a composite web page that combines certain visual elements of a 'host' website with content of a third-party merchant'.[53] Answering the first Alice question negatively, the court concluded that the patent in question did not claim the performance of an abstract business practice and therefore did not attempt to claim an abstract idea. This being so, there was no need to continue to the second prong of the Alice test and examine whether the invention included an 'inventive concept' sufficient to 'transform' the abstract idea into a patentable invention. Key to the court's finding was its conclusion that the claimed e-commerce solution did not have any offline real-world equivalent. That fact allowed the court to distinguish it from its earlier post-Alice decisions, all of which applied Alice finding software-related invention to be patent ineligible.[54]

In *Enfish* the CAFC was required to assess patent eligibility of two patents, which were 'directed to an innovative logical model for a computer database, . . . [that] includes all data entities in a single table, with column definitions provided by rows in that same table . . . as the 'self-referential' property of the database'. The district court found that the claimed process was an abstract idea of storing, organizing, and retrieving memory in a logical table. Overturning this decision, the CAFC concluded that the claimed 'self-referential' database software did not constitute an abstract idea within the meaning of *Alice*. After stressing that claims directed to software are not inherently abstract and therefore do not always necessitate analysis under the second step of the *Alice*, the CAFC explained that in the case at hand the claimed software contributed to improvements in computer functionality such as improving the way a computer stores and retrieved data in memory. This being so, the claimed software did not constitute an abstract idea and, therefore, there was no need to examine it under the second step of *Alice*. Thus, the invention was patent eligible. The case makes it clear that claims directed to software per se are not inherently abstract, even in the absence of specific physical components. This is especially the case where the claimed software improves the internal operation of a computer, such as providing faster search times and smaller memory requirements.

---

[52] *DDR Holdings, LLC v. Hotels.com, L.P.* 773 F.3d 1245 (Fed. Cir. 2014); *Enfish, LLC v. Microsoft Corp*, No. 2015-1244, 2016 WL 2756255 (Fed. Cir. 12 May 2016); *BASCOM Global Internet Services, Inc. v. AT&T Mobility LLC*, No. 2015-1763, 2016 WL 3514158 (Fed. Cir. June 27, 2016).

[53] See 773 F.3d 1245 (Fed. Cir. 2014).

[54] Judge Mayer's strong dissent should be noted in this case, as it appears that in addition to the merit of each case, the judicial panel's composition also plays its part in the case's outcome.

Just over a month after *Enfish*, the CAFC issued another decision in *BASCOM* upholding patent eligibility of a software-related invention.

In *BASCOM* the court was concerned with an invention that related to a 'system for filtering Internet content'. At the district court, the invention was found to be patent ineligible since the claims were directed to the abstract idea of 'filtering content'. According to the district court this was so since the content provided on the Internet was essentially not different from content provided offline such as in films, magazines, books and television. Turning to the second step of the *Alice* test, the district court concluded that the limitations at issue, either in isolation or in combination, were non-inventive since they consisted of well-known, generic computer components or a standard filtering mechanism. Thus, the claims did not contain something 'extra' that transformed them into patent-eligible matter. On appeal, the CAFC rejected the district court's conclusion regarding the second step of *Alice*. The court held that the claimed specific arrangement or combination of conventional and generic features constituted an inventive concept. The court explained that the claims did not merely recite the abstract idea of filtering content along with the requirement to perform it on the Internet, but instead were directed to a technology-based solution to filter content on the Internet in a manner that solved existing problems with prior art filtering systems. Distinguishing the case from numerous post-*Alice* decisions in which the CAFC found patent-ineligibility on the basis of the second *Alice* step, the court explained that the claims at issue:

> do not preempt the use of the abstract idea of filtering content on the Internet or on generic computer components performing conventional activities, [but] carve out a specific location for the filtering system (a remote ISP server) and require the filtering system to give users the ability to customize filtering for their individual net work accounts.[55]

At that point of time, any enthusiasm about the CAFC's rekindled patent-friendly leaning was short lived.[56] On 30 September 2016, a differently composed CAFC[57] issued its decision in *Intellectual Ventures v. Symantec*, where exceptions to patentability under Section 101, as articulated in *Alice*, were read in Judge Mayer's concurring view more expansively than ever before.[58] The dispute concerned the validity of three patents relating to: 'Distributed Content

---

[55] *BASCOM Global Internet Services, Inc. v. AT&T Mobility LLC*, No. 2015-1763, 2016 WL 3514158, (Fed. Cir. 27 June 2016) 8.

[56] See *Intellectual Ventures I LLC v. Symantec Corp. and Trend Micro Incorporated et al.*, No. 2015-1769 (Fed. Cir. 30 September 2016).

[57] Before Dyk, Mayer, and Stoll, Circuit Judges.

[58] As expressed by Judge Mayer in his concurring opinion.

6.1 Computer-Implemented Inventions

Identification' (050 patent), 'Automated Post Office Based Rule Analysis of E-Mail Messages and Other Data Objects for Controlled Distribution in Network Environments' (142 patent), and 'Computer Virus Screening Methods and Systems' (610 patent). The district court found that while two of the three patents were invalid under Section 101, the remaining patent was valid. The CAFC affirmed the district court's ruling in relation to the said patents, and reversed in relation to the third one, thus finding all three patents to involve patent-ineligible subject matter under Section 101. In relation to the 050 patent, the court agreed with the district court that 'receiving e-mail (and other data file) identifiers, characterizing e-mail based on the identifiers, and communicating the characterization—in other words, filtering files/e-mail is an abstract idea'.[59] It found that 'the patent merely applied a well-known idea using generic computers 'to the particular technological environment of the Internet'.[60] Proceeding to the second step of *Alice*, the court referred to the Supreme Court judgment in *Alice* and stated that claims that 'amount to nothing significantly more than an instruction to apply [an] abstract idea [. . .] using some unspecified, generic computer' and in which 'each step does no more than require a generic computer to perform generic computer functions' do not make an abstract idea patent-eligible'.[61] After clarifying that any novelty embodied in the claimed process has no relevance to the patent-eligibility inquiry under Section 101, the court went on to establish that the patent at stake did not improve the functioning of a computer or computer technology. Thus, the claims of patent 050 were not patent eligible.

Similarly, the court found in relation to the claimed subject matter in patent 142 that 'the concept is well-known and abstract. Furthermore, with the exception of generic computer-implemented steps, there is nothing in the claims themselves that foreclose them from being performed by a human, mentally or with pen and paper.'[62] Turning to the second step in Alice, the court had little hesitation in finding that the patent did not involve an inventive concept since it did not 'improve the functioning of the computer itself', nor did it 'solve a 'challenge particular to the Internet'.[63]

Finally, turning to patent 610, which was held valid in the district court, the CAFC found the relevant claims therein to be directed to computer-implemented, well-understood, routine, and conventional activities previously known to the industry. Finding the relevant claims to be patent ineligible, the court stated:

> unlike the claims at issue in Enfish, which involved a 'specific type of data structure designed to improve the way a computer stores and retrieves data in memory',

---

[59] See *Intellectual Ventures I LLC v. Symantec Corp. and Trend Micro Incorporated et al.*, No. 2015-1769, (Fed. Cir. 30 September 2016) 8.
[60] Ibid, 10.   [61] Ibid, 11.   [62] Ibid, 17.   [63] Ibid, 18.

claim 7 of the '610 patent does not improve or change the way a computer functions. Nor does claim 7 overcome a problem unique to the Internet as was the case in DDR Holdings.[64]

It was Judge Dyk that gave the leading opinion. Although finding all three patents to be invalid under Section 101, this might be explained on the basis of the specific facts of the case. After all, throughout its post-Alice judgment, the court stressed that each of the said patents differed from those allowed by the CAFC in some of its post-Alice previous decisions. However, what is less reconcilable with some of these earlier decisions was the concurring opinion by Judge Mayer. After expressing his agreement with the rest of the court's finding that all the claims fell outside the scope of Section 101, Judge Mayer stressed two additional points: (i) patents constricting the essential channels of online communication run afoul of the First Amendment, and (ii) claims directed to software implemented on a generic computer are categorically not patent eligible.[65] The radical stance expressed in point (i) suggests that Internet patents which, by definition, restrict essential channels of scientific, economic, and political discourse, violate core First Amendment rights. Turning to software patents as a whole rather than only Internet—related patents, Judge Mayer states: 'Most of the First Amendment concerns associated with patent protection could be avoided if this court were willing to acknowledge that Alice sounded the death knell for software patents.'[66] Continuing his avid attack on software implemented on general computers, Judge Mayer further contended:

> Because generically implemented software is an 'idea' insufficiently linked to any defining physical structure other than a standard computer, it is a precursor to technology rather than technology itself . . . . It is well past time to return software to its historical dwelling place in the domain of copyright. Software development has flourished despite—not because of—the availability of expansive patent protection.[67]

In his advocacy for patent reform, Judge Mayer listed four fundamental problems he identified in relation to software patents: (i) their scope is generally vastly disproportionate to their technological disclosure; (ii) they provide incentives at the wrong time, since they are typically obtained at the 'idea' stage, before any real inventive work has been done; (3) their sheer number makes it virtually impossible to innovate in any technological field without being ensnared by the patent thicket; and (iv) generically implemented software invariably lacks the concrete borders that patent law demands since software is akin to a work of literature or

[64] Ibid, 23.   [65] Ibid, 1.   [66] Ibid, 6.   [67] Ibid.

a piece of music, being too unbounded (i.e. too 'abstract,' to qualify as a patent-eligible invention). At last, Judge Mayer completed his attack on patents relating to software implemented on general computers by opining that 'Declaring that software implemented on a generic computer falls outside of section 101 would provide much needed clarity and consistency in our approach to patent eligibility.'[68]

The decision in *Intellectual Ventures v. Symantec* muddied the software patent waters. If one was under the impression that the software patent-friendly CAFC decisions in *Enfish* and *BASCOM* may have signalled more ways for software patents to survive, *Intellectual Ventures v. Symantec* threw that into serious doubt. While, arguably, *DDR Holdings* and *Enfish* may be distinguishable on the facts, it is hard to see how *BASCOM* is essentially different. Thus, it is debatable whether performing BASCOM's 'abstract idea' remotely, 'on a specific location', in a manner that improves the operation of the Internet, should be sufficient to overcome the second step in *Alice*, while claim 7 of patent 610 alleged improvement of the telephone network and, as a consequence, improvement of a computer as tools, should not.[69] In fact, Judge Dyk's lack of sympathy to the *BASCOM* decision was thinly veiled.[70]

The post-*Alice* record of the CAFC makes it clear that the outcome of Section 101 assessment of software patents is not only a consequence of the manner in which the claims were drafted and the subject matter claimed, but also dependent on the composition of the CAFC.[71] At present it appears that while some circuit judges are more generous in their interpretation of *Alice*, others clearly demonstrate a stricter approach.[72]

Notwithstanding such discrepancy between some of the CAFC judges and panels, it could be concluded that at present the emerging jurisprudence of the CAFC suggests that claims directed to broad, high-level functionality rather than

---

[68] Ibid, 13.
[69] See Judge Stoll's dissenting view at 5, where he argues the claims under patent 610 are patent-eligible for the same reasons as in *BASCOM*.
[70] For example, although the decision of CAFC in *BASCOM* established that the claims at issue improved an existing technical process and solved a technical problem, Judge Dyk appears to be less convinced. In *Intellectual Ventures v. Symantec*, he is referring to BASCOM's *alleged* improvement of a technological process and to BASCOM's solution of an *alleged* technical problem; see 13 and 23, respectively.
[71] Approximately one month after *Intellectual Ventures v. Symantec*, a split panel of the CAFC found in favour of patent eligibility in relation to patents that concern the solving of accounting and billing problems faced by network service providers in *Amdoc (Israel) Ltd v. Openet Telecom, Inc*. No. 15-1180 (Fed. Cir. 1 November 2016). The CAFC reversed the decision of the lower court and found that the patent claims at issue, to the extent that they were directed to an abstract idea, nevertheless contained sufficient inventive concept to render them patent eligible—thus successfully passing the *Alice* test.
[72] It appears that Judges Dyk, Mayer, Wallach, and Hughes more often than not adopt a tougher stance on patent eligibility under Section 101.

reciting details about how exactly that functionality is to be implemented, while providing little information about the structure of the software, stand little chance to satisfy Section 101.

6.2 COMPUTER-IMPLEMENTED INVENTIONS AT THE EUROPEAN PATENT OFFICE

6.2.1 Background

Regardless of its name, the EPO is distinct from EU institutions, with the European Patent Convention (EPC)[73] being an intergovernmental treaty.[74] Once the EPC comes into force in a signatory state, the domestic patent legislation is amended and modelled on the EPC (in particular the rules on patentability and validity). The EPC provides a legal framework for the granting of European patents, via a single, harmonized procedure before the EPO.[75] A single patent application may be filed at the EPO at Munich, at its branch at The Hague or at a national patent office of a Contracting State, if the national law of the State so permits.

As mentioned, issues of validity and patent eligibility are currently decided both at the EPO level, in relation to European patents, and at domestic level, in relation to national patents. Although decisions of the EPO are not strictly binding on national patent offices, they are highly persuasive. Thus, although deviations from the EPO line on patent eligibility are possible, they are rare.[76] The ensuing discussion therefore focuses on the jurisprudence of the EPO.

Article 52 stipulates the general patentability requirements under the EPC. It reads: 'European patents shall be granted for any inventions, in all fields of technology, provided that they are new, involve an inventive step and are susceptible of

---

[73] Convention on the Grant of European Patents (European Patent Convention), of 5 October 1973, as revised by the Act revising Article 63 EPC of 17 December 1991 and the Act revising the EPC of 29 November 2000.

[74] In terms of membership, it is also distinct, with signatory states of the EPC comprising EU Member States, plus Switzerland, Liechtenstein, Turkey, Monaco, San Marino, Serbia, Norway, Former Yugoslav Republic of Macedonia, Iceland, and Albania.

[75] It is noteworthy that the EPO grants a bundle of national patents, rather than a pan European patent (as in the case of a Community Trademark), although the setting up of the European Unitary Patent system will enable supranational protection for inventions in 26 countries across Europe; see http://www.epo.org/law-practice/unitary.html.

[76] One example is the United Kingdom's continuing adherence to the so-called contribution approach, many years after the EPO has discarded it. Notwithstanding, the actual effect of that difference is not significant in most cases; for a detailed discussion on the difference between the EPO and UK approaches on exclusions to patentability, see N Shemtov, 'The characteristics of technical character and the ongoing saga at the EPO and the English courts' (2009) 4(7) J. Intell. Prop. L. & Prac.

industrial application.'[77] It then provides a list of subject matters that are excluded from the definition of 'Invention' under the EPC; these include: '[. . .] mathematical methods [. . .] [78]schemes, rules and methods for performing mental acts, playing games or doing business, and programs for computers[79] [. . .] presentations of information'.[80] Finally it provides that the said exclusions 'shall exclude the patentability of the subject-matter or activities referred to therein only to the extent to which a European patent application or European patent relates to such subject-matter or activities as such'.[81]

6.2.2 Trends and case-law development

Article 52 provides that patent applications comprising claims directed to one of the excluded subject matters are excluded from patentability as 'non-inventions'. However, it goes on to provide that such exclusions apply only to the extent that the claims at issue are directed to one of the excluded subject matters *as such*. It was for the EPO to determine the circumstances and the legal test under which an excluded subject matter is considered to be claimed 'as such'.

6.2.2.1 *The contribution approach*

The starting point of the present discussion is the Technical Board of Appeal landmark decision in *Vicom*.[82] This case concerned claims directed to a method of digitally filtering a two-dimensional data array (representing stored image) and to an apparatus, which may be a general-purpose computer, for carrying out that method. The Technical Board of Appeal stipulated that an invention is patentable if it satisfies the normal requirements for patentability under the EPC and should not be prejudiced against simply because its implementation requires modern technical means in the form of a computer program. The Board then went on to state that 'decisive is what *technical contribution* the invention as defined in the claim when considered as a whole makes to the known art' (my emphasis). This later became known as the 'technical-contribution approach'. According to the said approach, when examining a patent application one should disregard the form or kind of claim and concentrate on its content in order to identify the real contribution, which the subject matter claimed, considered as a whole, adds to the known art. Thus, the examiner was required to identify the contribution made to the state of the art by the claimed subject matter and then to evaluate whether that contribution lay exclusively within one of the excluded areas of Article 52(2)

---

[77] Art. 52(1), pp 506–14. [78] Art. 52(2)(a). [79] Art. 52(2)(c).
[80] Art. 52(2)(d). [81] Art. 52(3).
[82] *Vicom/Computer – Related Inventions* [1987] OJ EPO 14; (1986) T208/84, [1987] 2 EPOR 74, para. 16.

(e.g. method of doing business). Where that was the case, the excluded subject matter was considered as being claimed 'as such', the application labelled as relating to a non-invention and therefore rejected. Whether or not the claims at issue were drafted by reference to technical equipment and/or environment was of no relevance, and such drafting could not imbue the claims with the requisite technical character and contribute towards a finding of technical contribution. Up to the *Pension Benefit* decision that is discussed below, the so-called contribution approach was considered as the prevailing legal test for evaluating patent eligibility in relation to excluded subject matters under Article 52.[83]

6.2.2.2 The 'any-hardware' approach

The first clear break from the so-called technical-contribution approach took place in the *Pension Benefit*[84] decision. In this case the objection raised by the EPO was that the claims in the application related to a computer-implemented method of doing business, one of the categories excluded from patentability by Article 52(2) EPC. The examining division maintained that since the contribution that the claimed subject matter made to the known art was solely within the 'business' field, this contribution was to be regarded as non-technical and the application was to be refused as a non-invention under Article 52(2). However, on appeal the Board rejected the application of the so-called contribution approach. In the Board's view, this approach confused the requirement of 'invention' with the requirements of 'novelty' and 'inventive step', since it compared the invention with the prior art and sought to identify the difference between the two. Consequently, the Board agreed with the appellant that the contribution approach was not appropriate for deciding whether an application relates to an invention for the purposes of Article 52(1) EPC. The Board went on to state that:

> In the Board's view a computer system suitably programmed for use in a particular field, even if that is the field of business and economy, has the character of a concrete apparatus in the sense of a physical entity, man-made for a utilitarian purpose and is thus an invention within the meaning of Article 52(1) EPC.[85]

Thus, rather than asking what type of contribution the subject matter is making to the state of the art, one should ask whether the claimed subject matter, as a whole, manifests a technical character. Consequently, a computer system must be regarded as a concrete technical apparatus rather than a non-technical method for doing business as such (which is excluded from patentability). In the Board's

---

[83] For example, the contribution was followed in *Koch and Sterzel/X-Ray Method for Optimum Exposure* (1987) T26/86; *IBM/Text Processing* (1988) T 115/85; *BM/Data Processor Network* (1988) T6/83.
[84] *Pension Benefit Systems* (T931/95) OJ EPO 441.   [85] Ibid, point 5.

6.2 Computer-Implemented Inventions

view, the fact that the said computer system was simply a general-purpose computer programmed to execute a business method was irrelevant for assessment under Article 52.

Interestingly, while the apparatus claims in *Pension Benefit Systems* were found by the Board to constitute an invention within the meaning of Article 52(1), the method claims were not. This was so since they literally corresponded to the 'method-of-doing-business' exclusion. However, in the end of the day the said apparatus claims did not fare much better. The Board held that where the contribution to the state of the art is made exclusively within an excluded field then, by definition, such contribution does not possess a technical character. Such non-technical contribution is therefore not to be taken into consideration when making an inventive step assessment under Article 56. Consequently, the Board was of the view that the said non-technical contribution should be considered as part of the state of the art, irrespective of whether or not it was in fact obvious to the person skilled in the art. As the non-technical contribution to the state of the art was not taken into consideration, the remaining features, beside the said contribution, were found to be obvious to the skilled person and hence the application was rejected.

The trend started in *Pension Benefit* was later extended in *Hitachi*.[86] Here too the 'technical-contribution approach' was rejected as inappropriate for assessment under Article 52. The Technical Board of Appeal stated that since, following *Pension Benefits*, apparatus claims in the case of computer-implemented inventions may not be caught by Article 52(2),[87] the corresponding method claims, likewise, should not be excluded where they involve technical means, even if such methods contribute solely to an excluded field. However, as in *Pension Benefit*, both types of claims failed under Article 56, since once the inventive but non-technical features were not taken into consideration in the Board's assessment of inventive step, the claims were found to be obvious.[88] The approach in *Hitachi* was further developed in *Microsoft*,[89] where the Board stated:

> [...] the claim category of a computer-implemented method is distinguished from that of a computer program. Even though a method, in particular a method of operating a computer, may be put into practice with the help of a computer program, a claim relating to such a method does not claim a computer program in the category of a computer program.

---

[86] *Auction Method/HITACHI* (T 258/03) [2004] OJ 2004, 575.
[87] Being physical entities, they manifest a technical character.
[88] That is, in both cases, the part concerning the excluded area was taken to form part of the state of the art for assessing inventive step.
[89] *MICROSOFT/Data Transfer* (T424/03) [2006] 40 EPOR 533.

Thus, such a claim is not directed to a computer program 'as such' and is not excluded as non-invention under Article 52.

Moreover, the Board in *Microsoft* went on to hold:

> Claim 5 is directed to a computer-readable medium having computer-executable instructions (i.e. a computer program) on it to cause the computer system to perform the claimed method. The subject-matter of claim 5 has technical character since it relates to a computer- readable medium, i.e. a technical product involving a carrier [...] Moreover, the computer executable instructions have the potential of achieving the above-mentioned further technical effect of enhancing the internal operation of the computer, which goes beyond the elementary interaction of any hardware and software of data processing.[90]

Interestingly, while relying on *Hitachi* and *Pension Benefit* to rule that both the method and the apparatus claims have the requisite technical effect in order to constitute an invention, the Board did not follow these decisions in its assessment of novelty and inventive step and took into consideration all aspects of the claimed subject matter.

Thus, under the *Microsoft/Data Transfer* approach, only the code constituting the program was excluded from patentability for being a computer program 'as such', while code as embodied in a physical medium which causes the computer to operate accordingly had a clear technical effect and therefore was neither excluded from patentability nor did it form part of the state of the art for the purpose of Article 56. Hence, although the contribution made by the invention to the state of the art was exclusively to the manner in which a computer operated, arguably, an excluded field under Article 52, such internal technical effect was acknowledged for the purpose of Article 56 and was not artificially taken to form part of the state of the art.

The EPO jurisprudence described above, which later became known as the 'any-hardware approach', provides that where the claim involves the use of any piece of physical hardware, whether or not commonplace, Article 52(2) does not apply. However, only technical features could be taken into account for an assessment made under Article 56 for an inventive step. Hence, where the differences between the invention and the closest prior art are wholly non-technical (namely, relating to non-technical activities listed under Article 52 such as method of doing business or a method for performing a mental act), an objection under Article 56 is likely to succeed.[91] This is so since the subject matter of a claim cannot involve an inventive

---

[90] Ibid, 5.3.

[91] However, it is noteworthy that non-technical features that interact with the technical subject matter of the claim for solving a technical problem may be taken into account for assessment of inventive step in formulating the problem to be solved (see *COMVIK/Two Identities* (T641/00) [2004] EPOR 10, reaffirmed in *Classification Method/COMPTEL* (T 1784/06) [2012]).

6.2 Computer-Implemented Inventions

step where there is no technical contribution to the state of the art or no technical problem solved by the claimed subject matter. This approach was subsequently confirmed by later boards of appeal,[92] as well as by the Enlarged Board of Appeal.[93]

Shifting the focus of investigation for the presence for excluded matter from Article 52 to Article 56 has been described as 'The Lord Giveth, the Lord Taketh away.'[94] Thus, although an application may be allowed to pass the Article 52 hurdle with relative ease, the ultimate question of only allowing claims that involve inventive technical features is still faced by the applicant under Article 56. In fact, both the contribution approach and the any-hardware approach have been described by the UK Court of Appeal as leading to the same outcome in the vast majority of cases, since the underlying question in both cases is the same.[95]

It is submitted that the abovementioned 'formula' by which the EPO resolves questions relating to compliance with Articles 52 and 56 in the case of computer-implemented inventions is fairly clear and its outcome could be predicted with reasonable certainty. What is sometimes less clear and predictable while applying this formula is the concept of *technicality*.

A technical effect for the purpose of patentability assessment can be either 'external' or 'internal'. Simply put, 'external' technical effect occurs where software controlling hardware makes something happen better in the real world. Examples of such 'external' technical effect could be the processing of physical data parameters or control values of an industrial process, such as voice/audio codecs. Such technical effect has been recognized for many years at the EPO as an improvement over the state of the art that merits patent protection. The EPO, however, also acknowledges 'internal' technical effect for the purpose of patentability assessment. Such 'internal' technical effect occurs where the program makes something happen better in the computer itself or its interfaces. Examples for such technical effect could be seen where the program at issue affects the efficiency or security of a process, the management of computer resources required or the rate of data transfer in a communication link.[96]

Subject to the abovementioned general principles, on occasions the EPO was prepared to stretch the scope of the term *technical* to encompass subject matter which it felt merits patent protection. In *Circuit Simulation/Infeneon Technologies*,[97] the patent application concerned a computer-implemented simulation or a modelling method for testing the performance of an integrated circuit under the influence of a

---

[92] For example, *DUNS LICENSING ASSOCIATES/ESTIMATING SALES ACTIVITY* (T154/04) [2007] E.P.O.R. 38.
[93] G 3/08. [94] See *Aerotel Ltd v. Telco Holdings Ltd & Ors Rev* 1 [2006] EWCA Civ. 1371, 28.
[95] *Symbian Ltd v. Comptroller General of Patents* [2008] EWCA Civ. 1066, para. 11.
[96] See EPO Guidelines for Examiners, G.II 3.6. [97] T 1227/05 [2007] OJ EPO 574.

1/f noise. It was based on a mathematical formula that generated random numbers that produced an exact 1/f noise into the simulation. The claimed method required shorter computing time and less storage space in designing integrated circuits. Thus, the claimed method made it possible to simulate noisy circuits on smaller computer systems, which were previously not powerful enough for that purpose, or to simulate large circuits, which previously could not have been simulated on any computer system whatsoever. After concluding that the application complied with Article 52, the Board went on to find that the claimed method, which comprised a mathematical method implemented in a computer program, involved a further technical effect since its outcome allowed a realistic prediction of the performance of a designed circuit and therefore allowed it to be developed accurately so that a prototype's chance of success could be assessed before it was built. At this point the Board turned to discuss the importance of computer-implemented simulation methods for virtual trails. In the Board's view, such methods are a practical part of the electrical engineer toolkit, rather than being a purely mathematical theory or a mental act. For this reason, the Board held that all steps relevant to the circuit simulation, including the mathematically expressed claim features, contributed to the technical character of the claimed subject matter. Obviously, this finding proved crucial for the assessment of inventive step.[98]

6.3 CONVERGENCE OF THE PRESENT APPROACHES IN THE UNITED STATES AND EUROPEAN PATENT OFFICE

The position at the EPO has been consistent and fairly predictable for the last decade and a half. As mentioned, both internal and external technical effects are taken into consideration while the actual filter of computer-implemented inventions, whose contribution to the state of the art lays in non-technical activities such as method of doing business or method of performing a mental act, is Article 56 rather Article 52. Thus, owing to the 'formula' described above, it is the inventiveness hurdle that effectively 'filters out' non-technical subject matters as listed under Article 52, rather than Article 52 itself.

As we have seen, the position under US law went through significant changes in the last few years. As the empirical data mentioned above suggests, the scope of patentable subject matter in relation to computer-implemented inventions has narrowed markedly.

---

[98] For a more detailed discussion of this decision and the manner in which the Board's decision was informed by public policy considerations, see N Shemtov, 'The characteristics of technical character and the ongoing saga in the EPO and English Courts' (2009) 4 J. Intell. Prop. L. & Prac. 506.

6.3 Convergence of the Present Approaches

It is suggested that US law, or at the very least the CAFC, effectively aligned itself largely with the position endorsed by the EPO. First, it appears that similar to the EPO, the CAFC recognizes both improvements taking place internally and externally to the computer as patentable subject matter. While improvements taking place outside a computer were patentable since the early days of *Diamond v. Diehr*,[99] the post-*Alice* approach suggests that improvements taking place within a computer, computer network or other programmable apparatus may also be patentable.

As we have seen, when assessing a computer-implemented invention, the EPO will seek to determine what is 'technical' in the claimed invention. It is suggested that this is not un-similar to the first step of *Alice*, where a court will examine whether or not the claims are directed to an 'abstract idea', which is excluded from patentability. Where they are so directed, the application could be rescued if, and only if, there is something else in the claims that 'transforms' the nature of the claim to a patent-eligible subject matter. It is clear that routine implementation of such 'abstract idea' as a computer program or its 'computization' does not generate the requisite transformation. As we have seen, this is not unlike the position at the EPO where although non-technical features cannot contribute to inventive step, their interaction with technical features, such as technical implementation by non-obvious means, can.[100] In this sense, there is a 'parallel' between what is abstract in the United States and 'non-technical' at the EPO. As the scope of what may constitute 'abstract' in the United States and 'non-technical' at the EPO is far from clear, it is yet to be seen to what extent the two concepts overlap.[101]

In *I/P Engine, Inc. v. AOL, Inc.*, Judge Mayer observed: '*Alice* thus made clear that abstract ideas untethered to any significant advance in science and technology are ineligible for patent protection [...].[102] He further opined that the claimed system in *Alice* fell outside the scope of Section 101 since 'it did not improve the functioning of the computer itself or effect an improvement in any other technology or technical field'.[103] Thus, according to Judge Mayer *abstract* appears to mean *non-technical*. If such construction of *Alice* is to gain acceptance, the approaches in the United States and the EPO are likely to converge in a non-insignificant manner.

Another area of significance where some convergence could recently be seen relates to claim drafting by reference to the result to be achieved. Previously, so-called functional claiming, where applicants do not claim the machine itself, or the series of steps for achieving a goal but the goal itself, was prevalent in the

---

[99] *Diamond v. Diehr* 450 U.S. 175, 209 USPQ 1 (1981).   [100] See T 641/00, (Two identities/COMVIK).
[101] On its face, it appears that 'abstract idea' is a somewhat narrower category than 'non-technical'.
[102] *I/P Engine, Inc. v. AOL, Inc.* 576 Fed.Appx. 982 (Fed. Cir. 2014), Judge Mayer concurring opinion at I.
[103] Ibid.

United States.[104] Claims written in functional terms have the potential of enabling patentees to 'own' the function, irrespective of the mode of implementation. Such a broad monopoly may have significant anticompetitive effects.[105] However, it appears that US courts finally decided to clamp down on this practice. Thus, in *Nautilus v. Biosig*, the Supreme Court raised the standard of definiteness under 35 U.S.C. 112(b), requiring that the scope of patent claims be 'reasonably certain' to the person skilled in the art.[106] Hence, pure functional claiming, without corresponding 'structure' accompanying the claims in the specifications, may not provide the requisite 'reasonable certainty'. Indeed, the CAFC appears to have begun to apply this approach to computer-implemented inventions. In *Eon Corp. v. AT&T Mobility*, the CAFC clearly indicated that reciting the structure of a computer-implemented invention, claimed in functional terms, to be a 'computer' would simply not do.[107] The CAFC explained:

> A general purpose computer is flexible it can do anything it is programmed to do. Therefore, the disclosure of a general purpose computer or a microprocessor as corresponding structure for a software function does nothing to limit the scope of the claim and 'avoid pure functional claiming'. As such, when a patentee invokes means-plus- function claiming to recite a software function, it accedes to the reciprocal obligation of disclosing a sufficient algorithm as corresponding structure.

Hence, since the disclosed microprocessor in the claims at issue did not provide the requisite structure, Eon's patents were invalidated.

At the EPO an applicant needs to comply with Article 83 and disclose the invention in a manner sufficiently clear and complete for it to be carried out by a person skilled in the art. Article 84 requires that the claims clearly define the matter for which protection is being sought. As regards inventions that are to be defined by reference to their result or benefit, the EPO's Guidelines for Examination provide:

> The area defined by the claims must be as precise as the invention allows. As a general rule, claims which attempt to define the invention by a result to be achieved should not be allowed [. . .]. However, they may be allowed if the invention either can only be defined in such terms or cannot otherwise be defined more precisely without unduly restricting the scope of the claims and if the result is one which

---

[104] This refers to the term *functional claiming* as its being used in the United States, especially in the context of 'means-plus-function' claims. At the EPO, functional claiming has a somewhat different meaning, where individual elements of the claim are described by function; for example, where a claim refers to 'means for resilient biasing' rather than to 'spring'. This is not considered as overall problematic, as it can still be clearly worked out what elements meet that requirement, that is, the claim is 'clear'.

[105] For a detailed discussion on functional claiming in software patents in the United States, see M Lemley, 'Software patents and the return of functional claiming' (12 October 2012) Stanford Public Law Working Paper No. 2117302, SSRN, https://ssrn.com/abstract=2117302.

[106] *Nautilus, Inc. v. Biosig Instruments, Inc.* 134 S.Ct. 2120 (2014).

[107] *Eon Corp. IP Holdings LLC v AT&T Mobility LLC* No. 14-1392 (Fed. Cir. 6 May 2015).

6.3 Convergence of the Present Approaches

can be directly and positively verified by tests or procedures adequately specified in the description or known to the person skilled in the art and which do not require undue experimentation.[108]

Thus, although it is possible to define an invention by reference to its result, it is necessary for it to be accompanied by a description of the relevant steps in a detailed enough fashion so that the skilled person, without undue burden, could put the invention into effect. Hence, merely reciting a general-purpose computer or a microprocessor together with the result to be achieved is clearly likely to contravene Article 84 EPC. However, defining the claim steps at some level of abstraction, without providing the actual mathematical algorithm, but describing enough of the process so the disclosure is clear under Article 84 and enabling under Article 83 should suffice.

This may be illustrated by an example.[109] Let us assume that we have an invention that relates to reducing power and bandwidth consumption in a Wi-Fi router that might receive packets including a packet header and data, the packet header indicating that it should be multicast or broadcast to all equipment connected to the Wi-Fi router (e.g. laptops, mobile phones, etc.). However a limited subset of the laptops and mobile phones may have a communication session with the Wi-Fi router to say that they are the only ones that want certain kinds of data so that the Wi-Fi router can strip off the 'multicast' header and replace it with a 'unicast' header just for equipment that has requested that kind of data (e.g. video data). As a result, the bandwidth consumption and power consumption of the individual devices is reduced.

The description of a patent directed to such invention would have to give enough detail of how this was achieved and might have to go into a bit more detail about the protocols, algorithms and so forth. However, both in Europe and the United States, a relevant claim might have the following basic components: a wireless network equipment (router); configured to receive an incoming packet having a header and data; configured to remove the header if it is a multicast header and replace it with a unicast header; depending on criteria set by the equipment.

Thus, although a mathematical algorithm is not being claimed, neither is the actual result or benefit (reduction of power/better use of bandwidth)—as might be the case with pure functional claiming.[110] Rather, such claim defines the functional features and steps that give rise to the benefit. Putting aside issues pertaining to novelty and inventive step, such a claim could prove allowable at both the EPO and the United States PTO.

---

[108] Guidelines for Examination, F.IV 4.10.
[109] I am very grateful to Gwilym Roberts, a leading UK and EPO patent attorney, partner, and Chairman of Kilburn & Strode Patent Attorneys, for sharing with me his thoughts and invaluable experience in this field.
[110] Referring to *functional claiming* in the sense used in the US.

7

PROTECTING USER INTERFACES

7.1. Copyright Protection Over 'Look-and-Feel' Elements	190
7.1.1 GUI protection under US copyright law	190
7.1.2 Look-and-feel protection under EU law	193
7.2. Trade-Mark, Trade-Dress, and Unfair-Competition Protection For GUIs	195
7.2.1 United States: trade-mark and trade-dress protection to GUIs	196
7.2.1.1 *Rules on eligibility and scope of protection*	196
7.2.1.2 *Applying the rules*	202
7.2.2 European Union: trade-mark protection for GUIs	203
7.2.2.1 *Distinctiveness*	203
7.2.2.2 *Functionality*	204
7.2.2.3 *Infringement*	206
7.2.3 A brief note on unfair-competition laws in the European Union	206
7.3. Design Patents and Registered Designs	207
7.3.1 Design patents in the United States	208
7.3.1.1 *Eligibility*	208
7.3.1.2 *Infringement*	210
7.3.2 Registered designs in the European Union	211
7.3.2.1 *Eligibility*	211
7.3.2.2 *Infringement*	213
7.4. A Brief Note on Patent Protection for GUIS	214
7.4.1 Utility-patent protection in the United States for GUIs	214
7.4.2 Protecting GUIs at the EPO	216

But for the breakthrough innovators of the 21st century, design has moved onto a much larger stage. It is where high function meets high style. And the traditional disciplines of IP—patents, trade-marks and copyrights—are no longer ends unto themselves but are now viewed as component parts of a larger whole. This 'design in the large' is driving new business strategies and success as never before, as leading-edge companies harness the power of converging IP disciplines to deliver

Chapter 7   Protecting User Interfaces   189

brands, inventions and content that differentiate not just their products in the market, but the companies themselves.[1]

'With a familiar Ribbon-style interface, Corel® Office looks like the office software you're used to, making it easy to get to work right away.'[2] Should a competitor be able to appropriate the look and feel of a competing product's graphical user interface (GUI), as exemplified in this ad by Corel?[3] During the last decade or so, computerized devices developed significant capabilities to process, manipulate, and store information.[4] Obviously, such capabilities would be of little benefit if users could not access and make use of them with ease. Thus, market actors in this area made large investments in developing GUIs that would enable users to do just that and, in so doing, render their device, their software or their service more appealing to consumers. A manufacturer would often use a similar if not identical GUI across a variety of devices, so that users become accustomed to its 'look and feel', which helps in building consumers' loyalty to that particular manufacturer.[5] The investment in developing GUIs is primarily protected through intellectual property laws. As GUIs are more often than not both functional and ornamental, their protection poses a particular challenge to our intellectual property regime. This chapter examines the scope of such protection.

Considering the term *look and feel* in the context of this chapter, the 'look' aspect of this term encompasses features such as layout, typeface, and colour, while the 'feel' aspect comprises dynamic behavioural elements such as buttons and menus. GUIs were defined by the CJEU as 'interaction interface which enable communication between the computer program and the user'.[6] Most user interfaces, whether touch screen-based or otherwise, involve GUIs whose importance to the success or failure of a software product could not be overestimated.[7] Various intellectual property rights play different roles in protecting GUIs and software products' look and feel: trade-marks, unfair-competition laws, design rights, copyright, and patents. This chapter will explore the scope of protection to which GUIs may be eligible under the abovementioned sets of rights. As we shall see, perhaps surprisingly,

---

[1] D Kappos, 'The new frontier of intellectual property' (2012) NLJ, April, https://www.cravath.com/files/Uploads/Documents/Publications/3407702_1.pdf (Accessed 2 June 2016). Mr Kappos is the former undersecretary of Commerce for Intellectual Property and Director of the United States Patent and Trademark Office (USPTO) from 2009 to 2013, and former vice-president for Intellectual Property for IBM.

[2] Part of Corel's advertising, as referred to in Microsoft's claim against Coral, filed in the Northern District Court of California on 28/12/2015; see http://www.protectingdesigns.com/images/Nguyen-2015-12-28-microsoft/2015-12-28-microsoft-v-corel.pdf.

[3] With the ongoing move towards a cloud environment, the only software element that a competitor may have access to is the user interface, as the code itself is not distributed to the user. Thus, it is the interface that is becoming most susceptible to imitators.

[4] In particular, portable devices.   [5] For example, see Apple's GUI in its iPhone, iPod, and iPad.

[6] Case C-393/09 *Bezpečnostní softwarová asociace – Svaz softwarové ochrany v. Ministerstvo kultury* (2011) 3 ECDR 70.

[7] For example, a smartphone is entirely manipulated through its touchscreen, which has an overwhelming impact on the phone's popularity.

copyright is not necessarily the most effective vehicle for protection in this context, with either design rights or design patents being the most promising one.

7.1 COPYRIGHT PROTECTION OVER 'LOOK-AND-FEEL' ELEMENTS

Some may judge a user interface to be nothing more than a functional tool through which a user seeks to interact with a programmed device; viewed in this manner a GUI could be argued to be ineligible for copyright protection. On the other hand, others may convincingly maintain that such GUIs often represent both investment and creative effort and thus should, in principle, be eligible for copyright protection.

7.1.1 GUI protection under US copyright law

Arguments regarding the protectability of user interfaces in the United States usually relate to: '(1) look and feel; (2) selection and arrangement; and (3) individual elements of the interface, including icons and images'.[8] Such arguments are usually examined under the scope of Section 102(b), which iterates what is usually referred to as the idea expression dichotomy. It reads: 'in no case does copyright protection for an original work of authorship extend to any idea, procedure, process, system, method of operation, concept, principle, or discovery, regardless of the form in which it is described, explained, illustrated, or embodied in such work'.

In its early days, copyright protection for computer software appeared to encompass the overall user experience when using a program; thus, not only the look aspects of GUIs were protected, but also the 'feel' aspect. Hence, the Third Circuit in *Whelan v. Jaslow*[9] suggested that user experience in interacting with a program is not dissimilar to a book's plot, both eligible to copyright protection.[10] This somewhat simplistic and overly broad approach towards copyright protection, according to which the purpose or function of a utilitarian work is the work's idea and everything that is not necessary to that purpose or function would be part of the protected expression did not last long. Six years later, this approach was explicitly rejected by the Second Circuit in *Computer Associates v. Altai*.[11] Instead, the Second Circuit employed the so-called abstraction-filtration-comparison

---

[8] Michael J Schallop, 'Protecting user interfaces: not as easy as 1-2-3' (1996) 45 Emory L. J. 1533.

[9] *Whelan Associates, Inc. v. Jaslow Dental Laboratory, Inc.* 797 F.2d 1222, 1248 (3rd Cir. 1986).

[10] A practical approach to protection of graphical user interfaces in the United States of America, Intellectual Property Owners Association (White Paper prepared jointly by Software and Business Methods & Design Rights Committees 2008–2009), http://www.visiond.com/IPO2012/MATERIALS/Dougal_Durkin_Kirincich_Strand_GroupPaper.pdf (Accessed 10 May 2016) 42.

[11] *Computer Associates Intern., Inc. v. Altai, Inc.* 982 F.2d 693, 706 (2nd Cir. 1992).

7.1 Copyright Protection Over 'Look-and-Feel'

test (AFC test), as developed by Professor Melville Nimmer;[12] the court commented: 'Professor Nimmer suggests, and we endorsed, a "successive filtering method" for separating protectable expressions from non-protectable materials.'[13] As mentioned in Chapter 4, the AFC test requires a court, first to construct a hierarchy of abstractions for the allegedly infringed program and decide on the level of abstraction at which the alleged infringement took place, second to consider whether the software features at that level were protectable or not on the basis of whether they were (i) constrained by external factors such as the relevant hardware or software environment in which the program was to operate, (ii) dictated by efficiency considerations, or (iii) constrained by standard programming techniques or public domain elements. Third, the court is to compare the remaining 'core of protectable expression' of the original program with the allegedly infringing program and look for substantial similarities. Over the years, the AFC text became the prevalent criterion for assessing copyright protectability of software's non-literal elements amongst most circuits.[14] As we have seen, the application of the AFC test to a dispute involving a program's user interface was rejected in the First Circuit decision of *Lotus v. Borland*,[15] according to which the predominant question asked by the court should be whether the allegedly reproduced elements constitute one of the non-protectable subject matters under Section 102(b): idea, procedure, process, system, or method of operation. In that case, a GUI menu command hierarchy was held to be a non-protectable method of operation; there was therefore no need to engage in an AFC type of examination. It is suggested that on the basis this approach, a large number of GUI aspects are likely to be classified as non-protectable subject matters, as they are likely to constitute either one, some, or all of the following: procedure, process, system, or method of operation. Under the *Lotus* rationale, features of a format that is intended to enable a user to interact with a device are likely to be characterized as one of the members of the abovementioned list of non-protectable subject matters.[16]

We have seen that the Federal Circuit in *Oracle v. Google*[17] rejected the *Lotus* approach. In its critique of *Lotus*, the Federal Circuit opined, 'notably, no other

---

[12] For a more detailed discussion of the AFC test and its application in computer programs cases, see Chapter 5 in this text.

[13] *Computer Associates International, Inc. v. Altai*, Inc. 982 F.2d 693, 704 (2nd Circ. 1992).

[14] For example, the Tenth Circuit decision in *Mitel Inc. v. Iqtel, Inc.* 24 F.3d 1366 (10th Cir. 1997); the Federal Circuit decision in *Oracle America, Inc. v. Google, Inc.* No. 13-1021 (Fed. Cir. 2014)

[15] *Lotus Development Corporation v. Borland*, 49 F.3d 807 (1st Circ. 1995).

[16] This does not apply to GUI aspects that are mainly ornamental, such as the background in a video game. Such aspects are eligible for copyright protection as if they were created in the offline sphere.

[17] *Oracle Am., Inc. v. Google, Inc.* (2014) 750 F.3d 1339, 1364 (Fed. Cir.).

circuit has adopted the First Circuit's "method of operation" analysis'.[18] Although the *Oracle* decision concerned the copyright ability of APIs rather than that of GUIs, the principles established and elaborated upon in this decision are clearly applicable to scenarios involving GUIs. The Federal Circuit clarified that irrespective of the functionality of the interface at issue, or whether or not it later becomes an industry standard, the key question regarding copyright-eligibility in this context is whether the said interface or part thereof could be designed in other ways in order to achieve the same function. If the answer to this question is affirmative, then the said interface constitutes a protectable expression of a procedure, process, system, or method of operation. Citing with approval from the Tenth Circuit decision in *Mitel*, who expressly rejected the *Lotus* 'method-of-operation' analysis, in favour of the Second Circuit's AFC test, the Federal Circuit stressed that 'although an element of a work may be characterized as a method of operation, that element may nevertheless contain expression that is eligible for copyright protection'.[19] It is the fact that functionality considerations did not dictate the choices made by the author of the interface, in the sense of having a plethora of other design options that would achieve the same function, which renders such interface or part thereof a protectable expression. Thus, the Federal Court in Oracle stressed: '[. . .] *we conclude that a set of commands to instruct a computer to carry out desired operations may contain expression that is eligible for copyright protection*'.[20] It further suggested that if a GUI or any part thereof becomes an industry standard owing to post-design and creation circumstances, it may and should be taken into account in infringement contexts under a fair use analysis. Thus, although the defendant's wish to have its program easily interacted with by its users, who are already familiar with the claimant's GUI, may be irrelevant to copyright-eligibility analysis, such pro-competitive objective may prove significant in a fair use inquiry.

In conclusion, should the Oracle approach prove prevalent and be adopted across the different US circuits, disputes involving alleged infringement of GUIs could commence with an AFC analysis of the different features of the said GUI. Where such features are found not to be dictated by a certain hardware or software environment, efficiency considerations, standard programming techniques, etc., their eligibility to copyright protection would be established. Reproducing such features to a degree that results in substantial similarity between the defendant's and claimant's GUIs may give rise to a finding of prima facie infringement. At this point it would be for the defendant to convince the court that notwithstanding the above, the said reproduction constitutes fair use.

---

[18] Ibid, 1405.   [19] Ibid, 1404.   [20] Ibid, 1407.

7.1 Copyright Protection Over 'Look-and-Feel'

The fact that elements of the claimant's GUI may now be so popular that they effectively became an industry standard may be taken into consideration under such fair use inquiry.

A note of caution: what is not yet clear is to what extent courts would be prepared to consider dynamic behavioural aspects of GUIs as a protectable expression of one of the excluded subject matters under Section 102(b). Although single elements of GUIs, such as icons, may be protected as graphic works and a combination of such single elements may protected as a compilation, the GUI as a whole might be protected as an audio-visual work. In fact, the Ninth Circuit in *Apple v. Microsoft* explicitly recognized this to be the case. It commented that GUIs are very similar to 'videogames, which are audiovisual works' and that 'graphical user interface audiovisual works are subject to the same process of analytical dissection as are other works'.[21] However, although the 'look' aspect of such GUIs is eligible to copyright protection, it is questionable whether the more amorphous 'feel' aspect of it is similarly eligible to copyright protection.[22] As we shall see, where possible, such 'feel' aspects may be suitable for protection as trade dress, protectable designs, or utility patents.

7.1.2 Look-and-feel protection under EU Law

The legal position in the EU in relation to copyright eligibility of GUIs is somewhat more straightforward than that in the United States, owing to the CJEU decision in *BSA*.[23]

First, the CJEU found that a GUI is not protectable as a component part of a computer program under the Software Directive.[24] The court reasoned that the aim of the Software Directive is to provide protection to the 'expression in any form of a computer program which permits reproduction in different computer languages, such as the source code and the object code'.[25] It followed that since '[. . .] the [GUI] does not enable the reproduction of the computer program itself, but merely constitutes one element of that program by means of which users make use of the features of that program',[26] GUI do not constitute a form of protectable expression under the Software Directive.

---

[21] *Apple Computer, Inc. v. Microsoft Corp.* 35 F.3d 1435, 1445 (9th Cir. 1994).

[22] See e.g. R Stigler, 'Ooey GUI: the messy protection of graphical user interfaces' (2014) 12 Nw. J. Tech. & Intell. Prop. 215, 228 (arguing that 'while copyright protection once could have extended to the non-literal elements of a GUI, i.e. its "look", case law over the years has long abandoned protecting the "look and feel" of software graphics').

[23] *Bezpečnostní softwarová asociace–Svaz softwarové ochrany v. Ministry of Culture of the Czech Republic* C-393/09.

[24] Ibid. [25] Ibid, para. 35. [26] Ibid, para. 41.

This, however, does not mean that GUIs are not eligible to copyright protection in general. The CJEU explained that GUIs might be protected as an authorial work under the Information Society Directive. Addressing the copyright-eligibility question of GUIs or parts thereof under the Information Society Directive, the court stated: 'where the expression of those components is dictated by their technical function, the criterion of originality is not met, since the different methods of implementing an idea are so limited that the idea and the expression become indissociable'.[27] Thus, the court suggests that where functionality-related constrains may lead to a limited number of design options, any GUI element that results from such limited options may not be considered as an original expression as it does not spawn from the author's intellectual creation but rather from the said design constraints. Where, on the other hand, the design choices in the GUI at issue were not dictated by their technical function, a GUI might *'be protected by copyright if it is its author's own intellectual creation'*.[28]

It is suggested that many design choices made in the process of designing a GUI are not dictated by their technical function *stricto sensu* and might have a number of alternatives. Of course, this hinges on how one defines 'technical function' in this context. Say, for example, that *technical function* is defined as enabling a user to interact with a device for a particular purpose. Under such formulation, many choices may be considered as protectable original expression, as other alternatives for achieving the same overall function exist. In contrast, *technical function* could also be defined more narrowly: for example, as enabling the user to interact in the most user intuitive fashion, or by using only one hand, or in the quickest possible manner, etc. Defined in such a manner, many more design choices are likely to be considered as non-protectable elements, as the number of options for achieving such more restrictively defined objectives shrinks. Thus, the definition of the term 'technical function' at issue may have a considerable impact on the outcome of the copyright-eligibility inquiry established by the CJEU. In this regard the court merely said that it is for the national court to make this assessment.

Unlike the position in the United States, a defendant that reproduced GUI elements that are copyright-eligible, does not have a fair use defence to fall back on. As mentioned above, an argument that a certain GUI or a part of it became an industry standard and its reproduction, therefore, has a pro-competitive objective as users are now accustomed to it, may be taken into consideration under a fair use inquiry.[29] There is no fair use equivalent under EU copyright law. Conceptually,

---

[27] Ibid, para. 49. [28] Ibid, para. 46.

[29] On a GUI that becomes an industry standard, which may therefore justify its reproduction owing to pro-competition considerations, see Judge Boudin's concurring view in *Lotus v. Borland* on freeing Lotus customers who might be 'locked in' to Lotus owing to their familiarity with its menu, stating:

the closest pro-competition provision addressing the promotion of interaction, Article 6 of the Software Directive, relates to interaction between and interoperability of different pieces of software and not between software and a human being. Furthermore, being a provision of the Software Directive, Article 6 is not a part of the Information Society Directive.

7.2 TRADE-MARK, TRADE-DRESS, AND UNFAIR-COMPETITION PROTECTION FOR GUIS

The United States is unique in having a trade-mark system that is based on the first to use principle rather than first to file.[30] Its registered and unregistered[31] trade-mark protection frameworks operate in parallel, both governed under the Lanham Act.[32] Although Federal registration provides some clear strategic benefits, in the present context courts have largely treated the substantive inquiry into protectability of both registered and unregistered marks in a similar fashion. Therefore, most of the discussion concerning the United States will address jointly the laws of registered trade-marks and unfair competition. In this respect, the position in the European Union could not be more different. While the law of registered trade-marks is harmonized across the European Union, unfair-competition laws and laws protection against the appropriation of unregistered insignia are jurisdiction-specific and vary from one Member State to another. This being so, the main discussion on the legal position in the European Union would address GUI protection in relation to registered trade-marks, as a detailed discussion of the different laws of unfair competition across the EU goes beyond the scope of this title. The present part of this chapter concludes with a brief note on the position under some laws of unfair competition in the European Union.

But if a better spreadsheet comes along, it is hard to see why customers who have learned the Lotus menu and devised macros for it should remain captives of Lotus because of an investment in learning made by the users and not by Lotus. Lotus has already reaped a substantial reward for being first; assuming that the Borland program is now better, good reasons exist for freeing it to attract old Lotus customers: to enable the old customers to take advantage of a new advance, and to reward Borland in turn for making a better product. If Borland has not made a better product, then customers will remain with Lotus anyway. *Lotus Development Corporation v. Borland*, 49 F.3d 807 (1st Circ. 1995), para. 78.

[30] *United Drug Co. v. Theodore Rectanus Co.*, 248 U.S. 90, 97 (1918) (stating, 'The right to use a particular mark grows out of its use, not its mere adoption.').

[31] Sometimes referred to as unfair-competition law in the US context.

[32] Sections 2 and 32 govern register ability and protectability of registered trade marks, while Section 43(a) concerns unregistered insignia.

7.2.1 United States: trade-mark and trade-dress protection to GUIs

Trade dress has been described by the Supreme Court as follows: '[t]he "trade dress" of a product is essentially its total image and overall appearance', and '[i]t involves the total image of a product and may include features such as size, shape, colour or colour combinations, texture, graphics, or even particular sales techniques'.[33]

In order to prevail in a federal trade-dress violation action, a plaintiff is required to establish: (i) the inherent distinctiveness or secondary meaning of its trade dress, (ii) the essential non-functionality of its trade dress, and (iii) the likelihood of customer confusion as to its origin, sponsorship, or approval owing to similarity between its own and the defendant's trade dress.[34] For convenience purposes, eligibility for protection and infringement will be discussed separately below, and the outcome of this analysis will be applied to the individual aspects of GUIs: the desktop as a whole, the individual static components that comprise the desktop, and any transitional or animated features.[35]

7.2.1.1 *Rules on eligibility and scope of protection*

Trade-marks' primary function, whether registered or unregistered, is source identification or indication of origin. For the purpose of registration, such identifying insignia must also have sufficient specificity so it is capable of being described in a trade-mark application with sufficient clarity. One key hurdle for establishing eligibility for protection as trade dress is distinctiveness.

Distinctiveness When it comes to GUIs, one of the key questions in relation to distinctiveness is whether it is necessary in all instances to establish that a secondary meaning was acquired. A GUI is clearly part of a software product's trade dress. Although the Supreme Court appeared to suggest in *Two Pesos*[36] that both categories of trade dress (product design and product packaging) could be inherently distinctive, it subsequently came up with a more restrictive approach. Thus, in *Samara Brothers*, the Supreme Court held that unlike product packaging, product-design trade dress could never be classified as 'inherently distinctive'.[37]

---

[33] *Two Pesos, Inc. v. Taco Cabana, Inc.* 505 U.S. 763 (1992) 764.

[34] *Al-Site Corp. v. VSI Intern., Inc.* 174 F.3d 1308 (1999).

[35] For this distinction between the various aspects of a GUI, see *A Practical Approach to Protection of Graphical User Interfaces in the United States Of America, Intellectual Property Owners Association* (White Paper prepared jointly by Software and Business Methods & Design Rights Committees 2008-2009), http://www.visiond.com/IPO2012/MATERIALS/Dougal_Durkin_Kirincich_Strand_GroupPaper.pdf (Accessed 10 May 2016) 37.

[36] *Two Pesos, Inc. v. Taco Cabana, Inc.* (91-971), 505 U.S. 763 (1992).

[37] *Wal-Mart Stores, Inc. v. Samara Brothers, Inc.* 529 U.S. 205 (2000).

But does a GUI constitute a product design or product packaging trade dress? The answer is not clear-cut, as a GUI does not fall neatly into either of these categories.

Since following *Samara Brothers*, the rules as per each category are different, it is more likely that the courts will prefer to err towards the stricter category of product design. The implications of having to establish secondary meaning are quite significant, as the 'secondary-meaning' threshold is high. It essentially means that it would be up to the right owner to show that its GUI is so well known that consumers associate it with a particular source.[38] High protection threshold it may be, but as mentioned above it is clearly reachable where the product design in question is sufficiently known and serves as an indication of origin. Such was the case in *Tetris*, where, inter alia, the court found that the Tetris video game's user interface had in fact acquired such a secondary meaning, which ultimately led to the court's finding of federal trade-dress violation.[39]

Does this mean though that where a right holder with an inherently distinctive GUI, which did not yet gain the level of familiarity necessary in order to establish secondary meaning, remains defenceless against a competitor who reproduces its GUI or parts thereof? The Supreme Court in *Samara Brothers* suggested that the answer to this question is negative, although it may not lie within the realms of federal trade-dress law. The court suggested that such inherently distinctive product-design trade dress might be successfully protected under copyright law or as a design patent. The court explained:

> [T]he producer can ordinarily obtain protection for a design that is inherently source identifying (if any such exists), but that does not yet have secondary meaning, by securing a design patent or a copyright for the design—as, indeed, respondent did for certain elements of the designs in this case. The availability of these other protections greatly reduces any harm to the producer that might ensue from our conclusion that a product design cannot be protected under §43(a) without a showing of secondary meaning.[40]

This being so, a right holder of a product with a newly introduced GUI may rely on copyright and design patents until its GUI acquires a secondary meaning. Once secondary meaning is acquired, our right holder's offensive arsenal grows as he may now also look to the Lenham Act for protection of its GUI as protectable trade dress.

Infringement There are two types of infringement applicable to a Lenham Act violation in relation to trade marks or trade dress: confusion and dilution. Arguing

---

[38] This is usually established through consumer surveys.
[39] *Tetris Holding, LLC v. Xio Interactive, Inc.* 863 F.Supp.2d 394 (D.N.J. 2012).
[40] *Wal-Mart Stores, Inc. v. Samara Brothers, Inc.* 529 U.S. 205 (2000) 214.

confusion, a right holder is required to show that there is likelihood that owing to the infringer's use of GUI features, consumers will confuse the infringer's product with its own.[41] A dilution claim should prove rare in a GUI trade-dress context, as it is usually argued in relation to non-competing goods and therefore less likely to be relevant in the present context.[42]

On the issue of confusion, the court's assessment is no different from its evaluation of confusion in trade-mark cases in general.[43] For example, in *Tetris v. Xio*,[44] where the court was required to decide, inter alia, whether Xio infringed the trade dress of Tetris;[45] the court had little hesitation in finding that the requisite level of confusion was present. In *Baby Be Mine*,[46] the court engaged in a more detailed discussion of the confusion element in a trade-dress violation action in relation to the look and feel of a website. On the basis of the facts of the case, the court concluded that the look and feel of the defendant's website could produce a likelihood of confusion when compared to Baby Be Mine's website, and there existed substantial similarity between the two sites, as illustrated by screenshots entered into evidence.

When it comes to an action for trade-dress violation by dilution, the author of this title is not aware of a binding judicial opinion in this context in relation to the look and feel of GUIs. However, in principle there is no reason inherent to GUIs that should preclude such an action. In fact, this was the view expressed in *Apple v. Samsung* at the district court level,[47] before the Court of Appeals for the Federal Circuit (CAFC) overturned it. Although part of the trade dress at issue concerned the iPhone 3G and 3GS hardware, another part of it was described as follows: 'when the device is on, a row of small dots on the display screen, a matrix of colorful square icons with evenly rounded corners within the display screen, and

---

[41] Section 43(a)(1)(A) of the Lenham Act refers to the defendant's behaviour which 'is likely to cause confusion, or to cause mistake, or to deceive as to the affiliation, connection, or association [. . .] or as to the origin, sponsorship, or approval of his or her goods, services, or commercial activities by another person [. . .]'.

[42] In essence, there are two types of harm addressed by the dilution provision under Section 43(c) of the Lenham Act: (i) dilution by blurring (impairment of the mark's distinctiveness), namely reduction of the mark's capacity to designate a single commercial source (the mark is associated with more than one commercial source); (ii) dilution by tarnishment (impairment of the mark's reputation), namely tarnishing or degrading the positive associations of the mark as a result of the defendant's use in connection with 'wholesome or degrading' goods/services.

[43] The main factors in determining likelihood of confusion were set out in the *Polaroid* decision, although the specific standard itself is defined by a large body of law and varies between the different circuits; *Polaroid Corp. v. Polarad Elect. Corp.* 287 F.2d 492 (2nd Cir. 1961).

[44] *Tetris Holding, LLC v. Xio Interactive, Inc.* 863 F.Supp.2d 394 (D.N.J. 2012).

[45] The said trade dress comprising 'the brighly-colored Tetriminos [falling bricks], which are formed by four equally-sized, delineated blocks, and the long vertical rectangular playfield, which is higher than wide'.

[46] *Ingrid & Isabel, LLC v. Baby Be Mine, LLC* F.Supp.3d, 2014 WL 4954656 (N.D. Cal. 2014).

[47] *Apple, Inc. v. Samsung Electronics Co., Ltd* U.S. District Court for the N.D.Cal, Case No. 5:11-cv-01846-LHK.

an unchanging bottom dock of colorful square icons with evenly rounded corners set off from the display's other icons'.[48] At the district court, the jury found that Samsung's products were liable for trade-dress dilution. Although subsequently overturned by the CAFC, the basis for this reversal did not contrast the possibility that using a similar GUI could blur one's distinctive trade dress.[49]

Notwithstanding the court's reasoning for this reversal, its lack of enthusiasm for broad trade-dress protection was implicit from the outset. Thus, at the commencement of its analysis the court stressed:

> Protection for trade dress exists to promote competition. The protection for source identification, however, must be balanced against a fundamental right to compete through imitation of a competitor's product. This right can only be temporarily denied by the patent or copyright laws [but] in contrast, trademark law allows for a perpetual monopoly and its use in the protection of physical details and design of a product must be limited to those that are nonfunctional.[50]

Functionality Section 43(a)(3) of the Lenham Act provides that 'In a civil action for trade dress infringement under this chapter for trade dress not registered on the principal register, the person who asserts trade dress protection has the burden of proving that the matter sought to be protected is not functional.' The basis for this rule is the distinction between trade-mark and patent laws and the different policies that underpin these branches of intellectual property law. As the Supreme Court explained in *Qualitex*:

> It is the province of patent law, not trademark law, to encourage invention by granting inventors a monopoly over new product designs or functions for a limited time, after which competitors are free to use the innovation. If a product's functional features could be used as trademarks, however, a monopoly over such features could be obtained without regard to whether they qualify as patents and could be extended forever (because trademarks may be renewed in perpetuity).[51]

Such a monopoly would obviously have severe anti-competitive implications. The Restatement (Third) of the Law of Unfair Competition, paragraph 17 explains: 'The exclusion of functional designs from the subject matter of trade-mark law is intended to insure effective competition, not just by the defendant, but also by other existing and potential competitors.' According to McCarthy, functionality 'is

---

[48] *Apple, Inc. v. Samsung Electronics Co., Ltd* Case: 14-1355 (Fed. Cir. 18/05/2015) 10.
[49] The appellant court reverse on this point as it was of the view that elements of the aforementioned trade dress served a functional purpose of improving usability; on functionality, see below.
[50] *Apple, Inc. v. Samsung Electronics Co., Ltd* Case: 14-1355 (Fed. Cir. 18/05/2015) 7.
[51] *Qualitex Co. v. Jacobson Prods. Co.* 514 U.S. 159 (1995) 214.

a potent public policy, for it trumps all evidence of actual consumer identification of source and all evidence of actual consumer confusion caused by an imitator'.[52]

There are two branches of the functionality defence under US trade-mark law: utilitarian functionality and aesthetic functionality. Although aesthetic functionality could be relevant to GUIs under very limited set of circumstances,[53] it is utilitarian functionality that is most relevant to the present context. In *Inwood Laboratories* the Supreme Court elaborated on utilitarian functionality and elucidated that a 'product feature is functional if it is essential to the use or purpose of the article or if it affects the cost or quality of the article'.[54] In *Trafix* the Supreme Court applied the above to a product-design trade-dress scenario and explicitly stated that functional features of product design are not eligible to trade-dress protection.[55] The court explained that a feature is considered 'functional' if it is either 'essential to the use or purpose of the device' or 'affects the cost or quality of the device'.[56] In assessing whether a product design is functional, a court may take the following factors into account: (i) the existence of a utility patent which discloses the utilitarian advantage of the design; (ii) whether the originator of the design promotes the utilitarian advantages of the product through advertising;[57] (iii) whether there are alternative designs available; and (iv) whether the design is more economical than an alternative design.[58]

It is the first three aforementioned factors that are most relevant to the present discussion. The existence of a utility patent is a clear indication that features of the GUI design are utilitarian and thus functional. In addition, there is a clear public policy justification for refusing protection for features that were subject to

---

[52] J Thomas Mccarthy, *Mccarthy on Trademarks and Unfair Competition* § 7:63, (4th edn., Eagan, MN, Thomson Reuters 2013).

[53] Aesthetic functionality was described in the 1938 Restatement of Torts:

When goods are bought largely for their aesthetic value, their features may be functional because they definitely contribute to that value and thus aid the performance of an object for which the goods are intended. The determination of whether or not such features are functional depends upon the question of fact whether the prohibition of imitation by others will deprive the others of something which will substantially hinder them in competition. So for example a candy or a chocolate box in the shape of a heart could be functional in an aesthetic sense.

The Restatement (Third) of Unfair Competition (1995) Section 17, comment (c) did not reject the doctrine of aesthetic functionality as such but narrowed down its scope by redefining it: 'A design is functional because of its aesthetic value only if it confers a significant benefit that cannot practically be duplicated by the use of alternative designs.'

[54] *Inwood Laboratories, Inc. v. Ives Laboratories* 436 US 844 (1982).

[55] *TrafFix Devices, Inc. v. Marketing Displays, Inc.* 532 U.S. 23 (2001).   [56] Ibid, 33.

[57] Protection becomes even more difficult when the promotional material focuses on the functional, rather than the source-identifying attributes of trade dress. In *Bose Corp.* 772 F.2d 866, 227 U.S.P.Q. 1 (Fed. Circ. 1985), the promotional material for Bose loudspeakers concentrated on their pentagonal shape as a functional part of the sound system. Consequently, it was held to be functional within the meaning of the functionality exception to trade-mark protection.

[58] See, *In re Morton-Norwich Products, Inc.* 671 F.2d 1332, 1340-41 (C.C.P.A. 1982).

utility-patent protection, which has now lapsed. As the *Trafix* court explained: '[a] utility patent is strong evidence that the features therein claimed are functional'[59] and is therefore highly likely to be excluded from trade-dress protection.[60] Therefore, a right holder that seeks to protect its GUI should consider which branch of the law, utility patents, or trade dress, offers a better form of protection under a given set of circumstances and focus its efforts accordingly. Of course, GUIs may comprise functional and non-functional features. Where possible, it would be beneficial to claim only the functional features as part of the utility-patent application, while leaving the non-functional features to be protected under different intellectual property regimes. For example, Google has a utility patent (U.S. Pat. No. 7,146,358), design patent (U.S. Pat. No. D533,561), and trade-mark (Reg. No. 2,806,075) directed to searching the web and displaying search results.[61] Thus, each intellectual property right is protecting a different facet of Google's product/service in this field.

An interesting question in relation to point (iii) above is whether similarly to the case under copyright law, the availability of alternative designs is assessed from the perspective of the originator of the design, rather than from that of the defendant.[62] For example, would a design of a GUI that becomes very popular and, as a result, has many consumers 'locked in' since they are now used to this GUI's layout and its associated manner of operation, be considered as functional?[63] While a competitor may argue that the number of alternative designs it could adopt in order to compete in a viable manner with the originator of the design is limited if not non-existent, the originator of the design could maintain that the number of alternatives that were available to it when creating the said design was considerable and its design choices were therefore arbitrary. Since trade-dress law has different objectives than copyright law does and since the functionality doctrine is applied with clear pro-competition objectives in mind, it is suggested that it is the position of competitors and not the

---

[59] *TrafFix Devices, Inc. v. Marketing Displays, Inc.* 532 U.S. 23 (2001) 24.

[60] There is an apparent split between different circuits on whether there is a per se prohibition on allowing trade-dress protection to design features that were subject to a utility-patent protection or there is merely a strong hint that the features in question are functional, which is ultimately decided on the basis of a detailed examination of the nature of the said features (for the former, see *Vornado Air Circulation Systems, Inc. v. Duracraft Corp.*, 58 F.3d 1498, 1500 (10th Cir. 1995), while for the latter approach, see *Thomas & Betts Corp. v. Panduit Corp.*, 138 F.3d 277, 285 (7th Cir. 1998)). It appears that the Supreme Court in *Trafix* subscribed to the latter approach.

[61] See, *A Practical Approach to Protection of Graphical User Interfaces in the United States of America*, Intellectual Property Owners Association (White Paper prepared jointly by Software and Business Methods & Design Rights Committees 2008-2009), http://www.visiond.com/IPO2012/MATERIALS/Dougal_Durkin_Kirincich_Strand_GroupPaper.pdf (Accessed 10 May 2016) 36.

[62] In the case of copyright, this forms part of the court's assessment when applying the merger doctrine.

[63] For example, Apple's mobile GUI with square icons in a grid with a dock bar at the bottom.

design originator that should prove crucial.[64] Thus, if at the point of time when the defendant adopted features of the plaintiff's GUI it could be established that owing to the success of the plaintiff's product, the said GUI became an industry standard so there is strong reluctance by consumers to learn to use GUI that is laid out differently and therefore operates in a different manner, competitors should be able to argue that such GUI is de facto functional, and unless they are permitted to adopt it, they will be substantially hindered in competing with the plaintiff.[65]

7.2.1.2 Applying the rules

In principle, each facet of GUIs could be protected under the Lenham Act as long as it is distinctive (most probably by acquiring a secondary meaning) and non-functional.

The overall layout of the GUI   Whether registered or unregistered trade dress, in order to be protected under the Lenham Act, the subject matter of protection must be distinctive. Most overall layouts of a desktop might prove too general or generic to comply with the distinctiveness requirement, although some layouts might have a sufficient degree of distinctiveness in order to qualify for trade-mark protection.[66] One may also look, by analogy, at store layouts as protectable subject matter. Both Microsoft and Apple obtained trade-mark registration for their stores' layout, in 2011 and 2013, respectively.[67] In principle, a layout of a store, a layout of website, and a layout of a GUI are subject to the same criteria for the purpose of assessing their eligibility for protection.

---

[64] Copyright is intended to protected authorial works with a creative aspect. It is therefore vital to assess eligibility at the point of time of creation. On the other hand, trade-mark law has no such objective and is intended to encourage effective competition. Thus, assessing eligibility with the needs of competitors in mind appears sensible. In addition, while copyright has a limited term of protection, trade-mark could potentially last perpetually.

[65] In *Rosetta Stone Ltd v. Google, Inc.* No. 10-2007 (4th Cir. 9 April 2012), the Fourth Circuit held otherwise, finding that the functionality doctrine was applicable only if the proprietor's use of the mark was functional, and any functional use of the mark made by the alleged infringer has no relevance to the analysis. It is noteworthy that this case, however, did not concern trade dress but a word mark and involved a set of facts that is very different from that discussed in this chapter.

[66] See, e.g. Reg. No. 3,495,193, for a customer-interface system that was registered on 8 September 2008.

[67] Microsoft's trade-mark registration certificate referring to '. . . three-dimensional trade dress depicting the interior of a retail store with four curved tabletops at the front and rear side walls and a rectangular band displaying changing video images on the walls'; Apple registration certificate referring to:

> . . . a primarily glass storefront, rectangular recessed lighting traversing the length of the store's ceiling, Cantilevered shelving and recessed display spaces along the front side walls, rectangular tables arranged in a line in the middle of the store parallel to the walls and extending from the storefront to the back of the store, multi-tiered shelving along the rear walls, and an oblong table with stools located at the back of the store below video screens in the back wall.

Individual static components GUI components usually represent graphics that are used by the user to interact with the device or the device's displays that are triggered in response to the user's interaction. The most common GUI components are pointers, icons, windows, and menus.[68] Although each of these components could be both distinctive and non-functional, it is mainly icons that are likely to satisfy both requirements. For example, AppleLink, Apple CarPlay, and Apple Remote Desktop are all icons registered as trade-marks.[69] In addition, it should be borne in mind that although some icons of more generic nature are not likely to satisfy the distinctiveness requirement, their combination in a particular manner could acquire a secondary meaning.

Transitional or animated features As above, each case is decided on its own facts, and as long as both aforementioned requirements could be satisfies, transitional and animated aspects of a GUI are eligible for protection. For example, the streaming services company HULU was granted registration for its animated GUI aspect, verbally described as:

> the mark consists of a moving image mark, consisting of an animated sequence showing a series of rectangular video screens of varying sizes, that fly inward in whirlwind fashion, as if from the viewer's location, toward the center of the viewer's screen, where they coalesce into the word 'hulu', the drawing represents three (3) stills (freeze frames) from the animated sequence.[70]

7.2.2 European Union: trade-mark protection for GUIs

As mentioned above, the EU trade-mark regime concerns only registered trade marks and leaves the protection of unregistered marks to EU Member States' domestic laws.

7.2.2.1 *Distinctiveness*

Unlike the United States, there is no bright line distinction between product design and product packaging in relation to the need to show acquired distinctiveness. Thus, in principle, a GUI may be inherently distinctive and eligible for registration

---

[68] *A Practical Approach to Protection of Graphical User Interfaces in the United States of America, Intellectual Property Owners Association* (White Paper prepared jointly by Software and Business Methods & Design Rights Committees 2008–2009), http://www.visiond.com/IPO2012/MATERIALS/Dougal_Durkin_Kirincich_Strand_GroupPaper.pdf (Accessed 10 May 2016) 35.

[69] See Apple's trade-marks list: http://www.apple.com/legal/intellectual-property/trademark/appletmlist.html.

[70] Granted on April 2012, for various goods and services; see https://trademarks.justia.com/779/81/n-a-77981717.html.

even without being previously used. Notwithstanding such general principle, the CJEU has stressed in the past that it is only in exceptional circumstances, where it departs significantly from the norm or custom in the sector, that a shape or design of a product could prove to be inherently distinctive.[71] Thus, it would have to be a fairly unique GUI, which is likely to be viewed as an indication of origin, in order to be considered as inherently distinctive. Otherwise, similar to the position in the United States, a GUI may acquire such distinctive character through prolonged and extensive use during which consumers are 'educated' to perceive the said GUI as an indication of origin.

7.2.2.2 *Functionality*

When it comes to the second main hurdle for protection under US law, namely functionality, EU trade-mark law differed significantly from its US counterpart until recently. While in the United States, the functionality doctrine clearly applies to any functional aspect of a product, in the EU, the functionality provisions were limited to three-dimensional shapes. It is only in the revised version of the trademark directive that passed on 16 December 2015, that the said limitation was removed and Article 4(1)(e)(ii) now refers to 'the shape, or *another characteristic* (my emphasis) of goods, which is necessary to achieve a technical result'.[72] Thus, it is clear that aspects of GUIs that are utilitarian in essence and perform a technical function are not registerable as trade-marks. Although the above provision is very recent and a decision on its scope is yet to be given, there is ample guidance by the CJEU on what constitutes 'necessary to obtain a technical result' in relation to three-dimensional shapes. Such principles should now equally apply to 'another characteristic of the goods', including GUIs.

In *Philips v. Remington*,[73] the CJEU concluded that where the essential functional characteristics of the shape of a product are attributable solely to the technical result, registration is precluded even if other shapes can achieve that technical result. In a subsequent decision the court further elaborated on the nature of the assessment that is to be carried out in this context and maintained that the expression 'essential characteristics' must be understood as referring to the most important elements of the sign.[74] Once the essential characteristics of the sign have been identified, it is only necessary to assess whether those characteristics perform the technical function of the product concerned. Thus, unlike the position in the

---

[71] C-24/05 P [2006] *Storck v. OHIM* para. 24 seq. (stating, 'Average consumers are not in the habit of making assumptions about the origin of products on the basis of their shape [. . .] only a mark which departs significantly from the norm or customs of the sector [. . .] is not devoid of any distinctive character [. . .].'

[72] Directive 2015/2436 of the European Parliament and of the Council of 16 December 2015 to Approximate the Laws of the Member States Relating to Trade Marks.

[73] Case 299/99, *Philips v. Remington*.   [74] *Lego Juris A/S v. OHIM, Mega Brands Inc.* Case 48/09.

United States, the availability of alternatives that may achieve the same technical result is not indicative of non-functionality. It is the objective and function of those essential characteristics that is decisive. The identification of those essential characteristics must be carried out on a case-by-case basis. Similar to the United States, supporting evidence such as patents or statements by the originator of the design may be given considerable weight in uncovering such objective. The above analysis suggests that first it is necessary to discern what are the essential and most important elements of a GUI. Once such elements are identified, it is then necessary to determine whether they are in essence functional or not. The fact that alternative designs to the GUI at issue could have achieved the same functional outcome is of little relevance. As mentioned, the decisive factor is the objective and function of the GUI at issue. It is suggested that this is likely to lead to more GUIs failing the functionality criterion in the European Union than in the United States.

The closest EU equivalent to the US aesthetic-functionality doctrine is found in Article 4(1)(e)(iii). In its present version, the provision states that a sign that consists exclusively of the shape, or another characteristic, which gives substantial value to the goods, is precluded from registration. *Bang & Olufsen* illustrates the manner in which a court may conduct its assessment under this exclusion.[75] In this case it was established that the design of the Hi-Fi speakers, the shape of which Bang & Olufsen sought to register as a trade mark, was very important to the consumers' choice, even if consumers also take other characteristics of the goods at issue into account. It was further established that the design was an essential element of Bang & Olufsen's branding and increased the appeal of the speaker, that is to say, its value. Furthermore, some promotional literature of distributors and online auction sites emphasized the aesthetic characteristics of the shape, which was perceived as a kind of pure, slender, timeless sculpture for music reproduction, which made it an important selling point. Thus, statements by third parties, not necessarily approved by the design originator, could also prove crucial to the court's assessment. Unlike the position in the United States, it is not necessary to show that the prohibition on imitation by others will deprive the others of something which will substantially hinder them in competition. It is merely necessary to show that the design at issue has an aesthetic appeal that increases the product's value in the eyes of the consuming public. Obviously, such increase in value must not be origin related.

The different facets of GUIs, namely entire desktops, individual components, and transitional and animated effects, are all potentially eligible for trade-mark registration. In fact instances where such elements were registered already exist in

---

[75] *Bang & Olufsen A/S v. OHIM* Case T-508/08.

the EUIPO trade-mark registry office.[76] What is less clear at present is how courts will apply the newly applicable functionality and aesthetic appeal based exclusions to GUIs.[77]

7.2.2.3 Infringement

The rules on trade-mark infringement under EU law differ substantially from their US counterparts. Although under both systems, consumer confusion,[78] blurring, and tarnishment[79] are actionable, the scope of each of these grounds for infringement in both jurisdictions is different. Moreover, EU trade-mark law may also be engaged where the defendant is using an identical GUI in relation to identical goods or services, without any need to show confusion.[80] Finally, unlike the position in the United States, a competitor in the European Union may be liable when using an identical or similar GUI in relation to any type of goods or service, identical – similar – or dissimilar, without any type of harm inflicted on the claimant, as long as the defendant's use constitutes the taking of unfair advantage.[81]

Although the abovementioned differences are of significant importance to any party engaged in a potential trade-mark dispute, GUI-related or otherwise, it is suggested that the GUI context does not merit a separate discussion on the application of these general rules.[82]

7.2.3 A brief note on unfair-competition laws in the European Union

Domestic laws against unfair competition across the EU could be grouped into two categories: common law and civil law models. Member States that follow the common law model do not have unfair-competition laws in a broad sense.[83] Thus, under the common law model the law of passing off, which, inter alia, may protect unregistered insignia, has misrepresentation that leads to consumer deception at its heart.[84] Thus, it may be more accurate to refer to passing off

---

[76] For example, CTM application No. 007114391 was granted by the EUIPO on 17/02/2009 for eGUI ergonomic graphic user interface (Figurative mark) by gateprotect GmbH. The goods and services in respect of which registration of the trade-mark was granted are in Classes 9, 38, and 42.

[77] The revised trade-mark legislation came into force in March 2016, two months before writing the present chapter.

[78] Art. 10(2)(b) or Directive 2015/2436.

[79] Art. 10(2)(c), governing both blurring and tarnishment of Directive 2015/2436.

[80] Art. 10(2)(a) of Directive 2015/2436. This is unlikely to take place in a GUI context unless the defendant's product is a counterfeit.

[81] Art. 10(2)(c) of Directive 2015/2436.

[82] For a detailed discussion on infringement under the EU regime from a UK perspective, see D Keeling et al., *Kerly's Law of Trade Marks and Trade Names* (15th edn., London, S&M, 2014).

[83] United Kingdom, Ireland, and Cyprus; the rest of the EU Member States follow a civil-law model.

[84] See, for example, *Reckitt & Colman Products Ltd v. Borden, Inc. and Others* [1990] 1 All ER 873 (the *Jif Lemon* case).

as a law of unfair competition by misrepresentation rather than merely as unfair competition law. Laws against unfair competition in civil law systems are broader in their application and are intended to shield competition against misappropriation of reputation and trade values, distortion, misrepresentation, and unfair practices in the interests of the competitors, consumers and other actors in the marketplace. Under the civil law model, liability could often be established even without any evidence of consumer confusion. For example, apart from instances giving rise to confusion, defamation, and misleading behaviour, French unfair-competition law may also apply in cases of 'parasitisme', where the defendant is engaged in parasitic exploitation of other parties' commercial achievements but without any misrepresentation and deception.[85]

Leaving unfair competition law not harmonized on the EU level means that it may be necessary for right holders to engage in jurisdiction-by-jurisdiction examination in order to determine whether a given situation gives rise to liability under unfair-competition law.[86] Thus, any similarity between GUIs which does not lead to misrepresentation and consumer deception, is not likely to give rise to liability under the laws of common law Member States. However, such similarity may nevertheless be actionable under the laws of some civil law Member States, where misrepresentation and consumer deception are not prerequisites for all types of unfair-competition violations.[87]

7.3 DESIGN PATENTS AND REGISTERED DESIGNS

Ornamental or aesthetic designs benefit from a tailor-made intellectual property right that grants protection to such design features in both the United States and European Union. Hence, the ornamental or aesthetic aspects of GUIs may be protected, inter alia, in the United States as design patents and in the European Union as registered designs.[88]

---

[85] Article 1382 of the French Civil Code the general tort law clause, which formed the basis for the development of unfair competition law on a case-law basis. There is now extensive jurisprudence in this area; for the development of French unfair competition law, see A Kamperman, *Unfair Competition Law: The Protection of Intellectual and Industrial Creativity* (Oxford, Clarendon Press, 1997).

[86] For a detailed analysis of the different laws against unfair competition in various EU Member States, see F Henning-Bodewig, *International Handbook on Unfair Competition* (Munich, C.H. Beck, 2012).

[87] See, for example, German law against unfair competition, Gesetz gegen den unlauteren Wettbewerb, § 4(3)(b) (stating that unfairness shall have occurred in particular where a person offers goods or services that are replicas of goods or services of a competitor if he unreasonably exploits or impairs the assessment of the replicated goods or services).

[88] The analysis below refers only to community-registered designs as eligibility to protection under the EU unregistered-design regime is subject to similar substantive requirements, while the scope of protection is

7.3.1 Design patents in the United States

For the last three decades, GUI designers have been using the design-patent system to protect the visual effect of software-generated icons, the overall imagery of GUIs, and other visual aspects of it. The USPTO has already granted thousands of such design patents for such designs.[89] Thus, design patents are granted to various aspects of GUIs: desktops, individual components, and transitional and animated effects.[90]

7.3.1.1 *Eligibility*

The scope of protection under design-patent legislation is set out in Section 171 of the US Patent Act: 'Whoever invents any new, original, and ornamental design for an article of manufacture may obtain a patent therefor, subject to the conditions and requirements of this title'[91]. First, it should be noted that GUIs, as such, are not eligible for design-patent protection, as they must be embodied in an 'article of manufacture'. Thus, in *Ex parte Strijland* the USPTO Board of Patent Appeals clarified that the referral of Section 171 to 'design for an article of manufacture' meant that an icon per se could not be claimed; rather, the icon design at issue must be claimed as embodied in the said article of manufacture and shown to be so in the design-patent application. The Manual of Patent Examining Procedure (MPEP) provides guidelines as to how to comply with the requirement of 'article of manufacture' in relation to GUI designs.[92]

Furthermore, in order to qualify for design patent, a design must be novel,[93] non-obvious,[94] and ornamental.[95] Overall, the novelty and non-obviousness requirements do not require special consideration in the context of GUIs. Hence, in order to satisfy the novelty requirement, a design must be new, original so that the 'average observer takes the new design for a different, and not a modified, already

---

narrower, since unlike registered designs, unregistered designs protect only against copying and not against independent creation.

[89] J J Du Mont and M D Janis, 'Virtual designs' (2014) 17 Stan. Tech. L. Rev. 107; R Stigler, 'Ooey GUI: the messy protection of graphical user interfaces' (2015) 12(3) Northwestern J. Tech. Intellect. Property 215–50.

[90] For example, see the design patent for screen display USD604305 S1 (a patent for the ornamental design for a graphical user interface for a display screen or portion thereof); on an icon USD404727 (an ornamental design for a computer icon for a computer monitor); on animated effects, see Apple's design patent for the genie dock effect, a user-interface feature that presents the illusion that application and Finder windows are shrinking into the system dock when minimized by the user.

[91] 35 U.S.C. §171(a)

[92] MPEP, § 1504.01(a)(I)(B) *'Procedures for Evaluating Whether Design Patent Applications Drawn to Computer-Generated Icons Comply with the "Article of Manufacture" Requirement'*.

[93] Ibid, Section 102.   [94] Ibid, Section 103.

[95] See ibid, Section 171(a), in combination with Section 171(b), which states: 'The provisions of this title relating to patents for inventions shall apply to patents for designs, except as otherwise provided.'

existing design'.[96] The non-obviousness requirement will be satisfied where the design in question is not anticipated by the prior art.

It is the requirement of ornamentation, however, that at first glance poses a challenge to GUIs as GUIs are designed in order to enable interaction with users; namely, often intended to achieve a utilitarian objective. However, this requirement is not as restrictive as it may appear to be. In order to contravene the requirement of ornamentation, the design at issue must be purely functional. Again, the MPEP provides some guidance on the matter: 'a distinction exists between the functionality of an article and the functionality of the design of the article that performs the function. Based on this distinction, the design of a computer-generated icon may not be dictated by the function associated with the computer-generated icon'. There are a number of tests being used in order to identify designs that are purely functional, all of which suggest that the functionality exclusion is narrow and that most GUIs should not fall within it ambit.[97] In fact, a GUI can obtain design-patent protection, even where it simultaneously ornamental and functional, as long as it is not 'purely' functional or unless the function is necessary to compete in the market.[98]

The *Apple v. Samsung* litigation illustrates that the functionality exception for design patents is considerably narrower than that under trade-dress law.[99] In this case, Samsung appealed against the decision of Northern District of California. In the appeal, the Federal Circuit, inter alia, upheld the infringement of Apple's deign patents but reversed the district court on infringement of Apple's trade dress in its iPhone. The basis for this reversal was the functionality of Apple's trade dress. Apple's registered trade-dress claim claimed the design details in each of the sixteen icons on the iPhone's home screen framed by the iPhone's rounded-rectangular shape with silver edges and a black background. The court found that the individual elements claimed by the trade dress were functional and, moreover, concluded that Apple failed to explain how the total combination of the sixteen icon design in the context of iPhone's screen-dominated rounded-rectangular shape, all part of the iPhone's 'easy to use' design theme, somehow negated the undisputed usability function of the individual elements.

---

[96] *Thabet Mfg. Co. v. Kool Vent Metal Awning Corp.* 226 F.2d 207, 212 (6th Cir. 1955).

[97] For example, see *High Point Design, LLC v. Buyers Direct, Inc.* 730 F.3d 1301, 1319 (Fed. Cir. 2013) (referring to both the alternative designs test and a broader multi-factor test that is similar to trade dress functionality); *Richardson v. Stanley Works, Inc.* 597 F.3d 1288 (Fed. Cir. 2010) (adopting a copyright-like approach to infringement where 'functional' features are not taken into consideration in the comparison).

[98] R Stigler, 'Ooey GUI: the messy protection of graphical user interfaces' (2015) 12(3) *Northwestern Journal of Technology and Intellectual Property* 240; M Risch, 'Functionality and graphical user interface design patents,' (2014) 17 STLR 53.

[99] *Apple, Inc. v. Samsung Electronics Co. Ltd et al.* Nos 2014-1335, 2015-1029((Fed Cir. 2015).

The Federal Circuit reached exactly the opposite conclusion when it assessed Samsung's arguments in relation to the functionality of Apple's design patents. Samsung argued that the district court should have instructed the jury when making the comparison between the two designs in the context of the design patent infringement claim, not to take into account the elements that were found to be functional for the purpose of its trade-dress assessment. The Federal Circuit disagreed and maintained that design-patent case-law did not give support to such an approach.[100] Rather, the comparison must be of the entire designs and individual elements in a design-patent claim, whether functional or not, should not be disregarded. It therefore appears that the functionality exception under design-patent law is narrower than trade-dress law is, and that GUI features that may be considered as functional for trade-dress purposes are not so considered under design-patent law.[101]

7.3.1.2 *Infringement*

A design patent is infringed if an ordinary observer would have been deceived: 'if, in the eye of an ordinary observer, giving such attention as a purchaser usually gives, two designs are substantially the same, if the resemblance is such as to deceive such an observer, inducing him to purchase one supposing it to be the other, the first one patented is infringed by the other'.[102] Actual deception is not required, and likelihood of deception suffices.[103] We have also seen that once the validity of the design patent is not at issue, the ordinary observer takes all features of the design into account when comparing both designs and not merely the ornamental features.

It appears that the scope of design patents is clearer in the United States than is copyright or trade dress, as such scope is informed by the design documents accompanying the application. Aspects such as colours and gradients can all be claimed, while immaterial aspects could be disclaimed. This enables right holders to focus protection on the more valuable aspects of their designs.[104] We also saw

---

[100] For a critique of the Federal Circuit's decision on this point and a detailed overall discussion on the role of functionality in an infringement inquiry, see M. Risch, 'Functionality and graphical user interface design patents' (2014) 17 STLR 53.

[101] It is noteworthy that the validity of Apple's design patents was not at issue at this stage, and the only question before the court was that of infringement.

[102] *Apple, Inc. v. Samsung Electronics Co. Ltd. et al.*, Nos 2014-1335, 2015-1029, (Fed Cir. 2015), reciting from *Gorham Co. v. White*, 81 U.S. 511, 528 (1872).

[103] Ibid, 530.

[104] For example, see *Graphical User Interface for a Display Screen of a Communications Terminal*, USD599,372 (where Google claimed its Internet home screen while disclaiming the term *Google* by using broken lines; this enables Google to have protection against a party that uses the same layout but replaces the tem *Google* with another).

that design patents are a preferable form of protection when it comes to the functionality exclusion. This demonstrates the value in obtaining design-patent protection to GUIs or features thereof rather than relying on a progressively acquired secondary meaning for trade-dress protection. Design-patent registration ensures that until such time as secondary meaning is acquired, the GUI in question is not susceptible to appropriation by competitors and, even when secondary meaning is acquired, the functionality doctrine that poses a constant risk to the enforceability of a GUI trade-dress claim proves to be less problematic for design-patent protection. Done in this way, when the term of protection for a design patent expires, trade-dress protection becomes of real value, having acquired a secondary meaning during this period.

7.3.2 Registered designs in the European Union

Similar to the position in relation to trade-marks, the European Union has a two-tier registered designs regime. Whether it is a national or a community-registered design, the substantive eligibility requirements are the same.[105]

7.3.2.1 Eligibility

The definition of a design eligible for registration is very broad. The Regulation provides: 'the appearance of whole or part of *product* resulting from features of, in particular, the lines, contours, colours, shape, texture and/or materials of the product and/or its ornamentation' (my emphasis).[106] The Regulation further provides that a *product* is: 'any industrial or handicraft item including parts to be assembled into complex product, packaging, get-up, graphic symbols,[107] and typographical typefaces, but excluding computer programs'.[108] Although computer programs are explicitly excluded from protection, GUIs, webpage designs and icons could constitute a 'product' and are therefore protectable.[109] Thus, unlike the position in the United States, GUIs or constituent parts thereof per se are protectable.

In order to be protected as a registered design, a design must be novel and have an individual character.[110] Similar to the situation in relation to US design patents, in the main these substantive requirements do not require special consideration

---

[105] Henceforth the discussion below refers to the Council Regulation (EC) No. 6/2002 of 12 December 2001, on Community designs (consolidated version) (hereinafter CDR).

[106] Art. 3(a)

[107] The protectability of typeface is obviously relevant in the GUI context as a particular type of typeface my constitute part of the look and feel of a GUI; for example see RCD 000130299-0001.

[108] Art. 3(b)

[109] See D Stone, *European Union Design Law: A Practitioners' Guide* (Oxford, OUP 2012), para. 4.76; for example, see RCD 930367-0002 registered for an icon for a portion of a display screen.

[110] Art. 4(a) RCD.

in the context of GUIs. Hence, in order to satisfy the novelty requirement, it must be shown that an identical design has not been made available to the public before the priority date.[111] The individual-character requirement will be satisfied where the overall impression it produces on the informed user differs from the overall impression of an earlier design made available to the public.[112]

One important limitation on the scope of protection in the present context is the technical-function exclusion. Thus, Article 8(1) CDR provides: 'A community design shall not subsist in features of appearance of a product which are solely dictated by its technical function.' Recital 10 explains: 'Technological innovation should not be hampered by granting design protection to features dictated solely by a technical function. It is understood that this does not entail that a design must have an aesthetic quality.' The reason is policy based: features solely dictated by a technical function should stand up to scrutiny of patent law rather than the more lax standards of registered designs, or else it is likely to stifle competition and innovation.[113]

It appears that at present, there is no uniform test to determine when is a feature of appearance 'solely dictated by its technical function'.[114] Three tests have been used in various EU jurisdictions in order to determine the scope of the technical-function exclusion.

The 'multiplicity-of-forms' test is somewhat similar to the US alternative-design test. If the related technical function could be achieved by at least one more design than the design at issue, the latter is not 'solely dictated by its technical function' and does not fall foul of the exclusion. This test is fairly lenient, as in most cases there is likely to be at least one alternative design that achieves the same technical function. The test has been endorsed in early OHIM decisions, by German, French, Spanish, Swedish, and British courts, as well as by the Advocate General in the trade-mark case *Philips v. Remington*.[115] While commenting on the differences between the functionality tests under trade-mark law and the CDR, the AG explained that while in order to fall foul of trade-mark law, the feature in question merely needs to be necessary in order to achieve the technical function; under design law, it should not only be necessary but essential in order to do so.[116] Therefore, while the availability of alternative designs would not be a decisive factor for trade-mark law

---

[111] Art. 5 CDR.   [112] Art. 6 CDR.
[113] U Suthersanen, *Design Law: European Union and United States* (London, Sweet and Maxwell 2010) 101.
[114] The CJEU is yet to rule on the matter.
[115] D Stone, *European Union Design Law: A Practitioners' Guide* (Oxford, OUP 2012) para. 6.11.
[116] *Koninklijke Philips Electronics NV v. Remington Consumer Products Ltd* Case C-299/99, [2002] ECR I-5475, para. 134 (AG Colomer).

purposes,[117] it may prove detrimental to a functionality argument under the multiplicity-of-forms test for CDR purposes. Thus, not unlike the position in the United States, features that may be considered as functional for trade-mark law purposes, may nevertheless be protectable as not solely dictated by their technical functional under the CDR.

The causative approach, sometimes referred to as the no-aesthetic-consideration test, has been used by the Board of Appeal and by Dutch courts.[118] According to this test, the key question is whether there were considerations other than the technically functional when designing the feature of appearance at issue. If the answer to the above query is negative, the feature of appearance in question is considered as solely dictated by its technical function. Clearly, the key question is designer motivation. This test is stricter than the multiplicity-of-forms test. Many features of appearance that may have been designed with a technical objective in mind but nevertheless have design alternatives, would fall foul of the former but not the latter.

A third test appears to have been adopted by the Invalidity Division around 2011, according to which if the designer had some design freedom during the design process, rather than being compelled to make the relevant design choices owing to functionality, the feature of appearance at issue is not considered as solely dictated by its technical function.[119] This test appears to be somewhat similar to the multiplicity-of-forms test in that alternative designs play an important role in the assessment. The availability of alternative designs may suggest that the designer had some creative freedom during the design process, as he could have opted for any of the said alternatives. Where there is some creative freedom, even if far from complete, the design of the feature of appearance at issue could not be said to have been exclusively determined by technical function.

7.3.2.2 *Infringement*

The test for infringement of a registered design is defined by Article 10 CDR: '(1) The scope of the protection conferred by a Community design shall include any design which does not produce on the informed user a different overall impression; (2) In assessing the scope of protection, the degree of freedom of the designer in developing his design shall be taken into consideration.' The essence of an action for infringement of a registered design, as opposed to unregistered design, was

---

[117] Ibid, para. 84 (stating, 'Moreover, the ground for refusal or invalidity of registration imposed by that provision cannot be overcome by establishing that there are other shapes which allow the same technical result to be obtained.').

[118] D Stone, *European Union Design Law: A Practitioners' Guide* (Oxford, OUP 2012) para. 6.11.

[119] See *ICD 8242 Nokia Corporation v. Kalwat Iwona Trak Electronics* (ID 28.10.2011); *ICD 8225 ASSTECH Assembly Technology GmbH Co KG v. Thomas Nagel* (ID 07.09.2011).

explained by Jacob LJ in the UK Court of Appeal decision of *Apple v. Samsung*: 'It is not about whether Samsung copied Apple's iPad. Infringement of a registered design does not involve any question of whether there was copying: the issue is simply whether the accused design is too close to the registered design according to the tests laid down in the law.'[120] In this context, it should be noted that design freedom, which may be affected by technical considerations and constraints, might have significant impact on the outcome of the assessment of 'overall impression'. Namely, where design freedom is limited, small differences between the designs at issue may be sufficient to constitute a different 'overall impression' on the informed user, and render the defendant's design non-infringing. In this context it should be borne in mind that a GUI is a utilitarian object that is ultimately designed to enable a user to interact with a device, and its design is therefore likely to be constrained by various functional considerations, which in turn limit design freedom.

7.4 A BRIEF NOTE ON PATENT PROTECTION FOR GUIS

We have seen that quite often, user experience one of the most valuable aspects of a software product or service. To what extent, if at all, can such an amorphous feature be protected by our patent system? As mentioned above, design patents in the United States or registered designs in the European Union may be available to ornamental product designs or features of appearance that are not solely dictated by functionality. However, where the design at issue is technical and functional, it may nevertheless be protected under patent law.[121] Chapter 6 above discusses software-patentability issues in general, but it does not touch upon patentability questions concerning GUIs; the discussion below does so.

7.4.1 Utility-patent protection in the United States for GUIs

A US patent may be granted with respect to 'any new and useful process, machine, manufacture, or composition of matter, or any new and useful improvement thereof'.[122] Sections 102 and 103 of the US Patent Act define the requirements of *novelty* and *non-obviousness*,[123] respectively. As a GUI per se is not a 'a process,

---

[120] *Samsung Electronics (UK) Ltd v. Apple, Inc.* [2012] EWCA Civ. 1339, para. 3.
[121] What is referred to in the United States as utility patents and in the European Union simply as patents; hereinafter 'patents' with respect to both jurisdictions.
[122] 35 U.S.C. § 101.
[123] It is noteworthy that although they share the same statutory reference to non-obviousness, the de facto obviousness standard applied by the courts in the case of design patents differs form that applies in utility patents context; see M Risch, 'Functionality and graphical user interface design patents' (2014) 17 STLR 18.

7.4 A Brief Note on Patent Protection for GUIs

machine, manufacture, or composition of matter', it may only be claimed indirectly by claiming '(1) the processes involved in the creation, display or interaction with the interface and (2) the computer equipment and memory devices (i.e. machines) that are loaded with software that control the creation, display or interaction with the interface'.[124]

We have seen that the scope of protection of software-related inventions in the United States appears to be cyclical: starting with the Supreme Court's restrictive interpretation in the 1970s,[125] its more liberal approach in the 1980s,[126] the Court of Appeals for the Federal Circuit's opening of the floodgate in the 1990s,[127] followed by the Supreme Court's rein-in in the 2010s,[128] as subsequently interpreted by CAFC.[129] Thus, the present discussion would be best served by looking at the more recent development at the Supreme Court and at the CAFC.

Patents protecting GUIs have been granted in large numbers.[130] The key question in the present context is to what extent the subject matter of such patents is still eligible for patent protection in light of *Alice*. We have seen that in *Alice*, the Supreme Court held that ineligible abstract ideas do not become patentable simply by being implemented on a computer. The court suggested that software-related patent-eligibility assessment under Section 101 is a two pronged exercise: first one needs to determine whether the claims at issue are directed to one of the judicial

---

[124] A Practical Approach to Protection of Graphical User Interfaces in the United States of America, Intellectual Property Owners Association (White Paper prepared jointly by Software and Business Methods & Design Rights Committees 2008–2009), http://www.visiond.com/IPO2012/MATERIALS/Dougal_Durkin_Kirincich_Strand_GroupPaper.pdf (Accessed 10 May 2016) 10.

[125] *Gottschalk v. Benson* 409 U.S. 63 (1972); *Parker v. Flook*, 437 U.S. 584 (1978).

[126] *Diamond v. Diehr* 450 U.S. 175 (1981).

[127] *In re Alappat*, 33 F. 3d 1526 (Fed. Cir. 1994) (en banc), to be followed by *State St. Bank & Trust Co. v. Signature Financial Grp.* 149 F.3d 1368 (Fed. Cir. 1998) and *T&T Corp. v. Excel Communications, Inc.* 172 F.3d 1352 (Fed. Cir. 1999), *cert. denied* 120 S. Ct. 368 (1999).

[128] See, *Bilski v. Kappos* 561 U.S. 593 (2010); *Mayo Collaborative Services v. Prometheus Laboratories, Inc.* 132 S. Ct. 1289 (2012) and *Alice Corp. Pty. Ltd v. CLS Bank Int'l.* 134 S.Ct. 2347 (2014).

[129] For example, *DDR Holdings, LLC v. Hotels.com, L.P.* 773 F.3d 1245 (Fed. Cir. 2014); *buySAFE, Inc. v. Google, Inc.* 2014 U.S. App. LEXIS 16987 (Fed. Cir. 3 Sept. 2014); *Eon Corp. IP Holdings LLC v. AT&T Mobility LLC* No. 14-1392 (Fed. Cir. 2015); *Enfish v. Microsoft Corp.* No. 2015-1244 (Fed. Cir. 12 May 2016); *TLI Communications, LLC v. AV Automotive, LLC* No. 15-1372 (Fed. Cir. 17 May 2016).

[130] USPTO patent classes 345 and 715 are considered as GUI-related classes ('Presentation Computer Graphics Processing and Saver Selective Visual Display Systems' and 'Presentation Processing of Document, Operator Interface Processing, and Screen Saver Display Processing (Data Processing)', respectively); for specific examples of such patents, see the patents asserted in the recent Microsoft's claim against Corel, filed in the Northern District Court of California on 28 Dec. 2015; see http://www.protectingdesigns.com/images/Nguyen-2015-12-28-microsoft/2015-12-28-microsoft-v-corel.pdf (the '828 patent –' 'Command User Interface for Displaying Selectable Software Functionality Controls'; the '036 patent' – 'User Interface for Displaying Selectable Software Functionality Controls that Are Relevant to a Selected Object'; The '501 patent –' 'Method for Displaying Controls in a System Using a Graphical User Interface'; and the '415 patent –' 'Computer Application with Help Pane Integrated into Workspace').

exceptions such as laws of nature, natural phenomena, and abstract ideas;[131] if yes, then evaluate the elements of the claim in order to determine whether they involve an inventive concept that is sufficient to transform the patent-ineligible concept into a patent-eligible one. In order to make the said transformation, the claims must recite additional elements that amount to significantly more than the judicial exception.

We have seen that although subsequent to *Alice*, the number of grants of software-related patents had been significantly reduced, and a large number of such patents that were granted before *Alice Corp* are now facing unfavourable invalidation prospects, some software-related patents could survive a post *Alice* examination. For example, applying the *Enfish* rationale to GUIs, one needs to enquire whether the claims purport to improve the functioning of the computer itself, or improve an existing technological process.[132] Where this is established, the application might not fall foul of the abstract idea exception. It is not clear how expansively the courts would be prepared to interpret 'technological process' or 'improvement of the computer itself' in the context of GUIs, as no decision on that point has yet been issued. In themselves, features of graphic designs that appeal to users do not concern the functioning of the computer itself nor do they concern a technological process. However, it is yet to be seen whether the courts would be prepared to entertain arguments according to which when such features are combined with interaction steps or means or when they concern technical information (e.g. internal machine states), they could be considered as improving a technical process: for example, by enhancing the precision of an input device or by lowering the cognitive burden of a user when performing certain computer interactions.[133]

7.4.2 Protecting GUIs at the EPO

In Chapter 6, we have seen that under the currently prevalent 'any-hardware' approach, an application is not likely to fall foul of Article 52 as long as the claimed subject matter as a whole manifests a technical character. Such technical character will be present for the purpose of Article 52 whenever the subject matter is claimed in relation to hardware (e.g. a computer) rather than in abstract. We have also seen that the excluded areas under Article 52 still play a vital role in assessing patentability, but the focus has now shifted to Article 56, which concerns the

---

[131] For a critique of the Supreme Court's 'abstract idea' exclusion, see D Chisum and J Mueller, 'Commentary: lax Section 112 standards won't help the case for software patents' SSRN (19 May 2015) http://ssrn.com/abstract=2624758.

[132] *Enfish v. Microsoft Corp.*, No. 2015-1244 (Fed. Cir. 12 May 2016).

[133] In a similar vein to EPO Guideline G-II 3.7.1 in the 2012 Guidelines for Examination, now replaced by a later version.

7.4 A Brief Note on Patent Protection for GUIs

requirement of inventive step. Thus, where the claimed contribution is made exclusively within an excluded field (e.g. the presentation of information), then by definition, it does not possess a technical character.[134] Consequently, as a legal fiction, the skilled person is taken to know about this contribution for the purpose of assessment under Article 56, regardless of whether or not the said contribution is de facto novel and inventive.[135]

There are numerous decisions of EPO Boards of Appeal concerning patent-eligibility of GUIs.[136] While some aspects of GUIs that may affect the ease of use of a GUI may involve technical considerations, other aspects might not be considered technical: for example, aspects that may be based on aesthetic factors or are designed to convey information.[137]

In T333/95 the Technical Board of Appeal was faced with 'a method of creating an animation by moving a graphics object around a graphical display under control of a pointing device', where the graphic object was a cursor. The said graphic object was held to have a technical character since it decreased 'both the necessary mental and physical effort of the operator, since the direct movement of the graphics object, obviously, does not need the concentration necessary when the operation must be performed by means of a normal cursor'[138] On the other hand, menu-based GUIs do not always fare as well because they are found not to involve technical considerations. However, in T49/04, the Technical Board expressed a relaxed and expansive view on what may constitute a technical character in GUI context. It stressed that:

> a feature which relates to the manner how the 'cognitive content', such as images, is conveyed to the user can very well be considered as contributing to a technical solution to a technical problem. This would in particular be the case when [. . .] this particular manner of *conveying* the information enables the user to perform their task more efficiently.[139]

Similarly, in T928/03, the Technical Board found, inter alia, that a graphical marker in a user interface of a video football game, said marker suggesting the orientation of another prospective team player, to which a player currently controlled by user passes a ball, solved a problem that contributed to the technical function of the display.[140]

---

[134] A feature may have a technical character if it has a technical effect either internal or external to the computer.
[135] The English Court of Appeal described this legal fiction as 'intellectually dishonest', see *Aerotel Ltd (a company incorporated under the laws of Israel) v. Telco Holdings Ltd, Telco Global Distribution Ltd, Telco Global Ltd* [2006] EWCA Civ. 1371, para. 27.
[136] For example, see T769/92 SOHEI, T333/95, T244/00, T49/04, T125/04, T643/00, T928/03, and T1741/08.
[137] T Young, 'The patentability of GUIs: moving goalposts at the EPO' (2014) 36(7) EIPR 409–12.
[138] T333/95 (Interactive animation/I.B.M.).   [139] T49/04 (Text Processor/WALKER).
[140] T0928/03 (Video game/KONAMI).

Subsequent to the above decisions, the EPO published its 2012 Guidelines for Examiners, where it suggested that although in most cases, features relating to GUIs do not have a technical effect, in some cases, they might nevertheless do. This would be the case, in particular, where they:

> combined with interaction steps or means or when they concern technical information (e.g. internal machine states), the examiner must check whether they are necessary for achieving a particular technical effect, for example by enhancing the precision of an input device or by lowering the cognitive burden of a user when performing certain computer interactions. The technical effect achieved might be a more efficient man-machine interface.[141]

Thus, the Guidelines gave an example of a technical effect being generated when the cognitive burden of a GUI user was reduced. This, of course, had the potential of treating features that improve the usability of a GUI as having a technical effect. However, following decision T1741/08,[142] where it was held that the lowering of the cognitive burden as a result of choices as to what or how to present information was not sufficient to generate a technical effect, the Guidelines were amended and the specific example of technical effect in the case of lowering the cognitive burden was removed.[143] In addition, the new version of the Guidelines stipulates that the colour, size, and shape of items of the screen do not usually amount to a technical aspect of a GUI. In conclusion, it appears that where a reduction in the cognitive burden is the only claimed benefit, the application is not likely to prove successful, and the vast majority of applications concerned with GUIs in general are likely to face the same odds.[144]

---

[141] Guideline G-II 3.7.1, in the 2012 Guidelines for Examination.   [142] T 1741/08 (GUI layout/SAP).
[143] Guideline G-II 3.7.1, in the 2013 Guidelines for Examination.
[144] T Young, 'The patentability of GUIs: moving goalposts at the EPO' (2014) 6(7) EIPR, 409 (suggesting that in order to strengthen one's position when making a GUI-related patent application, the applicant may 'seek to emphasise technical information (e.g. internal machine states), and the interaction steps or means by which the user interacts with the computer. He should then consider the technical effect achieved, stressing technical advantages of input as opposed to output if appropriate'.

8

TRADE SECRETS AND THE SOFTWARE INDUSTRY

8.1 Introduction	219
8.2 Trade Secrets: The Legal Basis of the Right	221
8.3 Trade Secrets Protection in the European Union	224
8.3.1 Protection in Member States prior to the Trade Secrets Directive	224
8.3.2 The Trade Secrets Directive	225
8.3.2.1 *Background*	225
8.3.2.2 *The Trade Secrets Directive's framework*	226
8.4 Trade Secrets Protection in the United States	233
8.4.1 Background	233
8.4.2 Legislative framework	234
8.4.2.1 *The Uniform Trade Secrets Act*	235
8.4.2.2 *A brief note on the Defend the Trade Secrets Act 2016*	243

8.1 INTRODUCTION

At the time of writing, trade secrets legislative initiatives appear to be in fashion. While the Trade Secrets Directive (TSD) was adopted by the European Council on 27 May 2016,[1] President Obama signed the Defend Trade Secrets Act (DTSA) into US law, effective immediately.[2] This chapter examines trade secrets regimes in both jurisdictions, with particular emphasis on their effect in relation to the software industry.

Almost every IP right originates in a secret. For example, an inventor keeps his inventive concept secret until he files for a patent; a writer keeps secret the

---

[1] Directive (EU) 2016/... of the European Parliament and of the Council of... on the undisclosed know-how business information (trade secrets) against their unlawful acquisition, use, and disclosure, See the final version: http://data.consilium.europa.eu/doc/document/PE-76-2015-INIT/en/pdf.

[2] Defend Trade Secrets Act of 2016, Public Law 114-153 114th Congress (11 May 2016), https://www.congress.gov/114/plaws/publ153/PLAW-114publ153.pdf.

Beyond the Code: Protection of Non-Textual Features of Software. First Edition. Noam Shemtov.
© Noam Shemtov 2017. Published 2017 by Oxford University Press.

detailed theme of his book until it is published; marketing personnel will do the same in relation to a new brand that is about to be launched. The same may apply to a designer in relation to a new product design until a registered design application or a design patent application is filed. These early stages of conception often require protection against misappropriation.

Right holders always considered trade secrets as useful tools in protecting their business assets and innovation. As regards software products that are circulating in the marketplace, trade secrets acted as a supplementary layer of protection. For example, software features that could not be uncovered through reverse engineering or decompilation, such as higher-level abstraction materials,[3] or new methods for delivering content, could be successfully protected by trade secrets law throughout the product's life cycle. But trade secrets could also be useful in relation to features that could be uncovered through reverse engineering, such as algorithms or data structures. As explained elsewhere in this title, reverse engineering is a time consuming and demanding practice whose result is often far from certain. Forcing one's competitors to go down the reverse engineering route, rather than poaching an employee that may disclose the sought-after information, could potentially have a number of consequences. First, it might be that the length of time and expense involved would be sufficient to deter a competitor from reverse engineering with the effect of such competitor either licensing the relevant information where possible, or abandoning his plans to access such information all together. Where a competitor nevertheless decides to practice reverse engineering and eventually successfully does so, a right holder may still enjoy his lead-time advantage owing to the time it takes to go through the reverse engineering process. Whether or not trade secrets law could and should be used to prohibit reverse engineering altogether is a question that is discussed in some detail below.

It should be borne in mind that some commercial software is not distributed to the public at all but is offered over the Internet as a service. Since the code of such software stays out of reach of competitors, its internal architecture might not be accessed through reverse engineering and decompilation. In such cases, trade secrets may serve as the main vehicle for protection against misappropriation of some of the innovative features of such software architecture.[4] Although patent protection, where possible, is an attractive option, it might not be the most attractive one under such circumstances. Even if a patent is likely to be obtained, which is at best difficult to predict in this sector, it carries with it a requirement of enabling disclosure, which a trade secret obviously does not. Admittedly, unlike trade secrets,

---

[3] For example, source code commentary and specification.
[4] For example, Google's search algorithm is one of the company's more valuable assets, ranking websites on the basis of factors such as anchor tags, page rank, inbound links, relevant text, etc.

patents also give protection against independent creation, but right holders should think long and hard whether the trade-off between that scope of protection and the secrecy inherent to trade secrets is worthwhile.

With software being available exclusively in the cloud environment becoming ever more common, the discussion above is only likely to increase in relevance.[5] After all, in a cloud environment no one has access to the sought-after software architecture except for the developers or other employees that may have access to the software.[6] Such persons could and should be subjected to a carefully drafted confidentiality agreement.

Finally, trade secrets law can be very effective against ex-employees. While labour laws vary from one Member State to another within the European Union, as well as amongst the various states in the United States, a well-drafted non-disclosure or secrecy agreement could prove more valuable, under the right circumstances, than a non-competition agreement. This is so since the latter is generally construed narrowly by the courts, and must contain time, geographic and/or industry limitation. In contrast, a non-disclosure agreement is not necessarily subject to narrow interpretation and does not have to include any of the above limitations. Of course, there must be trade secrets in the first place for such an agreement to be meaningful, while non-competition agreement may be valid irrespective of their existence.

Since both in the case of the EU and the US protection hinges upon recent legislative developments, the discussion below surveys this legislative framework in some detail, before examining its impact on the software industry.

8.2 TRADE SECRETS: THE LEGAL BASIS OF THE RIGHT

Prior to examining the legal regimes for protection against misappropriation of trade secrets in the United States and the European Union, it is necessary first to understand the legal nature of the right at issue. Unlike intellectual property rights that reside on the industrial side of the industrial/intellectual property divide, trade secrets do not require any procedural formalities as a precondition for protection. Although conditions for protection vary from one jurisdiction to another, some general standards for considering the information

---

[5] See B Butler, 'Gartner: cloud will be the "default option" for software deployment by 2020' (22 June 2016), http://www.networkworld.com/article/3087363/cloud-computing/gartner-cloud-will-be-the-default-option-for-software-deployment-by-2020.html.

[6] Of course certain types of black box reverse engineering are technically possible to practice in cloud environment, which might be useful in uncovering various behavioural aspects of the software at issue. Whether a licence that designates such aspects as trade secrets is likely to have the desired effect is discussed below.

in question as a protectable secret can be found in Article 39 of the TRIPS Agreement:[7]

- The information must be secret (i.e. it is not generally known among, or readily accessible to, circles that normally deal with the kind of information in question).
- It must have commercial value because it is a secret.
- It must have been subject to reasonable steps by the rightful holder of the information to keep it secret (e.g. through confidentiality agreements).

But before discussing the relevant conditions for protection of trade secrets and the circumstances under which such protection may be available, it might be useful to examine the legal basis for granting such protection in the first place. Namely, why do we grant protection against the appropriation of trade secrets under certain circumstances? Again, the legal position on this point varies greatly across various jurisdictions. First, it is not entirely clear what may be the doctrinal basis for protection. Is it based on relationship (e.g. contract, employment, and fiduciary), equity, property, or concepts of unfair competition and unjust enrichment? Or maybe there is no coherent theory behind trade secrets protection on the international level, and its justification could be traced to a collection of approaches and norms on protection of business information.[8]

Not only is there a divergence between different countries in relation to the approaches towards trade secrecy protection, but such divergence also exists between scholars as to the proper justification for such protection.[9] The differences in doctrinal basis for trade secrets protection amongst various countries flows from different normative and conceptual premises in such countries. The situation is not unlike other branches of law, which although recognized on an international level, are also based on different conceptual and normative bases in

---

[7] *TRIPS: Agreement on Trade-Related Aspects of Intellectual Property Rights* (Apr. 15, 1994, Marrakesh Agreement Establishing the World Trade Organization) 1869 UNTS 299; (1994) 33 ILM 1197.

[8] This explanation was originally suggested by Bone and was later described by Claeys as 'trade secrecy nihilism'. See R G Bone, 'A new look at trade secret law: doctrine in search of justification'(1998) 86 Cal. L. Rev. 241; E R Claeys, 'Private law theory and corrective justice in trade secrecy' (2011) George Mason Law & Economics Research Paper No. 11-14; 4(2) *Journal of Tort Law*, Article 2

[9] See, for example, on the debate in this context under US law in ibid; M Risch, 'Why do we have trade secrets?' (2007) 11 *Marquette Intellectual Property Law Review* 1; under UK and common law countries in general, in T Aplin et al., *Gurry on Breach of Confidence: The Protection of Confidential Information* (Oxford, OUP 2012). Ch. 3; under Italian law, in G Ghidini and V Falce, 'Trade secrets as intellectual property rights: a disgraceful upgrading - notes on an Italian 'reform', in R C Dreyfuss and K J Strandburg, eds, *The Law and Theory of Trade Secrecy: A Handbook of Contemporary Research* (Cheltenham, Edward Elgar 2011) 140-51.

8.2 Trade Secrets: The Legal Basis of the Right

various countries, which could be traced to these countries' unique history and legal traditions.[10] Irrespective of their different origin or doctrinal basis, recognition on international level of such branches of law is not in doubt; this is also the case with trade secrets. Thus, it has been noted in relation to trade secrets protection as early as the mid-nineteenth century:

> In some cases, it [the jurisdiction of the court] has been referred to property, in others to contract, and in others, again, it has been treated as founded upon trust or confidence, meaning, as I conceive, that the court fastens the obligation on the conscience of the party, and enforces it against him in the same manner as it enforces against a party to whom a benefit is given the obligation of performing a promise on the faith of which the benefit has been conferred; but, upon whatever grounds the jurisdiction is founded, the authorities leave no doubt as to the exercise of it.[11]

Generally speaking, it appears that under most legal systems, trade secrets protection does not constitute an exclusive right *stricto sensu*. Rather, it protects the veil of secrecy put up by the trade secret holder; it is not about generating incentives to create and develop per se, but about enforcing standards of commercial ethics.[12]

It is noteworthy that a discussion on the doctrinal basis for trade secrets' protection and its potential categorization as property is not of value only to legal theorists, but may be of real significance to businesses relying on trade secrets protection. For example, in *Ruckelshaus v. Monsanto*[13] the US Supreme Court recognized trade secrets as a type of property. This finding was instrumental to the court's holding that since a government agency, the Environmental Protection Agency, forced the disclosure of the said trade secrets, the applicant was entitled to just compensation under the 'Taking Clause' of the Fifth Amendment of the US Constitution. Similarly, the majority of EU Member States did not consider trade secrets as intellectual property,[14] thus precluding the application of the Enforcement Directive.[15]

---

[10] For example, see Barnett's survey of the different theories on contractual obligations, discussing autonomy of will, reliance, efficiency, fairness, and bargain theories and their prominence in various jurisdictions in R E Barnett, 'A consent theory of contract' (1986) 86 Colum. L. Rev. 269.

[11] *Morison v. Moat* (1851) 9 Hare 241, per Turner V-C.

[12] For example, see *Kewanee Oil Co. v. Bicron Corp.* 416 U.S. 470 (1974). Admittedly, enforcing such standards may ultimately generate incentives to innovate.

[13] *Ruckelshaus v. Monsanto* Co. (1984) 467 U.S. 986, 1002-3.   [14] With the exception of Italy.

[15] For the same reason, the Enforcement Directive was not extended in its application to the newly enacted TDS (The Impact Assessment explaining that 'trade secrets are not intellectual property rights', 267). This being so, the TSD includes harmonization measures on remedies.

8.3 TRADE SECRETS PROTECTION IN THE EUROPEAN UNION

On 26 May 2016, the European Council adopted the new TSD, which needs to be implemented by all Member States by mid to the end of 2018. The main objective of the TSD is to align protection against misappropriation of trade secrets across the different Member States.

8.3.1 Protection in Member States prior to the Trade Secrets Directive

At present the position on trade secrecy protection across the European Union varies significantly from one Member State to another. While Sweden is the only Member State that has specific legislation for trade secrets protection,[16] all other Member States offer protection through a piecemeal of civil and criminal laws. For example, countries such as Austria, Germany, Poland, and Spain rely on unfair competition law; Italy and Portugal have provisions on protection of trade secrets in their IP civil codes; the Netherlands uses tort law to provide protection; while the United Kingdom and Ireland rely on common law, contracts, and equity.[17]

Furthermore, there is currently no uniform definition on what constitutes a trade secret. In fact, most Member States have no clear definition, with only ten of them defining what constitutes a *trade secret*. It follows that each jurisdiction adopted its own eligibility standards for such protection, which resulted in fragmentation of protection of trade secrets across the single market. The same applies to the legal position in relation available remedies. Finally, a study on trade secrets commissioned by the European Commission found that the above-mentioned fragmented position is compounded by the risk of losing control over trade secrets for lack of efficient protection during court proceeding in the majority of Member States.[18]

Inter alia, the above led the European Commission to conclude that the single market would benefit from a unified regime for trade secrets protection.

---

[16] Act on the Protection of Trade Secrets (1990: 409).

[17] For an overview of the legal protection models of trade secrets across Member States, see Baker and Mackenzie, 'Study on trade secrets and confidential business information in the Internal Market', prepared for the European Commission (April 2013) 4, http://ec.europa.eu/internal_market/iprenforcement/docs/trade-secrets/130711_final-study_en.pdf.

[18] Ibid, 7.

8.3 Trade Secrets Protection: The European Union

8.3.2 The Trade Secrets Directive

The TSD was enacted following two commissioned studies,[19] a European Commission-led conference,[20] and a public consultation exercise.[21]

8.3.2.1 Background

These initiatives essentially identified the abovementioned fragmented protection in the single market against misappropriation of trade secrets as a major drawback, since it made handling and protecting trade secrets across the single market cumbersome and costly.

Two key problems were highlighted as justifying a harmonized regime: (i) business competitiveness being held back due to a fragmented trade secrets market, with some Member States, inter alia, offering weak and unpredictable level of protection. Since trade secrets allow creators and innovators to derive profit from their creation or innovation, in particular SMEs who rely on trade secrets even more so than larger companies do, lack of adequate and predictable protection of know-how and business information hinders competitiveness.[22] (ii) suboptimal cross-border collaboration in creating intellectual assets and innovation, which results from impeded incentives to invest in such collaborative efforts. Apparently, such incentives are partially impeded by the risk of trade secrets appropriation, especially in Member States where the level of protection is weak or unpredictable, and by the overall fragmentation of the market.[23] Thus, 'Cross-border network research and development, as well as innovation-related activities, including related production and subsequent cross-border trade, are rendered less attractive and more difficult within the Union, thus also resulting in Union-wide innovation-related inefficiencies.'[24] Both of these problems were considered to hinder potential employment growth and mobility, as well as to stifle competitiveness of businesses in the Internal Market.[25] According to the Commission, the flip side of these assumptions is that introducing to the Internal Market a harmonized trade secrets

---

[19] Hogan Lovells International, 'Study on trade secrets and parasitic copying (look-alikes)' (2012) *MARKT/2010/20/D: Report on Trade Secrets for the European*; Baker and Mackenzie, cited in fn. 17.

[20] 'Trade secrets: supporting innovation, protecting know-how', (Brussels, 29 June 2012).

[21] Launched on 11 Dec. 2012 and closed on 8 Mar. 2013, with 386 respondents taking part. See http://ec.europa.eu/internal_market/consultations/2012/trade-secrets_en.htm.

[22] Directive (EU) 2016/943 of the European Parliament and of the Council of 8 June 2016 on the protection of undisclosed know-how and business information (trade secrets) against their unlawful acquisition, use and disclosure [2016] OJ L 157, Recital 2. Hereinafter referred to as the TSD.

[23] Ibid, Recitals 3 and 8.   [24] Ibid, Recital 8.

[25] See Commission Staff Working Document Impact Assessment accompanying the document proposal for a Directive of the European Parliament and of the Council on the protection of undisclosed know-how and business information (trade secrets) against their unlawful acquisition, use and disclosure, (2013) SWD 471 Final, issued on 28 Nov. 34–6.

regime is likely to lead to a reversal of the abovementioned negative trends. The said assumptions were described as problematic by some scholars, who pointed out that the Commission appears to have relied on evidence selectively chosen to establish a case in favour of harmonization.[26]

8.3.2.2 *The Trade Secrets Directive's framework*

As a preliminary observation at this stage, it should be noted that the TSD does not follow the property model endorsed in other jurisdictions, such as in the United States.[27] The TSD's reference to trade secrets holders rather than owners further illustrates this point.[28] However, while the TSD does not consider trade secrets as property, it does not explicitly prescribe the manner in which Member States may choose to protect against their misappropriation. The same flexibility is also demonstrated in relation to the position under the TDS on the scope of protection granted by Member States. Thus, Article 1(1) provides, 'Member States may, in compliance with the provisions of the TFEU, provide for more far-reaching protection against the unlawful acquisition, use or disclosure of trade secrets than that required by this Directive, [. . .]'. In essence, the Directive does not provide for full harmonization, but rather sets minimal standards, subject to a number of safeguards.[29]

The definition of *trade secret* Article 2 provides a definition of what may constitute a trade secret. It stipulates in this context three conditions: (i) the information in question must not be generally known among or readily accessible to persons within the circles that normally deal with the kind of information in question; (ii) it has commercial value because it is secret; and (iii) it has been subject to reasonable steps under the circumstances, by a relevant person, to keep it secret. From a UK perspective, Condition (iii) and its focus on 'reasonable steps' should be

---

[26] For example, see T Aplin, 'A critical evaluation of the proposed EU Trade Secrets Directive' (18 July 2014) King's College London Law School Research Paper No. 2014-25, 5, SSRN, http://ssrn.com/abstract=2467946, arguing,

> While it is accepted that trade secrets are valuable assets and have an important role to play independently of and in tandem with patent, designs and copyright, in promoting innovation, the Commission seems conveniently to pluck out the evidence from the B&M Report that supports the case for harmonization while ignoring the evidence that might make us question such an approach.

[27] TSD, Recital 16 stating, 'In the interest of innovation and to foster competition, the provisions of this Directive should not create any exclusive right to know-how or information protected as trade secrets.'

[28] For example, see TSD, Recitals 23, 24, and 32, Arts 2, 4, and more.

[29] In particular, although Member States may provide for stricter protection than prescribed in the TDS, it must be done in conformity with the definition of *lawful disclosure* under Art. 3, exceptions defined under Art. 5, *the nature and proportionality of measures and remedi*es as defined under Arts 6 and 7(1), a limitation period not exceeding six years in accordance with Art. 8, the requirement of preservation of confidentiality in legal proceedings under Art. 9, and more; see Art. 1(1).

considered with care, as it has no equivalent under the current UK regime. Trade secrets holders should therefore ensure that the steps taken by them to keep the information at issue secret are sufficiently substantial to be considered as 'reasonable'. Clearly, the above definition may potentially capture numerous elements of software. Recital 14 provides that trade secrets' definition should 'be constructed so as to cover know-how, business information and technological information [...]'. Essentially, any aspect of software's design process, internal architecture, or source code that meets the above conditions could potentially qualify.

One of the hurdles that needs to be cleared in the software context would be how 'readily accessible' these software elements are. Can it be said that where a skilled person could uncover the said information through reverse engineering, such information should be considered as readily accessible to 'persons within the circles that normally deal with the kind of information'? It appears that the answer to this question is negative. First, it is arguable whether pieces of code or fragments of architecture that could only be uncovered through reverse engineering or disassembly are *readily* accessible. Thus, the emphasis under these circumstances should be on the fact that such access would be far from effortless and therefore would not comply with the 'readily' part of the definition. Second, if such information is to be regarded as 'readily accessible' and therefore outside the scope of a trade secret's definition, why include specific reference to reverse engineering activities in Article 3(1)(b) and define these as examples of lawful acquisition of trade secrets?

Another interesting question that relates to the above is whether a trade secret loses its trade secret status, if a person lawfully reverse engineers a piece of software and then circulates or makes the uncovered information available to 'persons within the circles that normally deal with the kind of information'? It appears that once this takes place, the trade secret status would be lost.[30]

Would the outcome of such assessment change where the original acquisition was unlawful, such as through decompilation for reasons other than achieving interoperability?[31] Article 4(4) reads: 'The acquisition, use or disclosure of a trade secret shall also be considered unlawful whenever a person, at the time of the acquisition, use or disclosure, knew or ought, under the circumstances, to have known that the trade secret had been obtained directly or indirectly from another

---

[30] T Aplin, 'A critical evaluation of the proposed EU Trade Secrets Directive' (18 July 2014), King's College London Law School Research Paper No. 2014-25, SSRN, 11, http://ssrn.com/abstract=2467946.
[31] Even where decompilation is practised in order to achieve interoperability, Art. 6(2)(b) of the Software Directive states that it must not be given to another except where necessary to achieve interoperability. Thus, making available over the web the information that was obtain in order to achieve interoperability amounts to violation of Art. 6 and it constitutes copyright infringement. Such acquisition is not likely to be considered as 'lawful' under Art. 3 of the TSD.

person who was using or disclosing the trade secret unlawfully.' Thus, Article 4(4) essentially provides that where the circumstances under which information in question was circulated or made available put the recipients on actual or constructive notice that the information at issue was originally obtained unlawfully, its acquisition by the recipients is deemed unlawful.

However, it should be noted that in order for the acquisition to be considered as unlawful in the first place, the subject matter must comply with the definition of a *trade secret*. It is suggested that, if at the point of time of acquisition the information was readily available, it is not a trade secret irrespective of whether it was a trade secret in the past but was then unlawfully publicly disclosed. Thus, it is suggested that if the information loses the secretive quality necessary under Article 2(1)(a) by the time the contested acquisition takes place, it appears that there is little that the former trade secret holder could do in relation to such acquisition.

Lawful acquisition Article 3 describes what may constitute lawful acquisition, use, and disclosure of trade secrets. The provision states that lawful acquisition takes place where a trade secret has been acquired, inter alia, as a result of: (i) independent discovery or creation; (ii) a variety of reverse engineering activities carried out on a subject matter that has been made available to the public, or is lawfully in the possession of the acquirer of the information—who is not bound by a valid legal duty to refrain from acquiring the trade secret; (iii) any other honest commercial practice. While (i) and (ii) are self—explanatory to an extent, at first glance Article 3(iii) is less clear. It is suggested that what might constitute 'honest commercial practices' is a fact specific query and may vary greatly from one industry sector to another. Moreover, that which may be acceptable in one segment of the software industry may be considered as non-customary in another segment and vice versa. In the sphere of trade-marks, the CJEU defined *honest use* in the context of what constitutes 'honest practices in industrial or commercial matters', as 'a duty to act fairly in relation to the legitimate interests of the trade-mark owner'.[32] This was followed by the court providing a number of examples of what does not constitute honest use in this context. It is yet to be seen whether similar guidelines will be provided in relation to trade secrets.

Reverse engineering As far as software products or services are concerned, the most interesting part of the definition of *lawful acquisition* relates to reverse engineering. It is suggested that in this context, one Recital and three provisions of the TSD should be read in conjunction: Recital 16 and Articles 3(1)(b), 4(2), and 4(3)(b).

---

[32] Case C-228/03, *The Gillette Company and Gillette Group Finland Oy v. LA- Laboratories Ltd Oy*, para. 41.

8.3   Trade Secrets Protection: The European Union

The general position of the TDS on reverse engineering is stipulated in Recital 16, which provides, 'Reverse engineering of a lawfully acquired product should be considered as a lawful means of acquiring information, except when otherwise contractually agreed. The freedom to enter into such contractual arrangements can, however, be limited by law.' Article 3(1)(b) stipulates that the following should be considered as lawful acquisition of a trade secret: 'observation, study, disassembly or testing of a product or object that has been made available to the public or that is lawfully in the possession of the acquirer of the information who is free from any legally valid duty to limit the acquisition of the trade secret'. Article 4(2) defines *unlawful acquisition* as being without the consent of the trade secret holder and results from:

(a) unauthorised access to, appropriation of, or copying of any documents, objects, materials, substances or electronic files, lawfully under the control of the trade secret holder, containing the trade secret or from which the trade secret can be deduced; (b) any other conduct which, under the circumstances, is considered contrary to honest commercial practices.

Finally, Article 4(3)(b) defines *unlawful use of a trade secret* as one that is carried out without the consent of the trade secret holder, while 'being in breach of a contractual or any other duty to limit the use of the trade secret'.

It is clear from the above provisions that, as such, the practice of reverse engineering is not restricted by the TDS. It is equally clear that a contractual provision that prohibits reverse engineering is likely to be ineffective in relation to the Software Directive and thus in relation to the TSD. But could a restrictive licensing provision defining the sought-after information as a trade secret and limiting access to and use of that information change this position? Could it then be argued that a breach of such secrecy clause would render reverse engineering 'unlawful' and thus amount to unlawful acquisition?

It is arguable whether such a licensing provision is likely to be enforceable in light of the Software Directive. We have seen that Articles 5(3) and 6 of the Software Directive enable a party, under certain circumstances, to engage in black box reverse engineering and decompilation respectively. As mentioned, the TSD does not affect the permissions granted under these provisions. Article 8 of the Software Directive further provides that any contractual provision that seeks to prohibit that which Articles 5(3) and 6 permit is void and null. However, Article 8 also provides that the Directive shall be without prejudice to any other legal provisions such as those concerning, inter alia, trade secrets.

It is suggested that it would make little sense if it would be possible to circumvent the effect of Article 8 by contractually defining the *sought-after information* as a trade secret, rather than simply prohibit reverse engineering. That would clearly defeat the pro-competition considerations that stand at the basis of Articles 5(3), 6, and 8, and courts would be well advised to bear these in mind when considering reverse engineering in the context of the TSD.

When it comes on the position under the TDS, Recital 16 suggests that although reverse engineering is lawful, this might be restricted by contract. However, it goes on to stipulate that 'the freedom to enter into such contractual arrangements can, however, be limited by law'.[33] Hence, a contractual provision that limits reverse engineering may not be effective under the TSD, since such a contractual provision is limited by law; namely, void under the Software Directive.[34] Examination of Articles 3(1)(b), 4(2), and 4(3)(b) leads to the same conclusion.

Article 3(2)(b) defines the lawful acquirer as someone who engages in reverse engineering activities while he 'is free from any legally valid duty to limit the acquisition of the trade secret'. Since a contractual provision that defines the *sought-after information* as a trade secret, which may be used only for a specific limited purpose, might be ineffective under the Software Directive, it may not be considered as a 'legally valid duty' that limits the acquisition of the trade secret. By the same token, reverse engineering done in violation of such contractual provision is not likely to be caught under the definition of *unlawful acquisition* of Article 4(2). Thus, the said contractual provision, ineffective under Article 8 of the Software Directive, is not likely to render the access gained to the sought-after information 'unauthorized', neither is it likely to render it 'contrary to honest commercial practices'. Finally, although on literal interpretation of Article 4(3)(b) it is at least arguable that using the information for a purpose other than the one narrowly defined under a confidentiality clause may render it 'unlawful', it is suggested that where such information has been obtained in accordance with Articles 5(3) or 6 of the Software Directive, courts are not likely to opt for such interpretation. When faced with such a question, courts should look at the overall impact of such a confidentiality clause. Holding such clause enforceable could enable right holders to defeat the pro-competition policy considerations embodied in Articles 5(3), 6, and 8. This being so, it is argued that courts are likely to find such clauses ineffective under the TSD.[35]

---

[33] It is noteworthy that the position in the United States is different. Since anti-reverse engineering contractual provisions are not necessarily void, uncovering information in breach of such provision may render such acquisition 'improper' under Section 1(1), UTSA 1985.

[34] That is, the ability to enter such a contract is limited by law.

[35] The rationale that courts are likely to employ in this instance may be similar to that applied by the CJEU in C-406/10 *SAS Institute Inc. v. World Programming Ltd* para. 47–59, finding that a person that carried out acts covered by a click-wrap licence with a purpose that went beyond the framework established by that licence did not infringe the copyright in the computer program following acts of reverse engineering.

8.3 Trade Secrets Protection: The European Union

However, while the rationale behind exempting reverse engineering and decompilation from copyright infringement is hardly in doubt, it is argued that the same rationale does not always hold in relation to liability for misappropriation of trade secrets. Most people would agree that it should not be possible to use trade secrets law as a means to defeat the intended effect of Articles 5(3), 6, and 8. However, there are potential scenarios where it could be convincingly argued that trade secrecy rules should be able to prevent a party from using the information uncovered through reverse engineering, whether or not permissible under copyright law.

A useful example to such a scenario is the relationship formed between the parties in the context of beta testing.[36] Let us assume that ABC is a developer that just completed the development of its newest product, a potentially successful application program of one type or another. Cost of development was significant, and the new application program is predicted to generate substantial returns. ABC's marketing department would like to contact potential customers and arrange for fifty of them to receive the beta version of the new application program, and accompanying documentation; the beta-testing period is predicted to last six months. The risks that ABC face should one of the beta-version recipients decide to reverse engineer the program are obvious. While it could be argued that reverse engineering a program that is already circulating in the marketplace is permissible as the right owner is enjoying a lead-time advantage, the same could not be said in the case of a beta-version scenario. ABC's software could be reverse engineered, its logic and underlying functionality uncovered and cloned before ABC had a chance to enjoy its lead-time advantage and recoup its development cost.

While it is hardly arguable that from a copyright perspective such a scenario does not justify a change to the general rule that reverse engineering is a permissible practice,[37] whether or not taking place during beta-testing period, the same cannot be said in relation to trade secrets protection. Unlike copyright law, trade secrets protection is informed, inter alia, by the type of relationship that exists between the trade secrets holder and the recipient, as reflected both in the definition of what constitutes a trade secret[38] and what does or does not amount 'lawful acquisition'. Where the relationships were such that a recipient agreed to the terms of a licence under which a beta version was given to him, not to reverse engineer or use any information uncovered through reverse engineering for any purpose

---

[36] A beta version of software is a version that is made available for testing, usually by users outside the right holder's organization, before a market release.

[37] This is so since being an exclusive property right, copyright protection is not dependent on the type of relationship existing between the author and members of the public.

[38] 'Reasonable steps', under Art.2(1)(c) of the TSD, may entail the inclusion of a confidentiality clause that limits the use of the uncovered information.

other than that which is strictly defined, the rationale for holding such a clause unenforceable, and, consequently, acquisition or use as 'lawful' is questionable. Therefore, it might be preferable if courts would attempt to maintain some flexibility in this context rather than hold that since such a contractual obligation is not enforceable under Article 8 of the Software Directive, it is also ineffective in relation to the TSD.

Since the public policy considerations that underpin our copyright and trade secrets regimes are quite different, it is perfectly justifiable that a contractual provision that has no effect for copyright purposes is nevertheless effective for trade secrets purposes. The first paragraph of Article 8, which states that the Directive is without prejudice to trade secrets law, may enable the courts to make the above distinction between the two regimes concerning the effect of a contractual provision that limits reverse engineering or the use of the information resulting therefrom. Of course, this does not mean that every time such contractual provision is used it should be found effective under trade secrets law and render reverse engineering or use unlawful. What ideally should be developed is a flexible mechanism that enables the court to take into account the particular circumstances of the case. For example, the courts may use the reference to 'conformity to honest commercial practices' under the Article 3 definition of *lawful acquisition*, or 'contrary to honest commercial practices' under the Article 4 definition of *unlawful acquisition*, as a means to make such assessment. As mentioned, under trade-mark law, the CJEU has held that acting in accordance with 'honest practices in industrial or commercial matters', means that a party is under 'a duty to act fairly in relation to the legitimate interests of the trade-mark owner'.[39] Applying the same rationale in the present context, courts may employ a similar formula: in order to act in 'conformity to honest commercial practices', a party would be under a duty to act fairly in relation to the legitimate interests of the trade secret holder. As argued above, the legitimate interests of the trade secret holder may be jeopardized where a beta version of its software would be reverse engineered and cloned during the beta-testing period.

Some of the issues highlighted above call upon special consideration in the context of the software industry, and were therefore discussed in detail. However, the TDS in general contains numerous provisions whose impact on businesses that derive competitive advantage from trade secrets, whether software related or not, is likely to be significant. Thus, issues pertaining to secondary infringement and third parties,[40] treatment of infringing goods, employees and ex-employee,[41]

---

[39] Case C-228/03, *The Gillette Company and Gillette Group Finland Oy v. LA- Laboratories Ltd Oy* para. 41.
[40] Art. 4(4) TSD.
[41] Inter alia, see Recital 14 TSD (stating, 'The definition of trade secret excludes trivial information and the experience and skills gained by employees in the normal course of their employment [. . .]')

limitation period,[42] preservation of confidentiality during legal proceedings,[43] and measures and remedies,[44] to name but a few, are all of utmost importance to a successful operation of a harmonized legal regime in relation to trade secrets across the Internal Market.[45]

8.4 TRADE SECRETS PROTECTION IN THE UNITED STATES

Traditionally, the US patent system has provided comprehensive and arguable excessive protection to software-related inventions. However, recent developments in US patent law jurisprudence suggest that the software protection landscape has changed.

8.4.1 Background

The Supreme Court decision in *Alice v. CLS Bank*[46] significantly narrowed available protection for software-related inventions. Although it is still possible to obtain a patent for a software-based product or service, it is more difficult to do so. The court in *Alice* made it clear that in order to be eligible for patent protection, the invention at issue needs to manifest an inventive concept that goes beyond mere implementation by computer. Consequently, software developers may conclude that under certain circumstances, it is trade secrecy that offers the best vehicle for protecting their innovation and business assets.

Until recently, trade secrecy was considered purely a matter of state law, and the legal regime governing the protection of trade secrets varied, to an extent, between states. The National Conference of Commissioners on Uniform State Laws proposed a Uniform Trade Secrets Act (UTSA) in 1979. The vast majority of states, the District of Columbia, the US Virgin Islands, and Puerto Rico have all adopted the Act either 'as is' or in modified version, with the States of New York and Massachusetts[47] being the only exceptions; the latter relying on common

---

[42] Art. 8 TSD (not exceeding six year).

[43] Art. 9 TSD (the Impact Study, 152, found that inadequate mechanisms to maintain confidentiality during legal proceedings reduce the motivation to seek legal relief).

[44] Issues pertaining thereto are addressed in Arts 6, 7, 10, 12, 13, 14, 15, and 16 of the TSD.

[45] For a general overview of the text of the Trade Secret Directive, see P L C Torremans, 'The road towards the harmonisation of trade secrets law in the European Union' (20 January 2016); 'Revista La Propiedad Inmaterial', No. 20, Julio-Diciembre de 2015, SSRN, <http://ssrn.com/abstract=2719015>; T Aplin, 'A critical evaluation of the proposed EU Trade Secrets Directive' (18 July 2014), King's College London Law School Research Paper No. 2014-25, SSRN, <http://ssrn.com/abstract=2467946>; D N D Pereira, 'The European Trade Secrets Directive (ETSD): nothing new under the sun?' (25 July 2015) *Lex Research Topics on Innovation 2015-1*, SSRN, http://ssrn.com/abstract=2635897.

[46] *Alice Corp. Pty. Ltd. v. CLS Bank Int'l* 134 S.Ct. 2347 (2014).

[47] With Massachusetts expected to adopt the UTSA in 2016; see Uniform Law Commission, Trade Secrets Act: Legislative Tracking, http://j.mp/1sGUTVv.

law.[48] The discussion below concerns the legal protection, its nature and scope, granted under the USTA. However, this state of affairs, where trade secrets protection is governed exclusively under state laws has recently changed. The DTSA was signed into law with immediate effect by President Barak Obama on 11 May 2016. It is intended to supplement state law rather than to pre-empt or replace it.[49] Finally, there is one more piece of federal legislation that may be mentioned in brief in this context—The Economic Espionage Act 1996,[50] which deals not only with industrial espionage but also with trade secrets theft. However, the Economic Espionage Act deals almost exclusively with the criminality of various practices in relation to, inter alia, trade secrets theft and thus will not be discussed in detail.[51]

Being based on state law has one potential major repercussion in the present context, with particular relevance to the software industry; the possibility of pre-emption. Thus, in a similar vein to copyright pre-emption discussed in Chapter 2, where a state law-based trade secret-right clashes with federal policy in relation to the same subject matter, congressional will prevails. Since trade secrets and intellectual property rights, such as copyright, sometimes occupy the same space, questions of pre-emption may arise.[52] The discussion below addresses such questions, in particular in relation to anti reverse engineering licensing clauses that identify the relevant information as a trade secret and limit its use accordingly.

8.4.2 Legislative framework

As mentioned, the vast majority of states opted for adopting UTSA either fully or in a modified version. Where state law jurisprudence does not provide guidelines in relation to a given scenario, a court may turn to generally accepted principles of trade secrecy law, which are to be found in the Restatements of Torts 1937. Thus, before examining the UTSA is some detail, it may be beneficial to survey the general principles of protection against misappropriation of trade secrets, as

---

[48] It is an interesting fact that both states are commercial and technology hubs, respectively.
[49] Although the DTSA largely mirrors UTSA, there are a number of differences between the two; these are described below.
[50] Recently amended by the DTSA 2016.
[51] On the effect of the Act on innovation, see R C Dreyfuss and O Lobel, 'Economic espionage as reality or rhetoric: equating trade secrecy with national security' (19 January 2016) *Lewis & Clark Law Review*; San Diego Legal Studies Paper No. 16-207, SSRN, http://ssrn.com/abstract=2718557.
[52] In the case of copyright, two types of pre-emption should be considered: statutory pre-emption under USC 17 § 301 and constitutional pre-emption under of 'supremacy clause' within the US Const. Art. VI.

stipulated under the Restatement of Torts.[53] Section 757, comment (b), therein provides the generally acceptable definition of trade secret:

> [a] trade secret may consist of any formula, pattern, device or compilation of information which is used in one's business, and which gives him an opportunity to obtain an advantage over competitors who do not know or use it. It may be a formula for a chemical compound, a process of manufacturing, treating or preserving materials, a pattern for a machine or other device, or a list of customers.

Section 757 further indicates that other factors could also be taken into account in determining whether a trade secret exists; these are: (i) the degree of secrecy both within and without the plaintiff's business; (ii) the efforts by plaintiff to develop the process and to preserve its secrecy; (iii) the value of the process to the plaintiff and its competitors; and (iv) the difficulty with which the process could be duplicated by others.[54]

8.4.2.1 The Uniform Trade Secrets Act

Initially, trade secrets protection was recognized by courts under common law. With the adoption of the UTSA by most states there is now a level of uniformity in relation to the protection afforded against the misappropriation of trade secrets.

The definition of *trade secret* Section 1(4) of the UTSA definition of *trade secret* is based on what was the generally accepted common law definition. It provides that a:

> 'Trade secret' means information, including a formula, pattern, compilation, program, device, method, technique, or process, that: (a) derives independent economic value, actual or potential, from not being generally known to, and not being readily ascertainable by proper means by, other persons who can obtain economic value from its disclosure or use; and (b) is the subject of efforts that are reasonable under the circumstances to maintain its secrecy.

Thus, in order to constitute a trade secret, the subject matter at issue must satisfy two conditions: it must have economic value owing to it being kept secret and reasonable efforts must be made to protect it as secret.[55] Although Article 2 of the EU TSD

---

[53] Restatement of Torts, Section 757 Liability for the Disclosure of Another's Trade Secrets (Am. Law Inst. 1937).

[54] Ibid.

[55] Depending on the circumstances, such reasonable efforts may comprise security measures at a workplace or confidentiality clauses in a licence. For a detailed discussion on the requirement for reasonable secrecy efforts, see R G Bone, 'Trade secrecy, innovation, and the requirement of reasonable secrecy precautions' (3 September 2009). R C Dreyfuss, P Newman, and K J Strandburg, eds, *The Law and Theory of Trade Secrecy: A Handbook of Contemporary Research* (Cheltenham, Edward Elgar Press, 2010); Boston Univ. School of Law Working Paper No. 09-40.

lists three rather than two conditions, in essence there is no significant difference between the two since the first two conditions under the TSD appear to address the same points covered by the first condition under Section 1(4)(a) of the UTSA.

It is hardly arguable that various aspects of software products, such as algorithms, data structure, interface specifications, or other valuable but hidden parts of software' internal architecture could potentially be covered by the above definition. As is the case with the TSD, it appears that the fact that a program is being distributed in object code, but might subsequently be legitimately reverse engineered to uncover internal aspects of it, does not destroy the secrecy element therein. Thus, such sought-after elements are not considered as *'generally known'* or *'readily ascertainable'* for the purposes of Section 1(4) UTSA merely because they are discoverable through reverse engineering. For example, in *Gates Rubber* the Court of Appeals for the Tenth Circuit had no hesitation in concluding: 'Although there is some evidence that some of the constants might be "reverse engineered" through mathematical trial and error, that fact alone does not deprive the constants of their status as trade secrets.'[56] However, it appears that once legitimate reverse engineering takes place and the uncovered information is then circulated to members of the public, any secrecy may be vitiated of the information at issue.[57] It also appears that an unauthorized public disclosure, such as information uncovered through unlawful reverse engineering that is subsequently and unlawfully made available to members of the public, with the effect that the information at issue had become 'generally known'—should equally destroy the secrecy in the said information. As mentioned elsewhere in this chapter, trade secrecy law protects the veil of secrecy erected by the trade secret holder; once this veil is removed and the information behind it becomes part of the general knowledge, there is nothing left to protect. Of course, if information that was obtained though 'improper means' is subsequently disclosed to an innocent party or parties, rather than to the public at large, and that party only later becomes aware of the circumstances of the disclosure, the position is similar to that under the EU TSD. In other words, where the circumstances are such that prior to disclosure or use, a third party is considered to be under actual or constructive notice that the information at issue was obtained through improper means or breach of confidentiality duty, a subsequent use or disclosure by that party may constitute actionable 'misappropriation'.[58]

---

[56] *Gates Rubber Co. v. Bando Chem. Indus., Ltd.*, 9 F.3d 823, 848 (10th Cir.1993)
[57] For example, see *Servo Corporation of America v. General Electric Company* 393 F.2d 551 (4th Cir.1968) (finding that public disclosure destroyed the confidentiality element on which trade secrets protection is based).
[58] Section 1(2)(b), UTSA.

8.4 Trade Secrets Protection: The United States

Misappropriation and 'improper means' Section 1(2) of UTSA provides that 'misappropriation' of trade secrets takes place, inter alia, where either the acquisition itself occurred while employing 'improper means' or the disclosure or use of a trade secret was by a person who:

> (a) used improper means to acquire knowledge of the trade secret; or (b) at the time of disclosure or use, knew or had reason to know that his knowledge of the trade secret was a consequence of another person employing improper means or breaching a confidentiality duty. Thus, in order to establish 'misappropriation', it is necessary to examine whether or not the defendant, or the person from whom the defendant derived his knowledge, employed 'improper means'.

Reverse engineering Improper means are defined under Section 1(1) as including 'theft, bribery, misrepresentation, breach or inducement of a breach of a duty to maintain secrecy, or espionage through electronic or other means'. Of particular interest in the present context is the question of whether or not reverse engineering or decompilation, carried out in violation of a restrictive licensing clause, constitute 'breach of a duty to maintain secrecy' and, therefore, amounts to 'improper means', which in turn results in misappropriation.

The general juridical approach under US law towards reverse engineering is overall accommodating. Not only is it sometimes tolerated in the eyes of the law, but in many cases, it is viewed as outright desirable. As the Supreme Court commented in *Bonito Boats*:

> Reverse engineering of chemical and mechanical articles in the public domain often leads to significant advances in technology [. . .] Moreover, [. . .] the competitive reality of reverse engineering may act as a spur to the inventor, creating an incentive to develop inventions that meet the rigorous requirements of patentability.[59]

It is hardly surprising therefore that reverse engineering is considered a legitimate way to uncover otherwise hidden information or know-how that is embedded in a product or service that circulates in the marketplace.

The Supreme Court in Kewanee Oil observed, 'A trade secret law, however, does not offer protection against discovery by fair and honest means, such as by independent invention, accidental disclosure, or by so-called reverse engineering [. . .].'[60] In fact, the comment on Section 1 of UTSA states that 'proper means' may include:

---

[59] *Bonito Boats Inc. v. Thunder Craft Boats Inc.* 489 US 141, 160; 109 S Ct 971, 982 (1989).
[60] *Kewanee Oil Co. v. Bicron Corp.* 416 U.S. 470 (1974).

Discovery by 'reverse engineering', that is, by starting with the known product and working backward to find the method by which it was developed. The acquisition of the known product must, of course, also be by a fair and honest means, such as purchase of the item on the open market for reverse engineering to be lawful.

This, however, does not explicitly address the issue of contractually imposed secrecy obligation. Thus, although reverse engineering is a proper means to uncover information that may otherwise be considered a trade secret, it is not clear whether a breach of a contractually imposed duty of secrecy renders the said instance of reverse engineering 'improper'.

There are numerous US decisions that address this issue, but there is no uniform approach to it. However, before looking at the approach adopted by some courts, it might be useful to recall the legal position on anti reverse engineering licensing provisions in the United States outside the realm of trade secrecy laws. We have seen that reverse engineering and decompilation may amount to fair use where they were carried out in order to gain access to unprotectable ideas and concepts that are embedded in a given software product.[61] Under such circumstances, it may not constitute copyright infringement. It should also be recalled that unlike the position under the Software Directive in the EU,[62] the fair use exception to copyright infringement appears to be contractually waivable. Namely, in most cases a copyright proprietor should be able to limit or prohibit fair use activities through the use of restrictive licensing provisions.[63] This state of affairs suggests that the impact of such restrictive clauses on trade secrecy might be somewhat different from their impact in the European Union under the TSD.

In *Secure Services v. Time and Space Processing*,[64] the US District Court for the Eastern District of Virginia opined on the legal position in relation to a defendant that reverse engineered a program in contravention of an anti reverse engineering clause. In this case the plaintiff essentially argued that the defendant

---

[61] *Sega Enterprises Ltd. v. Accolade, Inc.* 977 F.2d 1510 (9th Cir. 1992); *Atari Games Corp. v. Nintendo of Am., Inc.* 975 F.2d 832 (Fed. Cir. 1992); *Sony Computer Entertainment, Inc. v. Connectix Corp.* 203 F.3d 596 (9th Cir. 2000).

[62] Art. 8, TSD.

[63] It is noteworthy that a licensing provision that prohibits reverse engineering might not be enforceable in the end owing to the operation of the copyright misuse doctrine. However, at present the copyright misuse doctrine has only been effective against copyright infringement claims but not against breach of contract claims. Thus, even where the doctrine has been argued successfully, it had excused the defendant from copyright infringement claims but left him susceptible to actions for breach of contract. In essence, the copyright misuse doctrine does not render a restrictive term void, but, at best, does not enable the licensee to enforce its copyright. See J P Herrell, 'The Copyright Misuse Doctrine's role in open and closed technology platforms' (2011) 26 BTLJ 441–90; B Frischmann and D Moylan, 'The evolving common law doctrine of copyright misuse: a unified theory and its application to software' (2000) 15 BTLJ 865, 901–2.

[64] *Secure Services Technology v. Time and Space Processing* 722 F.Supp.1354 (E.D. Va. 1989).

misappropriated trade secrets by analysing a facsimile machine that was loaned to it by a customer of the plaintiff. The court found that there was nothing wrong with the defendant's actions, which constituted 'proper means'. The court stressed that the plaintiff failed to take the necessary steps to maintain the secrecy of its facsimile protocol. Thus, the court observed, 'Since SST failed to indicate in any way that it retained proprietary interest in information contained in its facsimile machine, it waived trade secret protection in the protocol variations.'[65] Essentially, the court suggested that an explicit statement of proprietary interest could have been sufficient. Would the terms of a licence constitute such an explicit statement?

The answer may vary across the different jurisdictions in the United States; different courts in the United States reached different conclusions when addressing the tension between the desirability of reverse engineering as a whole, and restrictive licensing provisions that seek to limit if not outright prohibit it. For example, the court in *Telerate Systems v. Caro*[66] found that a licensing provision was sufficient to render the defendant's reverse engineering 'improper', even though the defendant was not the licensee. In this case the defendant uncovered the plaintiff's communication protocol by attaching a protocol analyser to equipment obtained from the plaintiff's licensee. The court found that the defendant's actions constituted 'improper means' since the plaintiff's licence explicitly forbad the use of such analyser with the plaintiff's equipment without the latter's consent. As regards the defendant's actions being essentially a type of reverse engineering, the court commented: 'the term "reverse engineering" is not a talisman that may immunize the theft of trade secrets. The relevant inquiry remains whether the means used to obtain the alleged trade secret, including reverse engineering, were proper'.[67] Hence, the court made it clear that *reverse engineering* is not a synonym to *proper means*; it is necessary to enquire into the circumstances under which such reverse engineering was carried out. However, it does not appear that the court in this case is referring to the circumstances under which the object that was reverse engineered was obtained; there was nothing improper in this context. Rather, it appears that the court is referring to reverse engineering that was carried out in violation of the explicit terms of the licence and that this, irrespective of the defendant not being a party to the licence agreement, was sufficient to render the reverse engineering at issue 'improper'.

The above decision could be contrasted with *Acuson Corp. v. Aloka*,[68] where an explicit statement made by the plaintiff in its licensing agreement was not deemed sufficient in order to protect its trade secret against reverse engineering, since the

---

[65] Ibid, at 1361   [66] *Telerate Systems Inc. v. Caro* 689 F.Supp.221 (S.D.N.Y. 1988).   [67] Ibid, 233.
[68] *Acuson Corp. v. Aloka Co.* 209 Cal. App. 3d 425, 257 Cal. Rptr. 368 (6th Dist.1989).

court found that the defendant, who was not a party to the licensing agreement, was not bound by an obligation of secrecy.[69]

A more recent Californian case addressed the issue from a different angle. Rather than focus on whether or not the defendant was bound by the terms of the licence agreement, it appears to suggest that contracts of adhesion should not be allowed to circumvent the public policy considerations that render reverse engineering permissible, by using trade secrecy laws in combination with such contracts. In *Aqua Connect v. Code Rebel*,[70] the plaintiff alleged that the defendant appropriated its trade secrets by reverse engineering its software, in breach of the End User License Agreement (EULA) that accompanied the trial version of its Terminal Server software. It was alleged that certain parts of the code were obtained through reverse engineering, in breach of an explicit provision that prohibited reverse engineering, and were used to develop and market a competing software product. Although the Californian Trade Secrets Act[71] defines *improper means*, inter alia, as 'a breach of a duty to maintain secrecy', the court was not ready to accept that a violation of an anti reverse engineering term in the EULA amounted to 'a breach of a duty to maintain secrecy' within the meaning of the CUTSA, and therefore constituted 'improper means'. While referring to the CUTSA,[72] the court stressed: ' "[i]mproper means" includes theft, bribery, misrepresentation, breach or inducement of a breach of a duty to maintain secrecy, or espionage through electronic or other means', but '[r]everse engineering or independent derivation alone shall not be considered improper means'.[73] This, of course, is hardly new; we have already seen that the UTSA itself contains a comment to that effect.[74] But what about the argument that, coupled with a violation of a licensing prohibition, reverse engineering no longer takes place '*alone*', and should therefore constitute 'improper means'? After all, the plaintiff argued that it was the breach of the anti reverse engineering clause that changed the status of the reverse engineering at issue from 'proper' to 'improper'.

---

[69] Overall, the plaintiff employed the following precautions: (i) the equipment was sold under a limited license for the internal software; (ii) sales persons and dealers were required to sign confidentiality agreements; and (iii) internal padlocks were included in the equipment, making it more difficult to examine the machinery. Nevertheless, these precautions were held to be inadequate under the Act in 'immunizing' the ultrasonic imaging equipment against reverse engineering.

[70] *Aqua Connect, Inc. v. Code Rebel, LLC et al.* Case No. CV 11-5764-RSWL (C.D. Cal., 13 Feb. 2012).

[71] The California Uniform Trade Secrets Act (CUTSA) is located at Sections 3426 to 3426.11 of the California Civil Code.

[72] Civ. Code. § 3426.1(a).

[73] Interestingly, like California, some States explicitly exclude reverse engineering from the definition of *improper means* (e.g. Illinois and North Carolina), while others do not (e.g. Michigan and Pennsylvania).

[74] See the comment on Section 1 of UTSA.

8.4 Trade Secrets Protection: The United States

The court, however, was not convinced. Citing with approval from Justice Moreno's concurring view in *DVD Copy Control Ass'n., Inc. v. Bunner*,[75] the court pointed out:

> Justice Moreno in his concurrence to a California Supreme Court decision, states that 'nowhere has it been recognized that a party wishing to protect proprietary information may employ a consumer form contract to, in effect, change the statutory definition of 'improper means' under trade secret law to include reverse engineering, so that an alleged trade secret holder may bring an action.[76]

It concludes: 'Though a breach of the EULA may support a cognizable breach of contract claim, the Court finds that the mere presence of the EULA does not convert reverse engineering into an "improper means" within the definition of California trade secret law.'[77] Thus, the court was reluctant to accept that a standard form contract may convert a permissible practice into a practice that constitutes 'improper means' which, in turn, supports a claim of misappropriation. This decision appears to be based more on public policy considerations rather than on literal or textual reading of the law. In essence, it is also public policy considerations that stand at the heart of the pre-emption doctrine, which may be used to render a state law–based trade secrecy claim unenforceable.

Pre-emption Chapter 2 discusses in detail both branches of pre-emption that are relevant in this context: statutory pre-emption and constitutional pre-emption, and their application to software's contract of adhesion in relation to copyright law. We have seen that post *Pro CD*,[78] most Circuits do not consider claims concerning breach of licensing terms that prohibit reverse engineering, to be pre-empted by copyright law. But can the same be said about possible pre-emption of state misappropriation of trade secret claims, where the latter is used to order to prohibit reverse engineering? Putting the question in pre-emption terms, a pre-emption argument in the present context would essentially run as follows. Since reverse engineering involves copying, a trade secrets–based claim that prohibits such copying should be pre-empted by federal copyright law,[79] since the latter permits reverse engineering under the fair use exception. We have seen that in order to survive a pre-emption argument, a claim must protect a right that is 'qualitatively different', with an 'extra element' that makes it distinct from a copyright action.[80] As discussed in Chapter 2, when a claim is based on state contract

---

[75] *DVD Copy Control Ass'n., Inc. v. Bunner* 31 Cal. 4th 864, 901 (2003) (Moreno J, concurring).
[76] *Aqua Connect, Inc. v. Code Rebel, LLC et al.* Case No. CV 11-5764-RSWL (C.D. Cal., Feb. 13, 2012) 4.
[77] Ibid, at 6.   [78] *ProCD, Inc. v. Zeidenberg* 86 F.3d 1447 (7th Cir. 1996).
[79] Section 301 of the Copyright Act.
[80] See e.g. *Data General Corp. v. Grumman System Support Corp.* 36 F.3d 1147 (1st Cir. 1994); *Katz Dochtermann & Epstein, Inc. v. Home Box Office* (1999) 50 U.S.P.Q.2d 1957, 1959.

law, it is usually the mutual assent and consideration present in a contractual relationship that constitute 'extra elements' and thus save such a claim from pre-emption.[81] Applying the same type of analysis to state misappropriation of trade secrets claims, Nimmer concludes: 'Actions for disclosure and exploitation of trade secrets require a status of secrecy, not required for copyright, and hence, are not pre-empted. This conclusion follows whether or not the material subject to the trade secret is itself copyrightable.'[82] It appears that in order to be on the safe side of a pre-emption argument, the licence at issue should therefore make it as clear as possible that the prohibited acts concern trade secrets and, while doing so, identify the information that constitutes the trade secret and the activities that are prohibited in relation to that information. The more this could be done while using non-copyright related terminology,[83] the more likely it is that a court would consider a claim based on state secrets law under such circumstances as containing the necessary 'extra elements'.[84]

It is noteworthy that some courts do not appear to follow Nimmer's analysis. At least two federal district court decisions concluded, inter alia, that a state misappropriation of trade secret claim was pre-empted under Section 301 of the Copyright Act.[85] However, these decisions contain little discussion in relation to the presence of 'extra elements', and the outcome therein might have been avoided if greater care would have been taken to emphasize the difference between a copyright infringement claim and trade secrets–misappropriation claim. A much more recent decision of the Fifth Circuit Court of Appeals also appeared to diverge from the aforementioned of analysis.[86] In this case the court found that state law–based trade secrets claims were pre-empted under Section 301. But a closer look at the court's decision makes it clear that it did not shut the door on state trade secrets–misappropriation claims in relation to software. What appears to have been pre-empted under the court's analysis were a state law–based conversion claim and a claim under the Texas Theft Liability Act that concerned theft of trade secrets. Again, emphasizing the difference between

---

[81] It is noteworthy that some courts refused to follow that analysis and held that a breach of a term incorporated into a contract of adhesion does not constitute an 'extra element', unless the promise creates a right that is 'qualitatively different' from a copyright infringement claim; e.g. see *Kabahie v. Zoland* 102 Cal. App. 4th 513 (2002).
[82] *Nimmer on Copyright* § 1.01[B][1][h], at 1-39 to 1-40.
[83] For example, confidentiality rather than copying.
[84] For example, in *Firoozye v. Earthlink Network* 153 F.Supp.2d 1115, 1130 (N.D. Cal. 2001), the court held that a trade secret misappropriation claim included an extra element of secrecy, that rendered it qualitatively different from a copyright infringement claim.
[85] *Jobscience v. CV Partners* (2014) WL 852477 (N.D. Cal. 2014) and *Videotronics v. Bend Electronics* 564 F.Supp.1471 (D. Nev. 1983).
[86] *Spear Marketing Inc., v. BancorpSouth Bank et al.* 844 F.3d 464 (2016), 2015 WL 3972246 (5th Cir. 30 June 2015).

copyright infringement claims and misappropriation of trade secrets claims, while highlighting the extra elements in the latter, such as the duty to maintain secrecy, should greatly assist a misappropriation of trade-secrets claim to survive a pre-emption argument.

A recent legislative development, however, could render the pre-emption question theoretical in many cases. A plaintiff that wishes to remove the risk of copyright pre-emption altogether may wish to bring a claim under the newly enacted DTSA. Being federal legislation, the latter is not susceptible to pre-emption challenge.

8.4.2.2 A brief note on the Defend the Trade Secrets Act 2016

The DTSA creates a federal private right of action for trade secrets misappropriation.[87] The new law does not pre-empt state trade secrets law and the two regimes operate in parallel.[88] A proprietor can choose to bring an action under DTSA where 'the trade secret is related to a product or service used in, or intended for use in, interstate or foreign commerce'.[89] Enacted in 11 May 2016, it is considered by some to be the 'most significant expansion of federal law in intellectual property since the Lanham Act in 1946'.[90] The law has been the subject of a scholarly debate regarding its various aspects, such as its potential to serve as an instrument of abuse by trade secrets 'troll'.[91]

In essence, the DTSA largely mirrors the UTSA, but differs from it in a number of important aspects, such as: (i) it provides for an ex parte seizure procedure where the defendant 'would destroy, move, hide, or otherwise make such matter inaccessible to the court, if the applicant were to proceed on notice to such person [. . .]";[92] (ii) it rejects the inevitable disclosure doctrine, prevalent in many jurisdictions, and requires proof of actual or threatened disclosure for injunctions against ex-employees;[93] (iii) it provides for punitive damages in case of wilful and malicious misappropriation;[94] and (iv) it provides for whistleblowing immunity under certain circumstances.[95]

---

[87] On the DTSA's objectives, structure and content, see J A Cannan, 'A (mostly) legislative history of the Defend Trade Secrets Act of 2016' SSRN, http://ssrn.com/abstract=2775390.

[88] DTSA, Section 2(f).   [89] Ibid, Section 2(b).

[90] J Gershman, 'Congress may be about to shake up trade secret law: is that a good thing?' (27 April 2016) Wall Street Journal http://blogs.wsj.com/law/2016/04/27/congress-may-be-about-to-shake-up-trade-secret-law-is-that-a-good-thing/.

[91] For example, see E Goldman, D S Levine, S K Sandeen, and C B Seaman, 'Professors' letter in opposition to the Defend Trade Secrets Act of 2015' (S. 1890, H.R. 3326) (17 November 2015) SSRN, <http://ssrn.com/abstract=2699760>; J Pooley, 'The myth of the trade secret troll: why we need a federal civil claim for trade secret misappropriation' (17 November 2015) 23 GMLR 2016, Forthcoming, SSRN, http://ssrn.com/abstract=2692382.

[92] DTSA, Section 2(b)(2).   [93] Ibid, Section 2(b)(3).   [94] Ibid.   [95] Ibid, Section 7.

As aforementioned, of particular importance to the context of the software industry is that being based on federal legislation, a trade secrets–misappropriation claim under the DTSA does not face the risk of copyright pre-emption challenge. Thus, unless more courts opt to eco the aforementioned approach established in Justice Moreno's concurring view in *DVD Copy Control Ass'n., Inc., v. Bunner,* anti reverse engineering clauses that are drafted by reference to trade secrecy, defining the sought-after information as trade secrets and, where possible, limit its use, are likely to successfully prevent a competitor from reverse engineering a licensed software product. Moreover, a trade secret holder that wishes to eliminate even the small risk of finding his trade secrets claim being pre-empted may opt to bring an action under the DTSA.

It is clear, therefore, that in contrast to the position under the EU TSD, a trade secrets holder in the United States may shield himself from otherwise permissible reverse engineering, by careful drafting of a confidentiality clause and its inclusion in the licensing agreement under which the software at issue is made available.

Index

10NES computer program 86

abstract idea 171-5, 177, 185, 215-16
abstraction-filtration comparison (AFC) test 128-30, 133, 190-2
abuse of dominant position 56, 59-64, 66-9
    freedom of contracts regulation 20
    intellectual property rights function 152
abuse of rights 34n, 138, 139-140, 158-9
access control mechanisms 4, 7, 23
acquisition, lawful/unlawful 228, 229-32
activation code 87
Adobe 11-12
algorithms 123, 127
    patenting 164-8, 187
    trade secrets 220, 236
Alice **test** 174
alphabetical codes and symbols 73
Altai **test** 131
anti-circumvention provisions 4, 25, 29, 31, 84
    European Union 5
    United States 6-9
anticompetitive agreements 57-9, 65-6
Antitrust Guidelines for Licensing Intellectual Property Law 65
antitrust policies 20, 144-6, 162
any-hardware approach 180-4
Apple 12
Apple CarPlay 203
Apple Link 203
Apple Remote Desktop 203
application programming interfaces (APIs) 131-5, 192
architectural features of software
    entitlement to exclude access to ideas 94
    idea-expression dichotomy 128-9
    licence-created monopolies and software protectability 84
    trade secrets 236
art
    prior 180, 182, 209
    skilled in the 186-7

    state of the 181, 182, 183, 184
    technological 163
artistic copyright infringement 112-13
artistic elements 29
Aspen **conditions** 68
Atari Games Corp. v Nintendo of America 86-93
Australia 98-9
Austria 224
authentication handshakes 4
authorial works 107, 194, 202n
autonomy of will principle 15-16, 21

bare licences 25
barriers to entry 29-30
Beebe, B. 92
Belgium 50
bespoke agreements for use and service obligations 2-3
beta testing 231-2
binary form 72-3
    see also **object code**
black box reverse engineering 71-2, 76, 101, 221n, 229
Blizzard Battle.Net 8-9
Blizzard End User Licensing Agreement and Term of Use notices 8-9
bnetd.org servers 9
box-top licences 39-44
brand loyalty 30
breach of contract 34
breach of licence terms 9
breaking down software suites 36
Brief, B. 131n
browse-wrap licences 3n, 13, 44-6
business methods patents 166-8, 171-2

C++ 73
Calabresi, G. 93-4
chain of title 35
chilling effect 8, 134
'Chinese wall' 74

Index

civil law 106, 158, 206–7, 224
classic contract model 15
'clean room' 74–5
click-wrap licences 3n, 4, 13, 24–5, 37, 44–6
   pre-emption-based mechanisms 52, 54
cloud agreements 13, 24
cloud environment
   contract law-based mechanisms 34–5
   decompilation entitlement 96
   idea-expression dichotomy 134
   reverse engineering 101
   trade secrets 221
Coase theorem 15
code
   activation 87
   alphabetical 73
   compliable 78
   declaring 131–2
   obfuscation 4, 9–10, 29
   signing 4
   see also **object code; source code**
command structure 133
commercial licences 148
common law 206–7, 224
Communicator (Netscape) 45
competition
   distortion 21, 58–9, 207
   free 16, 20, 21
   legitimate 91–2
   prevention 21, 58–9
   restriction 21, 58–9
   see also **competition law-based mechanisms; unfair competition**
competition law-based mechanisms 56–69
   copyright and restrictive licensing 138
   decompilation and interoperability 97
   European Union and prohibitions on reproduction of functional features 57–64
   freedom of contracts regulation 20
   United States antitrust law 65–9
compliable code 78
comprehension aid 78
compulsory licensing 62
Computer & Communication Industry Association: Amicus Curiea 132
confidentiality and trade secrets 221, 230, 236, 244
consumer confusion 197–8, 206, 207

consumer welfare 56–7
contra proferentem doctrine 22
contract law-based mechanisms 4, 34–50
   competition law-based mechanisms 56–69
   content 46–50
   formation 38–46
   licensing or sale 34–8
      breach of contract 34
      European Union 38
      United States 35–7
   pre-emption-based mechanisms 51–6
   United States copyright-misuse doctrine 148
contracts
   breach of 34
   classic 15
   content 46–50
      Directive on the Legal Protection of Computer Programs (European Union) 46, 47–50
      Directive on Unfair Terms in Consumer Contracts (European Union) 46, 47
      Uniform Computer Information Transactions Act (UCITA) (United States) 46–7
   digital 23
   formation 38–46
      box-top licences 39–44
      browse-wrap licences 44–6
      click-wrap licences 44–6
      conclusion of contract 42–3
      negotiable licences 46
      shrink-wrap licences 39–44
   non-negotiable 24
   privity of 16, 42–4
   relative effect 16
   see also **contracts of adhesion; freedom of contracts**
contracts of adhesion 17–19
   regulating enforceability of 21–2
   and technological protection measures 23–6
   trade secrets 240–1
   see also **standard form contracts**
contractual prohibitions on reverse engineering and reproduction 11–13
contractual provisions
   for licence-created monopolies 10–14
   prohibitive 4
contractual terms, standard 23
contribution approach 179–80, 183

Index

copying 116
  commercial purpose 91
  control mechanisms 4
  of functional ideas and logic 120
  by inference 117
  intermediary 72, 90-1, 96
  literal and non-literal copying 130, 131
copyright 4
  competition law-based mechanisms 56-7, 59-62, 66-7
  contract law-based mechanisms 34, 37, 38, 48, 50
  entitlement to exclude access to ideas 94
  European Union 138-39
  European Union: abuse of rights 158-59
  exercising right in manner that runs contrary to objectives and social function 138-40
  grants 36
  GUIs 188, 189
  infringement 7-8, 23, 25, 26
    see also **idea-expression dichotomy**
  intellectual property rights function 149-58
  interoperability 80, 82-3, 97-8
  legal mechanisms 33
  licence-created monopolies and software 29, 31
  pre-emption-based mechanisms 51, 52, 53-5
  and restrictive licensing 33, 136-59
  reverse engineering in cloud environment 101
  reverse engineering and decompilation 71-2, 74-9, 95-6
  trade secrets 232, 234, 238, 241-3
  trade-mark and trade-dress protection for GUIs 197
  United States 137, 138-9, 155, 158
  United States copyright misuse doctrine 140-49
copyright-misuse doctrine 34n, 139, 140-9
copyright-patent dichotomy, collapse of 26-7
Corel Office 189
counterfeit products 37

data file formats 122, 123, 127, 130-1
data structure 220, 236

deception 206-7, 210
declaring code 131-2
decompilation *see* **reverse engineering and decompilation**
defamation 207
default rules 16
Defend the Trade Secrets Act 243-4
design
  alternative 213
  freedom 213-14
  intellectual property rights function and trade-marks 152
  licence-created monopolies and software 29
  ornamental or aesthetic 207-9
  rights for GUIs 189-90
  see also **design patents**
design patents
  for GUIs in United States 208-11
    eligibility 208-10
    infringement 210-11
  trade-mark and trade-dress protection for GUIs 197
Determann, L. 101
digital contract 23
dilution 197-199
  by blurring 198n, 206
  by tarnishment 198n, 206
direct-conflict pre-emption *see* **pre-emption, statutory**
Directive on the Legal Protection of Computer Programs (European Union) 46, 47-50
Directive on Unfair Terms in Consumer Contracts (European Union) 46, 47
disassembly 73, 76, 227
  see also **reverse engineering and decompilation**
disclosure requirement 68, 83, 243
dissemination of information 87
distinctiveness 196-7, 202
distortion of competition 21, 58-9, 207
Dolan, M. 148
dominant position 29-31
  see also **abuse of dominant position**
dominant undertaking 60
double prohibition 33
double-identity provision 153-5
downstream sales 2
Drassinower, A. 107-8
dressing up 34, 38

ecosphere innovation 29
Edelman, Benjamin 8
efficiency considerations 191
electronic gateway 4
eligibility rules and scope of
    protection 196–202
encryption system 8, 29
end user 18
End User License Agreement (EULA) 38, 240
Endicott, T.A.O. 105, 117
entitlement in case of decompilation of
    computer programs 94–6
entitlement to exclude access to ideas 93–4
equivalence 52
essential element 167
    of copyright 151–2
    of infringement action 114
    of patent 150–1
    trade-mark protection for GUIs 204–5
    of trade-marks 152–6
essential facilities doctrine 60–2, 66–9
essential function of right 139
ethics 15
European Patent Office (EPO)
    Guidelines for Examination 186–7, 218
    patent protection for GUIs 216–18
    patenting software 178–87
        any-hardware approach 180–4
        background 178–9
        contribution approach 179–80
European Union
    abuse of rights 158–9
    competition law-based mechanisms 66
    contract law-based mechanisms 42, 50
    copyright and restrictive
        licensing 137, 138–39
    decompilation 5, 72
        under copyright law 84–5
        entitlement 94
        and interoperability 98, 100
    design patents and registered designs for
        GUIs 207
    Directive on the Legal Protection of
        Computer Programs 46, 47–50
    Directive on Unfair Terms in Consumer
        Contracts 46, 47
    essential element of trade-marks 152–6
    European Commission 224–6

freedom of contracts regulation 15, 21, 22
GUIs and look-and-feel elements 193–5
idea-expression dichotomy
    application of idea in software-related
        disputes 121–4
    development of idea 115
    and natural laws systems 106
Information Society Directive 5
Intellectual Property Office (IPO) 206
intellectual property rights
    function 149–52, 156–7
interoperability 80
legal mechanisms and restrictive licensing
    provisions 33
licensing or sale 38
and prohibitions on reproduction of
    functional software
    features 57–64
    abuse of dominant position 59–64
    anticompetitive agreements 57–9
registered designs for GUIs
    eligibility 211–13
    infringement 213–14
restriction of licensees and
    technology-based solutions 4–5
reverse engineering, functional elements
    reproduction and contractual
    provisions 11, 72
Software Directive 5
trade secrets 224–33
    protection prior to Trade Secrets
        Directive 224
    see also **Trade Secrets Directive**
trade-mark and trade-dress protection for
    GUIs 195, 203–6
    distinctiveness 203–4
    functionality 204–6
    infringement 206
see also **European Patent Office (EPO)**
exceptional circumstances 61–2
exemption clause 43
exercising right in manner that runs
    contrary to objectives and social
    function 138–40
exhaustion of rights principle 2, 38
existence and exercise of a right
    distinction 23
expressive core of software 27–8

Index

external limits to a right 138-39
externalities, positive or negative 17
extra element 52-3, 170, 241-3

Facebook 3
FaceTime 30
fair-use
  contracts of adhesion and technological protection measures 26
  copyright protection for GUIs 192-3, 194
  decompilation under copyright law 85, 86-93
  idea-expression dichotomy 133-5
  interoperability 82
  legal mechanisms and restrictive licensing provisions 33
  pre-emption-based mechanisms 52-3, 55
  reverse engineering and decompilation 72
  reverse engineering, functional elements reproduction and contractual provisions 10
  trade secrets 238, 241
  United States 6, 7-8, 9
Feldman, R. 168
Feria, R. de la 159
Fewer, David 107
firmware 99
first sale doctrine 2, 35, 36, 38
first to use principle 195
fixation requirement 113
Flicker 3
form of expression 49
France 14, 158, 207, 212
free competition 16, 20, 21
free movement of goods 150-1, 153
Free and Open Source Software (FOSS) 80-3
Free Software Foundation (FSF): Freedom 1 81
freedom of contracts 14-17, 19
  contract law-based mechanisms 50
  contracts of adhesion and technological protection measures 25
  legal mechanisms and restrictive licensing provisions 33
  pre-emption-based mechanisms 53
  regulation 19-23
    contracts of adhesion, regulating enforceability of 21-2

  legal right, misuse of 22-3
  public policy, limitations based on 19-21
  supremacy 18
Freeman-Walter-Abele **test** 165-6
functional claiming 168, 185-7
functionality/functional elements
  aesthetic 200
  design patents and registered designs 209-11
  idea-expression dichotomy 122, 127-8
  legal mechanisms and restrictive licensing provisions 33
  licence-created monopolies 10-14
  patenting 160
  United States 199-202
  utilitarian 200-1

geographical maps 27
Germany 14, 158, 207n, 212, 224
Goldstein, P. 104, 118
good faith 21
Gordon, W. 107
Graham, L.D. 82-3
graphical user interfaces (GUIs) 188-218
  contract law-based mechanisms 49-50
  copyright and restrictive licensing 137
  European Union 5
  idea-expression dichotomy 121
  licence-created monopolies and software 29, 30
  look-and-feel elements 190-5
    European Union 193-5
    United States 190-3
  patent protection 214-18
    European Patent Office (EPO) 216-18
    United States 214-16
  reverse engineering, functional elements reproduction and contractual provisions 10-11
  trade-marks 189
  see also **design patents; registered designs for GUIs; trade-mark, trade-dress and unfair competition protection for GUIs**

hierarchy of abstractions 129, 191
honest commercial practices/honest use 228, 232
HULU 203

250 Index

IBM 100
idea, procedure, process, system or method of operation 29, 78, 83–4, 127,130, 190–2
idea-expression dichotomy 102–35
  copyright protection for GUIs 190, 194
  copyright-misuse doctrine in United States 143, 146
  critique 104–5
  decompilation under copyright law 83–4, 86, 89, 93
  decompilation entitlement 95
  economic and efficiency-based justifications 105–6
  emergence and development 108–35
    European Union 115, 121–4
    United Kingdom 109–10, 112–21, 123–4
    United States 110–11, 114, 119, 124–35
  intellectual property rights function and trade-marks 157
  licence-created monopolies and software 27
  natural laws systems 106–8
  patenting 160
  reverse engineering and decompilation 74
  reverse engineering, functional elements reproduction and contractual provisions 10
inalienability rules 93
incentives balancing test 63
incorporation by reference 43
individual character 211–12
individual static components 203
Information Society Directive 49–50
informational goods 25
initial inquiry results 131
innovative concept 164
inquiry notice 45–6
Institute of Electrical and Electronic Engineers (IEEE): Board of Directors Position Statement 81–2
Intel 12
intellectual creation 122–3
intellectual property rights
  competition law-based mechanisms 60–4, 66–7, 68–9
  contracts of adhesion 19
  copyright and restrictive licensing 139
  design patents and registered designs for GUIs 207
  entitlement to exclude access to ideas 94
  freedom of contracts 17, 20, 23
  function 149–8
    essential element of copyright 151–2
    essential element of patent 150–1
    essential element of trade-marks 152–6
    protectable functions 156–8
  graphical user interfaces (GUIs) 188–89
  idea-expression dichotomy and natural laws systems 107
  interoperability 81
  licence-created monopolies 14
  patenting 160
  reverse engineering and decompilation 74
  trade secrets 224, 234, 243
  trade-mark and trade-dress protection for GUIs 199, 201
intellectual spaces 95
intent test 66–7, 69
Interact computer program 142
interface-specification information 97–8, 100, 236
interfaces *see* **application programme interfaces (APIs); graphic user interfaces (GUIs)**
intermediary copying 72, 90–1, 96
internal limits to a right 138, 156
interoperability 79–83
  competition law-based mechanisms 63, 67–8
  copyright protection for GUIs 195
  decompilation under copyright law 85, 87
  decompilation entitlement 95
  Free and Open Source Software (FOSS) 80–3
  horizontal 79–80, 90
  idea-expression dichotomy 135
  reverse engineering and decompilation 96–101
  trade secrets 227
  United States 6, 8–9
  vertical 80
inventive concept 171, 173–4, 180, 216
inventive step 180–2, 185, 187, 217
invisible hand of the market 16
Ireland 224

Index

Italy 224
***ius quaesitum tertio* doctrine** 42

JAVA 73
Jones, R.H. 104
Josserand, L. 139-40, 157, 159
judicial exception(s) 167, 170-1, 216
jurisdiction-by-jurisdiction basis 50, 207

Kant, I. 107

labour theory (Locke) 107
layout of GUI 202-3
lead-time effects 30
Leaffer, M. 148
legal effect 14
legal mechanisms and restrictive licensing provisions 32-69
  contract law-based mechanisms 34-50
legal right, misuse of 22-3
liability rules 93, 94-5
licence-created monopolies 1-31
  barriers to entry 29-30
  breach of licence terms 9
  contracts of adhesion 17-19
  contracts of adhesion and technological protection measures 23-6
  contractual provisions 10-14
    prohibitions on reverse engineering and reproduction 11-13
  copyright-patent dichotomy, collapse of 26-7
  expressive core 27-8
  freedom of contracts 14-17
    regulation 19-23
  functional elements, reproduction of 10-14
  licence types 13
  restricting licensees through use of technology-based solutions 4-10
  reverse engineering 10-14
  vault-like nature 28-9
licences
  bare 25
  beach of terms 9
  box-top 39-44
  browse-wrap 3n, 13, 44-6
  commercial 148
  compulsory 62

  digital 14
  negotiable 32, 46
  network 3
  non-negotiable 32
  per-seat 3
  shrink-wrap 3n, 13, 24, 39-44, 52-5
  site 3
  so-many-users-at-a-time 3
  see also **click-wrap licences; licence-created monopolies**
licensing 2-3, 11
  conditions 84
  model 36
  or sale 34-8
  see also **restrictive licensing**
literary works 123, 156
Locke, J. 107
locked-in consumers 30, 301
look-and-feel elements 190-5
  European Union 193-5
  GUIs 189
  idea-expression dichotomy 120
  licence-created monopolies and software 29
  trade-mark and trade-dress protection for GUIs 198
  United States 190-3

McCarthy, J.T. 199-200
machine or transformation test 164, 169-70
Manual of Patent Examining Procedure (MPEP) guidelines 208-9
manual-to-manual claim 122-3
manual-to-program claim 122
market failures 56-7
Masiyakurima, P. 124
mass-market software products 18
mass-market standard form digital licences 14
master chip 86
***Mayo* test** 171
meeting of the minds 18, 21
Melamed, A.D. 93-4
mental-step doctrine 163
menu command hierarchy 130-2
merger doctrine 109n, 129, 131
method of doing business 167, 181, 182, 184

method of operation 130-3
  see also idea, procedure, process, system or method of operation
method of performing a mental act 182, 184
Microsoft: trade-mark and trade-dress protection for GUIs 202
misappropriation 236-7, 241-4
misleading behaviour 207
misrepresentation (and theft and bribery) 206-7, 237, 240
monopolies
  formation 20
  power 66
    abuse of dominant position
  see also licence-created monopolies
multiplicity-of-forms test 212-13
mutual assent and contractual considerations 53-4, 55, 242

N2HS Internet blocking program 8
Napster 12
National Conference of Commissioners on Uniform State Laws 47, 233
natural laws systems 170-1, 216
natural phenomena 171, 216
negotiable licences 32, 46
Netherlands 44, 158, 213, 224
network effects 30
network licences 3
new product requirement 63
Nimmer, D. 101
Nimmer, M.B. 111, 128-30, 191, 242
Nimmer, R. 36
no-aesthetic-consideration test (causative approach) 213
no-physical-limitation rule 168
Noerr-Pennington doctrine 69
non-Battle.Net servers 8
non-competition agreement 221
non-contracting parties 34
non-disclosure agreement 221
non-literal elements 122
non-negotiable contracts 24-5
non-negotiable licences 32
non-obvious design 208-9, 214
non-protectable material 129
  see also protectable expression and non-protectable ideas division

non-technical contribution 181
notable use restrictions 37
notice and contract formation 43
novelty 180, 182, 187, 208-9, 211-12, 214, 217

Obama, B. 219, 234
obfuscation of code and data structure 4, 9-10, 29
object code 26, 74, 76, 77
  copyright protection for GUIs 193
  decompilation under copyright law 89, 91
  decompilation entitlement 96
  interoperability 82
  licence-created monopolies and software 29
  reverse engineering in cloud environment 101
  trade secrets 236
offline copy 24
open source application (BnetD) 8-9
Open Source Initiative (OSI) 81
OpenStack platform 134
Oracle 12-13
originality criterion 49-50, 112, 117, 194

parallel importation 153
Pascal 73
passing off 206-7
patenting 160-87
  copyright-misuse doctrine 142-3, 147
  essential element 150-1
  European Patent Office (EPO) 178-87
    any-hardware approach 180-4
    background 178-79
    contribution approach 179-80
  freedom of contracts regulation 20-1
  GUIs 188, 189
    European Patent Office (EPO) 216-18
    trade-mark and trade-dress protection 199
    United States 214-16
  idea-expression dichotomy 113
  licence-created monopolies and software 29
  patent misuse doctrine 140-1
  Patent and Trademark Office (PTO)(United States) 162-6
    Board of Appeal 163
  trade secrets 220-1, 233

trade-mark protection for GUIs 205
United Kingdom 160n
United States 160n, 161-78, 184-7
　background 161-2
　business methods patents 166-8, 171-2
　copyright-misuse doctrine 141-2
　Freeman-Walter-Abele test 165-6
　policy trends 162-3
　Supreme Court trilogy of cases (*Benson, Parker v. Flook* and *Diamond v. Diehr*) 163-4
　Supreme Court trilogy of cases (*Bilski, Mayo* and *Alice*) 168-78
per se analysis 65
per-seat licences 3
physical transformation requirement 167
pirating works 7
'plot-borrowing' cases 124-5, 129
pointers, icons, windows, and menus 203
Poland 224
Portugal 50, 224
pre-emption 40, 51-6, 234
　constitutional 51, 54-6, 241
　statutory 51-4, 241
prior art 180, 182, 209
privity of contract 16, 42-4
product design/packaging 196-7
program-to-program claim 122-3
programming languages 122, 123
prohibitive contractual provisions 4
property rules 93-4
Property Rules, Liability Rules and Inalienability: One View from the Cathedral 93-4
protectable expression core 129
protectable expression and non-protectable ideas division 6, 84, 148, 191
protectable functions 156-8
protocol encryption 4
protocol language 9
PSD-1000 computer program 142
pseudo source code 76
public domain elements 191
public interest perspective 92, 107, 139
public policy considerations 19-21
　abuse of rights in European Union 159
　copyright and restrictive licensing 138
　decompilation under copyright law 92-3

idea-expression dichotomy 103, 114, 118, 124, 133
intellectual property rights
　function 152-7
　trade secrets 232, 240, 241-2
　trade-mark and trade-dress protection for GUIs 200-1
　United States copyright-misuse doctrine 141-3, 145-8
Puerto Rico 233

qualitatively different 52, 241

Reagan administration 164-5
registered designs for GUIs
　European Union 211-14
　　eligibility 211-13
　　infringement 213-14
rent seeking 106
reproduction for study and research 72
reputation and misrepresentation 198n, 207
Restatement (Second) of Contracts 18, 20
Restatement (Third) of the Law of Unfair Competition 199
restraint of trade 20, 34n, 60
restricting licensees through use of technology-based solutions 4-10
　European Union 5
　United States 5-10
　　judicial perspective 6-10
restrictive licensing
　contract law-based mechanisms 50
　licence-created monopolies and software 31
　trade secrets 238-39
　see also **copyright and restrictive licensing; licence-created monopolies**
result oriented claiming 168
reverse engineering and decompilation 4, 70-101
　cloud environment 101
　competition law-based mechanisms 67-8
　contract law-based mechanisms 38, 47-8
　contracts of adhesion 19
　contracts of adhesion and technological protection measures 23-4, 25
　copyright law 83-93

Index

reverse engineering and decompilation (*cont.*)
European Union 85
idea-expression dichotomy 84
United States 85–93
decompilation under copyright law 83–93
decompilation in order to achieve interoperability 96–101
entitlements in case of decompilation of computer programs 94–6
entitlements to exclude access to ideas 93–4
European Union 5
freedom of contracts regulation 22
idea-expression dichotomy 133–4
interoperability 79–83
legal mechanisms and restrictive licensing provisions 33
licence-created monopolies 10–14, 27–8, 30
motivation and methods 75–8
pre-emption-based mechanisms 53–5
reasons for and benefits of 78–9
restriction of licensees and technology-based solutions 4
software 71–3
stages 73–5
trade secrets 220, 227, 229, 231, 234, 236, 237–8, 244
Trade Secrets Directive 228–33
United States 5–6, 8–9
United States copyright-misuse doctrine 148
white box reverse engineering 71
see also **black box reverse engineering**
rights
abuse of 34n, 138, 139–40, 158–59
exercising right in manner that runs contrary to objectives and social function 138–40
exhaustion of rights principle 2, 38
external limits to a right 138–39
in personam (personal rights) 16, 25, 552
in rem (absolute rights) 16, 25, 53
internal limits to a right 138, 156
subjective 138–39
Roman law 158
royalties 34
rule of reason test 65

Samuelson, P. 98n, 99–100, 109n, 124, 131n
Scottish law 42
scrambling 29
secondary meaning 197, 202, 211
secrecy agreement 221
'secret handshake' 9, 29
Sega Enterprises v. Accolade 87–9
Seneca, L.A. 109n
shrink-wrap licences 3n, 13, 24, 39–44, 52–5
site licences 3
skill, labour and judgement of claimant 120–1
skilled in the art 186–7
slave chip 86
SmartDownload (Netscape) 45
so-many-users-at-a-time licences 3
social function 139
software-as-a-service (SAAS) agreements 3, 13, 24
software-related disputes *see* **idea-expression dichotomy**
software-to-hardware 99
software-to-software 99
Sony Computer Entertainment v. Connectix 90–3
source code 73, 74, 77
copyright protection for GUIs 193
decompilation entitlement 96
Free and Open Source Software (FOSS) 80–1
idea-expression dichotomy 122, 131
licence-created monopolies and software 29
pseudo 76
reverse engineering in cloud environment 101
Spain 212, 224
special purpose program (compiler or assembler) 73
Spence, M.J. 105, 117
standard contractual terms 23
standard form contracts 3, 4, 21, 25, 29, 241
mass-market digital 14
see also **click-wrap licences; contracts of adhesion**
standard programming techniques 191
state of the art 181, 182, 183, 184

store layouts as protectable subject matter 202
structure, sequence and organization (SSO) 131-3
subject matter 170-1, 215
subjective rights 138-39
substantial taking infringement test/ substantiality 114-15, 117
substantive law 17, 20, 21
successive filtration test 128-9, 131, 191
Sweden 212, 224
system of operation 132-3
'systems' cases 125-7

take it or leave it proposition 18
target programs 97
technical character 216-17
technical considerations 50
technical development restriction 63
technical effect 184, 218
   external 183, 184
   internal 183, 184
technical function 49, 194, 212
technical-contribution approach 179-181
technicality 183, 185
technological art 163
technological protection measures (TPMs) 4, 26
   and contracts of adhesion 19, 23-6
   European Union 5
   licence-created monopolies and software 29, 31
   United States 6-8, 9
textual elements 29
third parties
   contract law-based mechanisms 34, 44, 48
   legal mechanisms and restrictive licensing provisions 33
   patenting 170-1, 173
three-dimensional shapes 204-5
tort law 224
trade secrets 29, 84, 160, 219-44
   confidentiality 221, 230, 236, 244
   European Union 219, 221, 223, 224-33
      protection prior to Trade Secrets Directive 224
      see also **Trade Secrets Directive**

   legal basis of the right 221-3
   United States 219, 221, 223, 233-44
      background 233-4
      copyright-misuse doctrine 148
      Defend the Trade Secrets Act 243-4
      legislative framework 234-44
      see also **Uniform Trade Secrets Act**
Trade Secrets Directive 225-33
   background 225-6
   definition of trade secret 226-8
   framework 226-33
   lawful acquisition 228
   reverse engineering 228-33
trade values 207
trade-dress *see* trade-mark, trade-dress and unfair competition protection for GUIs
trade-mark, trade-dress and unfair competition protection for GUIs 195-207, 209, 211
   European Union 195, 203-6
      distinctiveness 203-4
      functionality 204-6
      infringement 206
   United States 195-203
      distinctiveness 196-7
      functionality 199-2
      individual static components 203
      infringement 197-199
      overall layout 202
      transitional or animated features 203
trade-marks
   essential element 152-6
   GUIs 188, 189
   indication of origin 196
   licence-created monopolies and software 29, 30
   registered 195, 196
   source identification 196
   unregistered 195, 196
   see also **trade-mark, trade-dress and unfair competition protection for GUIs**
trafficking in circumvention tools 5
Tran, J. 172
transaction costs 18
transfer of technology 60
transformative use 91
transitional or animated features 203

Index

Twitter 3
two-party deal 14, 25
tying arrangements 65

unbundling software 36
unclean hands doctrine 140
unconscionability doctrine 22
unfair advantage 206
unfair competition 124, 189, 224
   see also **trade-mark, trade-dress and unfair competition protection for GUIs**
Uniform Computer Information Transactions Act (UCITA)(United States) 46–7
Uniform Trade Secrets Act 235–43
   definition of trade secret 235–6
   misappropriation and improper means 237–41
   pre-emption 241–3
   reverse engineering 237–41
United Kingdom 212
   contract law-based mechanisms 42–4, 45–6
   idea-expression dichotomy 108
      application of idea in software-related disputes 120–1, 123–4
      development of idea 112–20
      emergence of idea 109–10
   patenting 160n, 183
   trade secrets 224, 226–7
United States 137
   antitrust law 65–9
      abuse of dominant position 66–9
      anticompetitive agreements 65–6
   contract law-based mechanisms 46
   copyright misuse doctrine 140–49, 155, 158
   copyright and restrictive licensing 137, 138–39
   decompilation under copyright regime 84, 85–93
      Atari Games Corp. v. Nintendo of America 86–93
   design patents for GUIs 207, 208–11
      eligibility 208–10
      infringement 210–11
   freedom of contracts regulation 15, 19–22
   functionality 204, 205

   idea-expression dichotomy 108–9
      application of idea in software-related disputes 127–35
      development of idea 114, 119, 124–7
      emergence of idea 110–11
   interoperability 80, 81
   legal mechanisms and restrictive licensing provisions 33
   licensing or sale 35–7
   look-and-feel elements of GUIs 190–3
   patent protection for GUIs 214–16
   Patent and Trademark Office (PTO) 172, 208
   pre-emption-based mechanisms 51, 55–6
   restricting licensees through use of technology-based solutions 4–10
      judicial perspective 6–10
   reverse engineering and decompilation 70, 72
   reverse engineering, functional elements reproduction and contractual provisions 10
   trade secrets 233–44
      background 233–4
      Defend the Trade Secrets Act 243–4
      legislative framework 234–44
      see also **Uniform Trade Secrets Act**
Uniform Commercial Code 14
Uniform Computer Information Transactions Act (UCITA) 46–7
Virgin Islands 233
user experience 214
user interface screen-display 121
utilitarian objectives 157, 209
utilitarian theory 106
utilitarian works 84, 110, 190
utilitarianism 15

Van Rooijen, A. 97–100
Vaver, David 107

Wharton, L. 147
whistleblowing immunity 243
white box reverse engineering 71, 101
Windows 63

Zerbe, R.O. 82–3